UNIVERSITY OF TORONTO STUDIES

LEGAL SERIES

EXTRA VOLUME

General Editor

W. P. M. Kennedy, Litt.D., LL.D.

Dean of the Faculty of the School of Law
of the University of Toronto

Monopolies & Patents

Dr. Fox has decided views on the benefits which are conferred on the industrial and commercial life of a country, and, indeed, on the public generally, by a strong patent system efficiently administered. In his view, the modern patent of invention is not a monopoly, in the sense in which that word is generally understood. He feels that the modern witch-hunt against monopolies is misdirected when it levels its attack on the patent system and predicates the opinion that, if the history of monopolies were better understood, much of the antagonism against them would tend to disappear. It is an exponent of this view that he examines, in this work, the reasons for the institution and development of monopolies, the factors which contributed to their growth in England in the sixteenth and seventeenth century, and the cause of their gradual decline and transition into the modern patent of invention.

The approach to the subject is not, however, merely antiquarian. In his opinion the patent system can be improved in the interests not only of the inventor but also of the public. With this thought in mind he proposes an amendment to the patent system designed to eliminate the indefinable element of inventive ingenuity from the content of patentability, a reform which would remove much of the uncertainty of result which in the past has been the main fault of the patent system and the chief curse of the inventor and patentee.

In this work Dr. Fox demonstrates an attitude toward monopolies and patents which reflects both his legal training and research and his practical industrial experience. Whether one agrees with his interpretation of the history of monopolies and his proposal for amendment of the patent system or not, this book will evoke much interest and possible controversy.

HAROLD G. FOX practised patent and trademark law as a member of the firm of Fetherstonhaugh & Fox. He was appointed King's Counsel in 1937 and is a Fellow and sometime President of the Patent Institute of Canada. He holds the honorary appointment in the University of Toronto Lecturer in the Law of Industrial Property and, in 1945, in recognition of his contributions to Canadian legal scholarship, the University conferred on him the honorary degree of Doctor of Letters.

MONOPOLIES AND PATENTS

A Study of the History and Future of the Patent Monopoly

By

HAROLD G. FOX

M.A., Ph.D., Litt.D.

One of His Majesty's Counsel
Lecturer in the Law of Industrial Property
in the Faculty of the School of Law
of the University of Toronto

TORONTO

1947 THE UNIVERSITY OF TORONTO PRESS

London: Geoffrey Cumberlege
Oxford University Press

Reprinted 2017
ISBN 978-1-4875-9874-7 (paper)

To

E. C. F.

PREFACE

THE present work had its beginning as a comment on the confusion attendant upon the definition of invention in the law of patents. For many years, the legal profession in the common law countries has been troubled by the wide divergence of views which have been held in the patent offices on the one hand, and the courts of law on the other, on the subject of inventive ingenuity. Much disquiet also has been occasioned by the obviously arbitrary differences which exist between various judges on the question of invention *versus* mechanical skill. Uneasiness and a sense of frustration have been suffered by lawyers and industrialists alike at the spectacle of many obviously worthy inventions, proved by years of commercial success and public approbation, being destroyed by judicial holdings of invalidity, based upon a mystical concept of invention which was nowhere defined but which operated entirely as a value judgment.

Feeling that in this there existed the germ of an idea, the discussion of which might prove useful not only to lawyers but to inventors and industrialists as well, I commenced to examine the much disputed question of invention. When, however, I endeavoured to trace the trend of decision from the present to the obviously different basis for the grant of letters patent contained in the Statute of Monopolies, I found the tide of investigation carrying me inexorably back to the common law and then to the very beginnings of the history of monopolies. Once embarked upon a study of the history of the genesis of the patent system, I found myself so absorbed by its interest that I felt it not out of place to assemble the material and present it to my colleagues in chronological and collected form. In doing so, I hope I shall be acquitted of the charge of mere antiquarianism. I have always felt that not only is the historical development of any branch of the law from its roots upward to the present a most interesting and pleasurable subject of investigation, but that no full understanding of the theory and philosophy and inner meaning of law can be had without it. It is with the idea of tracing the development of the patent system from the monopoly policy, as well as of showing the full meaning back of the word "invention" in its historical development and the distortion of meaning which it has undergone in the last century, that I have undertaken the present study.

The second part of this work consists of an examination of the doctrinal trend in the law of patents from the simple principles contained in the Statute of Monopolies toward the constantly increasing emphasis placed on inventive ingenuity as an essential ingredient of patentability. This doctrinal trend may be said to have reached its culmination in 1941 in the "flash of genius" principle enunciated by the Supreme Court of the United States in *Cuno Engineering Co.* v. *The Automatic Devices Corporation.*

The patent system may be outworn, as suggested by Judge Learned Hand in the Second Circuit Court of Appeals in the United States. Many attacks are being levelled at it. But it is, after all, as President Roosevelt has said, the key to our technology. Its overthrow, which would be a deplorable calamity, will not be hindered or prevented by anything other than sincere efforts to understand it, both from a practical and from a historical viewpoint, and to suggest its reform where reform is necessary and proper.

Much of the discredit presently attaching to the patent system is attributable to the lack of predictability which flows from the judicial law-making which has set aside the clear principles of the common law and the Statute of Monopolies on the necessary ingredients for patentability of inventions. The problem is one of pressing import and any discussion that can in any way aid in its solution may be considered as being not quite without merit.

If the small studies contained in this volume prove of utility to my colleagues, and if they serve to stimulate, in any lay minds to whose notice they may come, some interest in the patent system and a just appreciation of its worth and of the benefits which flow from its application, I shall be well rewarded for my labours. D'Ewes, the great reporter of the proceedings of Parliament from the time of Queen Elizabeth to the Long Parliament, stated in the preface of his first *Journal:* "These things I have proposed to myself to labour in . . . like him that shoots at the Sun, not in hopes to reach it, but to shoot as high as possibly his strength, art, or skill will permit . . . if I can but finish a little in each kind, it may hereafter stir up some able Judgments to add an end to the whole." Such has always been the urge behind the pen throughout the ages; and, while I am conscious of having attempted much, and keenly aware of having failed to accomplish more, that urge must be my apology and my reason for again presenting for the consideration of my brothers of the law another work on that branch of legal science which, to my mind, blends all that is practical and beneficial with so much that is of great historical interest.

HAROLD G. FOX

School of Law,
University of Toronto,
March 15, 1946.

CONTENTS

APPENDIXES

TABLE OF ABBREVIATIONS

A.A.L.H.	Select Essays in Anglo-American Legal History
A.C.	Law Reports, Appeal Cases
App. Div.	Appellate Division
Ass. Pl.	Le Liver des Assises et plees del Corone, 1580
B. & Ald.	Barnewall and Alderson's Reports, King's Bench
B. & S.	Best and Smith's Reports, Queen's Bench
Bac. Abr.	Bacon's Abridgement
Bing. N.C.	Bingham's New Cases, Common Pleas
Bl. Com.	Blackstone's Commentaries on the Laws of England
Blatch.	Blatchford's Reports, United States Circuit Courts, Second Circuit, 1845-1881
Bridg. Rep.	Bridgman's Common Pleas Reports
Brownl. & Golds.	Brownlow and Goldesborough's Reports, Common Pleas
Bull. N.P.	Buller's Nisi Prius Reports
Bulst.	Bulstrode's Reports, King's Bench
Burr.	Burrow's Reports, King's Bench
C.A.	Court of Appeal, England
C.B.N.S.	Common Bench Reports, New Series
Cal. Pat. Roll.	Calendars of the Patent Rolls
Cal. Rot. Pat.	Calendarium Rotulorum Patentium in Turri Londinensi, with Indexes by Ayscough
Can. Bar. Rev.	Canadian Bar Review
Ch.	Law Reports, Chancery
Ch. D.	Law Reports, Chancery Division
Ch. Lancs.	Chancery of the County Palatine of Lancaster, England
Co. Inst.	Coke's Institutes
Co. Rep.	Coke's Reports
Com. Dig.	Comyn's Digest
Comb.	Comberbach's Reports, King's Bench
Cott. MS	Manuscripts of the Cottonian Library deposited in the British Museum. Catalogue published by British Record Commission
Cott. Post.	Cottoni Posthuma: Divers Choice Pieces of that Renowned Antiquary, Sir Robert Cotton
Cout. Dig.	Coutlee's Digest of Cases in the Supreme Court of Canada
Cro. Eliz.	Croke's Reports *temp.* Elizabeth, King's Bench and Common Pleas
Ct. of Sess.	Court of Session Cases, Scotland

D.L.R.	Dominion Law Reports, Canada
Dav. P.C.	Davies' Patent Cases, England, 1785-1816
D'Ewes	D'Ewes Journals of Parliament. *See* Bibliography
East	East's Reports, King's Bench
Ec. Hist. Rev.	Economic History Review
Eng. & Amer. Pat. Cas.	English and American Patent Cases (Abbott)
Eq.	Law Reports, Equity Cases
Ex. C.R.	Reports of the Exchequer Court of Canada
Ex. D.	Law Reports, Exchequer Division
Ex. C.C.	Exchequer Court of Canada
F. Fed. Rep.	Federal Reporter, United States
F 2d.	Federal Reporter, Second Series, United States
F. Supp.	Federal Supplement, United States
Firma Burgi	Madox: Firma Burgi. *See* Bibliography
Fisher	Fisher's Reports of Patent Cases in the Circuit Courts of the United States 1848-1873
Fitz. Nat. Brev. F.N.B.	Fitzherbert's Natura Brevium
Foed.	Thomas Rymer: Foedera. *See* Bibliography
Fox Pat. C.	Fox's Patent, Trade Mark, Design and Copyright Cases, Canada
Godb. R.	Godbolt's Reports, King's Bench, Common Pleas, and Exchequer
Goodeve P.C.	Goodeve's Patent Cases, England
Gr.	Grant's Upper Canada Chancery Reports
Griff. P.C.	Griffin's Patent Cases, England, 1884-1887
H. Bl.	Henry Blackstone's Reports, Common Pleas
H.C.J.	High Court of Justice, England
H.L.	Law Reports, House of Lords. (In some cases the reference is to the House of Lords as a forum)
H.L.C.	House of Lords Cases
Hardres	Hardres's Reports, Exchequer
Harv. L. Rev.	Harvard Law Review
Hawarde	Hawarde's Reports del Cases in Camera Stellata
Hawk. P.C.	Hawkins's Pleas of the Crown
Hob.	Hobart's Reports, Common Pleas
Holt	Holt's Reports, King's Bench
How.	Howard's Reports, U. S. Supreme Court, 1843-1860
Hulme	History of English Patent System. *See* Bibliography
J.C.P.C.	Judicial Committee of the Privy Council
J.P.O.S.	Journal of the Patent Office Society, United States
Jo. H.C.	Journals of the House of Commons
Jo. H.L.	Journals of the House of Lords
Johns.	Johnson's Reports, Chancery

Keb.	Keble's Reports
Kent's Comm.	James Kent, Commentaries on American Law
Le. Leon.	Leonard's Reports, King's Bench, Common Pleas and Exchequer
L.J.C.P.	Law Journal, Common Pleas
L.J.Ch.	Law Journal, Chancery
L.Q.R.	Law Quarterly Review
L.R.	Law Reports, England, since 1865
L.T.N.S.	Law Times, New Series
M. & G.	Manning and Granger's Reports, Common Pleas
M. & W.	Meeson and Welsby's Reports, Exchequer
Macg. Cop. Cas.	Macgillivray's Copyright Cases
Mason	Reports of the United States Circuit Courts, First Circuit, 1816-1830
Mod.	Modern Reports
Mod. L.R.	Modern Law Review
Moo. P.C.	Moore's Privy Council Cases
Moore K.B.	Moore's Reports, King's Bench
N.Y.U.Law Q. Rev.	New York University Law Quarterly Review
Noy	Noy's Reports, King's Bench
O.A.R. Ont. A.R.	Ontario Appeal Reports
O.G.	Official Gazette of the United States Patent Office
O.L.R.	Ontario Law Reports
O.R.	Ontario Reports
Otto	Reports of the U. S. Supreme Court, 1875-82
O.W.N.	Ontario Weekly Notes
Ont. C.A.	Ontario Court of Appeal
Ont. Ct. of Ch.	Ontario Court of Chancery
Ont. Q.B.	Ontario Court of Queen's Bench
Ont. H.C.J.	Ontario High Court of Justice
Ow.	Owen's Reports, King's Bench and Common Pleas
P. Williams P. Wms.	Peere Williams' Reports, Chancery and King's Bench
Parl. Hist.	Parliamentary or Constitutional History of England from the Earliest Times to the Restoration of Charles II
Pat. Roll.	Patent Rolls: The Official Records of Royal Charters and Grants from the Reign of King John to Recent Times
Q.B.	Law Reports, Queen's Bench
Que. Ct. of Q.B.	Quebec Court of Queen's Bench
Que. S.C.	Quebec Superior Court

R.P.C.	Reports of Patent Cases, 1884-1946
R.S.O.	Revised Statutes of Ontario
Reg. Brev.	Registrum Brevium
Rev. St.	Revised Statutes of the United States
Riley Lib. Cust.	Munimenta Gildhallae Londoniensis; Liber Albus, Liber Custumarum, et Liber Horn
Roll. Abr.	Rolle's Abridgement des plusieurs Cases et Resolutions del Common Ley, 1668
Roll. R.	Rolle's Reports, King's Bench
Rot. Parl.	Rotuli Parliamentorum
Rush.	John Rushworth's Historical Collections, 1640-44
S.	Shaw, Court of Session Cases (Scotland) 1st series
S.C.C.	Supreme Court of Canada
S.C.O.	Supreme Court of Ontario
S.C.R.	Reports of the Supreme Court of Canada
S.D. & B.	Shaw, Dunlop and Bell, Reports of Cases in Court of Session, Scotland (1st series)
Salk.	Salkeld's Reports, King's Bench
Sc. Jur.	Scottish Jurist
Shep. Abr.	William Sheppard's Abridgement of the Common and Statute Law of England
Skin.	Skinner's King's Bench Reports
Sol. J.	Solicitor's Journal
S.P.D. S.P. Dom.	State Papers, Domestic
S.P. Docq.	State Papers Docquet
S.P. For.	State Papers, Foreign
St. at L.	Statutes at Large of the United States
St. Tr.	State Trials
Steele Proc.	Steele's Tudor and Stuart Proclamations, 1485-1714
T.L.R.	Times Law Reports
T.N.E.C.	Temporary National Economic Committee, Washington
T.R.	Term Reports (Durnford and East)
U.C.C.P.	Upper Canada Common Pleas Reports
U.C.Q.B.	Upper Canada Queen's Bench Reports
U.S.	Reports of the Supreme Court of the United States
U.S.C.—R.S.	United States Code, Revised Statutes
USPQ	United States Patents Quarterly
Vent.	Ventris's Reports, King's Bench and Common Pleas
Ves.	Vesey, Junior's, Reports, Chancery
Vin. Abr.	Viner's Abridgement of Law and Equity
W. Jones	Sir William Jones' Reports, King's Bench and Common Pleas
W.P.C.	Webster's Patent Cases, England, 1603-1855
Y.B.	Year Books

TABLE OF CASES CITED

C

T

U

V

W

Y

Z

Part One

HISTORY OF MONOPOLIES & PATENTS OF INVENTION

I. INTRODUCTION

TO know truly is to know by causes. Francis Bacon thus pointed the way to his "vantage ground of truth." So in examining the development of the patent system, we can know and understand it truly only by extending our investigation back through the story of the policy of monopolies into the dim recesses of the mediaeval guild system, and, by interpreting those early events in their causal relationships, arrive at an unprejudiced opinion of the nature and purpose of monopolies, and the merit and virtue of the resultant patent system. Of considerable importance in that history is the part played by the great Sir Francis Bacon, Viscount St. Albans, Lord High Chancellor of England, Lord Keeper of the Privy Seal, the story of whose fall from the zenith of power, wealth, influence, and honour makes the saddest and sorriest reading—a fall engendered by and traceable directly to his own corruption and venality. It has always been a paradox to historians that this man of such great culture and ability should have stooped to such shocking abuse of his powers and such perversion and prostitution not only of his authority but of his honesty of intellect and opinion. Macaulay has summed up his career as "a checkered spectacle of so much glory and so much shame." There is a parallel between the story of Bacon's career, as exemplified by that quotation, and the story of monopolies with which, during the most important part of their development, he was intimately concerned. For if monopolies have borne the opprobrium and contempt of their contemporaries and of subsequent historians, they, nevertheless, shared in the glory of the Golden Age of England and contributed in no small measure to its greatness. It seems fitting, therefore, that the history of that much maligned institution, the monopoly, should be written in an endeavour to show the benefits, as well as the disadvantages, which monopolies have contributed to the development of trade and industry and to demonstrate that along with the shame, they have carried a measure of glory.

The interest which the history of monopolies must have for the modern reader lies in the development of the monopoly from being a royal grant based upon prerogative right, regulated and enforced by courts of conciliar jurisdiction, to its position as a creature of parliamentary procedure subject to control by common legal process. In this transition lies the story of the part which this legal and social element has taken in the causative factors contributing to the development of law into a system for the use and service of the people. Cicero's eulogy that *Lex est vinculum civitatis, fundamentum libertatis et fons æquitatis* has no better illustration than in this branch of the law where a legal incident has been transformed from a master into a servant of the people. From a device conceived as a utility for trade promotion and regulation, but permitted to degenerate at times into a means of annoyance and grievance, the patent of monopoly has, through the operation of law, developed into one of the greatest factors of service to the people through its application to the progress of invention and the improvement of industry.

Industrial property is probably the least understood form of property known to the law. Indeed, there have been times when it has been denied that it constitutes property at all.[1] This misunderstanding as to its nature has caused much lack of perception of its beneficent qualities, not alone to its owners but to the public at large. While much of this misunderstanding is in many cases caused by the demagogues endeavouring to coin political capital out of flogging the whipping boy of monopoly, the unfortunate fact is that very few have any clear idea of what constitutes industrial and intellectual property, the reasons and bases for its creation, and the propriety of the monopolies flowing from it. It should never be forgotten that the origin of this type of property is in production and is based upon the theory that every man is entitled to the fruits of his own labour.[2]

This hiatus of understanding in our legal and social thinking is enhanced by the fact that the law of industrial property is only a

[1]Cf. Jefferys v. Boosey (1854) 4 H.L.C. 815 at 867 per Erle, J.; Tennyson v. Forrester (1871) 43 Sc. Jur. 278; Singer Mfg. Co. v. Wilson (1877) 3 A.C. 400; Tatem & Co. Ltd. v. Gaumont Co. Ltd. (1917) 34 R.P.C. 181 at 188 per Cozens-Hardy, M. R.; Attorney-General v. Lord Oswald (1848) 2 S., X, 969.

[2]Jefferys v. Boosey, supra; Millar v. Taylor (1769) 4 Burr. 2303 at 2359 per Yates, J.

very small part of the sum total of law with which the practising lawyer must familiarize himself. In addition, the lawyer meets cases involving this branch of the law only very occasionally, if at all, in his practice, and is therefore inclined to put the whole matter aside as of no importance, or at least of no pressing concern. But the social aspect of the subject is of far greater importance. Despite assertions that great scientific minds will work and strive without thought of hope or reward[3] the solid fact remains that, in essence, the mainspring of human activity is self-interest.[4] Inventions are pressed to conclusion and reduced to practice by the hope of material reward far more than by the hope of posterity's acclaim. This is equally true in other creative fields, for who will deny the truth and common sense of the old statement that he who engages in writing a laborious work will do it with more spirit if he thinks it may be a provision for his family.[5] Deliberate misrepresentation of and apathetic indifference toward the nature of this type of property may well have the result of limiting or even destroying it. The present methods of attack on patents for inventions are not only proof of this statement, but are so well known as to call for no furnishing of examples. If such results occur, the world will be a poorer place, for industrial and intellectual property monopolies are the life blood of rational endeavour.

Jenks has spoken[6] of the touching absence of curiosity among English lawyers. Institutions which are the very heart of modern business life, the fountain-head of not ungrateful streams of litigation, are accepted as though, like the image of Ephesus, they fell direct from Heaven for the benefit of a deserving profession. The legal questions to which they give rise are studied with minute care; the legal relationships which they create are made the occasion of microscopic analysis. But the subject itself, the really interesting and important matter, is left untouched. In no branch of the law is this so true as in that relating to patents and monopolies. It, therefore, seemed that a study of the sources from which our patent system was evolved, treating and discussing in a connected and continuous manner the play of the legal, constitutional, and

[3]See post 295.

[4]Cf. Taussig, *Inventors and Money Makers.*

[5]Millar v. Taylor (1769) 4 Burr. 2303 at 2335 per Willes, J.

[6]Jenks, "Early History of Negotiable Instruments" (1893) 9 L.Q.R., 70.

economic forces in their interdependent and inter-connected relation, the one upon the other, until this connection and interplay finally crystallized into a systematic national patent policy, might prove of some interest.

For this reason I have spent some time preparing a history of the evolution of the law relating to patent monopolies, written not only from the viewpoint of a connected and continuous economic and legal development, but weaving into that story something of the constitutional aspects both of law and history which form a background. I have done so in the hope that it will shed some light on the reasons, not only legal but economic, why a patent system was ever established in the first place. It is my feeling that the attacks on the present patent system, if they are not dictated for reasons entirely of personal political advancement without regard to truth, propriety, or national expediency, are the product of ignorance and a failure to know the necessity upon which history demonstrates the patent system to be based, coupled with an inability to understand the significance of the historical factors. When Holmes said that the history of the law is of much importance to the understanding of the law[7] he was merely making a statement that almost every lawyer is ready to accept without argument, even if, as Jenks points out, he is not so ready to carry it into practice. But when Holmes said that historic continuity with the past is not a duty, it is only a necessity,[8] he was uttering a profound truth that some may have dimly seen but never before placed in words. If then there is no duty, but only necessity that we have historical continuity with the past, nowhere perhaps is that necessity more alive and more properly applied than as it affects the patent system, which has become today the target for abuse of greater virulence and much wider scope than it ever suffered in the days when it was the focal point of assault upon, and limitation of, the Crown prerogative. If we understand the history of monopolies, we shall understand that our present patent system is in the logic of history. Before we rashly venture upon the sea of change advocated so strenuously by the ill-informed and the politically-minded, let us pause and examine causes and effects. Then, perhaps, we shall perceive that a system is not to be con-

[7]Holmes, *Collected Legal Papers*, 388.
[8]*Ibid.*, 138.

demned merely because it is based upon tradition; that a policy is not bad merely because it results from evolution; that new systems and policies are not to be welcomed with open arms and accepted merely because they are alleged to be more scientifically geared to the needs and manners of a changing world; and that, perhaps, we might do worse than to remember and to emulate the barons of England when, in the Statute of Merton in 1236, they exclaimed with united voice: "*Nolumus mutare leges Angliæ.*"

The lesson to be drawn from the history of the monopoly system is apparent. As a systematic policy it received a full and fair trial. In its operation and effects it was generally found wanting. Whatever may have been the motives which inspired its institution, it failed of its purpose in an expanding commercial world. It hampered enterprise and harmed the individual purchaser and consumer. The attacks upon it were virulent and widespread. At the time of the Long Parliament it had few friends except those who personally profited by holding monopolies. It was subject to almost universal condemnation, and nothing that could be said against it was left unsaid. Amid all this welter of abuse and condemnation, one element alone stood unchallenged—the propriety of a monopoly grant to the inventor of a new manufacture. That element, the foundation of our present patent system, was left unchallenged and unassailed at a time when all monopolies were suspect and almost all were condemned. That one feature remained acceptable in the minds of the people, producer and consumer alike. If, therefore, at such a time and under such stress of thinking, the system of granting patents to meritorious inventors was left without criticism, how much more should it be an object of respect at the present time when we have been able to acquire perspective and to see the continuity of its encouraging effect on the progress of industry and science and the development of new devices, processes, and techniques.

II. DEFINITION OF MONOPOLY

THE basic theory underlying the grant of letters patent for inventions is a part of the larger theory of monopolies. Patents constitute an element of what Chapman[1] characterized as legal monopolies in his classification of monopolies into those which are natural, social, legal, and voluntary. That they constitute a reasonable exception to otherwise objectionable forms of state bounty is generally accepted by such writers on economics as Marshall, Chapman, Mead, and Chamberlin, and indeed even such a socialistic writer as Thorstein Veblen states that "It is very doubtful if there are any successful business ventures within a range of modern industries from which the monopoly element is wholly absent."[2] Veblen is, of course, referring to the wider types of monopoly—not only to Chapman's legal type of monopoly characterized by patents and copyrights and other forms of industrial property, but also to those based on social and economic conditions. A clear understanding, therefore, of the underlying theory of this legal form of monopoly will hardly be possible without some reasonable appreciation of the historical aspect of the growth by which the patent monopoly came to be accepted as a legal and proper exception to the great body of objectionable monopolies.

A monopoly has been defined by Coke[3] as "an institution or allowance by the King, by his grant, commission, or otherwise, to any person or persons, bodies politic or corporate, of or for the sole buying, selling, making, working, or using anything; whereby any person or persons, bodies politic or corporate, are sought to be restrained of any freedom or liberty that they had before, or hindered in their lawful trade."[4] This definition, as will appear

[1]Chapman, *Outlines of Political Economy*, 139.

[2]Veblen, *Theory of Business Enterprise*, 54.

[3]Co. 3 Inst. 181, c. 85.

[4]Standard Oil Co. v. United States (1911) 221 U.S. 1; Coke also gives a further and shorter definition in his reports: "A monopoly is, when the sale of any merchandize or commodity is restrained to one or a certain number," 11 Co. Rep. 86b.

from our discussion, embraces only those monoplies which were improper and illegal at common law and against the commonwealth.[5] To this extent, therefore, it is only a partial definition, and does not include those monopolies or grants of privilege which were held valid at common law and formed the basis of the exceptions stated in the Statute of Monopolies of 1624.

Monopolies constitute an interference with the common law right possessed by every member of the community to carry on any trade or business he chooses in such a manner as he thinks most desirable in his own interests. Inasmuch as every right connotes an obligation, no one can lawfully interfere with another in the free exercise of his trade or business unless there exists some just cause or excuse for such interference. Just cause or excuse for interference with another's trade or business may be found in the existence of some additional or substantive right conferred by letters patent from the Crown or by contract between individuals. In the case of letters patent from the Crown this additional or substantive right is generally described as a monopoly. In the latter case, the contract on which the additional or substantive right is founded is generally described as a contract in restraint of trade. Monopolies and contracts in restraint of trade have this in common, that they both, if enforced, involve a derogation from the common law right in virtue of which any member of the community may exercise any trade or business he pleases in such manner as he thinks best in his own interests.[6]

Bl. Com., bk. IV, chap. XII, 158, defines monopoly as "a licence or privilege allowed by the king for the sole buying and selling, making, working, or using of any thing whatsoever; whereby the subject in general is restrained from that liberty of manufacturing or trading which he had before."

Com. Dig. (Tit. Trade D. 4) gives the following definition: "A monopoly is when the sale of any merchandise or commodity is restrained to one or a certain number."

Hawk. P.C., c. 79, s. 1, "A monopoly is an allowance by the king, to any person or persons, of the sole buying, selling, making, working, or using of anything whereby any person is sought to be restrained from any freedom which he had before or hindered from his lawful trade."

See also Wheeler, *Treatise of Commerce*, 101.

[5]Cf. 1 W.P.C. 5 n.

[6]Attorney-General of Australia v. The Adelaide Steamship Co. Ltd. et al. (1913) A.C. 781 at 793 per Lord Parker of Waddington.

This is not the proper place to engage in a general discussion of monopolies from an economic standpoint. Nor is the present author sufficiently skilled in the principles of economics to discuss the merits or demerits of monopolies which take their origins from the interplay of economic forces. Natural monopolies which originate from limitation of the source of supply, and voluntary monopolies arising from the absorption of competing businesses and the consequent destruction of competition are matters which need not concern us here, for the legislator is powerless to alter or remedy the first class, and whatever may be his opinion as to the propriety of interfering in and regulating the second class, experience has shown that, so long as private enterprise is preferred to communism, little if anything can effectively be done about it.

I venture to think, however, that a few words might usefully be added in discussion of those monopolies of a type which have social implications because, in many cases, they are surrounded with legal incidents and, in a number of cases, are the creations of legislative action. Those monopolies which owe their causation to legal action, although of a collective type, nevertheless operate by an exclusionary process upon the great majority of the public. These are the monopolies which constitute the so-called "closed corporations" of the professional classes. The Medical Act of the Province of Ontario[7] will furnish an example. Provision is made for the maintenance of a register of all those entitled to practise medicine and surgery within the Province. Those persons only whose names are inscribed in the register shall be deemed to be qualified and licensed to practise, and no person not so registered shall practise medicine, surgery, or midwifery for gain or hold himself out to be so registered under pain of penalties prescribed by the statute. Most of the professions are equally protected[8] and while it may with justice be said that the

[7]R.S.O. (1937) c. 225, ss. 18, 47, 48.

[8]The references here given are to the laws of the Province of Ontario, but substantially similar statutes prevail in most jurisdictions:

Barristers, R.S.O. (1937) c. 222, s. 2, 4a, as amended by 8 Geo. VI, c. 58, s. 1; Solicitors, *ibid.*, c. 223, s. 6; Dentists, *ibid.*, c. 227, s. 20; Pharmacists, *ibid.*, c. 228, s. 21; Drugless Practitioners, *ibid.*, c. 229, s. 5; Nurses, *ibid.*, c. 230, s. 2; Land Surveyors, *ibid.*, c. 231, s. 2; Architects, *ibid.*, c. 233, s. 18; Chartered Shorthand Reporters, *ibid.*, c. 234, s. 13; Chartered Accountants, *ibid.*, c. 235, s. 16; Certified Public Accountants, *ibid.*, c. 236, s. 10; Professional Engineers,

imposition of these restrictions is primarily in the public interest, monopolies are nevertheless thereby created. In this sense the professions and many other occupations today occupy a position in no way different from the mediaeval craft guilds and in truth cannot be distinguished from them so far as the right of exclusive privilege is concerned. As the early guilds increased in wealth and power, they started to organize their trades, crafts, and mysteries in such a way as to form monopolies, and prevent all competition from outsiders. They began, in early times, to draw up ordinances which gave them power over their own trades, with a right to institute searches and punish infringements of their privileges. They claimed the right to control the standard of workmanship, the wages of the journeymen, and the number and treatment of apprentices. Although in the beginning their authority was derived from the municipal courts to which they could appeal in case of dispute, they gradually tended to seek charters from the Crown giving them definite legal power over all the incidents of their trades.[9] In essence, the only distinction between the guilds and the professional and occupational monopolies of which we have been speaking lies in the fact that, while the early guilds sought protection by way of royal charter, the modern method is to seek protection by way of statute.

But perhaps the true successor of the ancient guilds is to be seen not so much in these "closed corporations" of professional and occupational classifications as in the trade unions. The Statute of Apprentices, 1562,[10] which superseded the Statute of Labourers,[11] was designed to institute a statutory system of wage fixing by the justices of the peace. The Act was passed as a direct result of the decay of the guilds which themselves constituted the earlier wage fixing authority. It fixed hours of labour and required a servant to obtain a testimonial from his master that his work had been finished before he sought work in a new district.

---

ibid., c. 237, s. 33; Veterinary Science Practitioners, *ibid.*, c. 239, s. 4; Embalmers and Funeral Directors, *ibid.*, c. 242, s. 11; Private Detectives, *ibid.*, c. 245, ss. 1 and 2; Optometrists, *ibid.*, c. 246, s. 8; Real Estate Brokers, 10 Geo. VI, c. 84, s. 3; and others.

[9]Cf. Pooley, *Guilds of London*, 12.

[10]5 Eliz., c. 4.

[11](1349) Close Roll, 23 Edw. III, 25 Edw. III, st. 2.

The act of Elizabeth, which provided minute regulatory details, and was limited to certain crafts, was extended to all labourers so far as the fixing of wages was concerned by statutes of James I and Charles I.[12] These acts, however, gradually became obsolete, and during the eighteenth century, workmen who had formerly resisted the state regulation of labour, began to realize that such regulation would prevent competition from unapprenticed men, women, and children. They thereupon began to petition Parliament for the enforcement of the Statute of Apprentices. Trade combinations inevitably followed on the failure of Parliament to accede to these petitions. The history of the trade union movement since that time shows a constant and steadily continuing gain of strength by the unions until today they wield a monopoly power of enormous proportion and significance, regulating wages and conditions and hours of work and controlling, by their rules and ordinances, the right of admission to gainful employment over the field of their jurisdiction. This monopoly of the right of admission to employment has now received statutory sanction.[13]

In a sense most voluntary associations which occupy that obscure intermediate region between the individual and the corporation are monopolistic in their nature in that the general public is excluded from the benefits flowing from membership therein. It is now, of course, a question how far trade unions may be considered to be purely voluntary associations,[14] or whether the tendency is not towards an extension of their power to one of complete monopoly control over the field of their activities.

In the field of social monopolies, some receive legal support. Railways, both urban and inter-urban, enjoy monopolistic franchises as do certain public utilities, e.g., telephone companies, gas supply, and electricity. These are obviously founded on reason and common sense because where one street railway would pay, two or more in competition would probably fail or give service at an uneconomical cost. Utility services can only be adequately

[12] 1 Jac. I, c. 6; 16 Car. I, c. 4, s. 2.

[13] See, e.g., Canada, Wartime Labour Relations Regulations, Order-in-Council, P.C. 1003, Feb. 17, 1944; Ontario Collective Bargaining Act (1943) 7 Geo. VI, c. 4; Ontario Labour Relations Board Act (1944) 8 Geo. VI, c. 29.

[14] See, e.g., the decision of Mr. Justice Rand as arbitrator in the industrial dispute between the Ford Motor Co. of Canada Ltd. and the U.A.W.-C.I.O. promulgated in January, 1946.

and efficiently handled if one of each type is permitted to occupy the entire field to the exclusion of all others. This is probably best illustrated by the development along monopolistic lines of Ontario's hydro-electric power resources.[15] These social monopolies are those which are inevitable for economic reasons. Then, too, there are those monopolies, also of a social type, which are operated under governmental ownership and supervision as in the case of the sale of alcoholic liquor in all the provinces of Canada and some of the states of the American Union[16] and the copyright residing in the Crown in such works as the Bible, the Book of Common Prayer, and acts of Parliament.[17] These latter types of social monopolies are not dictated by economic causes but rather by a combination of the factors of public welfare, popular desire, and political pressure.

While all these forms of restricted control differ in many of their incidences they have this in common, that they operate by way of exclusive privilege, excluding therefrom those who are not grantees of the monopoly right or members of the body exercising the monopoly power. In few, if any cases, however, are they seriously attacked and if attack or criticism is levelled at them it is not against them as monopolies *per se*. It seems to be only in the field of industrial grant that the onslaught against monopoly is at all virulent.

In modern industrial and commercial usage, there exist certain monopolies which take the form of industrial or intellectual property and I venture to think it may not be without merit to compare and in some senses to contrast the rights embodied within these forms of property more commonly known as patents, trade marks, industrial designs, and copyright. These forms of industrial and intellectual property differ in their essentials. On the one hand, rights in patents and copyright protect the substance of the article itself. The prohibition contained in these rights extends to any unauthorized manufacture or reproduction so long as the monopoly lasts. A trade mark, on the other hand, differs both from a patent and from a copyright. In a trade mark the property and right to

[15]Cf. Ontario Hydro-Electric Power Commission Act, R.S.O. (1937) c. 62.

[16]See, e.g., The Liquor Control Act of Ontario, R.S.O. (1937) c. 294.

[17]Cf. Fox, *Canadian Law of Copyright*, 274; Rex v. Bellman (1938) 3 D.L.R. 548; Attorney-General for New South Wales v. Butterworth & Co. (Australia) Ltd. (1938) N.S.W.R. 196; Canadian Copyright Act, R.S.C. (1927) c. 32, s. 11.

protection are in the device or symbol attached to the goods to be sold and not in the article itself which is manufactured or sold. The article is open to the world and the owner is only entitled to prevent the use of his mark in such a manner as to lead purchasers to believe that they are buying his goods when they are in fact the goods of a rival trader. But the grounds of obtaining legal recognition have a common element. Patents and copyright rest on the theory that the results of the original labour of the author or inventor are, both on the grounds of justice and public policy, to be protected against piracy. "Every man is entitled to the fruits of his own labour" is a sentiment that has long been approved.[18] Similarly, the law of trade marks is based on a man's right to have guaranteed to him the profit derivable from his own property. There is, in addition, a certain similarity between copyright and the protection accorded to industrial designs and of this more will be said hereafter.

While all these forms of industrial and intellectual property bear a certain resemblance to each other there are striking differences. They are all personal and incorporeal property, and are all, to a certain extent, monopolies, but there the resemblance practically ceases.

A patent is an absolute monopoly during its term, prohibiting the putting into use, by others than the patentee, of a new manufacture invented by the patentee. A copyright is a limited monopoly having its origin in production[19] and, closely analogous to patent rights, protecting the fruits of an author's exertion in literary, dramatic, artistic, or musical composition. But the monopoly is limited to the right to prevent copying. If an independent author arrives at the same results by independent means, the copyright owner has no right to prevent to that extent the invasion of his monopoly. The difference between the monopoly conferred by patent and by copyright will be immediately perceived. If it could be shown, as a matter of fact, that two precisely similar works were in fact produced wholly independently of one another, the author of the work published first would not be entitled to restrain the publication by the other author of that author's independent original work. What is given is the merely negative

[18]Per Yates, J., in Millar v. Taylor (1769) 4 Burr. 2303 at 2359.

[19]Jefferys v. Boosey (1854) 4 H.L.C. 815 at 867 per Erle, J.

right to prevent the appropriation of the labours of an author by another.[20] A patent right, on the other hand, is quite different. The monopoly is absolute, and once an inventor has complied with the provisions of the Patent Act, and a valid patent has issued to him, he can prevent the exercise of that invention by anyone else who has, quite in the belief that he was actually inventing something new, and without knowledge of the patentee's patent, invented the same thing, even simultaneously with the patentee.[21]

A trade mark, again, is a limited monopoly, but it is much more limited than either of the preceding types. There can be no monopoly in a trade mark in the abstract—that is, apart from goods. The monopoly only extends to prevent the use of similar trade marks on similar classes of goods. There is, for example, nothing to prevent a manufacturer of motor cars calling his car "The Quaker" although a good deal of valuable goodwill has been built up by the manufacturer of "Quaker" food products.

An industrial design, while having similarities to all three preceding types of property, is neither a minor patent nor a variety of trade mark, nor again is it a copyright. It is an exclusive right to a new and original idea of shape or configuration applied to an article of commerce and appealing to the eye. It has no existence apart from an article of commerce and cannot be infringed by being applied to articles of a different class. It is obvious that neat questions may arise as to whether a given subject matter falls within the protection accorded to artistic copyright or to industrial designs.

All forms of industrial and intellectual property are, to a certain extent, negative rights to prevent the appropriation of individual property by another. Indeed, it may be said that all forms of property exhibit this negative aspect, and therefore, as to the suggestion sometimes made that copyright is a personal privilege of monopoly, the answer is that it is the same right as is incidental to all ownership, which in its nature prohibits the use of the property against the will of the owner, and, considered in that light, is no more a monopoly in case of copyright than in the case of other possessions.[22] In the case of patents, there exists this negative right to

[20]Corelli v. Gray (1913) 29 T.L.R. 570 per Sargant, J., and see cases cited post 16, n. 23.

[21]See Landeker & Brown v. Wolff & Co. Ltd. (1907) 52 Sol. J. 45.

[22]Jefferys v. Boosey (1854) 4 H.L.C. 815 at 878 per Erle, J.

prevent the appropriation of the labour of the patentee by an infringer. There is, of course, the additional right, as mentioned above, that the patentee can prevent another person using his invention even though that other person has arrived at the same result by quite independent means. To this extent the law of copyright differs from the law of patents, for while both are monopolies, the patent monopoly is an absolute one, while copyright is only a limited monopoly in the sense that if a second author arrives at the same result by quite independent means, the first author cannot, by virtue of his copyright, prevent the second author from publishing his work.[23] To this extent there is no such thing as anticipation in the law of copyright as there is in the law of patents. A work which is the result of independent composition may be original and the subject matter of copyright notwithstanding that there is in existence an earlier work which is similar or identical to it.[24] In the same way the owner of a trade mark can prevent the appropriation of that mark by any other party and can enjoin a dishonest or even an innocent trader from capitalizing upon the goodwill in the mark built up by him and using it as an indication of origin of the same class of goods.

The charge of "monopoly" sometimes levelled against those forms of property should, however, be completely disregarded. The modern view was expressed by Sargant, L. J. in *Harms Inc. & Chappell & Co.* v. *Martans Club Ltd.*

> The word "monopoly" has been used, but I think all suggestions that lie in the word "monopoly" adverse to the principle of monopoly, are singularly wanting in the case of the protection of the property of authors and composers. I suppose there is no property which juristically speaking is more entirely the property of an individual than work which has been the direct result of the labour and the talent or genius of the author or composer who has given it to the world; and the copyright which is given to him is not in derogation of the right of any other person to perform something similar which has come from the brains and intelligence of that person, but it is merely the right to prevent other people from copying and appropriating that which is the true property and the true invention of the original author or composer.[25]

[23]Corelli v. Gray (1913) 29 T.L.R. 570 per Sargant, J.; Rees v. Melville (1914) Macg. Cop. Cas. 168; Wesman v. McNamara (1925) Macg. Cop. Cas. 121; Fischer v. Dillingham (1924) 298 F. 145; Arnstein v. Marks (1936) 28 USPQ 426; Seltzer v. Sunbrock (1938) 22 F. Supp. 621; Carpenter v. Peoples-Pittsburgh Trust Co. (1943) 57 USPQ 141.

[24]Fred Fischer Inc. v. Dillingham (1924) 298 F. 145.

[25](1927) 1 Ch. 526 at 535.

In this sense, therefore, there is a close analogy between the law of copyright and the law of patents. The modern theory of patent law is one of bargain between inventor and state.[26] The consideration for the grant is twofold; first, there must be a new and useful invention, and secondly, the inventor must, in return for the grant of a patent, give to the public a sufficient description of the invention with sufficiently complete and accurate details as will enable a workman, skilled in the art to which the invention relates, to construct or use that invention when the period of the monopoly has expired.[27] In considering copyright it is apparent that the public is interested in the development and promulgation of all new and wholesome ideas. Without publication and some exclusive right thereto the products of authors would prove comparatively profitless. The public, then, for the addition to its general stock of knowledge, and the author in consideration of the pecuniary profits derivable therefrom, are jointly interested in the publication of new works. The exclusive right for a limited time to intellectual productions and creations is therefore conferred upon authors as a compensation for their contributions to the promotion of general knowledge.

In discussing the similarity of copyrights and patents, Lord Brougham in *Jefferys* v. *Boosey*[28] said:

> Whatever can be urged for property in a composition, must be applicable to property in an invention or discovery. It is the subject-matter of the composition, not the mere writing, the mere collection of words, that constitutes the work. It may describe an invention, as well as contain a narrative or a poem, and the right to the exclusive property in the invention, the title to prevent anyone from describing it to others, or using it himself (before it is reduced to writing) without the inventor's leave, is precisely the same with the right of the author to exclude all men from the multiplication of his work.[29]

In *Millar* v. *Taylor*[30] Yates, J., gives an interesting summary of this similarity in the following terms:

[26]Harmar v. Playne (1807) 14 Ves. 130; 11 East 101; Dav. P.C. 311; Fox, *Canadian Patent Law* at 176 and 261.

[27]Prentice v. Dominion Rubber Co. Ltd. (1928) Ex. C.R. 196; French's Complex Ore Reduction of Canada v. Electrolytic Zinc Process Co. (1930) S.C.R. 462; Western Electric Co. Inc. et al. v. Baldwin International Radio Co. of Canada (1934) S.C.R. 570; B.V.D. Co. Ltd. v. Can. Celanese Ltd. (1936) Ex. C.R. 139; (1937) S.C.R. 221, 441.

[28](1854) 4 H.L.C. at 966.

[29]See also (1854) 4 H.L.C. at 957 per Lord Brougham.

[30](1769) 4 Burr. 2303 at 2386.

Both original inventions stand upon the same footing in point of property; whether the case be mechanical or literary; whether it be an epic poem or an orrery, the inventor of the one as well as the author of the other has a right to determine "whether the world shall see it or not"; and if the inventor of the machine chooses to make a property of it by selling the invention to an instrument maker the invention will procure him benefit. But when the invention is once made to the world it is laid open; it is become a gift to the public; every purchaser has a right to make what use of it he pleases. If the inventor has no patent any person whatever may copy the invention and sell it. Yet every reason that can be urged for the invention of an author may be urged with equal strength and force for the inventor of a machine. The very same arguments "of having a right to his own productions" and all others, will hold equally, in both cases; and the immorality of pirating another man's invention is fully as great as that of purloining his ideas. And the purchaser of a book and a mechanical invention have exactly the same mode of acquisition and therefore the *jus fruendi* ought to be exactly the same.

III. MONOPOLIES IN THE ANCIENT WORLD

THE history of monopolies is usually treated as having its rise in England, but that country was in fact a late-comer in the art of exercising exclusive privilege. The term "monopoly" originated, so far as we know, with the Greeks. The word μονοπωλία was used in 347 B.C. in the *Politics* of Aristotle as signifying an exclusive sale,[1] being derived from μόνος (alone) and πολεῖν (to sell).[2] Monopolies, in the sense of exclusive rights

[1]Aristotle, *Politics*, bk. I, chap. XII, 48. "There is the anecdote of Thales the Milesian and his financial device, which involves a principle of universal application, but is attributed to him on account of his reputation for wisdom. He was reproached for his poverty, which was supposed to show that philosophy was of no use. According to the story, he knew by his skill in the stars while it was yet winter that there would be a great harvest of olives in the coming year; so, having a little capital, he gave earnest-money for the use of all the olive-presses in Chios and Miletus, which he hired at a low price because no one bid against him. When the harvest-time came, and many wanted them all at once and of a sudden, he let them out at any rate which he pleased, and made a quantity of money. Thus he showed the world that philosophers can easily be rich if they like, but that their ambition is of another sort. He is supposed to have given a striking proof of his wisdom, but, as I was saying, his device for getting money is of universal application, and is nothing but the creation of a monopoly. It is an art often practiced by cities when they are in want of money; they make a monopoly of provisions." Aristotle then goes on to speak of a man of Sicily who bought up all the iron from the iron mines. When merchants came to buy, he was the only seller, and without much increasing the price he gained 200 per cent. "And," says Aristotle, "statesmen ought to know these things; for a state is often as much in want of money and of such devices for obtaining it as a household, or even more so." Obviously Aristotle saw nothing harmful or immoral in monopolies.

See also Aristotle, *Oecon.*, II, xviii; Pliny, *Hist. Nat.*, lib. 8, c. 37; Procopius, c. 25; Diogenes Laertius, lib. 1, c. 26; cf. Collier, *Law of Patents*, 2 et seq.

[2]Riezler, *Finanzen und Monopole im alten Griechenland*, 50; Francotte, *Industrie dans la Grèce Ancienne*, bk. III, chap. I, 143; Aristotle expressly mentions the establishment of monopolies by cities (Aristotle, *Politics*, bk. I, chap. XII, supra) in order to raise revenue, and in consequence a rise in the price of commodities (cf. Aristotle, *Oecon.*, II, viii, ix, xiv). He mentions a monopoly of lead and other commodities in the hands of the state as well as the monopoly of transport and banking (Francotte, *Industrie dans la Grèce Ancienne*, 144;

both from a state and a private standpoint, existed in Egypt both before and after its occupation as a Roman province.[3] There were royal monopolies of brick, of syenite, and of papyrus in Egypt, and of wheat and purple among the Phoenicians.[4] There were various state monopolies in Rome, notably the monopoly of salt, by means of which the government derived a considerable part of its revenue. The spirit of monopoly pervaded foreign commerce and Rome was, in this sense, the great monopolist of the world, stripping its conquered provinces of sustenance for the benefit of the Roman people.[5] Under the Roman emperors the word "monopolium" was first used to describe the acquisition of exclusive sale of products by the process of what we now call

---

Boeckh, *Staatshaushaltung der Athener*, I, 66; Aristotle, *Oecon.*, II, xxxvii; Le Rossignol, *Monopolies, Past and Present*, 24). At Chios, both during the Turkish domination and afterwards under the Genoese there existed a monopoly of cement which could be sold only through government agency (Francotte, *Industrie dans la Grèce Ancienne*, 144).

[3]Wilcken, *Grundzüge und Chrestomathie der Papyruskunde Gewerbes im hellenistischen Ägypten*, 9; Persson, *Staat und Manufactur im römischen Reiche*, 18; Grenfell, *Revenue Laws of Ptolemy;* Wilcken, *Griechische Ostraka aus Agypten und Nubien*, 681 et seq. In earlier times trade in Egypt had been controlled by a temple monopoly of industry, but this had been destroyed by the earliest Ptolemies. A period of almost complete nationalization followed, the workmen being attached to a special branch of industry producing on behalf of the state. Finally, in the Roman period the ties of the state monopoly were relaxed; the shopowners began to work for themselves, using the labour of members of their families, of apprentices, and of hired men or slaves. But while it existed the state monopoly covered coinage and banking as well as trade and industry (Rostovtzeff, *History of the Roman Empire*, 169-170, 259, 380, 420. As to typical monopolies practised in Egypt see the references cited, *ibid.*, 540, n. 43. See also Francotte, *Industrie dans la Grèce Ancienne*, 145). There existed a monopoly of the trade of spinning yarn, and the oil monopoly exercised regulation of all operations from sowing to sale. The quantities produced were regulated, sale could only be effected through government agency at prices fixed by the state, with all others excluded from the trade, and importation of foreign oil was forbidden except at Alexandria. These monopolies were all created in the fiscal interest with the consumers rendering the profit. The consumers were, however, never troubled by monopolies or forestalling of grain, the state, in general, not indulging in that practice (But see Aristotle, *Oecon.*, II, viii, ix, xviii; Boeckh, *Stattshaushaltung der Athener*, I, 67). The protection of the consumers lay in their being ensured an adequate supply of the regulated commodities at the regulated prices (Francotte, *Industrie dans la Grèce Ancienne*, 148).

[4]Le Rossignol, *Monopolies, Past and Present*, 24.

[5]*Ibid.*, 25.

"cornering";[6] and this practice was prohibited by a decree of the

[6]This process was an offence at common law and was spoken of by Sir Thomas More in his *Utopia* as well as by Blackstone as "regrating and forestalling."

As noted by Cunningham, *English Industry and Commerce*, I, 250: "Common folk had a strong suspicion that the man who was able to secure a monopoly by engrossing or by buying up the available supply of any article, would retail on terms that were to his own profit but not to the advantage of the community."

By the laws of Athens the practice of secreting or hoarding corn was punishable by death. Among the ancient Swedes and Goths and in Lombardy no purchase could take place unless before witnesses.

In imitation of these laws, our Saxon ancestors and after them the Anglo-Danish and Norman Kings introduced into the laws of England regulations of the same nature. Upon a review of them, from the times of Lothario and Edric, Kings of Kent, and Ina, King of Wessex, down to the period of the Conquest, it is obvious that scarce a reign passed without some laws being enacted for the better regulation of an open and free traffic. The general import of these laws was that sales of any commodity should be held publicly at the market and that no market should be permitted except within walled cities and towns in the kingdom. By a law of Æthelstan all sales of a value over 20*d.* were to be made publicly, while Canute reduced the figure to 4*d.* Offences were punishable by fine and imprisonment and sometimes by forfeiture of goods.

After the Conquest, forestalling, which was among the offences mentioned in Domesday Book, was continued as an offence both at common law and by statute. A number of statutes was passed, commencing with that of 51 Hen. III, st. 6; 5 & 6 Edw. VI, c. 14; 5 Eliz., c. 12; 21 Jac. I, c. 22 and continuing to the present day.

The history of the law, with a full discussion of the statutes and the decided cases, is treated in Illingworth, *Inquiry into the Laws Respecting Forestalling*.

43 Ass. Pl. 38 Fitz. Ass. 354, cites a case where forestalling of land was punished by confiscation of all the offender's goods. This was an offence contrary to the statutes 4 Hen. VII, c. 19; 7 Hen. VIII, c. 1; 27 Hen. VIII, c. 22; 5 Eliz., c. 2.

Engrossing of corn was an offence provided by statute 5 Edw. VI, c. 14; 5 Eliz., c. 12; 13 Eliz., c. 22, as well as by various royal proclamations, e.g., that of June 2, 1608. See also proclamation of Elizabeth, Jan. 30, 1563-4 against the engrossing of hops; Steele Proc. no. 587, and cf. such cases as Crosse v. Westwood (1611) 2 Brownl. & Golds. 108; Fenn's Case (1634) W. Jones 320; Bedoe v. Alpe (1622) W. Jones 156; R. v. Smith and Carter (1618) 2 Roll. R. 33; Smith v. Bointon (1615) Bridg. Rep. 48; Rex v. Wheder (1614) 2 Bulst. 317; 1 Roll. R. 134; Company of Merchant Adventurers v. Rebow (1686) 3 Mod. 126 at 131.

The Court of Star Chamber severely punished those found guilty of engrossing, whether of houses and land or of corn or wool or any other commodity. See Hawarde, 76, 77, 78, 91, 104, 305.

Bacon, in his *Abridgement*, tit. Monopoly, says: "Monopoly and engrossing differ only in this, that the first is by patent from the King, the other by act of the subject, between party and party; but both are equally injurious to trade

Senate during the reign of Tiberius.[7] The Roman theory of trade was that of free competition, but the practice of obtaining exclusive sale was so widespread that the Senate received many complaints on the subject.[8] The later wars caused a change in the imperial economic policy, in order to raise revenue, and monopolies granted by the state became general, extending even as far as the food supply.[9] These were not monopolies exercised by the state but

---

and the freedom of the subject, and therefore are equally restrained by the common law. Skin. 169." See also Hawk. P.C., c. 79, 2; Townsend's Collection of Proceedings in Parliament, 244-5.

Bl. Com., bk. IV, chap. XII, 9, states that "monopolies are much the same offence in other branches of trade, that engrossing is in provisions."

Cf. East India Company v. Sandys (1684) 10 St. Tr. 371 at 422 per Pollexfen, *arguendo:* "That ingrossing any sort of merchandize is an offence at common law, *vide* 3 Inst. 196. And in the case *Dominus Rex vers. Crispe et al.* here was lately an agreement between copperas-makers and copperas-merchants, for the buying of all copperas; these copperas-makers should for three years make at so much a ton; and restrain them from selling to others. It was here adjudged as ingrossing, upon an information."

It is interesting to note that the Ontario Municipal Act, R.S.O. (1937), c. 266, s. 408, gives power to certain municipalities to pass by-laws for "prohibiting the forestalling, regrating or monopoly" of foodstuffs and all articles for family use.

As to penalties for combinations among victuallers or artificers to raise the price of provisions, or any commodities, or the rate of labour, see 2 & 3 Edw. VI, c. 15.

That monopoly of the type of engrossing, regrating, and forestalling was not unknown among the Israelites, refer to the story of Joseph and his grain dealings as a royal agent in Egypt. Cf. Proverbs, II, 26: "He that withholdeth corn the people shall curse him, but blessing shall be upon the head of him that selleth it."

[7]A.D. 14-37. Suetonius, *History of the Twelve Caesars*, I, 226. Suetonius mentions the use of the Greek word "Monopolium" in the Roman Senate as a "strange and foreign word."

[8]"The period of Augustus and of his immediate successors was a time of almost complete freedom for trade and of splendid opportunities for private initiative. Neither as a republic nor under the guidance of Augustus and his successors did Rome adopt the policy pursued by some Hellenistic states, particularly Egypt, of nationalizing trade and industry, of making them more or less a monopoly of the state as represented by the king. Everything was left to private management" (Rostovtzeff, *History of the Roman Empire*, 54).

[9]*Ibid.*, 138, 435. During the Anarchy, the third century A.D., there was a return to the Ptolemaic system of state monopoly. This concerned both manufacture and sale of cloth as well as the organization of some branches of industry and retail trade which were vital for the supply of the cities, for example, the

were monopolies granted to private individuals in return for a consideration. In the end this policy was controlled by an edict of the Emperor Zeno issued in A.D. 483 to the Praetorian Prefect of Byzantium, commanding "That no one may presume to exercise a monopoly of any kind of clothing or of fish or of any other thing serving for food or for any other use, whatever its nature may be, either on his own authority or under a rescript of an emperor already procured, or that may hereafter be procured, or under an imperial decree or under a rescript signed by our Majesty; nor may any person combine or agree in unlawful meeting that different kinds of merchandize may not be sold at a less price than they may have agreed upon among themselves."[10] This edict was later continued by the Emperor Justinian[11] in his Code.[12]

---

manufacture and sale of oil. Concessionaires were granted a monopoly of the retail trade, and appear as lessees of oil factories connected with the temples. Industry, which had become to a certain extent emancipated in the second century, was again subjected to state control, which was exercised in the manner peculiar to Ptolemaic times.

[10]Thornton, *Combinations in Restraint of Trade*, 32.

[11]A.D. 527-65.

[12]See Justinian's *Code*: 4, 59, 1. "Jubemus, ne quis cujuscunque vestis, vel piscis, vel pectinum forte, aut echini, vel cujuslibet alterius ad victum, vel ad quemcunque usum pertinentis speciei, vel cujuslibet materiae, pro sua auctoritate, vel sacro jam elicito, aut in posterum eliciendo rescripto, aut pragmatica sanctione, vel sacra nostrae pietatis adnotatione, monopolium audeat exercere. . . Si quis autem monopolium ausus fuerit exercere, bonis propriis expoliatus, perpetuitate damnetur exilii."

The following entries in the Digest of Justinian are interesting as showing the view of monopolies of the forestalling and regrating type held by the Roman law. Any person doing anything or entering into any contract to raise artificially the price of provisions was punished under the lex Julia de Annona (D. 48, 12, 2.) with a fine of 20 aurei (Digest: 48, 12, 2, 2). "Lege Julia de annona poena statuitur adversus eam qui contra annonam fecerit, societamve coieret, quo annona carior fiat": Cf. Bl. Com., bk. IV, chap. XII, para. 8.

Those who kept merchandise out of the market to enhance the price (Dardanarii) were prohibited from trading or were relegated (Digest: 47, 11, 6). "Annonam attentare et vexare vel maxime dardanarii solent: quorum avaritiae obviam itum est tam mandatis quam constitutionibus. Mandatis denique ita cavetur: Praeterea debebis custodire, ne dardanarii ullius mercis sint, ne aut ab his qui coemptas merces supprimunt, aut a locupletioribus qui fructus suos aequis praetiis vendere nollent, dum minus uberes proventus expectant, ne annona oneretur. Poena autem in hos varie statuitur: nam plerumque, si negotiantes sunt, negotiatione eis tantum interdicitur, interdum et relegari solent: humiliores ad opus publicum dare."

See also Illingworth, *Inquiry into the Laws Respecting Forestalling*, 1.

IV. TRADE REGULATION AND THE GUILDS IN ENGLAND

THE term "monopoly" came into use in Europe during the thirteenth century,[1] the Latin word "monopolium" being used on the Continent to mean the right of sole sale obtained from the sovereign for a given payment. Monopolies granted to individuals by the state were considered legal; and it was only when the exclusive sale of a commodity was obtained without licence that it was considered illegal.[2]

In England the word "monopoly" was first used by Sir Thomas More in his *Utopia* in 1516, originally in the Latin version and translated shortly after into English. "Suffer not thies ryche men to bye up all, to ingrosse and forestalle, and with theyr monopolye to kepe the market alone as please them."[3] The first use of the word in an original English context occurred in 1534 in More's *Treatise upon the Passion of Chryste*, where, speaking of the treachery of Judas in betraying his Master, he apostrophizes him in the words: "Thou hast a monopoly thereof." The first official use of the word occurred when it appeared in 1582 in a petition from

[1]Mund, *Monopoly*, 13.

[2]*Ibid.*, Du Cange, *Glossarium Mediae*, pt. V, 510. "Est etiam societas hominum qui sibi solis jus vendendi comparant, vel aliquod genus mercaturae universim emunt, quo carius vendant; quod ut obtineatur pensio interdum fit Principi, quod Monopolium etiam dicitur. Hinc denique eadem vox ad quasvis illicitas confœderationes fluxit, qua ultima notione sæpius occurrit." Du Cange cites examples of the use of the word from A.D. 1268 on.

[3]"Refrenate coemptiones istas diuitum, ac uelut monopolii exercendi licentiam." More, *Utopia*, bk. I, 42; More also has a more direct reference to monopolies when he said, at 41, "Quod si maxime increscat ouium numerus, precio nihil descrescit tamen; quod earum, si monopolium appellari non potest, quod non unus vendit, certe oligopolium est." In the translation by Robynson in 1551 the meaning is curtailed and neither *monopolium* nor *oligopolium* is translated into the English version. More was obviously making an antithesis between monopoly and oligopoly, or control by the few, with which modern writers on economics are familiar. As he said in effect "if they cannot be called a monopoly, because they are not sold by only one person, certainly it is an oligopoly." This antithesis, which distinguishes monopoly from other forms of control and privilege in which there were more than one seller, and which were not considered illegal at common law, was clearly pointed out in Fuller's argument in the case of Darcy v. Allin (1602) Noy 178; 1 W.P.C. at 5.

the Hanse towns to the Assembly of the Empire at Augsburg, transmitted to Elizabeth, charging the Merchant Adventurers with "committing open Monopoly" in the cloth trade.[4] By the turn of the century it had come into common use and was widely employed in Parliament to describe the system of patents used by Elizabeth for the granting of exclusive rights.[5] The first recorded

[4]Wheeler, *Treatise of Commerce*, 65, 67, 84, 105.

A mandate issued by the Emperor Rudolph in 1597 prohibiting the Merchant Adventurers continuing to trade in the Empire on the ground of "committing open monopoly" in the cloth trade, recited that "Monopolish practises... according to the constitutions of us and the holy Empire deserve great punishment." Cf. *ibid.*, 86.

[5]Cf. D'Ewes 547; 554 *temp.* 39 & 40 Eliz.; thus, in 1601 Mr. Spicer of Warwick speaking in the Commons: "First, let us consider of the word Monopolie, what it is, *Monos* is *Unus,* and *Polis* is *Civitas*; so then the meaning of the word is, a restraint of any thing publick in a City or Common-Wealth, to a private use, and the User called a Monopolitan, *quasi cujus privatum lucrum est urbis et Orbis commune malum*" (D'Ewes 644). "The Monopolitans of Starch, Tinn, Fish . . . Salt, and I know not what" (*ibid.*, 646).

That the word and its significance had found general acceptance and usage by the end of the sixteenth century is shown by the following extracts:

1548. "Diuers other crymes were layde to his charge, as . . . gathering together and making a money polde of offices, fees, wardes, and fermes." Edward Hall, *Chronicle: The Union of the two Noble and Illustre Families of Lancastre and Yorke* (Henry VI), 158.

1549. "The ciuil lauis deffendis & forbidduis al monopoles and conuentions of the comont pepil." *Complaynt of Scotlande*, xvi, 140.

1576. "Master Merchant. . . Can finde the meane, to make Monopolyes of every ware, that is accompted strange." George Gascoigne, *The Steele Glas, a Satyre*, 753.

1580. "There is no such 'monopolish' trade used at Emden." *Calendar S.P. For.*, 366.

1587-8. "It becomes alwayes his majestie . . . to repres and stay all monopolles and factiounes." *Reg. Privy Council, Scotland*, iv, 253.

1589. "The said Companie . . . having reduced themselves to the nomber of xij, and so beeing now more notable Monopoliers than they weare beefore." Giles Fletcher, in *Letters of Eminent Literary Men*, 81.

1591. "You Marchant Mercers and Monopolites." Joshua Sylvester, *Du Bartas' Triumph of Faith*, I, III, 522.

1595. "He . . . makes a Monopoly of offices." Samuel Daniel, *The Civile Wares*, V, xcviii.

1596. "The intollerable licenses of Monopoles and Solesales." Bishop William Burlow, *Three Christian Sermons*, II, 49.

1596. "Now for my monapole, I would aske but this trifling sute." Sir John Harington, *The Metamorphosis of Ajax*, 92.

use of the word that we have in English law occurred in 1599 in the case of *Davenant* v. *Hurdis*[6] which will be considered more fully at a later stage.[7] It is apparent, however, from the manner in which the word was used by counsel in argument that it was by no means new in use, and that the principles relative to the legal position of monopolies had already become fairly crystallized.[8]

There are recorded instances of monopoly patents in Europe prior to those in England, as, for example, the monopoly for the manufacture and sale of paper in Berne and its jurisdictions in 1467;[9] the grant in 1469 to Johann von Speyer of the exclusive right of exercising the trade of printing in Venice for five years;[10] the exclusive privilege granted in Venice in 1507 for twenty years for the introduction of a secret process of mirror making;[11] and the establishment of the same industry in France by patent in

---

1596. "Then daily beg'd I great Monopolies." Michael Drayton, *The Legend of Piers Gaveston and Others*, III, 517.

1599. "To keepe out fell and black Monopolites." Thomas Moufet, *The Silkwormes and their Flies*, 58.

1600. "Merchants trafficke . . . from one Mart, hauen, promontorie, or Monopole to another." William Watson, *A Deacordon of Ten Quodlibeticall Questions*, 61.

1601. "Thou shalt have a monopoly of playing." Ben Jonson, *Poetaster*, V, iii.

By 1604 the word had acquired sufficient use to be accepted into Robert Cawdrey's *Table Alphabeticall of English Wordes: "Monopolie*, a licence that none shall buy or sell a thing, but one alone."

In 1611 it appeared in Randle Cotgrave's *Dictionary of the French and English Tongues:* "Monopolé, Monopoled or monopolized; ingrossed, as a commoditie, into one, or a few mens hands."

[6](1599) Moore, K.B. 576; Trin. 41 Eliz. rot. 92.

[7]See post 86, 214, 311.

[8]The Attorney-General Cook, as he is called in the report of the case, Coke as he is more generally known, argued that: "Et by by-law pur pontage, murage, et tiels semblables est bone, quia pur le publick bone: mes by-lawes que establish monopolies sont encountre common droit et void. Et pur ceo le Civil ley ad un text quod monopolistae omnes spolientur suis bonis et etiam rescripta eorum frangantur: et il define Monopolis del Greek parol ἀπὸ τὺ μόνυ κὶ πωλέομαι quel est en Latin solus vendere: et quia dapproppriater le sole vendicion al un et excluder auters est encounter common good, pur ceo il conclude que by-lawes faits pur enducer monopolies (come ceo est) sont void."

[9]Kohler, *Handbuch des deutschen Patentrechts*, 21.

[10]Klostermann, *Das Patentgesetz für das deutsche Reich*, 15.

[11]Nesbitt, *Glass*, 90.

1551 for a ten-year monopoly.[12] These industrial monopolies, originating in Italy, found their way to the Netherlands, and from there to England.[13] Acontius, a naturalized Italian, is reputed to have first suggested the adoption in England as a continuing policy, of this method of rewarding inventors.[14] The basis of the grant was that in return for the introduction of a manufacturing process, formerly unknown in England, the introducer was accorded a monopoly of using the process for a specified length of time, usually with conditions attached relating to the time within which manufacture was to commence, the teaching of the trade to English workmen, and the manufacture of a minimum quantity within a fixed period, the grant creating a monopoly only for the manufacture of the product and not for its sale, for monopoly as to sale did not appear as an essential part of the grant until a later period.[15]

The development of a patent system arising from the grant of exclusive privileges as a stimulation to invention and industrial expansion required a combination of factors which, during the Middle Ages, was present only in England. These factors were a reasonably integrated state with centralized authority over a broad area, with the concomitant of a reasonably broad market over which a monopoly could operate. The closely knit economic and governmental system of England constituted a field for the operation and growth of the monopoly system which was impossible

[12]Renouard, *Traité des brevets d'invention*, 79.

[13]Hulme, "History of the English Patent System" (1896) 12 L.Q.R., 144.

[14]Cal. S.P. Dom. Eliz., 1601-3; addenda, 1547-65, 495. "Jacobus Acontius to the Queen. Nothing is more honest than that those who, by searching, have found out things useful to the public should have some fruit of their rights and labours, as meanwhile they abandon all other modes of gain, are at much expense in experiments, and often sustain much loss, as has happened to me. I have discovered most useful things, new kinds of wheel machines, and of furnaces for dyers and brewers, which when known, will be used without my consent, except there be a penalty, and I, poor with expenses and labour, shall have no returns. Therefore I beg a prohibition against using any wheel machines, either for grinding or bruising, or any furnaces like mine, without my consent."

Doubt has been expressed of Acontius's claim to be the originator of this key-note of the patent law. Cf. Davies, "Further Light on the Case of Monopolies" (1932) 96 L.Q.R., 397. Certainly the grant to Smyth in 1552 shows that the expediency of rewarding invention as a common benefit was not a new idea when Elizabeth came to the throne.

[15]Holdsworth, *History of English Law*, IV, 345; Hulme (1896) 12 L.Q.R., 148, 151-3; (1897) 13 L.Q.R., 314.

in the isolated groups of states and small principalities existing in continental Europe.

At the time when England commenced, under the Tudors, to lay the foundations of the patent system, the Continent was divided into a complicated patchwork of petty principalities. Germany was hardly even a geographical term, being composed of numerous small states held together only by the shadowy overlordship of the Holy Roman Empire. Prussia, with its population of Slavic pagans had not yet emerged from a state of barbarism. Italy was, until the founding of the modern Italian state under Cavour and Mazzini, a muddled pattern of small, independent jurisdictions. France was a feudal association of provinces, and Spain was composed of four kingdoms warring against the Moors in Granada. Russia was just freeing itself from the domination of the Tartars, and the Scandinavian countries were only on the point of being christianized. These petty states of continental Europe could not offer an adequate breeding ground for the development of a firm policy of encouraging industry by monopoly.

While both France and England apparently offered an equal field for development, the tardier and later growth in France was due to the theoretical approach exercised by the French monarchs toward the system of monopolies which differed greatly from that exercised by the English sovereigns. Grants of exclusive privilege appeared as early as 1536 in France, when a concession by the consular government of Lyons was accorded to Etienne Turquette giving him and his workers safe conduct from Genoa and franchises for the establishment of the silk trade.[16] In 1551 a monopoly was granted to Theses Mutio, of Bologna, for glassware made in the Venetian manner; and in the same year a patent was granted to the Abbé Foullon, a French inventor. Thereafter, patents of exclusive privilege were granted in moderately substantial numbers, these being registered with the Parlement de Paris, which registration served to confirm the title. By royal decree of 1699, the French Académie des Sciences, established in 1666 by Colbert, was required to examine all machines for which privileges were solicited, and to certify whether they were new and useful. These patents had the character of property; and during the eighteenth

[16]Prager, "History of Intellectual Property" (1944) 26 J.P.O.S., 750.

century there grew up a patent system having marked similarities to the present system, except for the primary foundation—the right of an inventor to claim a patent for an invention.[17]

As in England and Germany, the origin of the protection of inventors is found in the individual privileges granted to them as acts of royal grace or favour. The obtaining of such privilege did not constitute a right of the inventor: it was a simple royal favour.[18] It was only in 1762 that an edict, providing generally for the protection of inventions, was passed laying down general rules in matters relating thereto. The purpose of the edict was "récompenser l'industrie des inventeurs ou exciter celle qui languissait." Like all other privileges, that of the inventor was abolished on the night of August 4, 1789; but a short time after, on January 7, 1791, the right of inventors was guaranteed by a decree of the National Assembly.[19] This was followed in due time by the act of July 5, 1844, which is the present law of France on the subject. Price[20] notes that, while France during the Middle Ages offered a field for the development of a patent system, its industrial progress being superior to that of England, its political, social, and economic integration had not gone so far. Economic organization in France tended to encourage local exclusiveness; and the efforts of the central powers were calculated to strengthen rather than supersede guild regulations. As will be seen hereafter, the establishment of a national monopoly policy was contrary in its trend to the development of the individual guilds and their regulations of trade, and must, to be successful, gradually cause the guilds to sink in importance and power. In addition to these factors, the French monarchy, while enjoying less real national power than did the English Crown, was at the same time tempted to engage in an active participation and intervention in industry; and this naturally tended to discourage the grant of monopolies to private individuals. Apparently the earliest systematic use of

[17]*Ibid.*, 727.

[18]Malapert and Forni, *Nouveau Commentaire des lois sur les brevets d'invention*, 8 et seq. Thus, the regulations of the Académie Royale des Sciences in 1699 provided: "L'académie examinera, si le roi ordonne, toutes les machines pour lesquelles on solicitera des privilèges auprès de Sa Majesté; elle certifera, si elles sont nouvelles et utiles, et les inventeurs de celles qui seront approuvées seront tenus de lui en laisser un modèle."

[19]Akerman, *Obligation d'exploiter en matière de brevets d'invention*, 161.

[20]Price, *English Patents of Monopoly*, 5.

patents in France dates from the closing years of the sixteenth century; and this may well have been in imitation of the English patent system, already well developed.

During the Middle Ages, industrial progress in England was far below that of the continental countries. On the Continent, owing to the higher civilization of the East, there was an infiltration of improved processes which accounted for much of the material progress, this progress being due more to the adaptation to European use of these improved processes than to original and individual experimental effort. Even as late as the time of Elizabeth, English society was mainly of an agricultural and mining type, dealing in natural products, exchanging its undressed cloth, wool, hides, tin, and lead for the manufactures of the Continent. The first substantial native manufacturing industry of England was the cloth trade, the improvement and expansion of which was fostered not alone by the grant of rewards and privileges from the Crown, but by the internal orders and regulations of the merchant and craft guilds and the Hanseatic League. The underlying aim behind these regulations and royal rewards was to make the country self-sustaining.

The theory of exclusive privilege probably takes its rise from the feudal system, under which the lord of the manor arrogated to himself the exclusive right of holding and controlling a market,[21] and of maintaining a mill, bakery, and other services.[22] These rights were established on the basis of immemorial custom, and the word "monopoly" was not generally used in the law books to describe this type of exclusive privilege.[23] The restrictions on

[21]Stubbs, *Constitutional History*, I, 426; Gibbins, *Industry in England*, 138; cf. the Case of Monopolies (1603) 11 Co. Rep. 84; see post 321.

[22]A survival of these exclusive rights may be seen by an examination of the seigneurial system under the Ancien Régime in Lower Canada. While *banalités* existed in profusion in France—no one but a seigneur could own a grist-mill, wine-press, slaughter-house, or even a dove-cot—in Canada, there was only one *droit de banalité*—the grist-mill right. While the operation of this exclusive milling privilege did not bear heavily on the people of the seigneuries, it shows a persistence of these exclusive rights well into the nineteenth century. Munro, *Seigneurs of Old Canada*, 98; Wrong, *Canadian Manor and its Seigneurs*.

[23]Fermor v. Brooke (1590) Cro. Eliz. 203; Hix v. Gardiner (1614) 2 Bulst. 195; Geffery at Hay v. William at Ford (1334) Y.B. 8 Edw. III, fo. 37 a, b; Dunstable v. B. (1433) Y.B. 11 Hen. VI, fo. 19, pl. 13; City of London's Case (1610) 8 Co. Rep. 121b, at 125a, 125b, 127a; Hilton v. Granville (1844) 5 Q.B. 701; London

sale within the manor to residents of the manor resulted in the establishment of markets and fairs, the holding of which was usually authorized by royal grant.[24] This power of the Crown to grant the franchise of fair often involved an element of exclusion, although the monopoly was thus strictly limited, there being within the market or fair, free competition of a number of buyers and sellers. Just as the right to trade in a particular town might be given to a particular body of persons, so, if the franchise of fair were granted, no rival fair could be set up within a certain distance.[25]

Corporation v. Cox (1867) 2 H.L. 239; Mercer v. Denne (1904) 2 Ch. 534; (1905) 2 Ch. 538.

Vin. Abr., XVII, 213, however, states that "custom may create a monopoly, as the case in the Register is, that none should exercise the trade of a dyer in Rippon without the Archbishop of York's licence. Vent. 196, Pasch. 24 Car. 2 in the case of Broadnox," citing Sir George Farmer v. Brook, Ow. 67; Mitchel v. Reynolds, 1 Le. 143. The case of Sir George Farmer v. Brook (1590) Ow. 67; Leonard 142, 8 Co. Rep. 127, held that, although the plaintiff and his ancestors had the sole right of maintaining a bake-house with a restraint to others against baking bread, such constituted a monopoly and was void. Cf. Merchant Adventurers Co. v. Rebow (1686) 3 Mod. 126 at 128.

[24]Maitland, *Domesday Book*, 193. In his judgment in the Great Case of Monopolies: The East India Co. v. Sandys (1684) 10 St. Tr. 371 at 524, Jefferies, L.C.J., approved the argument of the Attorney-General (Sir Robert Sawyer) which stated the prerogative basis of the grant of markets and fairs. Jefferies pointed out "that numbers of people could not meet to traffic or merchandise without being in danger of being punished as unlawful assemblies: the crown therefore granted the liberties of fairs and markets, for the sake of commerce and trade." Fairs and markets were, in the words of the Attorney-General (see 459) "no other than royal licenses to assemble for trade and traffic."

From counsel's argument in The Company of Merchant Adventurers v. Rebow (1686) 3 Mod. 126 it appears that the prerogative right of granting markets arose out of the statute of 27 Edw. III, c. 1 which confined the staple to certain places. The object of this, the first statute regulating trade, was "that persons might not go about in companies to trade without the King's licence; and from thence came markets."

[25]Holdsworth, *History of English Law*, VI, 327. The exclusive right to hold a fair was brought forward by counsel both for and against the patent in the Case of Monopolies (1603) 11 Co. Rep. 84b. See post 321.

In the Case of Monopolies (1602) Moore K.B. 674, the Solicitor-General cited a case where William the Conqueror granted to the City of Winchester a privilege in respect of a fair that none should sell elsewhere during the fair time save within a certain precinct and this continued in use until 18 Hen. VIII. This reference is to the Case of the Abbot of Westminster, Registrum Brevium fo. 107, which is again referred to by Jefferies, L.C.J., in the Great Case of Monopolies: East India Co. v. Sandys (1684) 10 St. Tr. 371 at 524. Post 321, 364.

With the rise of the towns in the eleventh century the merchant guilds began to be formed. These guilds obtained by charter the right of exclusive sale within the town of the goods made by them.[26] Under their charters they obtained the sole right of regulating and supervising trade within the town and so obtained a monopoly of all trade, not only of sale but of manufacture, within the town, subject, however, to the right of market or fair granted by royal charter or acquired by custom, this latter right serving in many cases to constitute the only competition against the monopolistic privileges held by the guilds.[27] By this police system, no one could obtain the freedom of the city unless men of the same mystery[28] were ready to undertake for him; and there is occasional evidence that this monopoly power was abused by the guild members.[29] The monopolies enjoyed by the guilds were, however, group monopolies, the sole right of sale never being granted to one person by any of the guild charters. Within the guild there was free trading and free competition, the privileges of the guild being those of restricting competition from strangers to the guild, the regulation of the trade, and the maintenance of price. The guild restriction was not upon competition but only upon the number of competitors. When the industrial monopolies were effectively controlled by local authorities, there seems to have been little trouble; what trouble there was arose in cases where any guild of craftsmen claimed to be independent of local authority.[30] The merchant guild, *gilda mercatoria*, *ceapmanne gild*, or *hansa*, to which all the traders of the town were, as a rule, obliged to belong,

[26]Brentano, *History of Gilds*, xciii; Gross, *The Gild Merchant*, I, 29; cf. Argument of Coke, A.-G. in the Case of Monopolies (1602) Moore K.B. 675.

From the time of William Rufus there was no reign in which political immunities or commercial franchises were not bestowed upon the towns. Hallam, *Middle Ages*, chap. VIII, pt. III.

[27]Maitland, *Domesday Book*, 193-4.

[28]It may not be amiss to note that our word mystery—sometimes spelled mistery—is derived from the French *métier*. Cf. Pooley, *Guilds of London*, 12.

[29]Cunningham, *English Industry and Commerce*, I, 292.

Instances of abuse of guild monopoly privileges usually occurred when several guild members combined to enhance and maintain prices unduly, as, e.g., the chandlers of Norwich in 1300, the London lime-burners in 1329, and the London pursers in 1344. Cf. Lipson, *Economic History of England*; Unwin, *Guilds and Companies of London*, 92.

[30]Cunningham, *English Industry and Commerce*, I, 341; Riley, *Liber Custumarum*, 424.

was of profound influence in the growth of the towns. At first independent of municipal authority, it gradually coalesced with it, monopolizing the rights which had originally belonged to all the free inhabitants. This development, arising before the Norman Conquest, occurred chiefly during the two centuries following so that "in the reign of Henry II there can be little doubt that the possession of a merchant-guild had become the sign and token of municipal independence; that it was in fact, if not in theory, the governing body of the town in which it was allowed to exist. It is recognized by Glanvill as identical with the *communa* of the privileged towns, the municipal corporation of the later age."[31] Thus, the charter granted by Henry II to Oxford distinctly laid down the principle that the merchant guild had an exclusive right of regulating trade except in specified cases[32] and in addition, it seems clear that it had also, originally, the right of regulating the craft guilds.

While the growth of the towns in England and of the merchant guilds as being the regulators and supervisors of trade and commerce and the privileges thereto appertaining within the towns, had much to do with the shaping and trend of the monopoly system, there existed also the influence of the great federation of towns and cities, the Hanseatic League. This was, during the Middle Ages, the most powerful of the commercial institutions. The League owed its origin to the establishment, during the discord and turbulence of the feudal period, of trading centres on the coasts of Europe, where exclusive privileges, in the form of patents and monopolies, were granted in order to procure the supply of some of the indulgences indispensable in an improving state of society. Commencing at the conclusion of the twelfth or the beginning of the thirteenth century near the coasts of the Baltic Sea, before the termination of the fourteenth, it consisted of sixty-four principal cities.[33] Its depot in London, the "Steel-yard" or "Stilliard," was the centre of its activity in England, London being the only port of England that was admitted to the

[31]Stubbs, *Constitutional History*, I, 453; Raumer, *Geschichte der Hohenstaufen*, V, 377-80; Gneist, *History of the English Constitution*, 124 n., 436; Taswell-Langmead, *English Constitutional History*, 16.

[32]Stubbs, *Constitutional History*, III, 582; *Select Charters*, 167.

[33]Collier, *Law of Patents*, 9.

dignity of membership in the Hanseatic League.[34] Wool was the staple commodity; and merchants, under the protection of the League, penetrated far into England, and in their dealings in the country towns spread the story of their own independence.[35] The merchants of the League had been encouraged to settle in London by Henry III; and England's fifteenth-century commerce was controlled principally by them, they having secured many special privileges for which they rendered particular services to the Crown and thereby obtained protection which enabled them to monopolize the trade. It is an anomaly in English history that until almost the end of the reign of Edward III, the policy of the government tended rather to discourage than to encourage trading abroad by its subjects. English merchants were practically excluded from foreign commerce; and their struggles against aliens were chiefly waged around the internal trade of the country.[36] The Hanseatics for a time constituted the strongest group of alien merchants in England, and, as such, claimed the exclusive enjoyment of the privileges granted by the *Carta Mercatoria* of 1303. As the guilds controlled and regulated trade within the towns, so the foreign trade of England was largely in the hands of the Merchants of the Staple who constituted the local constituent of the Hansa. The Merchants of the Staple controlled the export trade in wool for two and a half centuries after the accession of the Plantagenets. The system of the staple was founded upon the holding of regular and stable markets at fixed and settled places, usually the larger towns, both within England and in foreign countries. It was a useful and almost necessary device for the direction of the trade, the Staplers having a monopoly dictated by established and conservative principles. The monopoly in English hands was strengthened by the transfer of the staple from Bruges to England in 1353.[37] But as the manufacture of cloth grew up and gradually displaced the trade in raw wool, the usefulness of the system declined, and tended to become a clog on the progress of the expanding trade policies. During the fifteenth century

[34]Cf. East India Co. v. Sandys (1684), 10 St. Tr. 371 at 546 per Jefferies, L.C.J.

[35]Taswell-Langmead, *English Constitutional History*, 192 n.; Taylor, *Origin of the English Constitution*, 454 et seq; *Encyclopedia Britannica*, 14th ed., X, 964, tit. Guilds; XI, 162, tit. Hanseatic League; Hallam, *Middle Ages*, chap. IX, pt. II.

[36]Brodhurst, "The Staple" (1901) 17 L.Q.R., 56-76.

[37]27 Edw. III, c. 23.

the inevitable conflict between the new mercantile power, growing conscious of its national strength, and the old, standing insistent on the letter of its privileges, presaged the final withdrawal by Elizabeth of their privileges from the Hanseatics in favour of the English Merchant Adventurers.[38]

During the twelfth century, with the diversification of trades, there began a drift towards the formation of craft guilds, and as these became of more importance with the development of the cloth trade, the tendency during the fourteenth century was for the merchant guilds to give way to the craft guilds,[39] a craft guild usually comprising all the artisans in a single branch of industry in a particular town. When the merchant guild had become identified with the corporation or governing body, its power of regulating trade passed into the same hands. The craft guilds aimed at privileges of their own and possessed, each within the limits of its own art, directive and restrictive and regulative powers corresponding with those claimed by the merchant guilds.[40] Prior to Edward III the craft guilds secured their exclusive privileges by an annual payment to the King.[41] By the use of the royal prerogative, however, Edward III commenced the practice

[38]Cf. Trevelyan, *English Social History*, 198.

The great trading companies created by charter were the competitors and historical successors of the Hanseatic League. They were naturally monopolistic in their nature and activities because freedom of trade was not, in their day, considered advisable. Thus Bacon stated: "I dare not advise to adventure the great trade of the Kingdom, which hath been so long under government in a free and loose trade."

Among the chartered companies which displaced and succeeded the Hanseatic League as the exclusive repositories of the privileges of England's swiftly expanding foreign trade were the Company of Merchant Adventurers, chartered in 1407 with headquarters in London and branches at Exeter and Newcastle; the Levant or Turkey Company chartered by Elizabeth in 1581 with the exclusive right of trading with Turkey; the Eastland Company chartered in 1579 with exclusive rights of trade in the Baltic; the Muscovy Company in 1555 with exclusive rights to trade with Russia; and the Society of the Merchant Adventurers of Exeter chartered in 1560 with exclusive rights to trade with France. These were later followed by the great joint-stock companies such as the Royal African or Guinea Company of 1672 and the British East India Company of 1599.

[39]Unwin, *Industrial Organization*, 16.

[40]Stubbs, *Constitutional History*, III, 584 ff.

[41]Brentano, *History of Gilds*, cxxii. By 1500, twenty-five guilds had procured royal charters granting them corporate rights and powers of jurisdiction. Pooley, *Guilds of London*, 14.

of confirming the guilds' rights by charter in return for a fixed sum.[42] The craft guilds flourished because of the combination of ideas that the craftsmen in any industry desired to regulate their own affairs both of internal government and of quality and quantity of output, and that the people generally were willing to accord them special privileges and monopolies in order that quality might be maintained and prices regulated.

While it is not to be forgotten that, in many cases, the craft guild existed alongside the merchant guild, either as an integral part of the larger body, or, in some cases, in competition with it, the tendency was for the single organization, with a general monopoly of trade, to be replaced by a number of separate organizations representing the various trades and handicrafts.[43] The function of guarding and supervising the trade monopoly was gradually diversified by falling into the control of the separate organizations, the craft guild tending to supersede the old general guild merchant.[44] Economic forces, of course, caused this gradual transfer of the regulating authority from the larger organizations to the smaller but distinct bodies representing the individual crafts. The process was one of gradual but inevitable change, the merchant guild slowly losing its authority and decaying as the smaller and younger guilds gradually arrogated to themselves the individual powers peculiar to their crafts which had been embraced in the larger content of the older, inclusive type of guild. It was a process of natural growth and decay, the craft guilds rising to the height of their power in the fourteenth and fifteenth centuries.[45]

The craft guild represented the common interests of its members, and, subject to the general control of the municipality, it

[42]Pooley, *Guilds of London*, 13.

[43]Green, *History of the English People*, bk. III, chap. I. In a sense, the present grantee of a patent who, by his patent, is invested with the sole licence and privilege of making, using, and vending to others to be used, the subject matter of his patent, is incorporated and erected into a new mystery; he becomes in his own person the head of a new craft which is to comprise himself, his agents and licensees and no others. Cf. Gordon, *Monopolies by Patents*, 122.

[44]Examples of the monopolistic type of control which the guilds endeavoured to exercise may be seen by reference to the example cited in the case of Davenant v. Hurdis (considered post 86, 214, 311) and the decision in the Cloth Workers of Ipswich Case (post 89, 217).

[45]*Encyclopedia Britannica*, 14th ed., X, 964, tit. Guilds; Trevelyan, *English Social History*, 37 et seq.

managed the affairs of the craft within the town, fixing prices, wages, and conditions of work to the general satisfaction of masters and men,[46] and regulating the right to trade or work in the place in which its jurisdiction prevailed.[47] The craft guilds existed not only in London but also in provincial towns. They were mentioned as early as the time of Henry I, and seem to have existed from a much earlier date. By the fifteenth century they had become so universal that every trade which occupied as many as twenty men in a town had a guild of its own.[48] As well as trying to secure good work on the part of their members, the guilds attempted to suppress the production of wares by irresponsible persons who were not members of the craft.[49] An inherent feature of their organization was that they constituted monopolies; and in some cases this monopolistic factor tended to bring them into difficulties. The weavers' monopoly was considered a grievance in 1321,[50] and there were other difficulties in 1376. In 1437 it was charged that the guilds set the local authorities at defiance, and thus injured the public.[51] As a result, an act was passed[52] providing that their regulations and ordinances should, in the future, be submitted to justices of the peace, and be recorded by them. The craft guilds thus constituted an element in the national regulation of trade, Parliament using them as its agents for the purpose.[53]

The age of Chaucer was the great formative period of English capitalism—a time when the wool monopolists came into existence,[54] through the functioning of the Company of the Staple. The Staple was, in its beginning, concerned solely with the export of wool and constituted the only means of the export of that com-

[46]Trevelyan, *English Social History*, 38; Pooley, *Guilds of London*, 13.

[47]Trevelyan, *English Social History*, 190.

[48]Ashley, *English Economic History*, I, chap. II, 81. The thirteenth and fourteenth centuries were the periods of the greatest guild prosperity. Pooley, *Guilds of London*, 13.

[49]Ashley, *English Economic History*, I, chap. II, 72; Rogers, *Six Centuries of Work and Wages*, 107; Gibbins, *Industry in England*, 94 ff.

[50]Riley, *Liber Custumarum*, I, 416. Guild privileges were not, however, considered to be objectionable monopolies, unless the members conspired together to enhance prices. See *per* Fuller, *arguendo*, in Darcy v. Allin (1602) Noy at 182.

[51]Rot. Parl. IV, 507; cf. Pooley, *Guilds of London*, 19.

[52]15 Henry VI, c. 6.

[53]Cunningham, *English Industry and Commerce*, I, 445.

[54]Postan, "The Fifteenth Century" (1939) 9 Ec. Hist. Rev., 165.

modity, but later the export of cloth gained ground until, in the time of the Tudors, the export of cloth killed the export of raw wool.[55] So the capitalist system, with the rise of the entrepreneur, had its beginning during the same period in the business of cloth manufacture, for the manufacture of raw wool into cloth called not for one craft but for many, and the expansion of the cloth trade could not be organized by the craft guilds. For this there was needed capital and a standardized product. This early beginning of the capitalist system is one of the sign-posts in the history of monopolies. While it must be remembered that the guilds did not create other than group monopolies as opposed to private monopolies, the germ of the idea of exclusive sale was present, particularly in the case of the Staple.

The privileges granted to the boroughs and guilds are, however, to be distinguished from industrial monopoly licences in that they were commercial rather than manufacturing privileges.[56] They differed also in that the latter created a monopoly, and also because, in the former case, the Crown made the grant and then kept the privileged industry under its control. With the industrial monopoly the patentee obtained control.[57]

These commercial privileges granted to "a fraternity, society or corporation of merchants to the end that good order and rule should be by them observed for the increase and advancement of trade and merchandise, and not for the hindrance and diminution of it"[58] were considered valid restrictions on trade on the ground that "true trade and traffic cannot be maintained or increased without order or government."[59] These privileges were not regarded as grievances in the proceedings in 1601, and they were excepted from the prohibitions of the Statute of Monopolies.[60] *The Cloth Workers of Ipswich Case*[61] shows an example of this type

[55]Trevelyan, *English Social History*, 34.

[56]Cf. Darcy v. Allin (1602) Noy at 182; Hulme (1896) 12 L.Q.R., 153, n. 1.

[57]"With the acceptance by the Crown of the Monopoly policy advocated by Acontius in 1559, the responsibility for the introduction of new industries was by a gradual process of devolution shifted from the Crown to the patentee, upon the faith of whose representations the grant was both drawn and issued." Hulme (1896) 12 L.Q.R., 151.

[58]City of London's Case (1610) 8 Co. Rep. 125a.

[59]City of London's Case, supra.

[60]S. 9.

[61](1615) 11 Co. Rep. 53.

of exclusive privileges and the manner of their regulation by the courts of common law.[62]

Beginning with the fourteenth century, and continuing during the Tudor period, a transition occurred of the utmost importance. Gradually the export of wool declined, and the production of home manufactures increased, until they in turn were exported, in some cases the export of wool being prohibited. This transition became practically complete in the time of Elizabeth. At this time the number of employers of labour owning more than one loom became so great that an attempt was made by statute to stop the progress of this beginning of the factory system[63] by prohibiting the possession of more than one loom, or of two looms if the weaver lived in a town, or the letting and hiring of looms.[64] But the gradual decentralization of industry had commenced, and it was, in its way, a social revolution which nothing could stop. The craft guilds, as industry became more diversified and more national, gradually lost their jurisdiction and power. Industry became not only more diversified but more expanded as it was released from local custom. In Elizabethan England the old social ties were being swept away by the new wealth and the new discoveries; the new learning and the new religion were forces which were pregnant and prophetic of great social change. Although the craft guilds received their death blow only in the confiscatory legislation of Edward VI against guild property, they had already started to decline. The expansion of overseas enterprise was closely connected with the growth of merchant capitalism, inimical to the old municipal and guild system.[65] The guild system was not favourable to capital accumulation. The guild outlook was municipal, and its structure inelastic; and therefore it gave way to the system of merchant capitalism which, with its complementary domestic industry, lent itself to expansion and change.[66]

[62]See also Davenant v. Hurdis (1599) 11 Co. Rep. 88; Moore K.B. 576.

[63]2 & 3 Ph. & Mary, c. 11.

[64]Gibbins, *Industry in England*, 131, 236.

[65]Trevelyan, *English Social History*, 200. Until the reign of Edward VI, the foreign commerce of England was almost entirely in the hands of strangers, the merchants of the Steelyard. In 1551 their privileges began to be recalled, and from then on foreign commerce came more and more under the control of the English merchant companies, on whom monopolies of the same character were liberally bestowed. Hume, *History of England*, chap. XXV.

[66]Fay, *Great Britain from Adam Smith to the Present Day*, 127.

The external or commercial monopolies which were granted to groups of merchants for the export of the staples and manufactured products of England to foreign countries, of which the Merchant Adventurers and the East India Company are the best known examples, must not be confused with the internal monopolies with which we are concerned. These exclusive privileges, operating within the realm, subdivide into a classification such as the control of printing and censorship of the press[67] and of postal services; licences for relief from penal statutes; and the organizing of trade and industry under regulations designed for their protection and stimulation. Under the last of these classifications, industrial monopolies formed an essential element. We are concerned with monopolies granted for the purpose of establishing and encouraging new trades and industries and stimulating weak ones in the domestic sphere.

A further type of monopoly designed to promote trade was that which confined a particular manufacture to a particular town, and the restriction of the right to trade in a particular town to a particular body of persons.[68] Efforts of this type are, of course, evidence of the increase of manufacturing in the country districts and of the operation of increasing competition upon the older industries in the towns. Thus the manufacture of worsted cloth, first introduced by the Flemings, was restricted to the town of Worstead by a patent of 1315;[69] and in 1328 Edward III issued letters patent on behalf of the cloth workers of Norfolk.[70] In 2 Edw. III the King restrained all persons from importing sweet wines at any port except Southampton. A statute of 14 & 15 Hen. VIII, c. 1 prohibited country weavers from dealing with foreigners. In the same year a statute was passed protecting Norwich artisans against competition from the neighbouring countryside. This was

[67]See ante 68.

[68]Holdsworth, *History of English Law*, VI, 327.

[69]Gibbins, *Industry in England*, 129.

[70]Cal. Rot. Pat. 103, Prima Patent'de 2 Edw. III a Tergo; Gibbins, *Industry in England*, 130. An alnager was appointed the following year (Cal. Rot. Pat. 103, Prima Patent'de 3 Edw. III), but the patent was revoked and the alnager removed in 1348 (Cal. Rot. Pat. 156; Prima Pars Patent'de 22 Edw. III). The power of alnage was, however, restored in 1410 (Rot. Parl. iii, 637) and a further patent was granted to the worsted merchants and workers of Norfolk in 1377 (Cal. Rot. Pat. 197b; 1 Rich. II).

renewed by statute 5 & 6 Edw. VI, c. 24. In 1530[71] a monopoly was granted by Parliament to Bridport for the "making of cables, hawsers, ropes, and all other tackling," forbidding "the people of the adjacent parts" to make any kind of rope, it being alleged that the town would utterly decay without the monopoly. Again in 1534,[72] a monopoly was granted to the towns of Worcester, Evesham, Droitwich, Kidderminster, and Bromsgrove, restraining the persons "dwelling in the hamlets, thorps, and villages of the county" from making and finishing cloth. In 1544[73] a monopoly was granted to the citizens of York for the manufacture of coverlets and blanketings, on the representation that competitors had "withdrawn themselves out of the city into the country" and had competed with York.[74] In 1554[75] Parliament encouraged the foundation of a new industry by granting to certain citizens of Norwich, who had, at great cost to themselves, introduced the manufacture of satins and fustians from Naples, the right to be incorporated as a fellowship with power to survey the manufacture, which was to be carried on only at Norwich.

Again, there were the statutes which prohibited the practice of handicrafts until a defined period of apprenticeship in the craft had been undertaken.[76]

Grants of the general type we have been considering differed from the later grants of industrial privilege in that they did not create a sole monopoly in the hands of one individual but rather something in the nature of group privilege or restriction. They exhibited also the essential difference that the Crown retained control of the privileged industry.

As Gordon points out[77] it must have been very important for the early inventors to obtain dispensation from such disabilities,

[71]21 Hen. VIII, c. 12.

[72]25 Hen. VIII, c. 18.

[73]34 & 35 Hen. VIII, c. 10.

[74]Gibbins, *Industry in England*, 239. A list of exclusive rights which it was considered proper for the King to grant as an exercise of the prerogative is given by Coke in his argument in the Case of Monopolies (1602) Moore K.B. 674.

[75]1 & 2 Ph. & Mary, c. 14.

[76]Cf. 1 Mary, c. 7; 5 Eliz., c. 4, s. 4; and see also Charter to the Drapers Company of London, of Edward III: "We, willing . . . that none shall use the mystery of drapery in the City of London . . . unless he has been apprenticed." Herbert, *History of the London Livery Companies*, 480.

[77]Gordon, *Monopolies by Patents*, 29.

since in many towns throughout England there were chartered guilds of merchants and craftsmen whose privileges at the date of the Statute of Monopolies were effective and jealously guarded. On this account, royal licences were sought by those who desired to set up new industries, to countervail the earlier patents.[78] These grants obviously operated in derogation of trading privileges previously granted.[79] For this reason, the early grants of patents for inventions were carefully drafted to give "full power and authority . . . any law, statute, Act of Parliament, Proclamation, restraint or any other matter, cause, or thing whatsoever . . . to the contrary notwithstanding."[80] Under the organization of the craft guilds, the privileges and restraints granted by their charters prevented the exercise of many new trades and manufactures, and would have constituted an insurmountable barrier if not removed by some form of relief in the grant setting up the new manufacture. The inventor of a new manufacture was almost certain to find himself in conflict with some charter granting exclusive privileges to a craft guild which enabled the guild to make regulations for all persons exercising and using the mystery of the guild.[81] It was, therefore, a matter of strict necessity for the patentee to be relieved from these restraints and regulations laid down and exercised by the guilds, as is evidenced by the grants in the glass and smalt patents at the beginning of the seventeenth century.[82]

[78]See Mansell's Glass Patent (1623) 1 W.P.C. 20, 21. So also in the case of the Smalt Patent (1 W.P.C. 9) the grant was of "full, free and lawful power, license, etc., in all and every county, city, town corporate and other towns, villages, hamlets and other places exempt as not exempt to make, work and compound the said stuff called Smalt, etc."

[79]Vin. Ab., tit. Prerogative of the King (U.C.) 5.

[80]See the Smalt Patent (1606) 1 W.P.C. at 10.

[81]See Drapers' Charter of 4 Jac. 1; Herbert, *History of the London Livery Companies*, I, 489.

[82]Gordon, *Monopolies by Patents*, 122, notes that there is preserved in the library of the Corporation of London a complaint by the Stationers' Company of the patent granted to Roger Woode for printing on parchment, the gravamen of which complaint was that the patent enabled the patentee to set at naught the Company's charter and encroach upon its privileges.

V. THE USE OF MONOPOLY PRIVILEGE TO ATTRACT NEW MANUFACTURES FROM ABROAD

EVIDENCE of the early instances of the fostering influence of the Crown in favour of manufacturing industries in England is to be found in the Letters of Protection granted in 1331 to John Kempe.[1] These Letters granted to Kempe, a Fleming, together with his servants, apprentices, and other members of the Weavers' Mystery, and the fullers and dyers who might desire to come to England, "franchises as many and such as may suffice them." This was a grant which had as its object the express purpose of instructing the English in a new industry, and, in line with an earlier ordinance of 1326,[2] was designed to institute a policy of protection in favour of the new textile industry.[3] These letters patent were expressly confirmed by statute in 1337, which was designed for the general protection of the trade.[4] It offered protection to all foreign cloth workers who settled in England; and, in order to encourage home manufacture, it prohibited the export of wool and the import of foreign cloth. Whether all this protection was necessary to secure a footing for the new manufacture or not,[5] the interests of the consumer were not entirely forgotten, for the alnager and his officers were supposed to exercise a sufficient

[1]Pat. 5 Edw. III, 1 m. 25; Cal. Rot. Pat. Edw. III (1330-4), 161; and cf. Gibbins, *Industry in England*, 104 ff.

[2]Hulme (1909) 3 A.A.L.H., 119.

[3]Cf. Gibbins, *Industry in England*, 127. This grant is of importance in that it did not constitute a solitary instance of protection but, as Hulme points out ((1898) 16 L.Q.R., 142), the declaration of a distinct and comprehensive policy in favour of the textile industry; for the grant contains a general promise of like privilege to all foreign weavers, dyers, and fullers, on condition of their settling in the country and teaching their arts to those willing to be instructed therein. "Promittimus enim nos aliis Hominibus, de Mestero illo, ac Tinctoribus, et Fullonibus venire volentibus de partibus Transmarinis, ad morandum infra idem Regnum nostrum ex causa praemissa, consimiles litteras de Protectione fieri facere debere."

[4]11 Edw. III, cc. 3, 4, 5.

[5]Mill, *Political Economy*, bk. V, 1.

supervision as to the character of the cloth exposed for sale.[6] As Cunningham points out,[7] it is interesting to observe how closely subsequent efforts to plant new industries followed on the lines which Edward III laid down: they secured a monopoly to the craftsmen, while at the same time they tried to insist on a high standard of excellence in the wares produced.

This fostering influence upon trade is visible in several other grants in the fourteenth and succeeding centuries. They constitute examples of industrial grants designed to assist in the foundation and fostering of native industry by importation of artificers from abroad; and they are illustrative of the principle, then recognized, that the Crown had power to grant many privileges for the sake of the public good.[8] Thus, the grant in 1440 to John of Schiedame and his company was concerned with the introduction of a newly invented process of making salt on a scale theretofore never attempted in England, while the grant in 1452 to the Bohemian miners was based upon their possession of "meliorem scientiam in Mineriis."[9]

The influx of alien workmen left a deep and permanent influence on England. At the time of Edward III industry was but little advanced. Manufactures of everyday use were domestically made, but goods of the finer and more attractive sort were imported from abroad, English artisans not having sufficient skill and knowledge for the making of goods of the latter type. For these goods, the English exported surplus quantities of wool, corn, coal, hides, and tin.[10]

Such a condition provided a natural field for the development of a system of protection and its spontaneous transition into one of monopolies effectuated by patents and licences. Edward III was not slow to see the position and deliberately set himself to transform the country from a mere producer of raw materials

[6]Cunningham, *English Industry and Commerce*, I, 308. The office of alnager, however, did not serve to fulfil the intended function of public protector of quality. It later constituted one of the grievances against monopolies, particularly in connection with the sealing of the "new drapery." Cf. 1 Jo. H.C. 793; S.P. Dom. Jac. I, clxv, 26, May 22, 1624; clxv, 34, May 24, 1624. See chap. VI, n. 11.

[7]Cunningham, *English Industry and Commerce*, 309.

[8]Y.B. 40 Edw. III, XVII, XVIII.

[9]Foed. XI, 317; Martin, *English Patent System*, 10.

[10]Cunningham, *Alien Immigrants*, 101.

into one that would be capable not only of providing manufactured goods for its own requirements but for purposes of export as well. It was his genius to accomplish this result in the two ways which may seem obvious to us now, but needed then a statesman-like grasp of conditions and theories. Those two methods were by the enactment of progressive legislation and the inducements held out to those aliens who were skilled in the arts and had carried them to a state of perfection which it was desired to transplant to English soil.

The royal protection accorded to these foreigners, together with the permission to work their trade within the kingdom, was analogous to the rights conferred by charter upon the early guilds. While the protection of the immigrant workers was necessarily guaranteed by royal licence it was equally important that the workers be given permission to work in order to overcome the stringency of the law which prohibited working at a trade until a regular apprenticeship had been served.[11]

There was, therefore, nothing haphazard or accidental about the letters of protection accorded to John Kempe of Flanders in 1331. Those letters marked the beginning of a deliberate and vigorous policy which was pursued with substantial results, not only by the third Edward but by his successors. Letters of protection gradually gave place to letters patent conferring monopoly privileges. But the actuating motive for these grants was the same whichever form they took. In an earlier and cruder age the protection of the introducer of the trade, his family and workmen, was the desideratum. As conditions of life became more stable and international intercourse more prevalent, the need for protection gradually disappeared and the necessity for adequate reward took its place. The patent of monopoly was therefore the natural product of the protective policy instituted by Edward III. The significance of this factor on the development of the patent system should not be overlooked for it has left its impress on that development and endures to the present time, finding its expression, in Great Britain at least, in the accepted doctrine that a communication of a new invention from abroad is sufficient foundation for the grant of letters patent.[12]

[11]Martin, *English Patent System*, 10. The Apprenticeship Act of 1562, 5 Eliz., c. 4, s. 24.

[12]Cf. Statute of Monopolies, s. 6; Edgebury v. Stephens (1693) 1 W.P.C. 35; 2 Salk. 447: "The statute speaks of new manufactures within this realm, so that

The impress left upon the development of the patent system by the practice of rewarding foreign workmen and inventors for the introduction into the realm of new manufactures not before known or there used, has been so important that it may be useful to indicate in chronological order something of the history of the new trades and manufactures so inaugurated as a result of this policy of fostering and rewarding those responsible for their introduction. The list is not intended by any means to be more than illustrative and, while it breaks somewhat the historical continuity of the discussion and anticipates in some measure what we shall have to say later, it is felt that this aspect of the story is sufficiently important to justify a departure from the chronological factor.

Following the letters of protection given to John Kempe in 1331[13] and the confirming statute of 1337, determined efforts were made to foster the development of local cloth manufacture in an endeavour to reduce the earlier system of the export of raw wool and import of cloth manufactured abroad. Thus Rymer[14] speaks of the immigration from Brabant of foreign cloth workers and their establishment in London, York,[15] and Bristol,[16] royal authority for so doing having first been obtained.[17]

In the reign of Henry VIII there was a grant to John de Salvo and Anthony Spynile, permitting them to bring in foreign cloth makers[18] and in 1504 Anthony Bonvis, an Italian, received permission to introduce an improved method of spinning into Devonshire.[19] It is from the introduction from abroad of the new methods of weaving and finishing cloth within the realm that the term "new drapery" arose, a term which occurred with continuing frequency when the opposition to monopolies developed.

---

if it be new here it is within the statute, for the Act intended to encourage new devices useful to the kingdom, and whether learned by travel or by study it is the same thing." See also Boulton v. Bull (1795) 2 H. Bl. 463 at 491 per Eyre, C.J.; Plimpton v. Malcolmson (1876) 3 Ch. D. 531 at 555 per Jessel, M.R.; Marsden v. Saville Street Foundry and Engineering Co. (1878) 3 Ex. D. 203 per Jessel, M.R.

[13]Pat. 5 Edw. III, 2, m. 25; Martin, *English Patent System*, 10.

[14]Foed. III, 23

[15]Foed. II, 954.

[16]Foed. II, 1098.

[17]Foed. II, 954.

[18]Campbell, *Materials for the Reign of Henry VII*, II, 134, 528.

[19]Strype, *Annals*, 870.

The mining, metal working, and coining industries were developed by the importation of skilled foreign workers. By the end of the sixteenth century the tin and copper mines of Cornwall were being extensively worked by Dutch and German miners.[20] Henry VIII endeavoured to promote the working of the mineral resources of the country and in 1528 appointed Joachim Houghstetter of Augsburg principal surveyor and master of all mines in the kingdom. Gold and silver mining were set up by royal licence in 1564, a company of royal mines being formed by commission to Daniel Houghstetter[21] and Thomas Thurland, followed in the next year by a special licence according them privileges with respect to mining of gold, silver, etc.[22] On May 28, 1568, this company was incorporated by charter as the Society of the Mines Royal, which existed down to the eighteenth century.[23] In 1569 Houghstetter received a further grant for setting up and using engines for mine drainage,[24] this being one of the early grants of the reign of Elizabeth with respect to new inventions. In 1571 he became master of the royal mines.[25] The promoters of this project were accorded special privileges, among them remission of taxes.[26] In 1564 Cornelius de Vos obtained a licence to work alum and copperas[27] mines in the Isle of Wight.[28] Christopher Shuts, a German engineer, in association with William Humphrey, a paymaster of the Mint, obtained in 1565, two licences for mining calamine or zinc carbonate, an essential in the manufacture of latten or brass, which was proposed to be used for casting ordnance,[29] and for tin, lead, and other ores.[30] These grants covered geographically those parts not included in the grants of Houghstetter and de Vos.[31] In

[20]S.P. For. Edw. VI, nos. 245, 273; S.P. Dom. Eliz. clxiv, 4; clxviii, 13; clxix, 16; cxcv, 39, 50; clxxi, 4; xxiv, 59.

[21]Son of Joachim Houghstetter.

[22]Cf. Hulme (1909) 3 A.A.L.H., 124; S.P. Dom. Eliz. Add. xi, 94; S.P. Dom. Eliz. xviii, 18; *ibid.*, xxxv, 3; xxxvi, 25, 59; xl, 14.

[23]Cf. Hulme (1909) 3 A.A.L.H., 125.

[24]*Ibid.*, 128.

[25]S.P. Dom. Eliz. xxxiv, 59; xc, 48.

[26]S.P. Dom. Eliz. xxxvi, 43.

[27]Sulphate of iron.

[28]S.P. Dom. Eliz. xxxvi, 72, 82; *ibid.*, xlviii, 12.

[29]S.P. Dom. Eliz. viii, 14.

[30]S.P. Dom. Eliz. xxxvi, 73, 81-3; *ibid.*, xxxvii, 5, 40-4; *ibid.*, xl, 17.

[31]Hulme (1909), 3 A.A.L.H., 126.

furtherance of these grants Humphrey, with the assistance of his German associates, set up wire and battery works at Tintern.[32]

In other trades, foreign skill was equally relied on and Edward III pursued his same protective policy. Linen weavers were imported from Flanders[33] and clock makers from Delft in 1368.[34] The local silk trade, established by the earlier importation of foreign skilled work people, was protected against imports by a series of statutes beginning in 1329.[35] Proposals for establishing the manufacture of silk were brought by various foreigners for the consideration of Burleigh in 1559.[36] Ribbon weaving, the making of combs, jewellery, baskets, and embroidery were among the occupations practised by immigrants into the realm, as well as the arts of glazing and bookbinding, which were mostly done by foreigners.[37] The making of felt hats was introduced by Spaniards and Dutchmen at the beginning of Henry VIII's reign. In 1555 the merchants of Norwich obtained a statute granting them the monopoly of making satins, they having introduced Italians to teach them the method.[38]

The silk trade received a substantial stimulus at the time of the Huguenot immigration from France after the revocation of the Edict of Nantes. Large numbers from Tours, the Huguenot centre of the trade in France, emigrated to England and in 1692 a grant was made in favour of several Huguenots for the exclusive manufacture of certain silks and lustrings.[39] From this grant arose the Royal Lustring Company which was protected by acts forbidding importation of these fabrics.[40] The basis of these various protective measures was, however, not designed to further the use of domestic materials, but rather to supplant importation of foreign goods by their manufacture within the country.

[32]S.P. Dom. Eliz. xxxvii, 21; *ibid.*, xl, 11, *ibid.*, xli, 12.

[33]Madox, *Firma Burgi*, 197.

[32]S.P. Dom. Eliz. xxxvii, 21; *ibid.*, xl, 11, *ibid.*, xli, 12.

[33]Madox, *Firma Burgi*, 197.

[34]Martin, *English Patent System*, 10.

[35]3 Edw. III, c. 3; 22 Edw. III, c. 3; 1 Rich. III, c. 10; 19 Hen. VII, c. 2.

[36]S.P. Dom. Eliz. viii, 32-5.

[37]Cunningham, *Alien Immigrants*, 143.

[38]Martin, *English Patent System*, 12.

[39]Cunningham, *Alien Immigrants*, 235.

[40]7 & 8 Wm. III, c. 36; 3 & 4 Anne, c. 12; 6 Anne, c. 3.

It is in connection with the making of ordnance for the defence of the realm that considerable numbers of patents of monopoly privilege were granted to foreigners to induce them to settle in England. Under Henry VIII there had been created the post of "provider of the King's instruments of war," and this post was then filled by an alien in this as well as in the three following reigns. Gunners and armourers were brought over from France, Germany, and the Low Countries and Arcana, an Italian, established a gun foundry at Salisbury Court.[41] Burleigh was at great pains to foster the expansion of the domestic manufacture of ordnance with the results which will be hereafter noted, and, in doing so, he did not hesitate to authorize the grant of monopoly privileges, and, when called upon, to defend and justify them before Parliament.[42] Several of these grants were made as an inducement to the settlement of foreigners in the kingdom and as a reward for their introduction of new methods and equipment. While there were other grants of the same type to local residents it is with the former that we are for the moment concerned. As will be noted hereafter, they dealt not only with the making of cannon but also the mining of those substances necessary for the production of gunpowder. These latter have already been mentioned. It is, of course, not alone with grants to foreigners that we are here concerned, but grants with respect to the introduction of new arts from abroad, whether made to alien immigrants or to residents who had acquired the necessary skills by travel or communication. Thus in 1561, saltpetre, so necessary for the making of gunpowder, was not manufactured within the country, most of the imported material being imported *via* Antwerp, a port controlled by the Catholic King of Spain. Elizabeth therefore bargained with Gerard Honricke "an almaync[43] Captain" to come to England and teach her subjects the art of making saltpetre as good as that made "beyond the seas," stipulating that, in return for a cash award, the secret of its manufacture should be reduced to writing. On the arrival of Honricke, the Queen granted to two London tradesmen by patent, her share of the bargain.[44] The grants made by Elizabeth in 1564 to Cor-

[41]Cunningham, *Alien Immigrants*, 142.

[42]See post 170.

[43]German.

[44]Pat. 3 Eliz., 6; cf. Hulme (1909) 3 A.A.L.H., 122; cf. S.P. Dom. Eliz. cvi, 53.

nelius de Vos for the making of alum and sulphate of iron, in 1565 to Wade and Herlle for the manufacture of sulphur,[45] in 1565 to Humfry and Shutz for zinc carbonate, were examples of the inducements given by Burleigh for the introduction of new skills and techniques in the building up of the domestic defence industry.

Elizabeth made fifty-five grants of monopoly privilege, of which twenty-one were issued to aliens or naturalized subjects,[46] the subject matter of which included, in addition to those already noted, the making of soap,[47] machines for dredging and draining land, ovens and furnaces, oil, leather, grinding machines, salt, glass, drinking glasses, force-pumps for raising water, writing paper,[48] and processes for tempering iron, milling corn, extracting oil from rape-seeds, dressing and dyeing and calendering cloth.[49]

Another trade which owed its establishment in England to alien immigrants was that of glass making. Although attempts were made in 1552 and 1565 to introduce the art of glass making into England the results were meagre.[50] In 1552 Edward VI had made a grant of monopoly privilege for a term of twenty years to Henry Smyth, a London merchant, for the making of Normandy glass for windows, the patent reciting that the grantee proposed to bring over foreign workmen who were expert in its manufacture and would instruct local artisans in the necessary technique. The making of Normandy or any other glass fit for windows by others than the patentee was forbidden.[51] The later patent of 1567 to Anthony Beckie and John Carré, Low Countrymen, to make Normandy and Lorraine glass[52] may be said to mark the foundation of glass making in England. Seven years later a grant was made to James Verselyn, a Venetian, for the exclusive right to make drinking glasses, the patentee undertaking to teach native workmen the art. Further importation, which had before the date of the grant been considerable, was prohibited.[53]

[45]And its extension in 1577 for a further period of thirty years.

[46]Hulme (1909) 3 A.A.L.H., 138.

[47]Pat. 3 Eliz., p. 13, m. 1; S.P. Dom. Eliz. cxxvi, 45.

[48]S.P. Dom. Eliz. ccxvii, 70.

[49]S.P. Dom. Eliz. lxxvii, 65.

[50]S.P. Dom. Eliz. xxxvii, 3.

[51]Apr. 1552, Pat. Roll. 6 Edw. VI, p. 5.

[52]S.P. Dom. Eliz. xliii, 42-6; *ibid.*, xlvii, 56.

[53]S.P. Dom. Eliz. ccxli, 40.

The development of engineering works in the kingdom was also materially affected by the import of skills and techniques from abroad, several of these forming the basis of grants of privilege. The grant to George Cobham on May 26, 1562, for a machine to scour the entrance to harbours was accorded on the application of himself and an Italian and was designed to "give courage to others to study and seke for the knowledge of like good engines and devyses."[54] In addition to the grant to John Synertson of Amsterdam in 1573 to put into practice an instrument for land drainage and for the stopping of breaches in dams, considerable work in the harbour at Dover was carried on by Flemish workmen[55] under the advice of Humphrey Bradley, a Dutch engineer.[56] An Italian named Gianibelli projected waterworks for the city of London and was engaged on the defences of Gravesend at the time of the Armada.[57] In 1597 a grant for the term of twenty-one years was made to Thomas Lovell to drain and recover lands and to make peat, an art which the grantee is stated to have learned from the Dutch.[58] Giacopo Acontio of Trent was retained to reclaim the Plumstead Marshes[59] and the draining of the Lincolnshire fens was assisted by consultation with foreign engineers,[60] the undertaking by Vermuÿden under the early Stuarts being the most important of these projects.[61]

The art of clock making was introduced by French workers[62] and further improved by the Dutch. In 1368 a grant of privilege was made to three clock makers of Delft.[63] Improvements in pottery first became the subject of a monopoly privilege in 1571 when a grant was made to Richard Dyer for the making of "earthen furnaces, firepots and ovens transportable" an art which the grantee had learned while a prisoner of the Spaniards.[64] The Janssens of Antwerp petitioned in 1570 for a monopoly of the manufacture of

[54]S.P. Dom. Eliz. i, 56.
[55]S.P. Dom. Eliz. cliii, 56; *ibid.*, cl, 82; *ibid.*, clxxii, 18.
[56]S.P. Dom. Eliz. clxxiii, 96.
[57]S.P. Dom. Eliz. ccxvii, 4.
[58]Hulme (1909) 3 A.A.L.H., 137.
[59]S.P. Dom. Eliz. Add. xi, 99.
[60]S.P. Dom. Eliz. ccxiii, 28.
[61]Cunningham, *Alien Immigrants*, 209.
[62]S.P. Dom. Jac. I, cxxvii, 15.
[63]Cunningham, *Alien Immigrants*, 309; Martin, *English Patent System*, 10.
[64]Hulme (1909) 3 A.A.L.H., 129.

galley[65] tiles, and apothecaries' vessels[66] but there is no record of such a grant having been made. The great potteries of Staffordshire owe their importance in large measure to immigrants from Holland, who brought in the art of salt glazing as practised by the workmen of Saxony and Delft. In 1676 John Ariens van Hamme obtained a patent for "the art of making tiles, porcelain and other earthenware after the way practised in Holland."[67]

The manufacture of sugar in England also owes its origin to the introduction of processes from abroad. In 1598 the art of sugar making had been introduced by Gaspar Terlin, a German, and in 1622 another German, Martin Bigger, applied to the clerk of the Council for a patent for the making of double refined sugar.[68] A patent for the introduction of the manufacture of loaf sugar was solicited by certain foreigners in 1634.[69]

Another trade which Burleigh's policy of self-sufficiency was designed to foster was that of the making of sailcloth. All trades which had anything to do with national defence and the development of maritime power were stimulated to the utmost. Thus, in 1574, a monopoly licence was granted to John Collyns to make "brode clothes called Mildernix and Polledavies."[70] These sailcloths had formerly been imported from France and the grant recites the introduction of the manufacture and the training of apprentices therein. In 1590 the grant was reissued for an additional period of twenty-one years.[71] The trade was further stimulated by the immigration of French workers at the time of the Huguenot influx, but it gradually shifted to Ireland, along with the rest of the linen trade, being encouraged by the efforts of the Irish Parliament to stimulate its growth.[72] In the meantime, cotton having been imported from Antwerp in 1560, the cotton trade settled in Manchester where it was introduced after the sack of Antwerp in 1585 brought large numbers of refugees to England.[73]

[65]Glazed.

[66]Lansdowne MSS., XII, 58, 59.

[67]Jewett, *Ceramic Art*, 75 and 92.

[68]S.P. Dom. Jac. I cxvxxv, 49.

[69]S.P. Dom. Car. I cclxxix, 79.

[70]Hulme (1909) 3 A.A.L.H., 130.

[71]See also 1 Jac. I, c. 24 where these statements are confirmed.

[72]17 & 18 Car. II, c. 9; 7 & 8 Wm. & Mary, c. 39.

[73]Cunningham, *Alien Immigrants*, 180.

The domestic manufacture of writing paper also owes its origin to the introduction of French workers assisted by the grant of monopoly privileges. In 1585 Richard Tottyll, the Elizabethan law publisher, petitioned the Queen stating that the French, by buying up all the linen rags in the kingdom, had thwarted his efforts to introduce the manufacture. As a result[74] a grant for ten years was made to John Spilman, an alien who held the office of jeweller to the Queen, to buy all manner of linen rags, etc., to make white writing paper. The industry was established by Spilman at Dartford where he employed over six hundred workmen. The patent was reissued for fourteen years in 1597 and was extended to cover all kinds of paper.[75] The chief development of the manufacture was, however, due to the influx of French refugees in the seventeenth century. To the same period and to the same class of immigrants goes the credit for establishing in England the art of making sheets of plate glass,[76] while the introduction of lace making at Honiton and other centres is attributed to the refugees from the Low Countries at about the same time.[77]

Mediaeval monopolies for the furtherance of internal trade and domestic manufacture whether by local artificers or by the importation and encouragement of foreigners were, as we have seen,[78] by no means unique in the English system. Foreign precedents were not wanting, for the new art of printing was being not only encouraged but controlled and regulated throughout Europe by special licences.[79] The exclusive sale of salt had been assumed in Venice, Pisa, and Cyprus during the Middle Ages, and in Naples, during the thirteenth century, the King had reserved to himself the exclusive sale of salt, iron, steel, pitch, and gilded leather.[80] But the motive underlying the system of encouraging the entry into England and the subsequent protection of foreign artificers was not so much that of regulating trade, as of

[74]Cf. Hulme (1909) 3 A.A.L.H., 135.

[75]Arber, *Transcripts of the Registers of the Stationers' Company*, I, 242; II, 814. A grant of the monopoly of paper making was made in Scotland to "Petir Graet Heare, Almane" and his partners on Feb. 4, 1589-90. See Steele, Proc. no. S. 682.

[76]Cunningham, *Alien Immigrants*, 243.

[77]*Ibid.*, 177.

[78]Ante 26, 28.

[79]Price, *English Patents of Monopoly*, 7; Hulme (1909) 3 A.A.L.H., 121.

[80]Mund, *Monopoly*, 13.

making the realm self-sufficient, as evidenced by the statement of Chancellor Moreton in his message to Parliament in the reign of Henry VII wherein he expressed the desire "that our people be set on work in arts and handcrafts; that our realm may subsist more of itself; that idleness be avoided, and the drawing out of our treasury for foreign manufacture stopped."[81]

It will be seen from this short discussion that the development of English industry owed much to the importation of foreign skill, particularly in regard to the manufacture of textiles and hardware, and methods of mining, drainage, and refining of minerals, and that, in this development, the use of the monopoly patent played a substantial and significant role. So long as industrial skills and techniques were a matter of personal knowledge and experience combined with manual dexterity, the only manner of importing and fostering new trades and industries was by the importation of workmen possessing that knowledge and experience. However, as the art of printing gave rise to a wider spread of knowledge and interchange of ideas and experiences, the necessity of importing skilled workmen gradually disappeared when ideas and skills could be transferred by means of the printed page. The great upsurge of inventive ingenuity which created the Industrial Revolution at the close of the eighteenth century was therefore a natural phenomenon growing out of the accumulation of industrial skills and techniques brought in from abroad, not only by foreign workmen but also by the ever-expanding dissemination of ideas rendered possible by the printing press. This cumulative process of growth of the industrial arts found ripe soil for its development in England where, combining with the native genius of the people, it produced an admixture of practical skill with theoretical and imaginative genius which resulted in the flowering of invention marked by such names as Watt, Stephenson, Arkwright, Hargreaves, and Crompton. The genius of the English character was, throughout this period, displayed in its willingness to accept teaching from abroad, whether by the use of documentary communication, or from the example and direct examination of the exercise of manual operations of foreign immigrants. The Englishman's reserve, sometimes mistaken for a sense of arrogant superiority, never precluded him from learning from any who might contribute knowledge and skill to his ex-

[81]Martin, *English Patent System*, 11.

panding store. In this development the patent of monopoly played an ever increasing part. The letters of protection to foreign workmen of Edward III were replaced by the monopoly grants and licences of the Tudors and Stuarts.

From the letters of protection to the elimination of competition was nothing more than a natural step. Once the advantage to be gained from protecting the foreign workman in the exercise of his trade was perceived, it followed as a natural corollary that more important trades could be introduced by protecting the workers from competition. Once it was recognized that the alien immigrant was entitled to such protection in order to encourage the establishment of a new trade or industry, it was a logical extension of that policy to accord the same encouragement to the domestic worker, who by such means would be induced to establish new manufactures, whether they arose from the native intellect itself or were imported from abroad, thus reducing the necessity to import quantities of finished goods. This recognition of the benefits to be gained from the establishment of new industries flowed forward into a recognition that, by similar means, old and established trades and industries which were in a backward and languishing condition might be stimulated to further endeavour and ultimate success. By such means the shift of population from the agricultural areas to the towns could be balanced by opening up increased avenues of employment. It was to the recognition of these facts that the monopoly patent owes its origin and, before the system is condemned, as it so often is, this condition should be understood and analysed. Upon that basis alone, the monopoly system stands fully justified, whatever may have been the result in operation and later abuse. And so by slow degrees and out of hard experience, the early patent of trade and manufacturing monopoly solidified into the patent of invention, first justified by the common law, given parliamentary approval in the Statute of Monopolies, and becoming an accepted and rigidly restricted feature of our industrial system after the Restoration. The impress of this development, as has before been noted, has been left on the British patent system by the acceptance of the doctrine that a valid patent may be granted on a communication from abroad of a new manufacture, although the patentee himself may not have invented anything. This doctrine finds no place in the patent systems of North America, the significant factor in the light of the foregoing discussion being that the patent system of the United States was not called into being until the closing years of the eighteenth century, and of Canada until the beginning of the nineteenth. By that time the tide of invention evoked by the Industrial Revolution had swept away the recollection of, and the necessity for, the importation of foreign workmen possessing manual skills and dexterity. Henceforth those results were effected by the import of automatic machinery and the transference of techniques by means of the patent of invention.

VI. MONOPOLIES UNDER ELIZABETH: THE BEGINNING OF THE PATENT OF INVENTION

THE right of the Crown to grant monopolies of new trades or manufactures to inventors, i.e., persons introducing them into the realm, as a reward for the benefit thereby given to the community was always recognized as part of the common law prerogative.[1] The prerogative right to grant monopolies was theoretically limited at common law. A monopoly being a derogation from the common right of freedom of trade could not be granted without consideration moving to the public. In the case of new inventions the consideration was found either in the interest of the public to encourage inventive ingenuity or more probably in the disclosure made to the public of a new and useful article or process. In the case of sole rights of trading with foreign parts it might be found in the interest of the public in new countries being opened to trade. But for the validity of every monopoly some consideration flowing to the public was necessary.[2] In practice, however, the earlier sovereigns of England claimed and exercised the much wider prerogative right of granting all types of monopolies, some beneficial, others detrimental, some granted as royal favour, others as means of increasing the royal revenue.[3]

[1]Darcy v. Allin (1602) Noy 173; The Cloth Workers of Ipswich Case (1615) Godb. 252; Edgebury v. Stephens (1693) 2 Salk. 447; Reg. v. County Court Judge of Halifax (1891) 1 Q.B. 793; British Mutoscope Co. v. Homer (1901) 18 R.P.C. 177; Shep. Abr., pt. III, tit. Prerogative, 61; Hawk. P.C., pt. I, c. 79, s. 20; Com. Dig., tit. Trade (B).

Hawk. P.C., c. 79, s. 6: "It seemeth clear that the king may, for a reasonable time, make a good grant to any one of the sole use of any art invented or first brought into the realm by the grantee."

Bac. Abr., tit. Prerogative, F. 4, "It is agreed that the king may, for a reasonable time, grant to a person the sole use of any art first invented by him, and this it seems the king might do at common law."

A modern statement of the common law view appears from the reasons of Lord Parker of Waddington in Attorney-General of Australia v. The Adelaide Steamship Co. Ltd. et al. (1913) A.C. 781 at 793.

[2]Attorney-General of Australia v. The Adelaide Steamship Co. Ltd. et al. (1913) A.C. 781 at 793 per Lord Parker of Waddington.

[3]The right of the Crown to make such grants has been based upon its position as "*parens patriae et paterfamilias totius regni*, and, as it is said in 20 H. 7 fol. 7 as

These monopolies covered a variety of subjects which are somewhat astonishing to the modern reader acquainted with the strict limits within which the Crown prerogative may now be constitutionally exercised. But there were limits within which the royal prerogative could be constitutionally exercised even in those early days; and Parliament did not hesitate, upon occasion, to insist upon a true observance of the provision[4] of Magna Carta[5] which regulated, to some extent, the freedom of trade. Thus, when in 1373 Edward III granted to John Peachie the sole importation of sweet wine into London, the grant was adjudged void at a Parliament held 50 Edw. III.[6] The declaration of Magna Carta[7] that all merchant strangers in the realm should be able to buy and sell their goods by the old and rightful customs, is itself an illustration of the early attempts at limitation of the

---

Capitalis Justiciriaus Angliae." Case of Monopolies (1602) 11 Co. Rep. 85.

As to the practice which grew up under the Tudors and Stuarts of granting monopolies and regulating trade by proclamation, see the Case of Proclamations (1611) 12 Co. Rep. 74 where it was pointed out that "the King by his Proclamation or otherwise cannot change any part of the common law or statute law or the customs of the realm. Fortescue, *De Laudibus Angliae Legum*, c. 9. The king hath no prerogative but that which the law of the land allows him. . . . The law of England is divided into three parts, common law, statute law and custom; but the King's proclamation is none of them." See also The Zamora (1916) 2 A.C. 77 at 90 per Lord Parker of Waddington.

[4]C. 41.

[5]"Omnes mercatores habeant salvum et securum exire de Anglia, et venire in Angliam, et morari et ire per Angliam, tam per terram quam per aquam, ad emendum et vendendum, sine omnibus malis toltis, per antiquas et rectas consuetudines, praeterquam in tempore gwerrae, et si sint de terra contra nos gwerrina." In the version of the Charter granted by Henry III (9 Hen. III, c.30) and usually referred to in the cases, this provision appears in the following form: "Omnes mercatores, nisi publice ante prohibiti fuerunt, habeant salvum et securum conductum exire de Anglia et venire in Angliam, et morari et ire per Angliam praeterquam in tempore guerrae." In his observations on the consideration of this chapter of Magna Carta, Coke in 2 Inst. 63, states that this conclusion is necessarily gathered: "That all monopolies concerning trade and traffic are against the liberty and freedom granted and declared by this great charter, and against divers other acts of parliament, which are good commentaries on it." This provision in favour of merchants and for the advancement of trade has been justly eulogized, as showing great breadth and liberality in days when the feudal barons throughout Europe were accustomed to oppress and pillage commerce. Taswell-Langmead, *English Constitutional History*, 108.

[6]Cf. Darcy v. Allin (1602) 11 Co. Rep. 84; Noy 178; Vin. Abr. XVII, 210.

[7]C. 41.

prerogative right of granting monopolies; but notwithstanding this statutory provision, royal grants of monopolies were so common that merchants were scarcely able to indulge in general trade without the risk of interfering with some other trader's exclusive privilege. To remedy this state of affairs, the statutes 9 Edw. III, st. 1, c. 1; 25 Edw. III, c. 2;[8] 27 Edw. III, c. 10, and 2 Ric. II, st. 1, c. 1, were successively passed. Their main tenor, after a recitation of the grievous dearth of sustenance the citizens and burgesses were forced to undergo by reason of the prohibition upon foreign merchants from selling their wares in opposition to the various monopolies, was to grant freedom of trade to all merchants. The last noted statute is illustrative of them all in its provision that, "All merchants may buy and sell within the realm without disturbance, notwithstanding any Statutes, Ordinances, Charters, Judgments, Allowances, Customs and Usage made or suffered to the contrary, which Charters and Franchises, if any there be, they shall be utterly repealed and admitted as a thing made, used or granted against the common Profit and Oppression of the People."[9]

[8]Statute of Cloths.

[9]Thus, when King Philip and Queen Mary granted by letters patent to the burgesses of Southampton that that port should have the sole right of importing Malmsey wine, the grant was held to be against the laws of the realm, viz. Magna Carta, 29, 30; 9 Edw. III, c. 1; 14 Edw. III; 25 Edw. III, c. 2; 27 & 28 Edw. III, Statute of the Staple; 2 Rich. II, c. 1 and others. Cf. Vin. Abr. XVII, 210. See also Hawk. P.C. 231, c. 79, ss. 2, 3; 1 Rot. Parl. 1 Hen. V.N. 41; Roll. Abr. 214 tit. Prerogative le Roy, (D) Monopolies.

The common law view of freedom of trade was summed up by Pollexfen (afterwards Lord Chief Justice) in his argument for the defendant in East India Company v. Sandys (1684) 10 St. Tr. 371 at 421:

"By the common law, trade is free and open for the king's subjects; and for that the books that I shall cite are these, 3 Inst. 181 'Commercium Jure Gentium commune esse debet, et non in Monopolium et privatum pauculorum Quæstum convertendum; iniquum est alios permittere, alios inhibere Mercaturam.'

"The next book, my lord, is Fitzh. Nat. Br. fo. 85 that says thus; 'Note, That by the course of common law, every man may at his pleasure go out of the realm for merchandize, or to travel, or other cause, as shall please him, without demanding licence of the king; and shall not be punished for it.' And the Stat. of 5 R. II, c. 2, which prohibited all but the great men and merchants, to pass out of the realm without licence, has therein declared the law, when it excepted merchants, that they had a right to go without licence; but this statute is repealed afterwards by the statute of 4 Jac. cap. 1.

But, so long as these grants could be clearly shown to be for the welfare of the realm, they were considered as exceptions to the statutory prohibitions, and their validity was recognized by the mediaeval lawyers.[10] So, throughout the fourteenth and fifteenth centuries, there are instances of grants of privilege and protection in favour of the woollen and other industries.[11] There are occasional grants of such type in the early part of the sixteenth century, but it is not until 1552, with the grant of the glass patent to Smyth, that the new system of granting industrial monopoly licences, the precise origin of the present patent law, was introduced.[12] However, as we shall see later, the restraint upon the use of the prerogative was not frequently used and had practically fallen into desuetude until the temper of the Commons flared up once more toward the end of Elizabeth's reign.

The earliest reference we have extant to a grant of the type of the modern patent is that in the reign of Edward VI to Edward Smyth.[13] The patentee, a London merchant, according to the recital in the patent, intended to introduce foreign workmen "mete and experte" in the making of "brode glass of like fasshion and goodnes to that which is commonly called Normandy glass which shall not only be a great comoditie to our said realme and

---

"Then, my lord, there is Rolls, 1 Rep. fol. 4 the Taylor of Ipswich's case against Sherring. The words and sense of the books are, 'That no trade, mechanic, or merchant, can be hindered by the king's patent.' A patent to hinder trade at sea is a void patent; a patent that only a hundred persons shall use such a trade, is not good." (This latter point was decided against the defendant by the court.)

"Dyer 165, 'That every one may at his pleasure go with goods'; and cites F.N.B. for it. And F.N.B. 85 saith thus; 'Note, That by the common law, every man may at his pleasure go out of the realm for merchandize, or to travel, without demanding licence of the king'."

See also Mitchel v. Reynolds (1711) P. Williams 183; Company of Merchant Adventurers v. Rebow (1686) 3 Mod. 126 at 131. Cf. chap. VII, n. 1.

[10]Cf. Attorney-General of Australia v. The Adelaide Steamship Co. Ltd. et al. (1913) A.C. 781 at 793, Cott. Post. 185; Rot. Parl. 29 Hen. VI, n. 15.

[11]Holdsworth, *History of English Law*, IV, 344.

[12]*Ibid.*, 345.

[13]April 1552, Pat. Roll., 6 Edw. VI, 5 (Roll no. 846).

It will be noted that no serious mention is here made of the patent alleged to have been made 30 Edw. III to two aldermen of London for the sole making of the Philosopher's Stone. The patent was referred to by Coke in his argument in Darcy v. Allin (q.v. Appendix IV at 319) but it is felt that the historical basis of this study is worthy of a commencement a little less curious.

dominions but also bothe in the price of the glasse aforesaid and otherwise a benefite to our subjectes and besydes that dyvers of theym may be sett to worke and gett their lyvyng and in tyme learne and be hable to make the said glasse them selfe and so from tyme to tyme there to instructe the others in that science and feate." Smyth was granted a monopoly privilege for twenty years which forbade others without his licence or authority "to make any kynde of the said brode glasse commonly wount to be called Normandy glasse or any other fytte for wyndowes."[14]

This was followed by a grant made by Queen Mary in 1554 to Burchart Cranick of a twenty-year sole licence to mine, break open ground, melt, divide, and search for all manner of metals.[15]

The grant in 1561 by Elizabeth of a ten-year privilege to Stephen Groyett and Anthony Le Leuryer "to make white sope" may be said to have launched the policy of encouraging new manufactures so vigorously pursued by Elizabeth and Burleigh. The grant stipulated that at least two of the servants of the patentee should be of native birth and that the soap, which was to be of the white, hard variety, should be as good and fine as was made in the "Sope house of Triana or Syvile."[16]

In the early days of the Tudor dynasty we find, as we have seen, grants for the purpose of attracting skilled foreigners, such, for example, as German armourers, Italian shipwrights and glass makers, and French iron founders and sail makers. At the time of Elizabeth's accession, England was much behind the rest of Europe in all industrial arts, and could only hope to advance by importing skilled artisans, and encouraging enterprising men to undertake the risks of introducing new manufactures.[17] An examination of the grants of monopoly patents made in the reign of Elizabeth shows, however, a gradual reversal of that trend in favour of granting monopolies to resident subjects, monopoly patents granted during her reign constituting twenty-one to

[14]For the discovery of the details of this grant we are indebted to Mr. D. Seaborne Davies. See (1932) 96 L.Q.R., 396.

[15]See Pat. Roll., 3 & 4 Ph. & Mary 11; 4 & 5 Ph. & Mary 13; 3 Eliz. 6; Acts of the Privy Council V, 211-13, 294; *ibid.*, VI, 89, 109, 118, 226; Davies, "Further Light on the Case of Monopolies" (1932) 96 L.Q.R., 394 at 396; Hulme (1909) 3 A.A.L.H., 121.

[16]See Hulme (1909) 3 A.A.L.H., 122.

[17]Cunningham, *English Industry and Commerce*, II, 58.

foreigners and thirty to resident English. These grants, which have been collocated and placed in chronological, digested form by Hulme,[18] covered a wide variety of subject matter. Some of them were of a chemical, others of a mechanical nature; one for the making of sailcloth; some for mining rights; some for meritorious and new inventions;[19] others of questionable worth, such as the manufacture and sale of playing cards,[20] and so on. It is impossible, as Hulme pointed out, to subdivide them into grants of importation and invention, owing to the want of definition in the phraseology descriptive of the relation of the patentee to the subject of the grant. For the same reason it is impossible to classify them into those that were novel and beneficial and those that would now be regarded as abuses of the royal prerogative. This is largely occasioned by the contemporary meaning given to the words "inventor" and "invention" which was by no means co-terminous with the restricted mystical meaning placed upon them today by an ever narrowing judicial defining process. The patents themselves show that in some cases the grantee had no share in making any new discovery or invention as we understand the term today. In many cases they were granted merely to the first introducer, thereby showing the manner in which the prerogative of the Crown could be exercised, namely that patents could, in the words of the later *Case of Monopolies*[21] be granted to those who by their wit and invention, or by their charge and industry, had brought a new trade, or engine tending to the furtherance of a new trade, into the kingdom.

It is, however, possible to divide these grants into four main categories. First, there were those grants to which no exception could be taken. They were those which Bacon described, where "any man out of his own wit, industry or endeavour finds out anything beneficial for the commonwealth." In this class are to be included not only those for inventions, as we now understand them, made by native inventors but also those grants for importa-

[18]Hulme (1909) 3 A.A.L.H., 121. See also Fairman, "Early English Inventions" (1885) 12 Antiquary, 1 et seq.

[19]The word is here used in its widest sense, as including the first importation of known things.

[20]Patent of June 4, 1578 to Bowes and Bedingfield. Monopoly continued to Bowes for twelve years by proclamation, June 13, 1588. See Steele Proc. no. 801.

[21]See post 216, 323.

tion of new inventions and discoveries communicated from abroad which have always been recognized by the laws of England as constituting a "manner of new manufacture within this realm" as provided by the Statute of Monopolies. Nor must this class be taken as referring only to inventions of the type we now understand to be meant by that word. Many of the grants which were considered unobjectionable were for the introduction into the realm of new products not theretofore known, or for the carrying on of a new trade. Coke was of opinion that those who undertook "a new voyage for trade or merchandise that never was found out or undertaken before" were entitled to the same privileges as inventors of new manufactures.[22] From this conception flowed the monopoly grants to the great trading companies.[23]

At the opposite end of the pole were those which constituted the main grievance against monopolies. These were the cases where grants of the sole right to exercise an established trade were handed over to an individual or a group. The objection to this practice was exemplified in Coke's definition of illegal monopolies, the feature to which exception was taken being that they restrained people from a liberty which they had and enjoyed before the grant was made. Many of the monopolies granted by the Tudor and Stuart sovereigns were bad for want of any consideration moving to the public, and it was the vexatious interference with trade in the enforcement of these invalid grants which contributed to the enactment of the Statute of Monopolies. In a sense these first two types of grant were not mutually exclusive, for a monopoly of the second type might eventually result from a grant of the first type. Thus the grant in 1561 to Groyett and Le Leuryer of the monopoly of soap making was good at the time it was made in view of the novelty within the kingdom of the trade and manufacture covered by the grant. But, as we shall see at a later stage of this discussion, it degenerated into a series of additional grants, long after the manufacture and trade had ceased to be novelties, until it culminated in the patents to the London and Westminster Companies of Soap Makers. So with the grant

[22]S.P.D. Eliz. cclxxvi, 81, 82.

[23]See, e.g., the grant to the Company of the Levant Merchants, 1592, Pat. Roll 34 Eliz. 12.

in 1588 to Young to make starch, which was later reissued to Pakington and finally to the Company of Starch Makers.[24]

In the third category, and also objectionable in their nature, were those patents which granted a power of supervision over a trade or industry. The patents for the supervision of inns and alehouses, in respect of which Mompesson and Michell were impeached in 1620-1, are examples of this type of grant, which was responsible for by far the greatest part of the antagonism which developed against monopolies. Had it not been for this type of grant, and for the provision in most patent grants providing for the right of supervision, search, seizure, and arrest with respect to the trade or subject matter concerned in the grants, it is probable that the history of monopolies would have taken a much less stormy course.

Occupying a sort of *terra media* were those grants of special licences which dispensed with the rigour of the law forbidding import, export, and transport of certain commodities. The statutes setting up these prohibitions were found, at times, to be

[24]The starch monopoly had a chequered history. Originally granted on April 15, 1588, to Richard Young for a term of seven years (cf. Hulme (1909) 3 A.A.L.H., 134), the real motive of the grant was the suppression of the manufacture from grain, the patentee being confined to "bran of wheat." The manufacture of starch from grain was prohibited by a number of proclamations. (See, e.g., Proclamations of Elizabeth, July 31, 1596, Steele Proc. no. 884; Aug. 23, 1598, Rot. Pat. p. 16. m. 13. d. Steele Proc. no. 898; Proclamation of James I, Aug. 23, 1607; Rot. Pat. p. 26. m. 20 d. Steele Proc. no. 1046. S.P. Dom. Jac. I. Add. xxxviii, 1105. July 5, 1608: Rot. Pat. p. 30. m. 17. d. Steele Proc. no. 1062, Jan. 10, 1609-10, Rot. Pat. p. 8. m. 1. d. Steele Proc. no. 1089: Aug. 22, 1610: Rot. Pat. p. 30. m. 12. d. Steele Proc. no. 1095: May 5, 1620, Rot. Pat. p. 19, m. 14. d. Steele Proc. no. 1279.) The patent was reissued to Sir John Pakington for eight years on July 6, 1594, and again to the same party on May 20, 1598 (Steele Proc. no. 897). The Company of Starch Makers was incorporated in 1607 (S.P. Docq. Oct. 21, 1607; Dec. 23, 1607; March 14, 1608). It was reincorporated according to proclamation of May 16, 1622 (Rot. Pat. p. 16. n. 27. d. Steele Proc. no. 1330). This grant was confirmed by order of Charles I on July 5, 1629, (see Rush. II, 12), and a surveyor appointed. Letters patent of incorporation issued to the members of the company under date of Dec. 26, 1638, and the ordering and supervision of the trade were provided for in a proclamation of Feb. 9, 1638-9 (Rot. Pat. p. 6. n. 10. d. Steele Proc. no. 1793). They were re-incorporated on the Restoration in 1661 (see Proclamation of Aug. 3, 1661: Rot. Pat. p. 17. n. 20. d. Steele Proc. no. 3317) still preserving the monopoly which had been given them in early grants which had been made "owing to the waste of wheat caused by careless making of starch."

unworkable, and it was customary, rather than to repeal a statute, to grant special licences for its evasion. In the main, grants of this type were dictated by economic pressure of a temporary nature, and, although they were condemned by James I in his *Book of Bounty* and later by the Statute of Monopolies, they were reasonable expedients for the times and occasioned little objection.[25] The grants of industrial monopolies are not to be confused with these "grants . . . of the benefit of penal laws, and of power to dispense with the law or to compound with forfeitures" mentioned by James I in his *Book of Bounty*. These, while they constituted exclusive privileges, had nothing to do with, or were opposed to, trade restrictions. In such class were the export licences which were granted in contravention or suspension of statutes prohibiting certain exports, and the dispensing patents which granted dispensations from penal laws by authorizing patentees to issue pardons upon receipt of composition, to grant dispensations from the penalties of statutes upon receiving a fee, or to take the benefit of forfeiture. The first type constituted an effort, in many cases necessary, to escape the rigour of statutes prohibiting the export of commodities which, if the statute had been adhered to, would have served no useful purpose or, what was worse, would have glutted the market and ruined the trades concerned. The latter type enabled offenders to bargain for the right to break the law and to purchase immunity from the effect of penal statutes. They were nominally abandoned in 1605 when the judges, upon being consulted, gave advice against them to the Privy Council.[26] They were, however, continued by the commissions issued under James I and Charles I for compounding with transgressors, the declaration of 1605 having held that this power, while it could not be delegated, resided in and could be exercised by the King himself.[27]

As trade increased, monopolies multiplied. While their grant was sometimes abused by the Crown because they were bestowed upon the favoured few who often sold them to the highest bidder, in general, the grants of monopoly patents were quite justifiable either on the ground that they were necessary to the interests

[25]Cf. Lipson, *Economic History of England*, III, 352-6; Davies, "Further Light on the Case of Monopolies" (1932) 96 L.Q.R., 397.

[26]The Case of Penal Statutes (1605) 7 Co. Rep. 36. See Appendix V.

[27]See Appendix V, 327.

of the state, or in order to regulate or to stimulate an industry,[28] or to encourage a languishing industry.[29] In some cases the grants of monopolies by Elizabeth and her successors may have been aimed at an easy method of increasing royal revenues or of rewarding royal favourites,[30] but where grants of exclusive privilege were shown to be for the general good of the realm, their validity and propriety were never doubted by the contemporary lawyers, and they were considered as proper exceptions to such statutes as prohibited the grant of exclusive privileges and franchises. Grants of this class are illustrated by those for the sole printing of books[31] and for the production of saltpetre.[32] In the latter case, the government assumed complete control, and, though this occasioned an interference with private property, the monopoly was held to be legal, and was not objected to by the House of Commons, along with other grievances, because it was felt to be necessary for the defence of the kingdom.[33] The exclusive patents for the production of sulphur in 1565[34] and for saltpetre in 1561,[35] were issued in order to furnish native supplies of gunpowder, and, although the latter patent was regarded with some disfavour,[36]

[28]E.g., the patent granted in 1614 to Sir William Cockayne giving him the exclusive right of dyeing and dressing all woollen cloth, the object being to render the export of undressed cloth for the purpose of finishing abroad, unnecessary, S.P.D. Jac. I, lxxx, 112; see Gardiner, *History of England*, II, 386.

[29]Cunningham, *English Industry and Commerce*, II, 165. In general the grants made by Elizabeth between the years 1561 and 1603 *ex facie* conform strictly with the theories of the common law as to their validity, as declared by the statute of Monopolies. Hulme, "History of the Patent System" (1900) 19 L.Q.R., 44.

[30]E.g., Elizabeth's grant to Essex of the monopoly of sweet wines. Cf. Hallam, *Constitutional History of England*, I, 244, and see post 101.

[31]See Fox, *Canadian Law of Copyright*, 14.

[32]Proclamation of Elizabeth, Jan. 13, 1589-90. See Steele Proc. no. 820; Case of the King's Prerogative in Saltpetre (1607) 12 Co. Rep. at 14, 15.

[33]Cf. Holdsworth, *History of English Law*, IV, 331. It should be noted carefully that, all through the debate on monopolies in 1601 and the later debates on grievances the saltpetre monopoly was not attacked *per se*. The grievance that was attacked was the actions of the saltpetre men or searchers. It was of these that Cecil spoke when in discussing the saltpetre monopoly he said that "it digs into every man's house, it annoys the inhabitant, and generally troubleth the subject." 1 Parl. Hist. 936.

[34]Foed., XIII, 650.

[35]S.P. Dom. Eliz. xvi, 30.

[36]D'Ewes 653.

it constituted, on the grounds of national interest, one of the exceptions contained in the Statute of Monopolies. Although the patent was set aside by the Long Parliament in 1641,[37] a further patent for two years was re-introduced by Parliament during the Civil War.[38]

Thus, the necessities of the times were to some extent the measure of propriety of a number of monopolies. The pressing necessity of a means of supplying the realm with ordnance at the beginning of Elizabeth's reign[39] was the controlling force behind the patents issued at Cecil's insistence; and this resulted, before the end of the reign, in England's ordnance being recognized as the best in Europe.[40] The Crown, being unable to afford the expense of engaging in mining operations, issued a number of patents to develop and revive the mining and metallurgical industries. In July, 1561, a company was formed to work the mines of Northumberland and to search for copper at Keswick.[41] The Company of Royal Mines was incorporated in 1568, and resulted in the provision of iron and copper for the ordnance.[42] William Humphrey, in the same year, floated a company under the name of the Mineral and Battery Company to dig for iron, tin, lead, and calamine stone, and to erect a mill for drawing wire. The venture was encouraged by a patent issued under Cecil's authority.[43]

Cecil[44] had firmly fixed in his mind the policy of making the realm self-sufficient. His patents with respect to mining, ordnance, and gunpowder manufacture are examples. He desired to develop English industry of every kind; and to his way of thinking the best manner of accomplishing this lay in the direction of granting patents of monopoly to men who were sufficiently enterprising to invent a new art or to introduce a new manufacture. The encouragement resided in the special monopoly privileges which would be granted for limited periods. They were by no means issued indiscriminately, but, on the contrary, careful inquiry

[37]16 Car. I, c. 21.

[38]Gardiner, *History of England*, IV, 2-6.

[39]S.P. Dom. Eliz. vii, 5, Oct. 4, 1559.

[40]S.P. Dom. Eliz. ccxliv, 116.

[41]S.P. Dom. Eliz. xviii, 18.

[42]S.P. Dom. Eliz. xcv, 70, 79.

[43]S.P. Dom. Eliz. xxvi, 83; xxxvii, 30, 43, 44; xlviii, 43; xl, 30.

[44]Lord Burleigh.

seems to have been made as to the novelty of the subject and the possible eventual benefit to be gained by granting a monopoly. There was a discriminating and statesmanlike policy of introducing new industries without displacing the old. If many of them concerned commodities of daily life, it was because those were the very commodities whose domestic manufacture was most desired.[45]

Among the patents granted were those for the manufacture of window-glass in 1567, the patentees being required to teach the art to others in the trade. In 1565 a grant was made for a new process of manufacturing salt.[46] Most of these patents were granted for the introduction of a new process of manufacture. Novelty (not in the sense as we now understand it, but in the sense of whether the process or manufacture had previously been practised within the kingdom) was the test of the validity of the patent. Of such type were the patents for the making of white soap, saltpetre, ovens, and dredging machines. Cecil's aim was, by the grant of patents, to eliminate the importation and establish the domestic manufacture of alum, glass, soap, oils, salt, saltpetre, and latten. His obvious intent was to profit by the religious disorders on the Continent which constantly persuaded artisans to emigrate, and, by offering them safe conduct and the encouragement of a limited monopoly, to endeavour to have them instruct English workmen in the practice of arts which were new to them.[47]

The establishment of new industries was, in general, undertaken by men of substance, willing to wait for a return on their money. There was thus a capitalist undertaking; and the return on the capital employed was a necessary and proper ingredient of the transaction. It was only when manufacture became established, and the trade in what had eventually come to be ordinary commodities in common use was controlled by patentees, that the system became a grievance.

Any history of monopolies would be incomplete without some reference to the monopolies granted for the printing and publishing of books. In view of the fact that we are discussing mainly those monopolies of an industrial type which laid the foundation for our patent system, it is not necessary to consider in detail the

[45]Cunningham, *English Industry and Commerce*, II, 76.

[46]8 Eliz., c. 22.

[47]S.P. Dom. Eliz. xliii, 29.

type of monopoly of printing and publishing which constituted the foundation of our copyright system.[48] But, just as the Crown granted exclusive manufacturing and commercial privileges, as an exercise of the prerogative, so it made grants of the sole right of printing and publishing certain kinds of books for specified terms.[49] That these grants were not considered illegal may be seen by the provision in Section 10 of the Statute of Monopolies that it should not extend to "any letters patent or grants of privilege heretofore made or hereafter to be made of, for, or concerning printing."[50] Side by side with this monopoly by royal grant, which might confer the monopoly on any person named in the grant, grew up the system of exclusive right by registration with the Stationers' Company, in which case the monopoly belonged to the member of the Company who registered it. The first type was the progenitor of the author's copyright, while the second was the foundation of the system of copyright residing in the printer or publisher. Printer's copyright could not prove, in the end, to be satisfactory, because it resulted in the fact that all the most profitable books became the property of the favoured few. Widespread piracy was the inevitable sequel, and this naturally resulted in the government taking over direct and complete control of printing. This was effected by the ordinances of the Star Chamber in 1586 and 1637, which were followed by the Licensing Acts of 1662, 1685, and 1688,[51] and finally by the Copyright Act of 1709.[52] Although it was held in *Millar* v. *Taylor*[53] that copyright had

[48]The history of copyright is treated in Fox, *Canadian Law of Copyright*, 14 ff.; Holdsworth, *History of English Law*, VI, 365 ff.; cf. Millar v. Taylor (1769) 4 Burr. 2303.

[49]These grants have been collected by Arber, *Transcripts of Registers of Stationers' Company*. Cf. proclamations of Henry VIII, 1533; Nov. 16, 1538; Order of Privy Council, Aug. 13, 1549; Decrees of Star Chamber, 1556, June 29, 1566, and June 23, 1585; Incorporation of Stationers' Company, May 4, 1557. See Arber, *Transcripts of Registers of Stationers' Company*, I, xix-xxiv.

[50]The basis of restriction on the right of printing was placed on public welfare. This may be seen from the observation in the case of the Company of Merchant Adventurers v. Rebow (1686) 3 Mod. 126 at 129: "The case of sole printing is a manufacture, and so not in the power of the King to restrain, for it is a piece of art and skill; but when once it becomes of public concernment, then the prerogative interposes."

[51]13 & 14 Car. II, c. 33; 1 Jac. II, c. 7; 1 Wm. & Mary, c. 24.

[52]8 Anne, c. 19.

[53](1769) 4 Burr. 2303.

always existed at common law,[54] it may be said that the statute of Anne is the basis of the modern system of copyright.

While the regulation of trade, and the maintenance of quality and supply, constituted the main actuating motives of the systematic monopoly policy, it must be admitted that the Crown, in the grant of monopolies of the various kinds we have discussed, sometimes acted for purely mercenary reasons, attempting to obtain either a cash payment or a share of the profits from the grant or dispensation. In the hands of the corrupt courtiers, the system of monopolies, designed originally to foster new arts, tended to become degraded into a system of plunder, for the holders of the monopolies in some cases knew nothing of the arts and acted in the widest spirit of exploitation and extortion.[55] In some cases the monopolies were sold to companies of merchants, who enhanced the price to the utmost ability of the purchaser.[56] In practice, commercial operations were hampered by a number of the grants; and although many which had previously been given to foreign merchants were rescinded and bestowed upon English merchants, the tendency was towards a concentration of power in corporate hands, until free competition was practically destroyed, and almost all commodities were in the hands of a favoured few, who fixed prices, terms, and conditions, on such bases as would return them the greatest profit. Of necessity the general body of the citizenry suffered.

There was precedent for the use of monopoly grants as rewards to those who had, during these active and flourishing times, distinguished themselves in civil and military employment. Elizabeth, who was unable to grant from her revenue rewards comparable with the services rendered, made use of the expedient used by her predecessors. It is true that she carried this policy to greater lengths than had theretofore been the custom, but, as we shall presently see, the motive force of these grants was neither mercenary nor otherwise improper. That the monopoly grants were far too many and varied, and that they embraced a wide variety of commodities of everyday use and necessity to the subjects, cannot be denied. Under cover of the loosely defined

[54]See also Donaldson v. Beckett (1774) 4 Burr. 2408; Jefferys v. Boosey (1854) 4 H.L.C. 815.

[55]Price, *English Patents of Monopoly*, 17.

[56]Hallam, *Constitutional History of England*, I, 244.

prerogative possessed or assumed by the Crown of regulating all matters relating to commerce, Elizabeth had made lavish grants of patents to deal in a multitude of articles, including common necessaries of life.[57] The number and importance of the commodities assigned over to the patentees may be ascertained from the speech of Sir Robert Wroth during the debate on monopolies in 1601: "There have been divers patents granted since the last parliament; these are now in being, viz. the patents for currants, iron, powder, cards, ox-shin bones, train-oil, transportation of leather, lists of cloth, ashes, anniseeds, vinegar, sea-coals, steel, aquavitae, brushes, pots, salt-petre, lead, accidences, oil, calamin-stone, oil of blubber, fumachoes, or dried piltchers in the smoak, and divers others."[58] When the list was read to the House, Mr. Hackwell stood up and asked: "Is not bread there?" "Bread," cried everyone in astonishment, "this voice seems strange." "No," said Mr. Hackwell, "but if order be not taken for these, bread will be there before the next parliament."[59]

There can be no question that some of the monopolists at least used their power to charge exorbitant prices for their commodities, it being stated by Sir Edward Hobbie during the debate that salt, which before the patent had sold for 16*d*. a bushel, now sold for 14*s*. or 15*s*. a bushel. After the Privy Council took notice of this extortion, the patentee was imprisoned, and salt was reduced to 16*d*. a bushel as before. Hobbie stated that if the patent were

[57]Cf. Hume, *History of England*; Hallam, *Constitutional History of England*, 244.

[58]To this list may also be added salt, bottles, glasses, paper, starch, tin, sulphur, new drapery, transportation of iron ordnance, beer, horn, leather, importation of Spanish wool, and Irish yarn. See also list of patents compiled by D'Ewes at 650 of his Journal printed in Appendix, II, 314. See also list appearing in Lodge, *Illustrations of British History*, III, 6, from the Talbot Papers, K, fo. 79, appearing in Appendix III, 315. A further list may be obtained from a perusal of *Burghley's State Papers*, transcribed by William Murdin, at 782-811 *passim*. List of grievances presented by the Commons to James I in 1606 is contained in Appendix VI, 329. For lists of patents considered improper during the debates of 1620-1 see lists prepared by Sir Robert Heath, May 20, 1621, S.P. Dom. Jac. I, cxxi, 48, 49, 122-5. List of patents ordered to be brought in to the Privy Council April 10, 1640, appears in Appendix XII, 346. For lists of objectionable patents during the sitting of the Long Parliament see S.P. Dom. Car. I, cccclxxii, 16, Nov. 23, 1640, and cf. chap. X, 127.

[59]1 Parl. Hist. 930; D'Ewes 648.

called in there might well be £3,000 a year saved in the ports of Lyme, Boston, and Hull.[60] Such high prices naturally attracted competition from intruders upon the monopoly, and in order to enforce their patents the patentees were armed with high and arbitrary powers from the Council. Although these powers were designed to prohibit infringement and punish infringers, they were misused by the patentees and turned by them into a system of oppression and extortion. Thus, the patentees of saltpetre, having the power of entering into houses, stables, and cellars and of searching wherever they suspected saltpetre might be gathered, used this authority as a means of extorting money from those who desired to escape such trouble and damage.[61] In addition, as well as thus restraining domestic trade and industry, most of the foreign commerce was in the hands of trading companies who, operating under exclusive charters, traded in commodities at whatever price suited them.

But the slavish Parliament of Henry VIII grew into the murmuring Parliament of Queen Elizabeth,[62] the mutinous Parliament of James I, and the rebellious Parliament of Charles I.[63] The fact that discussions on monopolies were raised in the House of Commons is sufficient to indicate the growth of a competitive spirit in England which was unique in mediaeval history, and to show that industrial life was growing stronger and more self-assertive. Merchants and manufacturers were beginning to resent the interference of government with industry, and more especially that form of state interference which took the shape of granting either to individuals or to corporations the exclusive right of producing or trading in any particular commodity.[64]

Hume goes so far as to assert that, during the reign of Elizabeth, "in reality the Crown possessed the full legislative power by means of proclamations, which might effect any matter even of the greatest importance, and which the Star Chamber took care to see more vigorously executed than the laws themselves,"[65] and

[60]1 Parl. Hist. 930.

[61]Cf. *ibid.*, 956.

[62]Hallam, *Constitutional History of England*, I, 245, 246 speaks of the "growing spirit" and of the "lurking ill-humour" of the Commons at the time of the debate on monopolies in 1601; cf. D'Ewes 619, 644.

[63]Bagehot, *English Constitution*, 282.

[64]Gibbins, *Industry in England*, 243.

[65]Hume, *History of England*, V, 463.

there is strong evidence in support of Hume's view when one looks at the ordinances of 1559 and 1585 which, issued by the Privy Council, set up a complete licensing and censorship system of the press and all publications.[66] As an exercise of the royal prerogative, the Crown undertook to exercise this censorship through the Star Chamber, and the Stationers' Company was set up as a kind of literary constable.[67] "It was in the Parliament of 1601," states Macaulay, "that the opposition which had, during forty years, been silently gathering and husbanding strength, fought its first great battle and won its first victory."[68] This conflict arose concerning the abuse of monopolies. The weight of some of the monopolies granted by Elizabeth bore so heavily on the people that a political convulsion might have been the result had the affairs of state been in less skilful hands.

Despite the peculiar nature of some of the grants, despite their apparent hampering restrictions and the confused state of thinking, despite the mercenary motives which sometimes actuated them, it may be said that the history of monopolies is the history of the growth of trade and industry. By means of a study of that history we can trace the causative factors of the evolution of England from the feudal system, through the beginning of the patent system as we now understand the term, up to the Industrial Revolution and the scientific and mechanical development of our own time.

But this policy of systematic supervision and regulation of industry on a national scale and its corollary of reward for meritorious invention and introduction of new industries did not

[66]Hallam, *Constitutional History of England*, I, 244, states: "The Crown either possessed or assumed the prerogative of regulating almost all matters of commerce at its discretion."

[67]Millar v. Taylor (1769) 4 Burr. 2303 at 2310 et seq. per Willes, J.; Taylor, *Origin of the English Constitution*, II, 181 n.; Fox, *Canadian Law of Copyright*, 13 et seq; Gneist, *Constitutional History of England*, 499.

[68]Macaulay, *History of England*, I, 63.

Cf. East India Company v. Sandys (1684) 10 St. Tr. 371 at 428 per Pollexfen *arguendo:* "The proviso in the statute of 43 Eliz. cap. 1. sect. 9, shows also that monopolies were granted; but so far were they from receiving any allowance or approbation, that that statute that was made in the end of her reign, for confirmation of the queen's grants by a special proviso, does except and provide that it should not extend to make good any letters patent that did concern any licenses, powers or privileges, commonly called monopolies."

suddenly spring into being as a *fait accompli*. At no time could it be said that it was called into existence as a system of full growth or even as an understood and decided policy which had not existed during the period immediately preceding. It was a system which developed slowly with many setbacks and reverses. It was thus a system which owed its final perfection to a slow and painful evolution, passing through periods of reaction and of misunderstanding. An unfortunate element of this type of evolutionary progress was that for a time during the reign of Elizabeth the earlier view of the Crown in favour of invention was reversed, and grants of special privilege in return for the introduction of noteworthy inventions were refused, the benefits of those inventions being thus lost to the realm. Among those noteworthy inventions which this policy refused to protect were Stanley's invention of armour plate, Gianibelli's method of land reclamation, the water closet of Harington (which had to wait a century and a half for introduction and use), and the stocking frame of Lee which, in default of encouragement, went to France, where it was accepted and protected.

The refusal to protect meritorious inventions or at least those which were new and contributed to the amenities of the population, in contrast with the generous treatment accorded to favourites and those willing to pay, by the grant of quite improper special privileges, inevitably built up a resistance in the minds of those who have been characterized as having a genius for knowing the proper point at which to rebel. The first murmurings came in 1571 when a member named Bell brought the matter up for discussion in Parliament. In the debate on the subsidy he stated that "the people were galled by two means . . . namely by licenses and the abuse of promoters; for which, if remedy were provided, then would the subsidy be paid willingly; which he proved, for that by licenses a few only were enriched, and the multitude impoverished."[69] He was summoned before the Privy Council and reprimanded. The Queen followed this by sending a message to the House "to spend little time in Motions, and to avoid long Speeches."[70] The subject of monopolies was causing deep and universal discontent; and, in 1597, an address was presented to the

[69] 1 Parl. Hist. 735.

[70] D'Ewes 159.

Queen on the subject,[71] in reply to which she rebuked the Commons for their presumption, sending a message through the Lord Keeper that "Touching the monopolies her Majesty hoped her dutiful and loving subjects would not take away her prerogative, which is the choicest flower in her garden . . . but would rather leave that to her disposition, promising to examine all patents and to abide the touchstone of the law."[72] But far from the conditions being ameliorated they grew steadily worse. In at least one case, an action at common law in which the validity of one of the patents would have come into question, was stayed.[73] The grievance of grants of the exclusive right to deal in commodities had become altogether insupportable, and had caused the deepest ferment throughout the kingdom. This is not to be wondered at when it is borne in mind that "almost all matters of human consumption or commercial adventure were assigned over to monopolists, who were so exorbitant in their demands that they sometimes raised prices tenfold; and who, to secure themselves against encroachments, were armed with high and arbitrary powers to search everywhere for contraband, and to oppress the people at pleasure."[74]

On November 20, 1601, Mr. Laurence Hide brought in a declaratory bill to Parliament entitled "An Act for the explanation of the Common Law in certain cases of Letters Patent" which was designed to put down the grievance, and to restore common law freedom of trade. The debate on this bill is illuminating as showing the care and delicacy with which members of the House discussed any matter touching the royal prerogative. Francis Bacon[75] said:

[71]Hallam, *Constitutional History of England*, I, 244, notes this as being a remarkable occurrence.

[72]1 Parl. Hist. 906; Campbell, *Lives of the Lord Chancellors*, II, 209; D'Ewes 547; Hallam, *Constitutional History of England*, 244.

[73]Carr, *Select Charters of Trading Companies*, lxvi; Holdsworth, *History of English Law*, IV, 248.

[74]Campbell, *Lives of the Lord Chancellors*, II, 331. Lord Campbell, however, is not to be relied upon as an accurate historian.

"For such Boldness the Monopolists took, that often at the Council-Table, Star-Chamber, Chancery, and Exchequer Chamber, Petitions, Informations and Bills were preferr'd in the Star-Chamber &c., pretending a Contempt for not obeying the Commandments and Clauses of the said Grants of Monopolies, and the Proclamations &c. covering the same." Vin. Abr., XVII, 215; Co. 3 Inst. 182, 183, c. 85; Hawk. P.C. 232, c. 79, s. 11.

[75]Afterwards the celebrated Lord Chancellor.

For the prerogative royal of the prince, for my own part I ever allowed of it, and it is such as I hope shall never be discussed. The Queen, as she is our sovereign, hath both an enlarging and restraining liberty of her prerogative; that is, she hath power by her patents to set at liberty things restrained by statute law or otherwise; and, by her prerogative she may restrain things that are at liberty. For the first, she may grant *non obstantes* contrary to the penal laws, which truly, in my own conscience, are as hateful to the subject as monopolies. For the second, if any man out of his own wit, industry or endeavour find out anything beneficial for the commonwealth . . . her Majesty is pleased perhaps to grant him a privilege to use the same only by himself or his deputies for a certain time; this is one kind of monopoly. Sometimes there is a glut of things when they be in excessive quantities, as of corn, and perhaps her Majesty gives licence to one man of transportation: this is another kind of monopoly. Sometimes there is a scarcity or small quantity: and the like is granted also.

Sir George Moore observed: "We know the power of her Majesty cannot be restrained by any Act; why, therefore, should we thus talk?" And Mr. Secretary Cecil stated: "If you stand upon law and dispute of the prerogative, hark what Bracton saith, *Prerogativam nostram nemo audeat disputare.*" But there were stronger voices to be heard. Mr. Francis Moore asked "to what purpose is it to do anything by act of parliament, when the Queen will undo the same by her prerogative . . . . there is no act of hers that hath been or is more derogatory to her own Majesty, or more odious to the subject, or more dangerous to the commonwealth than the granting of these monopolies." The list of patents, mentioned earlier,[76] was enumerated by Sir Robert Wroth during the debate in committee, upon which the question relative to bread was interjected by Mr. Hackwell of Lincoln's Inn. Sir Edward Hobbie discussed the great abuse of the salt monopoly, stating that through its operation the price of salt had risen from 16*d.* a bushel to 14*s.* and 15*s.* a bushel.[77] Those who attempted to oppose the bill were overcome by a torrent of indignant and menacing eloquence on the part of its proponents and the open clamour of the public who declared that the prerogative should not be suffered to touch the old liberties of England. Raleigh, no small gainer himself by some monopolies, after making what excuse he could, offered to give them up.[78] After four days of eager debate, and more heat than

[76]See ante 71.

[77]1 Parl. Hist. 923 et seq; D'Ewes 644; Prothero, *Constitutional Documents*, iii, et seq.

[78]1 Parl. Hist. 928.

had ever been witnessed, this ferment was suddenly appeased by Elizabeth herself.[79] Bowing to the inevitable, the Queen[80] sent a message to the House through the Speaker that "she understood that divers patents, that she had granted, were grievous to her subjects; and that the substitutes of the patentees had used great oppression. But, she said, she never assented to grant anything which was *malum in se*.[81] And if in the abuse of her grant there be anything evil, which she took knowledge there was, she herself would take present order of reformation thereof . . . and that some should be presently repealed, some suspended, and none put into execution but such as should first have a trial according to the law for the good of the people."[82] Upon this pleasant but deceptive note the bill was withdrawn.[83]

Robert Cecil, the secretary, added the more direct assurance that all existing patents would be revoked and no others granted in the future except in accordance with law.[84] The Queen issued a proclamation concerning monopolies three days later,[85] in which,

[79]Hallam, *Constitutional History of England*, 244.

[80]November 25.

[81]In his argument in the Case of Monopolies (1602) Moore K.B. 671, Coke insisted upon the distinction between *malum prohibitum* and *malum in se* saying that the King could dispense in respect of the one but not of the other, citing as an example the report of 11H. VII, 11b. It is to be noted that the terms of the Statute of Monopolies in enacting that all monopolies "are altogether contrary to the laws of this realm" have the effect of declaring monopolies not *malum prohibitum* but *malum in se*. See Co. 3 Inst. 181.

[82]D'Ewes 652; Townsend's Journals, 230-49; 1 Parl. Hist. 933.

[83]Prothero, *Constitutional Documents*, 114, 116.

[84]1 Parl. Hist. 934; Taswell-Langmead, *English Constitutional History*, 382. Cecil stated: "There are no patents now of force, which shall not presently be revoked; for what patent soever is granted, there shall be left to the overthrow of that patent, a liberty agreeable to the law." He then went on to say that most of these patents had been supported by letters of assistance from the Privy Council. No more such letters should be granted and all should be revoked. He promised a general proclamation throughout the realm to the above effect and enumerated the patents which would be immediately revoked, namely, those for salt, aquavitae, aqua composita and the like, vinegar, alegar, train-oil, oil of blubber, brushes, bottles, pouldavy, oade, and starch. As to other patents, they would be subject to adjudication by law, being suspended in the meantime, namely, those for the New Drapery, Irish yarn, calf-skins and fells, steel, leather, cards, glasses. As to the patent for saltpetre, her Majesty proposed to take it to herself, and Cecil cautioned the House not to disturb it as there was a shortage of gunpowder. 1 Parl. Hist. 934.

[85]Nov. 28, 1601; Rot. Pat. p. 8. m. 2; Steele Proc. no. 922.

after setting forth that her subjects had been aggrieved by a number of grants which had been made upon false and untrue suggestions and had been notoriously abused, declared a number of monopolies to be void. These grants concerned salt, salt upon salt, vinegar, aqua vitae or aqua composita, the salting and packing of fish, train-oil, blubbers or livers of fish, poldavies and mildernix, pots, brushes, bottles, and starch. As to a further list of grants concerning new. drapery, Irish yarn, calf-skins, pelts, cards, glasses, searching and sealing of leather, and steel, and such like, the proclamation provided that if any person were thereafter grieved, injured, or wronged by any of the said grants, he should be at liberty to take his ordinary remedy by the laws of the realm notwithstanding any matter or thing in any of the grants to the contrary. The Queen also withdrew her authority from any letters of assistance previously written for the enforcement of such grants. It is to be noted that the Queen apparently did not revoke or suspend all the monopolies.[86] Many years had to elapse before the triumph of Parliament over the Crown prerogative came to pass, but these champions of the liberties and rights of the Commons were the fathers of those who, in the next generation, passed the Petition of

[86]Foed., XVI, 540; Carte, *History of England*, III, 712; Hallam, *Constitutional History of England*, 245. A list of them dated May, 1603 (Lodge, *Illustrations of British History*, III, 159) seems to imply that many were still existing.

Thus in the Calendar of State Papers, Domestic, 1601-3, 276, there appears the following note which indicates that the intent of the proclamation was to revoke the objectionable monopolies only, while leaving unaffected those which had justification. "Arguments to prove that Her Majesty's letters patent dated the 7th day of September, 1559, for the sole making of saltpetre and gunpowder throughout Her Majesty's Dominions as the same are made, are maintainable not only in policy for the preservation of the State, but also in equity, and by the common laws of the land, viz., 1, that the use of saltpetre and gunpowder is necessary; 2, that they should be made in the country; 3, that their sole making belongs to the Crown, and should not be exercised without the Queen's grant; with objections thereto, and their answers; 4, statement of the benefit of granting the sole making of saltpetre and gunpowder. Conclusion, that the patent therefore is not a monopoly, but useful in policy, equity, and common law; therefore that the Proclamation of 28 November 1601 does not impeach it, but only prohibits its abuse, and that all who call it in question should be punished. With note that the patent was drawn by Att. Gen. Coke; the discourse approved by Sol. Gen. Fleming, Fras. Bacon, and by Councillors And. Blundon, John Dodderidge, John Walter, and John Hele."

The patent above referred to is that granted to Gerard Honricke, transferred on August 8, 1561, to Cockeram and Barnes, and mentioned in chap. V, n. 44.

Right and assembled in the Long Parliament. But the character of Elizabeth is demonstrated at its best by the manner in which she handled the grievance of monopolies on this occasion. In a measure she took out of their mouths the words which the members of the House of Commons were preparing to address to her. She did not treat the nation as an adverse party but readily promised to redress their grievances and promptly put her promise into execution. As Macaulay so aptly observed:

If such a man as Charles the First had been in her place when the whole nation was crying out against the monopolies, he would have refused all redress. He would have dissolved the Parliament, and imprisoned the most popular members. He would have called another Parliament. He would have given some vague and delusive promises of relief in return for subsidies. When entreated to fulfil his promises, he would have again dissolved the Parliament, and again imprisoned his leading opponents. The country would have become more agitated than before. The next House of Commons would have been more unmanageable than that which preceded it. The tyrant would have agreed to all that the nation demanded. He would have solemnly ratified an act abolishing monopolies forever. He would have received a large supply in return for this concession; and within half a year new patents, more oppressive than those which had been cancelled, would have been issued by scores.[87]

It is difficult to arrive at an adequate assessment of all the factors leading to the origin of the patent system which arose out of the concerted policy of trade regulation of Elizabeth, and the contemporaneous increase in the number of grants of monopoly patents. At the same time it is not a simple matter to estimate the relative weight of the reasons which go to explain the large increase in the number of monopolies granted during the closing years of the Tudor period. Many writers have over-emphasized the pecuniary motivation of these grants. This, it is suggested, is to accept the weight of only one of the causative factors. There can, of course, be no doubt that the pecuniary interest of the Crown was a factor contributing to the increase in the grant of monopolies, but it is to be borne in mind that in many cases the Crown obtained only nominal or, at any rate, meagre returns from its grants.[88] Rather than charging Elizabeth with rapacity and financial greed it would be a truer appraisal of history to transfer the odium of those qualities to the courtiers, adventurers, and place seekers who in those times clung like barnacles to the royal favour. That the

[87]Macaulay, "Burleigh and His Times" (1832) April, Edinburgh Review.
[88]Cf. Gardiner, *History of England*, IV, chap. XXXIII, 6.

system could have been otherwise is to be doubted, for, in those days, there was no civil list, and the Crown was under the necessity of remunerating royal servants and officials from its own revenues. Salaries were unknown and one of the few means, therefore, of reward left to the sovereign, was by the grant of special privileges and monopolies.[89] That monopolies were abused should, therefore, not be charged solely against the sovereign, but rather against those who, by their importunities and demands, many of which were founded on the obligation arising from valuable services rendered, constantly clamoured for recognition. The sovereign was thus under constant pressure to extend the use of the prerogative, and the limitations with which the common law had surrounded its exercise were at times neglected. The unfortunate feature of this situation was that, in general, the influential and unscrupulous among those who had claim to royal recognition and reward were not identified with or interested in the improvement of trade and industry and the furtherance of new inventions. Their interest lay, rather, in those grants of exclusive privilege which interfered with and made a charge upon established industries and the regulation and supervision of the sale of everyday commodities.[90] But the abuse of monopolies, great as it may have been, appears on a careful scrutiny to be merely an unhappy incident in the formation and development of a policy wisely conceived and executed on a basis of sound judgment, and which laid much of the foundation for, and was inextricably bound up with, the growing power of England as it emerged from the Middle Ages to its position of commercial, industrial, and national supremacy.[91] To suggest, as seems to be the almost universal custom

[89]Thus, James I, in his proclamation of May 7, 1603, inhibiting the use of any charter or grant made by Elizabeth, of any kind of monopolies, speaks of "the queen our sister, deceased, finding some years before her death, that some things had passed her hands, at the importunity of her servants, whom she was willing to reward with little burden to her estate (otherwise by necessary occasion exhausted). . . ." S.P. Dom. Jac. I, i, 68, 69, 70.

[90]Cf. Gardiner, *History of England*, 7.

[91]Cf. *ibid.*, 6.

A perusal of the Elizabethan patent grants will clearly show that the policy back of the monopoly system was the introduction into the realm of the domestic manufacture of those commodities which had hitherto figured most prominently in the list of imports, namely, alum, glass, soap, oils, salt, saltpetre, latten, etc. The rights of the inventor were regarded as being derived from the importer. The rights of the first finder-out were not so highly regarded as those of the first

among writers on the law of patents, that the patent system was a direct outgrowth of the abuse of monopolies, is a fallacy. The abuse was nothing more than a minor incident in a national policy, the growth and perfection of which was inevitable and progressive. Once the policy propounded by Acontius—that those, who by searching have found out things useful to the public, should have some fruits of their rights and labours by being protected from copying by others—was accepted and acted upon as a national policy, the benefits of the underlying principle became obvious. Those who had the interests of the realm sincerely at heart—those whom we might call the economists of their day—had before them the experience of the guilds, and the benefits to be obtained from their monopolistic regulation of industry. The genius of Elizabeth lay in the application of that monopolistic regulation as a national policy rather than as a local phenomenon. Once perceived, its steady and forward development could not be stayed by the mere incident that it did not arrive at instant perfection.[92] Just as every other branch of the common law has behind it a record of inception and development, of progress and retrogression, and of trial and error, so the law of monopolies and patents endured a history of uneasy progress beset at times by uncertainties, reactions, and abuses. These factors are inevitable in any system of legal development, but they are not the causative factors of any legal system. They are nothing but incidents in its growth. In this sense neither the *Case of Monopolies* nor the Statute of Monopolies constitutes the foundation of the patent system.

Why the monopoly system culminated into a national policy in the time of Elizabeth is not a matter of speculation but one of drawing valid conclusions from established facts. More than one factor had its effect upon this development. The acquisition of

---

bringer-in. The inventor's rights flowed only from the connotation of sharing with the introducer the ability of importing a new industry within the realm. This principle was clearly continued in the Statute of Monopolies and is fully expressed in the Case of Monopolies and the Cloth Workers of Ipswich Case. A perusal of the statute and these two cases will clearly demonstrate that it was the introduction of a new device or industry that was important and not its invention as we understand the term today. The modern meaning attached by the courts to the meaning of invention is an illustration of judicial legislation at its very worst.

[92]Cf. *ibid.*, 7.

privileges of sole manufacture throughout the whole country tended to expand a monopoly over the entire country. Such acquisition also tended to amalgamate or affiliate several local guilds or companies each having its own monopoly within its limited sphere. Coincident with the suppression of domestic competition was the growing idea of a protective trade policy against foreign imports. While the decline of the guilds, the corresponding diversification of industry, and the development of industry with a national scope, all played their parts, there must not be overlooked the new elements which were infiltrating into the English mind and character. The consciousness of national power in both the internal and external field had a profound effect on the men of Elizabethan England. The exploits and narratives of the Merchant Adventurers were filling them with a new and broad national spirit, which was being fulfilled and expanded by the development of commerce and industry within as well as without the national sphere. The gradual development of political consciousness was causing them to examine anew the function of Parliament, not only as an initiatory legislative body but as a restraining influence upon the prerogative of the Crown. Along with this slowly developing change in the constitutional thinking of the people, we must not lose sight of the historical factors which called forth the qualities of mind and of action which built the golden age of England. In both these spheres the character of Elizabeth exercised a profound influence.

The Tudor monarchy, which attained to the culmination of its power in the reign of Elizabeth, depended on the willing support of the nation at large. That support, based in affection, respect, and necessity, was in essence the cause not only of the success of Elizabeth's rule but of the mighty progress of the nation during her reign. It sprang from two causes, the first, that a strong sovereign power was necessary to unity at home, and the second, that in face of the dangers which threatened the realm from abroad that power should be allowed a reasonably free hand. It was essentially a national monarchy popular with the multitude and actively supported by the influential and wealthy classes. The religious difficulties and troubles, the fact that Mary, Queen of Scots, constituted a constant source of danger and fear, the lack of an heir to the throne, the antagonism to the Papacy, combined with the fear of foreign invasion and conquest, caused the people through their representatives to vote without reluctance whatever taxes were required, and to abstain from criticisms and demands which might hamper or interfere with the interests of the state either in its internal or foreign relations.

In this difficult situation the character of Elizabeth was of supreme influence and importance. She had the ability not only to see clearly the source of her power but to understand its limitations. While royal influence was important, it was not excessive, and her Parliaments were neither servile nor venal. The chivalrous loyalty of her subjects to a woman existed side by side with growing confidence in her wisdom. Her character and firmness were respected as much as her ability to make concessions when concessions were needed. Elizabeth was strong because she was popular. Her power consisted in the willing obedience of her subjects, in their attachment to her person and to her office, in their respect for the old line from which she sprang, in their sense of the general security which they enjoyed under her government.[93] If she could confidently rely upon the support of her people, they in turn were able to rely upon her wisdom and the obvious sincerity of her patriotic fervour.

The government of the Tudors was generally a popular government under the forms of despotism,[94] but in the exercise of her prerogative Elizabeth showed a cautious policy of desiring to keep its exercise within the limitations imposed upon it by the common law. The privileges embraced within the prerogative of the Crown, resting as they do partly on statute, partly on custom and precedent, are not indefinite but capable of description.[95] Elizabeth, in exercising the prerogative, did not transcend the limits laid down by the common law; and she thereby avoided the pitfall into which James I fell.[96] She, on the other hand, while claiming to exercise

[93]Macaulay, "Burleigh and His Times" (1832) April, Edinburgh Review.

[94]*Ibid.*

[95]Bl. Com., I, 239, has defined prerogative as being "that special pre-eminence which the King hath, over and above all other persons, and out of the ordinary courts of the common law, in right of his regal dignity." This undefined power to override the law and act for the good of the state is what Blackstone regards in his definition as the essence of the royal prerogative.

[96]This improper extension of the prerogative, which characterized the reigns of James I and Charles I, is typified by the statement of Cowell that "the prerogative of the King is that especial power, pre-eminence or privilege that the King hath in any kind, over and above other persons and above the ordinary

her prerogative right over a wide area, nevertheless had the caution to restrain herself within the bounds set by Bracton.[97] Elizabeth, therefore, always showed some desire that her monopoly grants should be in accordance with the law. She always paid attention to that natural check on the power of the sovereign of which Macaulay, when writing of the English monarchy in the sixteenth century[98] said: "There was one great and effectual limitation on the royal authority, the knowledge that, if the patience of the nation were severely tried, the nation would put forth its strength, and that its strength would be found irresistible."

While there was no doubt as to the legislative supremacy of Parliament in its trinitarian concept,[99] the effect of this supremacy was reduced in practice by two recognized principles. These were that the sovereign could issue proclamations controlling the liberty of the subject so long as such edicts did not run counter to statute or common law, and that he could dispense with the action of the law in individual cases. This quasi-legislative authority of issuing proclamations covered a wide field, and was not restrained within reasonable limits until the petition of the House of Commons to James I in 1610, in which the starch monopoly was called in question.[100] The power of dispensing with laws in particular cases was widely exercised by Elizabeth in respect of commercial regulations. It was recognized by Bacon and by Sir George Moore in

courts of the common law, in the right of his Crown." Cf. Prothero, *Constitutional Documents*, 410, where it is pointed out that a different implication arises in the use of the word "above" in Cowell's definition and the use of the words "out of" in Blackstone's.

[97]Bracton, *De Legibus et Consuetudinibus Angliae.* "Ipse autem rex non debet esse sub homine sed sub deo et sub lege, quia lex facit regem . . . ; non est enim rex ubi dominatur voluntas et non lex."

[98]Macaulay, "Burleigh and His Times" (1832) April, Edinburgh Review.

[99]Cf. speech of Yelverton in the House of Commons, April 20, 1571: "It was fit for princes to have their prerogatives; but yet the same be straitened within reasonable limits. The prince . . . could not of herself make laws neither might she by the same reason protect laws." D'Ewes 175-6; see also Sir Thomas Smith on *The Parliament and the Authority Thereof.* Prothero, *Constitutional Documents*, 178.

Yelverton had always disliked having to defend monopolies. Cf. Church, *Bacon*, 119.

[100]Prothero, *Constitutional Documents*, 305.

the debate on monopolies,[101] and when used in moderation seems not to have been disputed.

A further incident of government in the time of the Tudors assisted in the establishment of a patent policy. This was the initiatory power with respect to legislation which at that time was held to reside in the Crown. As was demonstrated in the debate on monopolies, it is clear that the Crown not only had the right to initiate legislation but to deny to the Commons the right to interfere in matters other than those which were propounded to them for their attention. This theory of government was, however, already suspect in Elizabeth's reign, and it is to be remarked that the debates on monopolies were precipitated and motivated by the action of private members. But so long as it was accepted, it tended to allow the sovereign to exercise a strong control over the regulation of trade and the stimulation of industry by initiating only such legislation as was designed not to upset any delicate balance existing in connection with foreign commercial relations. An over-riding power of this type inevitably resulted in the setting up of certain monopolistic controls which might have been suspect in the minds of a wide group of legislators who were not acquainted with the broad details of trade policy and who might, therefore, have interfered with such a policy if they had had the right of initiating legislation and of discussing matters not propounded to them for their consideration by the sovereign.

It was, therefore, not by accident that the patent system had its origin in England nor that the industrial revolution was the inevitable sequel. Scientific curiosity and the fever of increased production applied to the solution of economic problems were the outward symbols of the Elizabethan lust of living and zest of discovery and accomplishment. That spirit of joyous pioneering, in the arts and sciences, in trade and commerce, in adventure, exploration, and discovery, in literature, drama, and poetry, in politics and government, in loving and living, was the hallmark of the golden quality of the age, in sharp and striking contrast to the dismal torpidity and shrinking fear of our own times, when the *summum bonum* seems to be nothing more attractive than the dead level of mediocrity which goes by the name of security, under the leaden hand of socialism.

[101]See ante 76.

VII. MONOPOLIES AND THE COMMON LAW

THE view of the common law concerning monopolies was that, in general, they were void unless for the common good.[1] This may be gathered from the arguments of counsel and the judgment in the case of *Davenant* v. *Hurdis* (sometimes known as the *Merchant Tailors' Case*)[2] heard in the Court of King's Bench in 1599. In that case the Company of Merchant Tailors in London had, by its charter, power to make ordinances for the government of the Company, and the charter and the powers therein contained had been confirmed by Parliament. The Court, however, held void an ordinance of the Company requiring every brother of the Company to put his cloths to be dressed, at least as to half thereof, to some brother of the same society under pain of forfeiture of 10*s*. It was held that every subject by the law had freedom and liberty to put his cloth to be dressed by what cloth maker he pleased and could not be restrained to certain persons, for that, in effect, would be a monopoly and void.[3] The arguments of counsel in this case

[1]Bac. Abr., tit. Prerogative, F. 14, "The King's grant of a monopoly, as of the sole buying, selling, working, making, or using of any commodity, is not only void by the common law, but the persons procuring such grants are said to be punishable by fine and imprisonment."

Com. Dig., tit. Trade, D. 4, "All monopolies are contrary to Magna Carta."

These statements by Bacon and Comyns are obviously inaccurate. The right of the Crown to grant patents of monopoly in case of new inventions was recognized at common law before the time of the Statute of Monopolies. Thus in the case of the Taylors de Ipswich v. Sherring (1615) 1 Roll. R. 4, it was held that the King can grant a patent for a new invention for a reasonable time. The judgment, at 5, gives the precise view of the common law on this point: "Mes lou nest ascun novell invention, le Roy per son patent ne polt hinder ascun trade."

To the same extent the statement in Merchant Adventurers v. Rebow (1686) 3 Mod. 126 at 131 that: "All patents prohibiting trade are void. 13 Hen. IV. pl. 14: 1 Rolle R. 4" is inaccurate unless its meaning is restricted as above indicated.

[2](1599) Moore K.B. 576. See also Norris and Stap's Case, Hob. 211 referred to in East India Co. v. Sandys (1684) 10 St. Tr. 371 at 437.

[3]In this case the word "monopoly" was defined as follows: "This word *monopolium, dicitur* ἀπὸ τοῦ μόνου χαὶ πωλέω *quod est cum unus solus aliquod genus mercaturae universum emit pretium ad suum libitum statuens.*"

show that, by the close of the sixteenth century, the common law had arrived at settled principles in its attitude on monopolies, and are, therefore, considered of sufficient importance to warrant a summary in the Appendix.[4]

In 1598 Elizabeth had made a grant to Edward Darcy for transporting and making cards for the term of twenty-one years, a subject of monopoly which was evidently a favourite of Elizabeth's, for it figured in several of her previous grants.[5] The case of *Darcy* v. *Allin*,[6] better known as the *Case of Monopolies*, was an inevitable milestone in the evolution of the patent policy as a national system. This case is deserving of careful consideration in that it is the first complete judicial pronouncement upon the common law principles concerning monopolies. The appearance of a case of this sort in the common law courts, touching as it did upon the delicate subject of crown prerogative, was due to the assurance that the Queen had given in her message to the House in 1601 that no monopolies should be put in execution but such as should first have a trial according to the law.[7] As late as 1603, actions had been prohibited against Darcy[8] but on this occasion Darcy brought the action himself, thus giving the courts of common law an opportunity which they might otherwise not have had for some time. The importance laid upon this case by the judges is demonstrated by their exhaustive treatment accorded to the principles and history of the law. Their expatiation upon the inconvenience of monopolies has become a classic; and the exposition of the law in the arguments of counsel and the reasons for judgment, having formed the basis of the patent systems of England, the British Dominions, the United States of America, and many foreign states, ranks as one of the most valuable contributions ever made to a theory of jurisprudence.[9] It is useful, as throwing some light on the type of monopoly which met with disapproval, to

[4]See post 311.

[5]Hulme (1909) 3 A.A.L.H., 137.

[6](1602) 11 Co. Rep. 84 b.

[7]The patent for cards was specifically mentioned by Cecil as one which was to be suspended and left to adjudication by the courts of law. 1 Parl. Hist. 936.

[8]Carr, *Select Charters of Trading Companies*, lxvi: Acts of the Privy Council, xxxi, 333-6, 346, 347; xxxii, 237; S.P. Dom. Eliz. cclxxxii, 8.

[9]Cf. a similar historical treatment given to the law of copyright by Willes, J., in Millar v. Taylor (1769) 4 Burr. 2303 at 2310 et seq; cf. Fox, *Canadian Law of Copyright*, 12 et seq.

examine the terms of the grant. Those terms, as well as the basis upon which the grant was made, may be gathered from the declaration in the case which claimed that Queen Elizabeth (intending that her subjects, being men able to exercise husbandry, should apply themselves thereto and not employ themselves in making playing cards, which had not been an English occupation within the realm, and observing that by reason of the making of a multitude of such cards, card playing was becoming more frequent, especially among servants, apprentices, and poor artificers, and to the end that her subjects might apply themselves to more necessary and lawful trades), by letters patent,[10] granted to the plaintiff full power, licence, and authority to buy beyond sea all such playing cards as he thought good and import them into and sell them within the realm; that he, his servants, factors, and deputies should enjoy the whole merchandise of all playing cards; and further that the plaintiff, his servants, factors, and deputies and none other should have the making of playing cards within the realm for twenty-one years; and further charged and commanded that no other persons should bring any cards or buy, sell, or make any cards, within the realm, under penalty of fine and imprisonment.

It was held by the court that such a grant as was claimed by the plaintiff was void for two reasons. First, because it was a monopoly, and against the common law; secondly, because it was against divers acts of Parliament. The arguments of counsel, as well as the judgment, merit the fullest consideration and scrutiny and these will be found summarized at length in the Appendix.[11]

[10]30 Eliz., June 13.

[11]See post 318.

Mr. D. Seaborne Davies has provided a most interesting sidelight on the card monopoly in his article "Further Light on the Case of Monopolies" (1932) 96 L.Q.R., 394. In his admirable study of the case Mr. Davies shows that the monopoly of cards had already been granted by Elizabeth to Ralph Bowes and Thomas Bedingfield in July, 1576. The patent was reissued in 1578 and again in 1588 to Bowes alone (Pat. Roll., 18 Eliz. 1; 20 Eliz. 7; 30 Eliz. 12). Upon the death of Bowes before the term of the grant had expired, it was reissued, in 1598 to Darcy (Pat. Roll., 40 Eliz. 9). The resistance to the grant is demonstrated by the records of the Courts of Star Chamber, Chancery, and Exchequer and of the Privy Council, which show a number of actions brought for infringement of the grant by Bowes and Bedingfield and later by Darcy. The proclamation of Nov. 28, 1601, by Elizabeth, promising to reform many of the abuses committed by patentees, and which nullified many of the existing patents, did not affect Darcy's patent which was left "to abide the touchstone of the law."

In discussing this case, Thomas Webster, the learned nineteenth-century author on the law of patents, observed: "In the preceding case, the consideration or motive is the restraining of people in one known occupation, in order that they might employ themselves in another; and this was to be effected by giving the exclusive privilege of manufacture and sale to certain persons. Such a grant is declared to be a monopoly, and against the common law. The principles of the above decision have been recognized in many subsequent cases of grants or restraints connected with some known manufacture or trade."[12] It is important to ascertain the sense in which the term monopoly is used because it must not be inferred from the case of *Darcy* v. *Allin* that all monopolies as the term is usually understood are against the law. It will thus be evident that Sir Edward Coke's definition of a monopoly[13] would appear to include such monopolies only as are, on the authority of the case of *Darcy* v. *Allin*, against common law and the commonwealth.

The next step in the history of monopolies as far as adjudication in the courts of common law is concerned was the decision in the *Cloth Workers of Ipswich Case* which was tried in the King's Bench in the year 1614.[14] That was an action for a penalty brought by the masters and wardens of the cloth workers or tailors of Ipswich. The declaration alleged that the King had incorporated the plaintiffs, and had granted them a charter by which no person might exercise the art or trade of a cloth worker or tailor within the town

---

An interesting and detailed study of the further history of the patent to Darcy is given by Mr. Davies in his article in the Law Quarterly Review. In the subsequent case of Allin v. Garrard, Allin, the defendant in the famous Case of Monopolies, alleged that he had defended that action on the assurance of Sir John Garrard, Lord Mayor of London, that the City Corporation would undertake to repay him his costs, as the action was fought for the direct benefit of the privileges of the tradesmen of London. Garrard refused to pay any of the costs, but it appears that Allin was largely successful in his action.

Later, in 1609, Darcy was sued by the Crown for failure to pay rent on his patent for cards for the previous seven years. Darcy pleaded the invalidity of his patent as established in the Case of Monopolies and he was accordingly discharged. Davies, "Further Light on the Case of Monopolies" (1932) 96 L.Q.R., 414.

[12]1 W.P.C. 4 n.

[13]Co. 3 Inst. 181, b. 85; see ante 8.

[14](1615) Godb. R. 252; 11 Co. Rep. 53a, *sub nom.* Taylors de Ipswich v. Sherring 1 Roll. R. 4.

of Ipswich, unless he had first served an apprenticeship; and that the defendant had exercised the trade in violation of this charter. It was held by the court that the ordinance was unlawful; and it was agreed by the court that the King might make corporations and grant to them the power of making ordinances for the ordering and government of any trade, but that thereby they could not make a monopoly, for that was to take away free trade, which was the birthright of every subject.[15] The court further went on to refer to a case in 2 Hen. V, c. 5, a case in debt upon a bond, upon condition that one should not use his trade of a dyer in the town which the plaintiff inhabited for a period of one year; and it was there held that the obligation was void because the condition was against the law.[16] It was resolved that, although such clause was contained in the King's letters patent, yet it was void. But it was also observed that where it is either by prescription or by custom confirmed by Parliament, there such an ordinance may be good, *quia consuetudo legalis plus valet quam concessio regalis*. The court pointed out that grants of this type were expressly against the Statute of 9 Edw. III, c. 1, and referred to the charter granted by King Henry VIII to the physicians of London which had the same clause in it, but pointed out that if it had not been confirmed by act of Parliament, made 33 Hen. VIII, it would have been void. The court, however, then proceeded to enunciate the principles which attached to monopolies at common law in the following terms:

> But if a man hath brought in a new invention and a new trade within the kingdom, in peril of his life, and consumption of his estate and stock, etc., or if a man hath made a new discovery of anything, in such cases the King, of his grace and favour, in recompense of his costs and travail, may grant by charter unto him, that he only shall use such a trade or traffic for a certain time, because at first the people of the kingdom are ignorant, and have not the knowledge or skill to use it; but when that patent is expired, the King cannot make a new grant thereof, for when the trade has become common, and others have been bound apprentices in the same trade, there is no reason why such should be forbidden to use it.

---

[15]"At common law no man could be prohibited from working in any lawful trade, for the law abhors idleness . . . and therefore the common law abhors all monopolies which prohibit any from working in any lawful trade and that appears in 2 H. 5, 5 B."

[16]Sometimes known as the Case of John, the Dyer, Year Book, 2 H. V, 5 B. Sir John Hull, in delivering judgment holding the bond against the common law added, "and by God, if the plaintiff was here he should go to prison till he paid a fine to the king."

The common law had thus arrived at the point where its principles were finding enunciation in a system similar in its essentials to that of the present. The royal publication of the *Book of Bounty* in 1610 gave evidence that the prerogative power was keeping step with the evolutionary process of the common law. Interwoven in these two forces was the expanding authority of the popular will which found increasing expression in Parliament. The stage was set for the culminating act. Regarded in this light, the Statute of Monopolies, enacted in 1624, was not a mere incident, but the final expression of an evolutionary process to which all factors of the times, legal, political and popular, made their contribution. Its climactic character is to be perceived by its presence on the pages of the existing statute books.

VIII. PARLIAMENTARY CONTROL OF MONOPOLIES

THE death of Elizabeth and the accession of James I occurred before the delivery of the judgment in the *Case of Monopolies*. The acuteness of the question of monopolies had been somewhat softened after Elizabeth's message to the House during the debate on the bill of 1601, and by her speech to her last Parliament on November 30, 1601.[1] But a policy of trade regulation under a sovereign who earned the almost universal respect of her subjects by her obvious attempts to keep constantly before her eyes the progress and good of her realm, was not a policy which could easily be continued with a change of dynasty. Under Elizabeth the power of the Crown in the direct and almost unquestioned regulation of trade was exercised through its own officials. Under the Stuarts the royal authority was delegated to privileged bodies, corporations, and patentees. There was necessary for its continuance a continuity of the personal element; and with the accession of the Stuarts the personality of the sovereign had a direct effect on the public attitude toward trade regulation. The great development of trade, the expansion of industry, and the establishment of new industries, tended to loosen the royal control. With the development of political thought toward a freer and more independent attitude, the existence of privileged classes with special rights was a cause of anger and constant agitation. The tendency under the Stuarts to pass the regulation of this expanded trade into the hands of corporations, as being more capable of handling and administering it, led to criticisms and agitations which attacked the fundamental policy rather than its maladministration. The practice of appointing supervisors of the monopolies, the manner in which their powers were abused, the practice of the Council in

[1]In the course of her speech the Queen said that "yet did I never put my pen to any grant but upon pretext and semblance made me, that it was for the good and avail of my subjects generally, though a private profit to some of my ancient servants, who have deserved well; but that my grants shall be made grievances to my people, and oppressions, to be privileged under colour of our patents, our princely dignity shall not suffer it."

directly interfering in the regulation of monopolies under the mistaken theory that infringement of a patent established by royal proclamation constituted a contempt of royal authority—all engendered economic grievances on the part of manufacturers and traders which required remedy. The sentiment gradually arose that commerce could look after itself without royal interference and regulation. Governmental regulation became more and more frowned upon as an unwarranted interference with personal liberty, and, instead of attacking the manner in which the system was abused, the system itself was attacked. And so the monopoly system, as a method of regulating trade and commerce was, except as to new inventions, swept out of existence at the end of the earlier Stuart period and monopolies so thoroughly discredited that we have not yet become economically emancipated from the thoughts associated with this popular feeling of revulsion. So thoroughly was the system destroyed and the new policy of trade independence fostered that the period of the Commonwealth can only be described as one of economic anarchy. The experience gained during those years resulted in a swing of opinion toward the re-establishment of the exercise of economic authority by the Crown subject to parliamentary criticism and control which has developed by slow and continuous degrees to that which obtains today.

Elizabeth's policy of trade interference formed an irresistible temptation to James I. He did, however, maintain a somewhat vacillating policy in regard to monopolies, at times allowing himself to be advised as to the permissible lengths to which the prerogative could be used as laid down in *Darcy* v. *Allin*, and at times making a considerable number of grants which led to much controversy[2] and to a number of annulments.[3] In 1603, he issued a proclamation[4] in which, after reciting that the late Queen had issued many grants for the purpose of rewarding her servants, he suspended all

[2]Thus in the debate in the House in 1620 Coke said that, "Monopolies are now grown like Hydra-heads: they grow up as fast as they are cut off." 1 Parl. Hist. 1193. See also "The poore men's petition to their King against monopolies." S.P. Dom. Jac. I. Add. April 17, 1603.

[3]Price, *English Patents of Monopoly*, 25-31; Mund, *Monopoly*, 22; S.P. Dom. Jac. I, ii, 4, 5; ix, 75.

[4]"A Proclamation inhibiting the use and execution of any Charter or Grant made by the late Queene Elizabeth, of any kinde of Monopolies, &c." Booke of Proclamations, 12. Cf. Hawarde, 182; S.P. Dom. Jac. I, i, 68, 69, and 70.

grants and charters of monopoly, together with all licences to dispense with penal laws, grants to corporations of arts or mysteries, and grants for enlarging trade, until examination could be had of them by the King with the advice of his Council. The terms of the proclamation with respect to the grants by Elizabeth are of much interest in that James characterized them by the use of the expression: "Though they had and might have foundation in princely prerogative, yet either by too large extending thereof, or for the most part in respect that they were of such nature as could hardly be put in use without hindrance to multitudes of people, or else committed to inferior persons, who in the execution thereof did so exceedingly abuse the same, as they became intolerable." In general, as Prothero puts it,[5] "too wise or too timid to commit himself to distinctly illegal courses or flagrant departures from precedent, he preserved for the most part a fairly good understanding with his subjects." James had a fixed belief in the propriety and efficacy of the full use of the royal prerogative, but in this he ran into collision with Coke who stepped forward on various occasions as the champion of the laws and constitution of his country, going so far as to say on one occasion[6] that "the King cannot change any part of the common law . . . without parliament." But James's extravagance, under the name of "the royal bounty" which he claimed to be necessary for the dignity of his position but which his critics regarded as a diversion of the flow of the wealth of England to his Scottish favourites, made great claims upon his supply of available funds. Impositions and the grant of patents of monopoly by virtue of the royal prerogative were apparently easy taps by which to set the golden fountain flowing. James was not reluctant to use the methods, but the people, remembering the extent to which these had been carried under Elizabeth, and the storms through which they had passed in placing some reasonable restraint upon their use, were inclined to be vigilant to protect their hard-won gains and to prevent a recurrence of the abuses with which they had been plagued. But the popular idea of this period of history must not be too readily accepted. That popular idea is exemplified in Macaulay's essays, where he states that James "resorted without scruple to the most illegal and oppressive devices for the purpose of enabling Bucking-

[5]Prothero, *Constitutional Documents*, xxii.
[6]1615.

ham and Buckingham's relations to outshine the ancient aristocracy of the realm. Benevolences were exacted. Patents of monopoly were multiplied. All the resources which could have been employed to replenish a beggared exchequer at the close of a ruinous war were put in motion during this season of ignominious peace." In commenting on this passage, Gardiner observes: "This is, in all probability, precisely what nine-tenths of those who read history believe. Yet in the whole passage there is not a single word of truth."[7]

James had apologized to his first Parliament for being so profuse in his gifts, and had undertaken to moderate his bounty.[8] He had set up an investigating body known as the Commissioners for Suits to examine upon all applications for grants. But by the time of the second session in 1606 patents of monopoly had become so great in number as to form one of the important matters considered by the Committee of Grievances, and a petition dealing with the monopolies was presented by it to the King at the close of the session.[9] When the House resumed its sittings at the third session,[10] the King replied to the petition by undertaking to revoke some of the monopolies. This not having been done, the Commons presented a petition on July 7, 1610, pointing out that not only had the grievances not been redressed as promised but that the King had failed in his undertaking that the courts should consider and judge of the validity of certain of the grants.[11] James replied in his usual adroit fashion. The grievances put forward at this time by the Commons related to the imposition on sea coal, the exaction for sealing the new drapery,[12] the imposition upon

[7]S. R. Gardiner, "On Four Letters from Lord Bacon to Christian IV, King of Denmark" (1867) 41 Archaeologia, 219 at 225.

[8]March 19, 1604.

[9]S.P. Dom. Jac. I, xxiii, 66 and 67. The list is contained in Hawarde, 436 and is reprinted in the Appendix, 329.

[10]November, 1606; cf. 1 Jo. H.C. 316-18.

[11]S.P. Dom. Jac. I, July 7, 1610, lvi, 10.

[12]The patent for the alnage of the new drapery caused strong protest and appears constantly in the proceedings of the House of Commons as one of the main subjects of grievance. The term "new drapery" arose from the introduction from abroad in the early years of the sixteenth century of new methods of weaving and finishing cloth. The original patent was granted by Elizabeth in 1594 for the supervision of worsteds, bays, fustians, and frisadoes. The alnagers were to collect a subsidy for the Crown in the form of a fee for sealing

alehouses, and the monopoly of licence of wines. The answers by the King met with a favourable reception by the Commons, for, though the *Journals* do not express so much, they sent up the bill of supply a few days later.[13]

That the assertion of his prerogative by James I was kept within reasonable limits during the earlier years of his reign may be ascertained by his publication in the year 1610 of a declaration against grants of monopolies which Coke observes to have been a result of the judgment in *Darcy* v. *Allin*.[14] It is also significant that Parliament protested in 1610 against the excessive granting of monopolies.[15] This declaration, or *Book of Bounty*, as it is more frequently styled, was entitled "A Declaration of His Majesty's Pleasure, etc." It was published in 1610 and was stated to be out of the King's zeal for law and justice. It declared that monopolies were things against the laws of the realm and therefore expressly commanded that no suitor presume to move the King to grant any of them.[16] The similarity of the language

---

and certifying the cloth. No cloth was to be exposed for sale without being sealed and defective material was to be destroyed. The Duke of Lennox procured the surrender of the patent and the grant to him of a new patent by James I. The unauthorized seizures of cloth and the extortions of his agents were the subject of complaint in the petition of July 8, 1610. The patent was called before the Committee of Grievances in the session of 1624 (1 Jo. H.C. 689) and on May 22, 1624 (1 Jo. H.C. 709, 793; S.P. Dom. Jac. I, clxv, 26; clxv, 34) the House resolved that the patent should be included in a petition of grievances to the King who should be asked to reform the abuses and punish the offenders. The House of Commons *Journal* for this date gives a summary of the abuses which were occasioned by this patent in the following words:

"The Abuses now of Four Heads: 1. Usurping upon the Subject: Extending his Office upon Stockings, Waistcoats, and Caps, made of wool. 2. Upon Cloths sealed before: Pressing the Retailer to seal, after the Clothier hath sealed. 3. Presseth the Seal upon Cloths less than half Cloths. They now sell their Seals by Bushels; so as the Seal, the Instrument of Right, now of Deceit. They sell these Seals for 1d. a-piece. 4. Exact Rents upon all that deal in Woollen Commodities; as Stockings; 10*s*. *per annum* yearly Rent: Their Fines uncertain."

The Statute of Monopolies put an end to the matter.

[13] 1 Parl. Hist. 1132.

[14] Cf. Co. 3 Inst. 182.

[15] Hallam, *Constitutional History of England*, 305.

[16] 11 Co. Rep. 88d. The *Book of Bounty* was published in facsimile form in 1897. Page 13 contains "A Memorial of Those Speciall things for which Wee expressly command that no Suitor presume to move Us, being matters either

in the book and in the judgment in the *Case of Monopolies* would seem to indicate that the case had been brought to his attention, and had had no inconsiderable effect on his attitude. The similarity with the language of the *Cloth Workers of Ipswich Case*[17] is even more striking, and shows that the judges were fully alive to the progress of thought on this subject. It is probable that the publication of the *Book of Bounty* was influenced by James's desire to convince the public that he did not wish to transgress the principles of the common law and the limits of the royal prerogative as they were ascertained in 1610; but the suspicion is inescapable that James was doing so, to a certain extent, with tongue in cheek, in an effort to lull the minds of the people into a feeling of security and with no real intention of limiting his own use of this facile tool for regulating trade.

While, as above stated, the judgment in the *Case of Monopolies* was the principal motive for the *Book of Bounty*, its publication in its turn, was a great motive for obtaining the royal assent to the Statute of Monopolies.[18] It is worthy of note that, amid all the clamour against monopolies on the one hand, and their continued issue under the Great Seal on the other, James apparently clung to his original opinions, and was at least consonant in that the declaration of the *Book of Bounty* was reprinted in 1619.[19] In this he may have been persuaded by the attraction of consistency, for he was not allowed to forget the statements to which he was committed. During the debate on the patent for inns in 1620 Noy

---

contrary to Our lawes, or such principall Profits of Our Crowne, and setled Revenue, as are fit to be wholly reserved to Our Owne use, until Our Estate be repaired.

"Things contrary to our Lawes.

1. Monopolies.
2. Graunts of the benefite of any Penal Lawes, or of power to dispence with the Lawe, or compound for the forfeiture."

Pages 17 and 21 contain: "A Memorial of Those Suits wherein We are contented to bee moved by Our Servants and Subiects, and to reward them according to the particular merit of the Suitor.

"9. Proiects of new invention, so they be not contrary to the Law, nor mischievous to the State, by raising prices of commodities at home, or hurt of trade, or otherwise inconvenient."

[17](1615) Godb. R. 252.

[18]See Co. 3 Inst. 182.

[19]Gardiner, *History of England*, IV, chap. CXXXIII, 14.

remarked: "Monopolies and powers of dispensation of penal laws are chief grounds of all the Grievances, and this ariseth and proceedeth *per importunitatem impetrantis*; and therefore let us examine, who these are, for the King by his Book, has published his distaste of these importunate suitors: and therefore it is good that we teach them more manners."[20] But the publication of the book had little practical effect, and, after the suspension of parliamentary government in 1614, the abuse of monopolies continued. Despite James's high-sounding words in the *Book of Bounty*, the use of the royal prerogative persisted practically unchecked, and, whatever may have been the motives actuating the grants, Parliament was fast becoming too conscious of its growing political power to regard with unconcern the continued regulation of trade and industry by royal action, unhampered by the check of parliamentary supervision.

During the sitting of 1614, the question of monopolies was brought up in the House on several occasions. There seemed, in the debates, to be some question of the right of Parliament to question the King's grants but Francis Moore cited the case of Peachie, when his patent for sweet wines was declared void by Parliament in 5 Edw. III, and the *Case of John the Dyer*,[21] from which he advised the House that monopolies were against the law. The glass patent which, according to the evidence presented, was causing prices to be maintained at an extortionate level, was declared to be a patent of monopoly and was ordered brought before the House for examination.[22] The patents for transportation of iron ordnance[23] and for dyeing and dressing cloth[24] also came up for discussion but the sudden message of the King on June 1, dissolving Parliament,[25] put an end to any attempt at reform for the time being.

The question of monopolies was, during this time, inextricably bound up with the subject of impositions. The duties on customs, tonnage and poundage, had been considered the ancient revenue of the Crown; and from the time of Richard II it had become

[20] 1 Parl. Hist. 1192.
[21] Y.B. 2 Hen. V, 5 B; 11 Co. Rep. 53.
[22] 1 Jo. H.C. 472, May 4, 1614.
[23] 1 Jo. H.C. 479.
[24] 1 Jo. H.C. 491.
[25] 1 Jo. H.C. 505.

customary for Parliament to vote these revenues to the Crown for life. They were, however, supplemented by impositions or additional duties placed upon certain imports by royal rather than by parliamentary action. Originally commenced in 1491,[26] the government was authorized to levy an extra duty for the purpose of the regulation of the trade in sweet wines. An act of Henry VIII[27] empowered the King, during his life, by proclamation, to regulate the course of trade by repealing or reviving any act of Parliament dealing with the import or export of goods. This power, conferred on the Crown originally for purposes of regulating trade, soon became little more than a means of raising royal revenue. The policy became recognized as a legitimate method of the Crown for such purpose and was confirmed by later statutes.[28]

The right of the Crown to regulate trade, partly by custom and party by statute, resulted in the close connection above mentioned between impositions and monopolies. Obviously, a trade could be retarded and discouraged by imposing upon it heavier duties; another trade could be founded or assisted and stimulated by granting a monopoly. Both methods were used by Elizabeth. Her good sense and obvious desire to exercise a sound commercial policy caused the question of monopolies to be discussed only during the closing years of her reign, and the matter of impositions to be accepted with little, if any, question. But under James the situation was different. James had neither the wisdom of Elizabeth nor her feeling of unity with the people. He had not gained the respect of the Commons; and the reasons for entrusting Elizabeth with wide powers which we have noted[29] had largely passed away. The tendency was not to extend but rather to limit royal power, particularly where revenue was concerned. This unparliamentary revenue could not long remain unchallenged, and in 1606 its legality was attacked before the Exchequer Court in *Bates's Case*.[30] Bates, a merchant, had refused to pay an imposition levied by the Crown on currants on the ground that the King had no right to take the duty without a grant from Parliament. The judges held that the Crown had power to levy such impositions, the doctrine

[26]7 Hen. VII, c. 8.

[27]26 Hen. VIII, c. 10.

[28]Cf. 23 Eliz., c. 7; 39 Eliz., c. 10.

[29]Ante 83.

[30]Prothero, *Constitutional Documents*, 340.

established by the case seeming to be that the King may not set impositions merely for the sake of revenue, but that he may do so for the protection of English merchants.[31] In this decision the Parliament of 1608 acquiesced. But the Parliament of 1610, after arguments addressed to it by several of its members, began to see that sovereignty resided not in the King alone, but in the King-in-Parliament. The dissolution of Parliament, however, caused the bill which had been prepared remedying the grievance to be dropped. The matter came up again during the sitting of the Addled Parliament in 1614, when it was clearly seen that parliamentary control of the Crown was being evaded by reason of the ability to raise revenue independently, without having to count on the vote of parliamentary subsidies. It was thus appreciated that impositions and the grant of monopolies, originally authorized for the proper and necessary regulation of trade and commerce, were being made to subserve other ends. But the session ended without accomplishing any action on either question. The Commons passed a unanimous vote denying the King's right of imposition. They refused to grant any subsidy until the grievances should be redressed; and James thereupon dissolved the Parliament.[32] Although the Parliament of 1621 undertook the impeachment of Mompesson, Michell, and others, and the Parliament of 1624 went far to settle the question of monopolies, the illegality of impositions was not established until the passage of the Tonnage and Poundage Act in 1641.[33]

The historical connection of these two means of raising revenue having been shown, we may now leave the question of impositions and pursue our examination of monopolies. Ellesmere, the Lord Keeper, was reputed to have been an uncompromising opponent of the grant of improper monopolies during the latter years of Elizabeth's reign and throughout the greater part of that of James. When, in 1616, overcome by illness, he failed to attach the Great Seal to two patents for the sale of woods and the licensing of inns, he was removed from office.[34] Bacon (who, in 1617, had been appointed Lord Keeper in succession to Ellesmere) in subservience

[31]Maitland, *Constitutional History of England*, 259.

[32]Prothero, *Constitutional Documents*, 340-53; Maitland, *Constitutional History of England*, 259.

[33]16 Car. I, c. 8.

[34]S.P. Dom. Jac. I, Feb. 23, 1614.

to Buckingham, the King's favourite, continued his complacency towards the grant of monopolies by royal prerogative which he had indicated in his speech as a member of the House of Commons in the previous reign.[35] He was well aware of the abuses of monopolies which had caused so much complaint during this and the previous reigns, and he had promised to stay such grants when they came to the Great Seal;[36] but Buckingham regarded them, mistakenly as we shall see, as a means of enriching his own family and providing for his dependents.[37] His part in this policy was unsavoury at its best, although it hardly deserves the strictures of some writers. In this, Bacon must bear his full share of the blame, for many of such grants passed under the Great Seal while it was in his possession. The most famous, from the proceedings to which it afterwards gave rise, was the patent issued on the solicitation of Sir Giles Mompesson and Sir Francis Michell[38] for the manufacture of gold and silver lace—with authority to search houses and arrest interlopers and other powers "as great as have ever been given to farmers of the revenue in the worst governed countries."[39] This, not only leading to gross frauds by the patentees, but their agents abusing the enormous powers conferred upon them, the public clamour was so great that a reference was made by the King to the Lord Keeper respecting the legality of such proceedings. Bacon gave a considered opinion (in which he had the Attorney-General and Solicitor concur) in favour of the gold and silver lace patent, as "a means of setting

[35]See ante 75.

[36]At the time of first taking his seat in court he had pledged himself to discharge this important part of his functions with the greatest caution and impartiality. Cf. Macaulay, "Lord Bacon" (1837) July, Edinburgh Review.

[37]If Bacon's character has been an enigma to subsequent historians, Buckingham's has likewise presented a fruitful field of enquiry. Amid all the opprobium poured on Buckingham in relation to his dealings with monopolies, the careful reader of history cannot overlook the significance of statements which show the paradox of his peculiar nature. Thus, Gardiner observes: "Yet it is certain that Buckingham, profuse as he was in his own habits, claimed, and justly claimed, the distinction of being the champion of economy in the State." S. R. Gardiner, "On Four Letters from Lord Bacon to Christian IV, King of Denmark" (1867) 41 Archaeologia, 219 at 220.

[38]The originals of Massinger's "Sir Giles Overreach" and "Justice Greedy." Cf. Macaulay, "Lord Bacon" (1837) July, Edinburgh Review.

[39]Cf. *ibid.*

many of his Majesty's poor subjects on work," and he continued to commit to prison all who infringed it.[40]

In 1620, Bacon, realizing how unpopular some of the monopolies were, and appreciating the necessity for the leaders of the government to occupy a position of reasonable harmony with the people, recommended that the patents should be examined by the Privy Council and that those against which exception could properly be taken should be recalled. But Buckingham refused to be convinced of the necessity of taking the step, and the patents were left to be considered by the House when it met.[41] The patents for inns and alehouses and for gold and silver thread were the chief ones concerning which the Committee on Grievances protested.[42] On March 26, 1620, in a speech to the Lords, the King undertook to revoke the patents.[43]

During the summer of 1621, complaints of the weight of monopolies were becoming widespread. A letter preserved among the state papers had this to say on the subject:

> Indeed the world is now much terrified with the Star Chamber, there being not so little an offence against any proclamation but is liable and subject to the censure of that Court; and for proclamations and patents, they are becoming so ordinary that there is no end, every day bringing forth some new project or other. In truth, the world doth even groan under the burden of these perpetual patents, which are become so frequent that whereas, at the King's coming in, there were complaints of some eight or nine monopolies then in being, they are now said to be multiplied by so many scores.[44]

To suppose that James was stubbornly persisting in the grant of improper monopolies over the objections of the members of the Commons and of his legal advisers is not an accurate view of the situation. In the autumn preceding the calling of the Parliament of 1620-1 James had issued a commission to survey the entire question of monopolies, and it was as a result of that commission that so much pressure on the subject developed at the opening of Parliament.[45]

[40]Campbell, *Lives of the Lord Chancellors*, II, 383. It should be emphasized that Bacon's opinion was fully consonant with that of all the other Crown lawyers of his day and of preceding times.

[41]Gardiner, *History of England*, IV, chap. XXXIII, 20.

[42]Cf. 1 Parl. Hist. 1192, 1198, 1204-5, 1218, 1224, 1228.

[43]1 Parl. Hist. 1226.

[44]S.P. Dom. cxvi, 13, Chamberlain to Carleton, July 8.

[45]See S.P. Dom. Jac. I, cxvii, 59, Nov. 4, 1620. Letter Chamberlain to Carleton, "the King called a Parliament for January and has issued a commission

As soon as Parliament met on January 30, 1620-1, the House proceeded in a temperate and respectful, but most determined, manner to discuss the public grievances. The first two days were occupied with routine business and on the third day of the sitting, February 5, a Committee on Grievances was moved for by Sir Edward Coke, the House at the same time directing that a petition be prepared for submission to the King on the subject of monopolies.[46] On the following day, a bill was introduced against promoters who were characterized as being "like the frogs of Egypt." The first attacks were directed against patents which had been so much abused by Buckingham and his creatures. The vigour with which these proceedings were conducted spread dismay through the Court.[47] Buckingham was advised not to attempt to defend the monopolies and Mompesson and Michell were abandoned as victims to the popular vengeance. Noy, seconded by Coke, who no longer held judicial office but was a member of the House, and still a fierce and patriotic adherent to the theory of the supremacy of the law over the royal prerogative, struck a decisive blow by moving for a committee to enquire into the grievance of monopolies, which the ministers found they could not attempt to resist.[48] It was resolved that a select committee be set up to examine all patents complained of, these to be referred to the Committee on Grievances upon which Committee no parties interested in the patents were to be allowed to sit.[49] The following week,[50] it was moved that all patents of privilege be brought in and examined, the member in so moving stating that "patents of privilege oft granted in respect of the time: but if granted upon false suggestion, void; or, if the execution not according to the grant: 3ly, if it be prejudicial to the Commonwealth, or if the

for survey of monopolies." See also letter from Sir Thomas Edmondes to Carleton, June 12, 1621, S. P. D. cxxi, 96: "His Majesty has declared his intention to revoke monopolies and redress grievances, which were grown to such a height that the kingdom would have been undone but for the calling of a Parliament."

[46]1 Jo. H.C. 509.

[47]Macaulay, "Lord Bacon" (1837) July, Edinburgh Review.

[48]Coke was himself the chairman of the committee of the House of Commons to which the bill was referred which afterwards became the Statute of Monopolies; cf. Gordon, *Monopolies by Patents*, 27.

[49]1 Jo. H.C. 511.

[50]Feb. 14.

Commonwealth shall receive more good, if the patent of privilege were not—To have therefore all these examined; because his majesty oft, by misinformation, misguided."[51] Two days later a motion was made to have all monopolies "sacrificed." The great trading companies, the East India, Spanish, and Turkey companies came in for their share of criticism, their monopolistic practices being condemned along with the monopolies of wines and tobacco, and the patent for gold and silver lace, one member indicating the spirit of the House by terminating his speech with the words "we in hand, first to sweep the House of monopolies, and patents, with proclamations, etc."[52] All patentees, whose patents were found to be grievances, were prohibited from sitting in the House, as well as all projectors, referees, prosecutors, and maintainers of such patents.[53]

A reading of the *Journals* of the House of Commons throughout the whole of the session demonstrates the temper and disposition of the House towards patents of monopoly. Almost daily, various patents were called in for examination and referred to the Committee on Grievances. Among those successively brought before the House—the list is by no means exhaustive, but indicates the almost universal application of patents to every feature of life—were the patents for the keeping of lighthouses, for inns and alehouses, for concealed tithes, for dispensing with pedlars and rogues, for engrossing of wills, dispensing with apprentices, forfeitures of all customs duties, armour, iron ordnance, hospitals, compounding for tolls, the sole signing of writs and covenants, writs of entry, etc., the taking of lobsters and salmon, gold foliate, the survey of sea coals, making of bills and letters, and glass.[54] Altogether some eighty petitions of grievance were presented to the Committee.[55] A report was speedily presented by the Committee showing the oppression that the monopolies were producing and it was resolved to demand a conference on the subject with

[51] 1 Jo. H.C. 521.

[52] 1 Jo. H.C. 528.

[53] 1 Jo. H.C. 603; Sir Giles Mompesson was expelled on March 3, 1620-1: cf. 1 Jo. H.C. 536; and Sir Robert Floyde on March 21: cf. 1 Jo. H.C. 567; Vin. Abr., XVII, 210.

[54] 1 Jo. H.C. 529 to 622.

[55] 1 Jo. H.C. 550. As Chamberlain wrote to Carleton, "They work hard at cleaning out the Augean stable of monopolies." S.P. Jac. I, March 24, 1621; cxx, 38.

the Lords. Several such conferences, in fact, took place, the final one being held on March 12, 1621 and in the course of the proceedings the Commons offered to prove "that the patents of gold and silver thread, of inns and alehouses, and power to compound for obsolete laws, of the price of horse meat, starch, cards, tobacco, pipes, salt, train oil and the rest were all illegal; howbeit they touched not the tender point of prerogative but, in restoring the subject's liberty, were careful to preserve the king's honour."[56]

James condemned all these monopolies in the warmest terms, saying that it made his hair stand upright to think how his people had been robbed thereby,[57] that his purpose was to "strike them all dead; and that time may not be lost I will have it done presently."[58] In the course of his address to Parliament on March 27, the King suggested that the members of the House should draw up the proclamation against the three most objectionable patents,[59] stating that he "would give Life to it, without alteration."[60]

When the House re-assembled after adjournment on April 17 the matter of patents was immediately brought forward by Coke.[61] Monopolies objected to were those of "Pins, Shreds and Lists, scouring Armor, Carmen, garbling Tobacco, Printing of Linen, General Remembrancer; Grants in the Custom-house," lighthouses, and shipbuilding.[62]

Although the patent for alehouses had been revoked by royal proclamation, the Commons were not satisfied and insisted that it should be revoked by parliamentary course saying that it was better to have "stood, than that it should be only taken away by Proclamation."[63]

On May 16 a committee was set up to reduce into writing details of the patents that had already been condemned and those that the House proposed to condemn, and on the following day[64] Coke moved that, in the petition for grievances, which was being

[56]Rush. I 24.

[57]Craik, *British Commerce*, II, 27; Gibbins, *Industry in England*, 244; see also Rush. I 26.

[58]Rush. I 26.

[59]Presumably those for gold and silver thread, for inns and for alehouses.

[60]1 Jo. H.C. 577.

[61]1 Jo. H.C. 578.

[62]1 Jo. H.C. 580, 582.

[63]1 Jo. H.C. 586.

[64]1 Jo. H.C. 623.

prepared for presentation to the King, there be included the request that all other patents of like nature as those condemned by Parliament should be recalled by the King. Coke assured the House that he would be able to satisfy the members that all the patents condemned by them were against the law and upon his motion it was forbidden to put into execution during the parliamentary recess any of the patents which had been condemned.[65] By the time Parliament adjourned on June 4 some thirty-five or thirty-six monopolies had been "removed."[66]

Early in the session[67] an act respecting monopolies was introduced into the House. Its terms, as nearly as can be gathered from the discussion in the House, were to declare the sole working, importation, or exportation of any commodity to be a monopoly and subject to heavy penalties. The power to dispense with laws was no longer to be a matter which could be the subject of grant and whether a thing did or did not constitute a monopoly was to be defined by the "Judges of the Law." Two of the members brought up the question of new inventions and it is reasonably certain from their warnings that no saving provision had been inserted in the bill regarding them. After some discussion the bill was referred to a committee and was reported back to the House on March 26.[68]

The bill was passed by the House on May 12[69] and sent up to the Lords. Evidently some consideration had been given to the question of new manufactures, for at this stage it contained a proviso saving the validity of grants in respect of them for a period of fourteen years which, on motion, was reduced to ten. The bill was apparently pending through the adjournment for, on December 15, 1621, Serjeant Ashley reported to the House that he had warrant from the Lords to say that the Lords generally approved the Bill of Monopolies.[70] This was obviously an overstatement because a few moments later one of the members, complaining about the many good bills they had passed only to have them thrown out by the Lords, said, "The Bill of Monopolies

[65] 1 Jo. H.C. 636.
[66] 1 Jo. H.C. 642.
[67] 1 Jo. H.C. 551, March 12, 1620-1.
[68] 1 Jo. H.C. 575.
[69] 1 Jo. H.C. 619.
[70] 1 Jo. H.C. 664.

cast out.—Many patents decried here, yet some stand still on Foot."[71] Nothing more appears in the *Journals* of the House of Commons and the session adjourned on December 18. But James, upon hearing that the Commons had placed upon its records the memorable Protestation of December 18, 1621, insisting upon their ancient liberties, sent for the *Journals* of the Commons, tore out the obnoxious protestation with his own hand and on February 8, 1621-2, dissolved Parliament.[72] The bill against monopolies thereupon became a dead issue.

The grant of monopolies, including licences for exclusively carrying on certain trades, was the most injurious to the subject of the methods which were used in an endeavour to compensate the King for the withholding of subsidies by Parliament. The patent to Mompesson of gold and silver lace had been misused to the extent of making the material from base metal.[73] But the patent for licensing alehouses and inns gave the most offence, for in its enforcement Mompesson used extreme violence and oppression aided by Michell, a justice of the peace.[74] Proceedings against Mompesson were instituted and vigorously pressed. Coke gave it as his opinion that both he and Michell could be punished by the House, whereupon he was brought to the Bar on February 27, 1620-1, and was ordered to "hold himself in readiness to appear at the House's pleasure."[75] The Commons thus revived the ancient right of parliamentary impeachment—the accusation of an individual by the Commons at the Bar of the House of Lords—a proceeding which had not been used since the case of the Duke of Suffolk in 1449.[76] Mompesson was committed to the custody

[71]For a short discussion of proceedings in the Lords, see the Buccleuch Papers, 222, 240; see also letter Locke to Carleton, Dec. 8, 1621, speaking of "ill feeling between the two Houses because Lords refuse to pass bills against monopolies and concealments, though needful by Commons." S.P. Dom. Jac. I, cxxiv, 20.

[72]1 Jo. H.C. 668; Rush. I 54.

[73]In his speech to the Lords revoking this patent in March of 1621 James stated that it "was most vilely executed, both for wrong done to men's persons, as also for abuse in the stuff; for it was a kind of false coin." Rush. I 26.

[74]The contempt which was felt for justices of the peace who were "commanded to assist the patentees" and the "great dishonour to those gentlemen which are in commission to be so meanly employed" may be gathered by reading the speech of John Pym in the Short Parliament. See 129, n. 29; 143; 144, n. 28

[75]1 Jo. H.C. 530.

[76]For the debates in the Commons on the proceedings against Mompesson refer to 1 Parl. Hist. 1198; for proceedings against Michell refer to 1 Parl. Hist. 1242.

of the Serjeant-at-Arms, although he was a member of the House, and was later, on unanimous vote, expelled from membership.[77]

The history of the patent for gold and silver thread was fully aired in the House on March 5 in a report given by one of the members[78] which recited the grant of the patent by the King in 1618[79] at the solicitation of Sir Edward Villiers and the abuses which it had since occasioned, two of them being the mixing of gold and silver thread with lead and, contrary to the basis of grant, making it from domestic instead of imported bullion. During the discussion on the history of the patent, feeling ran high and indignation can be perceived in all the speeches which were made on the subject. One member moved that a short bill be

[77]1 Jo. H.C. 536, March 3.

[78]1 Jo. H.C. 538.

[79]The first patent, however, with respect to the manufacture of gold and silver thread, had been granted in 1611 (Grant to Dike and others, June 5, 1611. Pat. Roll. 9, Jac. I, part 7.) It is important to observe that this patent was not granted to Mompesson or Michell and that it was not, in any way, engineered by the Buckingham group. Furthermore, it was not sealed by Bacon but by Ellesmere, who was Lord Keeper at the time. After various attempts had been made to infringe the patent (Proceedings and Debates in 1621, I, 120), the matter was heard by the Privy Council and a new patent was drawn up which passed the Great Seal on January 10, 1616. (Indenture between the King and Dike et al., January 10, 1616. Pat. Roll., 13 Jac. I, part 16.) Dike, and his co-patentee Fowle, surrendered their patent on April 6, 1618, and five days later fresh patents were granted, according to Fowle the sole right of making and selling gold and silver thread for a period of three years. (See Commons' charge against Mompesson, House of Lords MSS. and cf. Pat. Roll., 16 Jac. I, part 12—a commission for the discovery and punishment of infringers. The patent of 1618 was never enrolled.) A further patent was issued to Dike, Bennett, and Salter on April 5, 1620 (Pat. Roll., 18 Jac. I, part 19).

The basic reason for the grant of the original patent of 1611 will be gathered from a reading of its preamble, which was in the following terms:

"Whereas our loving subjects Richard Dike, Mathias Fowle, Humphrey Phipps, and John Dade of London, merchants, have undertaken and do undertake to establish and perfecte within this our realme of England, and for the service of the same, the arte, misterie, trade, or feate of making, beating, cutting, thredding, and spynning of gould and silver threed, and have begunne to use, exercise, practize, sett upp and putt in use the said arte, misterie, trade, or feate of making, beating, cutting, thredding, and spynning of gould and silver threed, within this our realme of England, in such manner and forme as gould and silver threed, commonly called Venice gold and silver threed, is or hath bene made, beaten, cutt, threeded, and spunne in Millaine, Naples, Florence, Bolonia, Italie, and France, or in all or any of them, which said arte, misterie, trade, or feate had not before bene used, exercised, practised, sett upp, or put in use within our said realme of England, and whereas the said Richard Dike, Mathias Fowle, Humfrey Phipps, and John Dade have already att their charge sett upp or praied

drawn providing for a declaration against all projectors and all referees[80] who should thereafter mislead the King, "that they may be branded to Posterity." Sir Edward Gyles was more forthright. "These Blood-suckers of the Kingdom," he called them, "and Vipers of the Commonwealth, which have misled the King." The Attorney-General was chided for his apparent fear of Mompesson and Villiers and the temper of the House may be gathered from the remark of Sir Edward Gyles: "Strange, Mr. Attorney must be afraid of Sir Edward Villiers and Sir Giles Mompesson.—Let no man's Greatness daunt us. The more we do to great Men, the more we prevent in future these Mischiefs." Speaking of Mompesson, Sir Henry Strange said, "The Plague of his Corruption did exceedingly poison the Country. That he masked all under his Service to the King.—These, like Worms, which ever eat out the Body of the State." The referees who had certified the patents came in for their share of trouble, Sir Francis Fane moving that the referees of all the patents be questioned "that so they bear their Load.—This to clear the King.—That the King hath restrained all unlawful suits for Monopolies: If that had been

---

to be sett up within this our said realme of England, and other our said dominions, divers frames, loomes, ingines, and other devises and meanes, and more will, for the better using, exercising, practising, setting upp, putting in use, and perfecting of the said arte, misterie, trade, or feate within our said realme of England, and other our said dominions, and doe likewise intende to teach and instructe, or to procure to be taught and instructed in the same arte or misterie, many of our people and subjects of this our said realme of England, and of other our dominions and countries, by meanes whereof the said gold and silver threed, which heretofore hath been brought into this our realme of England and other our domynions from forraine parts, may not only hereafter be made within our aid realme and other our domynions by our owne people and subjects, but many, of our said people and subjects may thereby be releeved, mainteyned, and sett on work. And forasmuch as the use, exercise, practize, and employment of our people in the said arte, misterie, trade, or feate is very likely in tyme to prove very benificiall and comodious to us and to our said subjects and comon weale, as well by the learning, teachinge, and instructing of our said subjects in the said arte, misterie, trade, or feate, as alsoe in setting in work, releeving, and maynteyninge themselves by a trade not heretofore used."

The patent granted to the persons named a monopoly of the manufacture for twenty years, and directed the Court of Exchequer to afford proper protection to the patentees. It will be observed that the reason for its grant, namely the setting up of a new industry within the realm, was fully in keeping with the laws relating to monopoly grants existing at the time, and, subject only to the evidence of a small prior user by a different method, accords with the principles of modern British patent law. (Cf. chap. XIV, note 9.)

[80]Those appointed by Parliament to examine and report on applications for monopolies or letters patent.

done, these Things had been prevented.—To take Notice of the King's Proclamation, Of the King's Book of Bounty."[81] It was moved that all the patents should be called in and suppressed, that none were to be thereafter granted and if they were, they should be void. Upon the question being put to the House, it was resolved that the referees as well as the projectors of the patents should be questioned by the Committee.[82]

On the following day[83] it was reported to the House that the Committee on Grievances had found that the patent for gold and silver thread, although not so general as that for inns, was more grievous in execution. The Committee pointed out that the King had been wronged in his judgment in issuing the patent by misinformation. He had been informed that it would cause a great increase of trade whereas this was an established trade of two hundred years' standing. He had also been informed that £5,000 would be imported whereas none had been brought in. White lead and arsenic had been used in the making of the thread which had caused serious injury and those who had charge of the patent used it as a means of oppression and extortion. Judgment against Mompesson was pronounced by the Lords on March 26. All charges were found to be true. He was degraded of knighthood, heavily fined, and his goods forfeited. The King in his address to Parliament the following day added to the punishment by banishing Mompesson "out of all his Dominions."[84] Michell was also found guilty, degraded from knighthood, fined, and imprisoned.[85] The patents for inns and alehouses and for the manufacture of gold and silver thread were thereupon revoked by the King.[86]

Bacon's case was then proceeded with. He was relieved of the Great Seal and deprived of all his offices, titles, and honours.[87] The part he played in issuing the monopoly patents, however, had very little, if anything, to do with his disgrace, for his main

[81]1 Jo. H.C. 539; this reference to the King's *Book of Bounty* is interesting as showing that none of the contemporary opprobrium for the grant of monopolies was cast upon the King.

[82]1 Jo. H.C. 539.

[83]1 Jo. H.C. 540, March 6.

[84]1 Jo. H.C. 576-7; Rush. I 27.

[85]Cf. S.P. Dom. Jac. I, cxxi, 21, June 23, 1621.

[86]Rush. I 28.

[87]Campbell, *Materials for the Reign of Henry VIII*, 395 et seq.; Hallam, *Constitutional History of England*, 333; 1 Parl. Hist. 1248; Church, *Bacon*, 124 ff.

guilt arose from the acceptance of bribes in his judicial capacity. The fact that emerges clearly from the proceedings is that, so long as the charge concerned Bacon's dealing with monopolies and patents which were alleged to be illegal, he defended himself with vigour. But once the attack was switched to the allegation of bribery, he ceased all defence and delivered himself up to his accusers.[88] We shall have more to say on Bacon's viewpoint and motives in this connection at a later stage, but the reminder may not be amiss that, during the debate on monopolies in the House in 1601, Bacon expressed his view on the legality of patents for new inventions which not only accorded with the view held generally by the common law lawyers of the day, but closely approximates their legal position today. Then too, when the King consulted the Council as to the disposition to be made of the patents in which Buckingham and Villiers were interested, Bacon, although he defended them both in law and policy, voted with the minority for their removal by act of Council.

On March 30, James had issued a proclamation cancelling the patents for gold and silver thread and for inns. Other patents such as those for the sole engrossing of wills, for the levying of lighthouse tolls, for the importation of salmon and lobsters, for the making of gold leaf, and for the manufacture of glass were voted to be grievances, but the adjournment of the House in June and its dissolution in December occurred before effective action could be taken. In the meantime, however, on July 10, 1621, James issued a proclamation[89] in which, as did Elizabeth in her proclamation of 1601, he recited that many privileges, licences, and letters patent had been obtained upon suggestions that they would tend to the common good and profit of his subjects, but that upon examination it appeared that many of the grants were not only obtained upon false and untrue surmises, but had also been notoriously abused. A reference to the *Book of Bounty* appeared in the proclamation when James spoke of his "having

[88]Rush. I 29.

[89]This proclamation was obviously prepared after the question had been thoroughly aired in the Council. Under date of June 23, 1621, the State Papers contain a list, "preferred for consideration in Council, of patents pronounced grievances; or questioned in Parliament, some of which the King absolutely condemns, and others he refers to the examination of Council, also list of ninety patents which are similar in character and therefore likely to be questioned." S.P. Dom. Jac. I, cxxi, 125.

heretofore published in print his dislike of such suits, together with his hatred and detestation of all importunities to obtain or procure the same." James thereupon proclaimed void some eighteen patents which concerned *inter alia* the making of gold and silver foliate, the sole making of tobacco pipes, the hot-press, the manufacture of playing cards, and the brogging of wool. Various commissions were revoked, among them those for the granting of leets, parks, free warrens, fairs, markets, tolls, tallages, etc. As to some seventeen patents of the type with which we are more particularly concerned, relating to manufacture and importation and enumerated according to subject matter in the proclamation, it was provided that if any subject should find himself grieved, injured, or wronged by reason of any of the said grants, he might take his remedy therefor by the common laws of the realm or other ordinary courts of justice, any manner or thing in the said grants to the contrary notwithstanding.[90] Apart from the specific nature of the subject matter of the patents concerned, the language of the proclamation is in striking similarity to Elizabeth's proclamation of 1601. This was followed by a proclamation of February 14, 1622-3, setting up a committee to sit once a week at least at Whitehall to receive the petitions and complaints of the King's subjects concerning their just grievances and to certify the same to him or to the Privy Council.[91]

[90]Proclamation of James I, July 10, 1621; Rot. Pat. p. 13. m. 17. d. See Steele Proc. no. 1314. For text see Appendix VIII, 336. Cf. S.P. Dom. Jac. I, cxxiii, 122, November 24, 1621; cxxiii, 134, November 28, 1621.

[91]Rot. Pat. p. 16. m. 14. d. Steele Proc. no. 1350. See Appendix IX, 337.

IX. THE STATUTE OF MONOPOLIES

THE proceedings in 1620 against Sir Giles Mompesson for abuse of patents of monopoly[1] brought matters to a head. A petition was presented to the King during the session of 1623-4[2] by the Commons, complaining of grievances occasioned by monopolies. Among those specifically mentioned were the grants relating to gold wire thread, sea coals, apothecaries, and the building and repairing of houses. The King, in his answer, said:

Touching my Patents in general, I am grieved that you have called them in and condemned them upon so short examination. I confess I might have passed some upon false suggestion and wrong information; but you are not to recall them before they be examined by the judges. And here I have heard it complained of by divers of my learned counsel in the law, that you will from time to time, delaying the patentees, still call for patents without just ground; and so put the subjects still to more charge, and so consequently put a scorn upon my patents.—Therefore I advise you to be careful, that you have a good ground before you call for your patents, that you do not defraud the patentees . . . . I say to you when you judge of patents, hear patiently, say not presently, it is against the law, for patents are not to be judged unlawful by you.[3]

The petition, above mentioned, was probably presented in the closing days of the session because the King's reply, which was delivered at the end of the session, is in some measure an answer to it. The King spoke concerning the monopolies named in the petition and his reference to his patents in general, when he said "I am grieved that you have called them in and condemned them upon so short examination," was apparently directed to the passing of the Statute of Monopolies, which took place on May 25, 1624. No one can quarrel with the King's view that Parliament is not the proper place to test the validity of patents but that they should be left to adjudication by the courts of law. That was, in fact, provided by Section 2 of the Statute; and it was a principle won by the Commons after considerable agitation and pressure.

[1](1620) 2 St. Tr. 1119.

[2]The date of the petition is unknown. Cf. 1 Parl. Hist. 1489. On Feb. 21, 1623-4, the Speaker of the House of Commons begged completion of the bill against monopolies. Cf. S.P. Dom. Jac. I, clix, 66.

[3]1 Parl. Hist. 1503.

Although it had first been promised by Elizabeth in 1601, the principle had by no means been strictly followed, and to find James urging the principle on the members of the House does much to defeat the charge so often levelled against him of the illegal grant of oppressive monopolies. Parliament, urged on not only by the evidence in those proceedings but by the publication of the King's own *Book of Bounty*, his proclamations of July 10, 1621[4] and February 14, 1623[5] proceeded to attack the subject of monopolies with vigour. The session opened on February 12, 1623-4. A committee for grievances was set up whose duty it was to take into consideration the patents condemned or questioned at the last session and whether and by whom any of them had since been "set on foot."[6] A perusal of the subject matter of the patents examined by the committee will illustrate the extent to which the monopoly policy was used. Among them were the patents for the survey of sea coals, the patent for the Hamper, that respecting the office of alnager with regard to sealing of new drapery, those of the Merchant Adventurers and the East India Company, those for printing, making red lead, glass, soap, iron ordnance, for the sole drying and packing of fish, for the keeping of gaols and lighthouses, and for gold wire drawing.[7] Some of these were forbidden to be put in execution, some were recommended to be left undisturbed but not to be renewed. Others were delivered up to the Bar of the House by the patentees. In

[4]See post 336. The repetition of the language of the *Book of Bounty* and the reminder of its publication are not to be overlooked as factors contributing to the zeal of the Commons in pressing the Statute of Monopolies to its final enactment. It is not too much to say that James, by his pompous philosophical disquisitions and pronouncements and his desire to impress others with his great wisdom and sense of justice, here found himself hoist with his own petard.

It is obvious that the King's *Book of Bounty* exercised considerable weight in the enactment of the Statute of Monopolies. When the abortive bill was presented in the House during the session of 1620-1, Coke, in reporting the result of the conference with the Lords on the question of the grievances of the patents for gold and silver thread, for inns and for alehouses, stated that he had brought to the attention of the Lords "the Grounds of the King's Book, concerning the King's granting Power to despense with penal Statutes" (1 Jo. H.C. 555, March 15, 1620-1). On Dec. 13, 1921, Coke characterized the bill "freeing us frome Monopolies" as being "grounded upon the King's own Book" (1 Jo. H.C. 663).

[5]Rot. Pat. p. 16. n. 14. d. Steele Proc. no. 1350. See Appendix IX, 337.

[6]1 Jo. H.C. 673.

[7]1 Jo. H.C. 685-794 *passim*.

some cases as, e.g., the patent of the alnager's office, they were to form the subject of a petition to the King requesting him to revoke them and punish the offenders. Some few which had been brought into the House and not condemned were delivered again to the patentees, and it is noteworthy that among these was Sir Robert Mansell's glass patent[8] which was also among those grants which were excepted from the rigours of the Statute of Monopolies by Section 13.

In pursuance of the vigorous anti-monopoly policy which characterized both this and the preceding sessions, the House proceeded with the enactment of the Statute of Monopolies.[9] The bill was introduced on February 26, 1623-4, and was sent to committee on May 1. On May 22, 1624, the Lords assented to the report of the Joint Committee of the two Houses and on May 25 the Commons adopted the report, the bill thus passing both Houses and receiving the royal assent as Chapter 3.[10]

Some writers have assumed that James is not entitled to any great credit either for the passing of the Statute of Monopolies, which will be later considered, or for his publication of the *Book of Bounty*. History has borne none too tender a testimony of his wastefulness and extravagance and even of what some unsympathetic writers have termed his Scottish habit of giving away that which was not his to give in his treatment of the monopoly privileges. He was little deterred by legal considerations, and only restrained in extreme cases by necessity and the strong use of common sense forced upon him at times by unpalatable advice. His attitude to legal considerations may be gathered by his retort to Coke over a matter of the King's right to issue writs forbidding certain proceedings in law suits if it were considered that the matter in question belonged to another court. While Coke supported the King in his view, he made the unhappy mistake of informing James that he was "defended by his Laws," to which the King replied in great fury "Laws! My Lord Chief Justice, ye speak like a fool. I am not defended by my laws, but by God. And see

[8]1 Jo. H.C. 798.

[9](1624) 21 Jac. I, c. 3.

[10]S.P. Dom. Jac. I, clxv, 39. The bill did not, however, have clear sailing in its passage through the Lords. Two days after its enactment, Locke wrote to Carleton that, "The Bill against monopolies is more minced than the Lower House expected." S.P. Dom. Jac. I, clxv, 33, May 24, 1624.

that ye forget it not in the future!" The royal assent was an act not entirely agreeable to the King, but his publication of the *Book of Bounty* was, as Coke intimated, a motive force actuating the King to grant his assent. The action of Parliament may have been somewhat repugnant to James, for the effects of the act embraced a territory in which the King was vitally interested. But this view of history is to lay blame at the wrong door. Not only did James issue a proclamation against monopolies in 1603, but he revoked a considerable number of them in his proclamation of July 10, 1621. He not only published the declaration against them in the *Book of Bounty* in 1610, but he caused this to be reprinted nine years later. Nor must it be overlooked that in the earlier part of the session of Parliament in 1621, he took the leading part in the movement against the patents. The true view probably is that James resented the action of Parliament, considering it to be a high-handed interference with his royal prerogative. He was unfavourably disposed to many of the monopolies, but he desired that their revocation should be an act of grace on his part rather than a display of parliamentary independence.

Many writers treat the subject as ending with the Statute of Monopolies,[11] but, unfortunately, the abuses continued in even greater measure, culminating in the revocation proceedings in the Long Parliament.

The Statute of Monopolies, the only legislative measure of importance gained by the Commons during a struggle of more than twenty years to restore and to fortify their own and their

[11]"Monopolies were made void and all questions of what constituted a monopoly were to be judged in the courts of common law. No longer would men like Sir William Garway and Sir Nicholas Salter be permitted to collect the customs on silks, velvets, lawns and cambrics at a rent of £16,000 a year, a sum which might or might not find its way into the Exchequer. No more would Edward Peshall and Edward White of London be allowed to collect two shillings on every pound of tobacco imported into England, for which privilege they were to pay the King £7,000 a year and were empowered to name the persons allowed to sell this commodity. Mediaeval commercial make-shifts were to be ended and England's imports and exports, manufacturing and production of raw materials were at last to be taken out of absolute control of private individuals, never too scrupulously honest, who for some reason or another had won favour at Court. The King would no longer be able to reward his friends with monopolies, or to deprive his enemies of these sources of income." Steeholm, *James I of England*.

fellow subjects' liberties,[12] began with a long preamble of an argumentative and explanatory type, reciting the publication in 1610 of the *Book of Bounty*, the declaration contained in which was stated to be "truly consonant and agreeable to the ancient and fundamental laws of this your realm." The preamble then recited the command contained in the *Book of Bounty* that no suitor should presume to move the Crown for matters of the nature which were there set out.

This first section of the Act which, it will be seen, incorporated the main principles of the *Book of Bounty* into the English statute law, thereupon declared as contrary to the laws of the realm and utterly void and of none effect and in no wise to be put into execution, all monopolies, grants, licences, and letters patent theretofore made or granted, or thereafter to be made or granted, to any person or persons, bodies politic or corporate, of or for the sole buying, selling, making, working, or using of any thing within the realm.[13]

Section 2 provided that monopolies, letters patent, licences, etc., and the force and validity of them should be tried and determined according to the common law and not otherwise.

By Section 3 all persons and bodies politic and corporate were declared to be disabled and incapable of using and exercising any monopolies, grants, letters patent, etc.

By Section 4 a party aggrieved by any monopoly or grant was to have the right to recover treble damages by action in the courts of common law with double costs; and if any person caused any such action or judgment therein to be stayed or delayed, he should suffer the penalties and forfeitures of the Statute of Provision and Praemunire of 16 Ric. II, c. 5.[14] This section has been invoked in only one case although it was republished in the statute law revision of 1888.[15]

Sections 5 and 6 are, however, the important sections for our purpose, because they carried into effect Item 9 of those matters in which in his *Book of Bounty* the King held himself to be content to be moved, and in furtherance of that statement, excepted from

[12]Hallam, *Constitutional History of England*, 346.

[13]For the terms of the Act see Appendix X, 338.

[14]Cf. Vin. Abr. XVII, 215; Co. 3 Inst. 183, c. 85; Hawk. P.C. 232, c. 79, s. 13.

[15]51 Vict., c. 3; see Gordon, *Monopolies by Patents*, 12. Peck v. Hindes (1898) 15 R.P.C. 113. Cf. Fox, "Abuse of Monopoly" (1945) 23 Can. Bar Rev., 353.

the nullifying effect of the enacting section of the statute, not only former grants for the period stated in Section 5 but also, as stated in Section 6, "letters patents and grants of privilege for the term of fourteen years or under hereafter to be made of the sole working or making of any manner of new manufactures within this realm, to the true and first inventor and inventors of such manufactures, which others at the time of making such letters patents and grants shall not use, so as also they be not contrary to the law, nor mischievous to the State, by raising prices of commodities at home, or hurt of trade, or generally inconvenient."

It is important to note that not only were monopolies declared to be void by the common law, but by Section 2 of the Act, it was provided that they should be examined, heard, tried, and determined in the courts of common law according to the common law. Prior to this act the Court of Star Chamber had considered all infringements of patents and grants of the Crown as contempts of royal authority, and on that principle supported any patent the Crown thought fit to grant.[16] As Coke noted in his Institutes "such boldness the monopolist took that often at the Council table, Star Chamber, Chancery and Exchequer Chamber, Petitions, informations, and bills, were preferred, pretending a contempt for not obeying the commandments and clauses of the said grant of monopolies and of the proclamations concerning the same."[17] After the passing of the Statute of Monopolies, such matters were to be determined not at the Council table, or by the Star Chamber, or any other forum of like nature, but only according to the common laws of the realm and not otherwise. This provision, and the limitation of the term to fourteen years, were the only changes made by the statute in the common law. The Council, however, notwithstanding this provision, continued to exercise the chief control over matters relating to patents; and it was not until the end of the eighteenth century that patent cases began to come

[16]See the debate in the House of Commons on monopolies, Nov. 20, 1601; D'Ewes 644, 652; 1 Parl. Hist. 924.

[17]Co. 3 Inst. 182-3; Vin. Abr., XVII, 215, after reciting the custom of bringing actions on patents before the courts of conciliar jurisdiction, proceeds to cite this section of the statute and adds: "For the preventing of which mischief this branch was added."

frequently before the common law courts.[18] It is interesting to note that a count of the cases contained in Webster's *Patent Cases* and in Abbott's *English and American Patent Cases* shows that, after the passage of the Statute of Monopolies, only one case is reported in the courts of common law during the seventeenth century and one in the first half of the eighteenth century, but that, commencing with *Dollond's Case*,[19] tried in the Common Pleas in 1766, there were twenty-one heard during the second half of that century. Thereafter, patent cases are met with in the reports with increasing frequency.

There will, no doubt, be cause for some surprise that, prior to the *Case of Monopolies*,[20] there were only four reported instances in which monopoly grants were considered by the courts of common law.[21] The reason for this singular lack of judicial consideration of monopolies is not difficult to find. It is explainable on the same basis as the absence, before the time of Lord Mansfield, of cases on commercial law, or the law merchant, in the common law courts.[22] The reason why there were so few cases dealing with

[18]Hulme (1909) 3 A.A.L.H., 146-7; Holdsworth, *History of English Law*, IV, 354; *ibid.*, VI, 331; cf. Edgebury v. Stephens (1691) Holt 475; 1 W.P.C. 35; Dwight's Patent (1684) L.Q.R. xxxiii, 74; Roebuck & Garbett's Case (1774) 1 W.P.C. 45; Morris v. Bransom (1776) Bull N.P. 76; 1 W.P.C. 51.

[19](1766) 1 W.P.C. 43.

[20]Darcy v. Allin (1602) 11 Co. Rep. 84.

[21]Case of John the Dyer (1414) Y.B. 2 H. V, 5 B; 11 Co. Rep. 53; Davenant v. Hurdis (1599) 11 Co. Rep. 86; Moore K.B. 576; Hasting's Case, Noy 183; Humphrey's Case, Noy 183; cf. 1 W.P.C. 6. Matthey's Case, also referred to in Noy 183, was heard by the Privy Council. It is to be borne in mind, however, that more cases were heard and determined than appear in the law reports as is evidenced by the speech of Bacon in the Commons on the debate on monopolies in 1601 (Prothero, *Constitutional Documents*, 112) when after discussing *non obstantes* and monopolies, both of new inventions and of the exclusive dealing in commodities, he said: "These and divers of this nature have been on trial, both in the Common Pleas, upon actions of trespass (where, if the judges do find the privilege good for the commonwealth, they then will allow it, otherwise disallow it), and also I know that her Majesty herself hath given commandment to her attorney-general, to bring divers of them, since the last parliament, to trial in the Exchequer; since which time at least fifteen or sixteen, to my knowledge, have been repealed; some upon her Majesty's own express command, upon complaint made unto her by petition, and some by *quo warranto* in the exchequer." Unfortunately we have little further record of these cases. Cf. 121, n. 30.

[22]"I am sure I rather go beyond bounds if I assert that in all our reports from the reign of Queen Elizabeth to the year 1756, when Lord Mansfield became

commercial matters in the reports of the common law courts is that such cases were dealt with by special courts and under special law. That law was an old established law based largely on mercantile customs.[23] The special courts were the old Court Pepoudrous, or Pie-Powder Court, established to administer speedy justice at the great markets and fairs, and the similar courts established at the seaports to give summary justice in matters of marine commerce. There were also special courts established by statute for the summary administration of the law merchant and the law of the sea.[24] In the same way, matters involving letters patent and grants of monopolies and other privileges were rarely, if ever, heard in the common law courts, and for a somewhat similar reason. Grants of this type were, generally speaking, based on an exercise of the royal prerogative, and it was not thought fitting or consonant with the royal dignity that questions concerning their propriety should be discussed and considered in the ordinary courts of common law. Instead, such questions were heard and determined either by the Privy Council itself or before one or other of the conciliar courts such as the Court of Star Chamber. Actions at law concerning patents were, to all intents and purposes, forbidden. Orders of restraint, staying actions at law, were issued not only by the Court of Chancery, but also by the Privy Council, and even by individual Privy Councillors.[25] During the proceedings against the patent for gold and silver thread, an information laid in the Court of Exchequer against the infringers was set aside by the appointment of a commission for the discovery and punishment of offenders against the proclamation of May 22, 1618, setting up the manufacture as a monopoly

---

Chief Justice of the King's Bench, there are sixty cases upon matters of insurance." Parke, *Law of Insurance*, I, pref. 43; to the same effect as to bills of exchange see *Chalmers on Bills*, pref. 36; as to charter parties and bills of lading, see Zouch, *Jurisdiction of the Admiralty*, 89. Cf. Scrutton, *Elements of the Law Merchant*, 4.

[23]Cf. Bl. Com., I, 273; IV, 67; Smith, *Mercantile Law*, 82; Scrutton, *Elements of the Law Merchant*, 5.

[24]Cf. the statute 43 Eliz., c. 12 establishing a court of eight "grave and discreet merchants" for the summary dispatch of insurance cases, without formalities.

[25]*Remembrancia of City of London*, 521; cf. Co. 3 Inst. 182.

of the King's.[26] The promise of Elizabeth to the Commons in 1597 to submit questions concerning patents to the judgment of the courts of law, and her proclamation to the same effect in 1601, show that she was sanctioning a departure from previous practice. In support of this view may be noted the striking fact that, in his argument to the court in the *Case of Monopolies*,[27] Fuller was able to cite only three patent cases,[28] two of which were determined in the Court of Exchequer Chamber[29] and the other of which was heard by the Council.[30] The delicacy of the question of interference with matters of prerogative, in which must be included monopoly grants, is illustrated by the reprimand given by the Privy Council to a member of the Commons in 1571 who dared to touch

[26]Cf. Gardiner, *History of England*, IV, chap. XXXIII, 12-17.

[27]See post 324.

[28]Noy 183.

[29]Hastings' Case, Noy 182; Humphrey's Case, Noy 183; see also 2 Brownl. & Golds. 108.

[30]Matthey's Case, Noy 183.

There are vague references to be found in contemporary documents of cases touching on monopolies but whether they were heard in the courts of common law or in the conciliar courts it is now impossible to ascertain. The cases are not reported in the law reports with the exception of those we have noted, and there is no record of them in the meagre available records of the Court of Star Chamber. Among those vague references, the following notes of a speech made by Coke on March 15, 1620-1 (1 Jo. H.C. 555) during the debate on the abortive bill respecting monopolies may give some indication of the view of the law on the subject. The probability is that these were decisions of the common law courts because the Star Chamber usually supported any patent.

"The King Phillip arriving at Southampton, when he married Queen Mary, granted them a Monopoly, to have all the sweet Wines landed there. In Queen Eliz. time, resolved by the Judges, this a Monopoly; and overthrown.—Got by importunity, that all Strangers should land their Wines there only." See also Vin. Abr., XVII, 210.

"Wm. Simpson in Queen Eliz. got a Patent for the sole Bringing in Stone Pots, Bottles, and Heath, to make Brushes. This, 39° Eliz. questioned, the Queen promised, *in verbo Principis* to reform what amiss. Hereupon he, Attorney General, brought Quo Warranto against Simpson, who justified by his Patent.—Called in, and cancelled.—

"Then Sir. Jo. Packington got a Patent of Starch, because a Vanity: Yet this adjudged void.—

"That Rich. Mompesson, and Alexander, got a sole Importation of Anyseeds, and Shoemake: This also adjudged void." [It appears from 1 Jo. H.C. 553

upon matters of prerogative.[31] This is not the place to discuss the composition or history of these courts of conciliar jurisdiction. Enough has been written on the subject to enable even the casual reader of history to recall the grave abuses and injustices that were constantly attendant upon the exercise of their jurisdiction. It is therefore, worthy of note that of the four common law cases discussed in Chapter VII only two were actions for infringement of patent. The *Case of John the Dyer*[32] was not concerned with a royal grant of exclusive privilege but only with a bond given by one private person to another; *Davenant* v. *Hurdis*[33] concerned an effort by the Merchant Tailors of London to enforce an ordinance for its own internal government; and the *Case of Monopolies, Darcy* v. *Allin*, [34] was not a proceeding brought to set aside or attack the validity of a grant of monopoly, but an action brought by the patentee against an infringer, the patentee being, in this case, the one who chose the forum. Eleven years elapsed before another case involving a royal grant of monopoly, that of the *Cloth Workers of Ipswich*, was reported in the common law courts[35] and there was

---

that this was a common law proceeding, Coke stating that he "brought a *quo warranto* and the defendant pleaded his grant which was adjudged void."]

"Sir Tho. Wilkes got a Monopoly, to make Salt only at Lynn, and Boston, because he had made a little Addition to the former making Salt: Adjudged void, because but an Addition.—

"44° Eliz. Sir Edw. Darcy—the sole Making and Importation of Cards, which prohibited by the Statute: Yet adjudged void, and the *Non obstante* also; because against the common Good: For an old Trade."

Again, during the same debate, May 3, 1621 (1 Jo. H.C. 606) Coke gave some further precedents as follows:

"21 Edw. III a patent made for alnaging and measuring of worsted, which spoiled by Opening; which, at the Parliament, declared to be void.

"13 H. IV a new grant, for measuring canvas, overthrown by the Judges, confirmed by Parliament.

"22 H. VI a prescription of an office for packing of wools.

"—Ed. IV a grant, for survey of victuals, void.

"21 Edw. Mowle, a broker, his patent adjudged void.

"When he Recorder, Tyler got a patent for survey of vinegar: Adjudged void." See also 119, n. 21.

[31]See 74.

[32](1414) Y.B. 2 H. V, 5 B; 11 Co. Rep. 53.

[33](1599) 11 Co. Rep. 86; cf. ante 816, post 214, 311.

[34]Cf. ante 87, post 215, 318.

[35]Cloth Workers of Ipswich Case (1615) 11 Co. Rep. 53; Godb. R. 253.

a hiatus of a further seventy-six years before there appeared the first reported case dealing with a patent for invention.[36]

But the reports of the courts of common law are not entirely devoid of references to actions concerning letters patent during this period. Thus in 1631, there appears the report of an action[37] in which the Court of King's Bench declared invalid a patent granted in 1607 for the sole making of bills and informations to be preferred before the Privy Council at York. In general, however, patents of this type seldom found their way into the courts for the reason that Parliament was actively concerning itself with the question of examining all patents issued and deciding as to their validity.[38]

That the conciliar jurisdiction of adjudicating patents was neither palatable nor satisfactory to the subject is plainly to be gathered from Elizabeth's proclamation concerning monopolies of November 28, 1601, which provided that if any subject found himself grieved, injured, or wronged by reason of any of the grants referred to in the proclamation, he should be at liberty to take his ordinary remedy by the laws of the realm notwithstanding anything in any such grant to the contrary. This provision was repeated almost *verbatim* in the later proclamations of James on the subject, under date of July 10, 1621, and of Charles I under date of April 9, 1639. It is to be recalled also that this was, with the limitation of the term, the only new principle of law enacted by the Statute of Monopolies in 1624. But neither the proclamations nor the Statute of Monopolies had the effect of displacing the conciliar jurisdiction over these grants, as an examination of the reports of the seventeenth century will clearly show. Thus,

[36]Edgebury v. Stephens (1693) 1 W.P.C. 35; 2 Salk 447; and cf. Mitchel v. Reynolds (1711) 1 P. Wms. 183 per Parker, C.J. It is, however, noteworthy that, in the course of the argument in East India Co. v. Sandys (1684) 10 St. Tr. 371 at 456, Jefferies, L.C.J., spoke of "all the actions that have been brought upon that statute of monopolies, by the patentees of new inventions, as there has been multitudes in my lord Hale's time, and at all times."

[37]Mounson v. Lyster (1631) W. Jones 231; Hawk. P.C. 231, c. 79, s. 4.

[38]See, e.g., The Case of Fludd's Patent, Vin. Abr. 2d. Ed., XVII, 209, tit. Monopoly. Leepton's Case, Roll. Abr. 214 (E). In 1690 it was enacted by 2 Wm. & Mary, st. 2, c. 9 that letters patent for the sole making of brandy and spirits from malted corn, etc., as a new invention, contrary to the fact, were declared void.

we find James on February 14, 1623, issuing a proclamation setting up a committee to hear and report on grievances which might be brought to its attention by any subject.[39] In the Grand Remonstrance of 1641 we find that: "The Court of Star Chamber hath abounded in extravagant censures, not only for the maintenance of monopolies and their unlawful taxes, but for divers other causes where there hath been no offence, or very small."[40]

The Statute of Monopolies had provided that existing monopolies for new inventions, some of which were named, were not to be prejudiced if granted for no more than twenty-one years. The Privy Council interpreted this provision as a statutory authorization of such monopolies, and quashed proceedings in the common law courts designed to test their legality.[41] Again, as we have noted, the Court of Star Chamber claimed jurisdiction over all patents which were authorized by proclamation, under the theory that defiance of a royal proclamation was a contempt of royal prerogative.[42] The order-in-council of March 31, 1639, and the proclamation of April 9, 1639, revoking a large number of monopolies, was an obvious attempt to stem the tide of public antagonism and indignation not only against the abuse of monopoly but against the exercise of jurisdiction concerning their enforcement by the Council and its Court of Star Chamber. The effort, however, was unavailing, for on July 5, 1641, the Long Parliament abolished the Court of Star Chamber.[43]

The Statute of Monopolies is usually taken as marking the beginning of the patent system as it is understood in its modern sense in England, and indeed has been said to have been the originating factor of the modern patent system throughout the world. But such is not the case. The patent system, not only of England, but of the modern world, is not of statutory origin. As pointed out by Hulme: "The statute must be interpreted as recapitulating limitations already assigned by the common law,

[39]See post 337.

[40]Par. 37.

[41]S.P. Dom. Car. I, Dec. 6, 1626.

[42]See, e.g., Bridgeman v. Glover et al. (1606) Hawarde, 302, where suit was brought on the patent granted by Elizabeth in 1601 to Brigham (Bridgeman) and Wemmes for pre-emption of tin. Cf. 1 Jo. H.C. 777.

[43]17 Car. I, c. 10.

which limitations in their turn . . . are such as were commonly prescribed in these grants for the purpose of safeguarding the powers with which the grantee was thus invested."[44] An examination of the *Journals* of the House of Commons[45] for April 20 to May 25, 1614, when the glass patents were considered by the House, will show that the objections to the validity of a patent at common law were substantially the same as those which were applied by the courts after the passing of the statute. The Statute of Monopolies was nothing more than a declaration of what the common law had always been,[46] for in those days Parliament entertained doubts as to whether it had any power to change the fundamental principles of the common law.

It is important to remember that the period covered by the reigns of Elizabeth and James I was not by any means the beginning of the system of monopolies for the regulation of trade. It was merely the period of culmination and crystallization of the system. As we have noted before,[47] the development of a patent system arising out of the combination of the ideas of the regulation, supervision, and stimulation of trade, and the introduction of new crafts, by the use and influence of exclusive privileges, was possible only in a reasonably well integrated state with some degree of economic unity under a sovereign who not only could control trade and industry over a wide area but who had sufficient authority as well as desire to exercise the prerogative for what was conceived to be the general good. Together with these factors there must not be disregarded the general and gradual decline of the power of the merchant and craft guilds, their regulations and supervision slowly giving way to a more national and diversified type of industry. This decline of the guilds, coincident with the gradual rise of the national, capitalist type of industry, naturally called for and required a national type of supervision and regulation.

[44]Hulme (1900) 16 L.Q.R., 55.

[45]Jo. H.C. 469-711.

[46]In his argument in East India Company v. Sandys (1684) 10 St. Tr. 371 at 410, Finch, the Solicitor-General, pointed out that "Patents for new inventions are not made good by the statute of 21 of king James, but left as they were before: only they are restrained to a number of years, and were always good, because they were for the encouragement of trade, and of useful inventions to increase them."

[47]Ante chap. IV.

Had such a system not been readily available, different results might have ensued, and the Industrial Revolution might conceivably have been postponed or have found its cradle in another country. Fortunately, the incidents necessary for the rise and development of a national patent system were present in embryo; and this opportunity was seized by the sovereign power for the development of the public good. In this sense, therefore, there was nothing adventitious in the fact that a systematic national policy of patent control first arose in England. It was an inevitability in the logic of the industrial and historical factors at play at the crucial time. The opportunity of stimulating old industries and founding new trades and crafts by increasing and standardizing the monopoly form of protection was seized upon by a sovereign who had sufficient absolute power to accomplish her purpose, together with a sincere desire to further the establishment and stimulation of industry for the public good. Where industrial monopoly had formerly been of a local character, it now assumed a national and systematic form. Assisted by the development of the capitalist forces in the changing type of industry, this policy laid the foundation for the patent system as it has developed to our time. What distinguished the monopolies of the period from their precursors was the fact that they bore a definitely capitalistic impress. They represented national industrial organizations as contrasted with the former trade monopolies of the guilds which were of a purely local character.[48]

To assume, however, that the Statute of Monopolies put an end to the grievances it was designed to prevent, is to neglect the facts. A note in the *Parliamentary History* at the close of the reign of James I[49] states that "the king had annulled, of his own accord, all patents for monopolies by which any species of domestic industry was fettered; but all foreign trade, that of France excepted, was possessed by exclusive companies; and hence the navigation and commerce of the kingdom were every day sensibly diminishing. At last an act was passed, by which all monopolies were condemned as contrary to law, and the known liberties of the people: an act which ought for ever to have put an end to so destructive a grievance." Unfortunately, the results were quite different.

[48]Levy, *Monopoly and Competition*, 4; Price, *English Patents of Monopoly*, 6; Unwin, *Industrial Organization*, 175.

[49]1 Parl. Hist. 1509.

X. RESURGENCE OF MONOPOLIES

DURING the reign of Charles I, Coventry, the Lord Keeper, was responsible for the revived monopolies. In direct violation of the statute, he passed many patents under the Great Seal for the exclusive manufacture and vending of soap, leather, salt, and other commodities, without any pretence of invention or improvement—merely in respect of the gains to be made from their grant. A Parliament was talked of to redress these grievances; but the King declared by proclamation, countersigned by the Lord Keeper, that "he would consider it presumption for any one to prescribe to him any time for calling that assembly."[1] Coventry was held in great discredit by the people for the illegal patents of monopoly which he had sealed, and, had it not been for his timely death, the Parliament summoned in 1639 would probably have dealt with him as the preceding Parliament had dealt with his predecessor, Bacon.[2]

The policy of Charles I with regard to trade was one of supervision and regulation which he considered not only proper but necessary in the interest of his subjects. In such a policy, regulation by means of monopolies formed a natural part, and these, forbidden by the Statute of 1624 to private persons, were granted to corporations in accordance with Section 9 of the Statute, that procedure being considered proper by contemporary legal opinion. They were, however, extended to such a variety of articles of common use that, a few years later, we find Sir John Culpeper telling the Long Parliament during the debate of November, 1640, that monopolies were:

> a nest of wasps, or swarm of vermin which have overcrept the land. I mean the monopolies and polers of the people. These, like the frogs of Egypt, have gotten possession of our dwellings, and we have scarce a room free from them. They sup in our cup.[3] They dip in our dish.[4] They sit by our fire.[5] We find

[1]Campbell, *Materials for the Reign of Henry VII*, II, 539.
[2]*Ibid.*, 551.
[3]Patent for £4 per tun on wine.
[4]Licence to dress meat in taverns.
[5]Imposition on coal.

them in the dye-vat, wash-bowl[6] and powdering tub.[7] They share with the butler in his box.[8] They have marked and sealed[9] us from head to foot. Mr. Speaker, they will not bate us a pin.[10] We may not buy our clothes without their brokage.[11]

When the second Parliament of Charles I met in February, 1625-6, the Commons complained of the fact that new impositions and monopolies had multiplied.[12] But despite this expression of parliamentary opposition monopolies continued to be granted over a wide range of subject matter which could only serve to provoke opposition of the strongest kind. Included in the list were grants with respect to saltpetre and the making of gunpowder,[13] the importation of alum,[14] iron,[15] glass,[16] whale oil or whale fins,[17] latten wire,[18] books printed abroad,[19] for lighthouses,[20] for the sealing of playing cards[21] and dice,[22] the regulation of printing,[23] and the manufacture and importation of soap and starch.[24] The holders of these grants were given wide powers of search and seizure, importation contrary to their terms was strictly forbidden,[25] and infringers heavily punished.[26]

[6]Patent for soap.

[7]Tax on salt.

[8]Patent for cards and dice.

[9]Beavers, felts, bone-lace, etc.

[10]Patent for pins. The pin monopoly is fully discussed by Unwin, *Industrial Organization*, 164-71, 176. Cf. S.P. Dom. Car. I, cccii, 22; S.P. Dom. Car. II, lxxix, 120; xci, 95; xciii, 60, 61.

[11]Rush. III 917, 1338; IV 33; 2 Parl. Hist. 656; S.P. Dom. Car. I, ccccIxxi, 63.

[12]Rush. I 207.

[13]Rush. II 38, 41, 286.

[14]Rush. II 38.

[15]Rush. II 81.

[16]Rush. II 318.

[17]Rush. II 323.

[18]Rush. II 883.

[19]Rush. II 321.

[20]Rush. II 45.

[21]Rush. II 104, 616, 883. It will be noted that this grant to the Company of Card Makers was in direct violation of the decision in Darcy v. Allin, and the terms of the Statute of Monopolies, its only possible justification, if it can be called such, being that the grant was made to a corporation.

[22]Rush. II 104, 883.

[23]Rush. II 321, 463.

[24]Rush. II 13, 136, 187, 286, 458, 607, 884.

[25]Rush. II 839.

[26]Rush. II 252.

Charles I met with an opposition more strenuous than he had expected and more determined than any which had been presented to his predecessors.[27] It would, however, be wrong to suppose that he was committed to a wilful pursuance of the monopoly policy without regard to the rights and conveniences of his subjects. Nor must it be supposed that the House of Commons was the sole repository of the desire for reform of the situation nor that the elected members of the legislature were carrying on a lone fight for the rights of the people. Not only is such a supposition disproved by the King's proclamation of April 15, 1639, revoking many of the monopolies, but further evidence is revealed by the fact that on April 10, 1640, the Attorney-General reported to the Privy Council that, despite the fact that many patents had been called in and declared void by the King's proclamation, many were still retained by the patentees who refused to surrender them. Thereupon an order was made immediately calling in those patents set forth in a list appended to the order.[28]

The relative importance of the grievances of the times should not be overlooked. Such matters as ship-money, impositions, and Star Chamber practices were the most obtrusive. But monopolies were, even though less onerous, among the grievances and Charles had to meet the complaints and opposition of men like Eliot, Hampden, and Pym concerning them. After an interval of eleven years from the dissolution of his third Parliament, the fourth, or Short Parliament was opened by the King on April 13, 1640. Four days later, a number of petitions was presented complaining "of ship-money, projects and monopolies, the star-chamber and high-commission courts and other grievances." In the course of a speech delivered in the House on that day on the subject of grievances John Pym voiced the general dissatisfaction of the members by referring to: "Monopolies and inundations of them, whereby a burthen is laid not only upon foreign, but upon native commodities: as soap, salt, drink, etc., the particulars whereof are fit for the Committee of Grievances."[29]

[27]See, e.g., Lonsdale Papers, 30, 53, 54.

[28]Rush. III 1103. For list see Appendix XII, 346.

[29]Adams, *British Eloquence*, I, 62.

The *Parliamentary History* is authority for two separate speeches by Pym on the subject of monopolies, the first during the sitting of the Short Parliament and the second four days after the commencement of the Long Parliament.

A conference with the Lords was requested and on April 24 a list of matters to be discussed was presented to the House, of which one of the main headings was "Monopolies and Restraint of

---

According to the *Parliamentary History*, on April 17 and 18, 1640, a number of petitions respecting grievances was presented to the House and of the grievances set forth in them monopolies occupied a conspicuous place. The quotation above set out from the speech of Pym is given in 2 Parl. Hist. 549. Rushworth agrees with the *Parliamentary History* as to the date of April 17. (Cf. Rush. III 1131, 1134; see also 2 Jo. H.C. 5; and also as to Nov. 7 cf. Rush. IV 23.) The State Papers confirm the date of April 17. Cf. S.P. Dom. Car. I, ccccl, 108.

On November 7 Pym numbered among the grievances "inundations of monopolies by the Soap Patent, undertaken by papists, full of mischief; 1. By impairing the goodness and enhancing the price of salt, soap, beer and coals. 2. Under colour of which, trade was restrained to a few hands. 3. Many illegally imprisoned." 2 Parl. Hist. 641; Rush. IV 23.

But Forster, when writing his life of Pym, discovered among the papers of the British Museum a report of the speech with corrections by Pym's own hand, in which it appears that the date of delivery was stated as April 5, 1640, and that the several extracts here given appeared in the speech made on that occasion. (Cf. Adams, *British Eloquence*, I, 35, and see S.P. Dom. Car. I, ccccl, 108, April 17, 1640; Forster, *Life of Pym*, British Statesmen, III, 89.) Rushworth, as noted, agrees with the *Parliamentary History* that Pym spoke to the subject both in April and November, and the *Journals* of the House of Commons show that the matter of grievances was brought up on April 17 (cf. 2 Jo. H.C. 5). While Forster dates Pym's speech as April 5, 1640, it is to be noted that the Short Parliament did not commence its sitting until April 13. It is probable that the manuscript discovered by Forster contained the draft of a speech which Pym intended to deliver at the opening of the sitting but was forced to separate into two speeches, the second and fuller part being delivered in November.

The temper of the Commons at this session seems to have been unanimously against monopolies. Notes of speeches made appear in a MS. Entry Book among the State Papers for the period April 15 to May 5, 1640, as follows:

Francis Rowse, member for Truro: "Thus break in the swarms and inundations of monopolies and projectors like the caterpillars of Egypt, upon which plague there is this other plague attending, that little of that money they bring in is now to be seen." S.P. Dom. Car. I, ccccl, 94.

Speech of John Pym, April 17, 1640, S.P. Dom. Car. I, ccccl, 108.

Proceedings in House, April 23, 1640, S.P. Dom. Car. I, ccccli, 66: "The great increase upon native commodities consumed within the realm."

Speech of E. Bagshaw, member for Southwark, November 14, 1640, "And if we examine the law it will tell us what has been the reward of those that have monopolized and abused the King's authority . . . what they deserve that have raised mountains of monopolies." S.P. Dom. Car. I, cccclxxi, 63.

Trade."[30] But the question of supply intervened[31] and on May 5 Charles dissolved Parliament.[32]

Under Charles I the local monopoly of civic corporations began to be used as a cover for national monopolies by obtaining a right of superintendence over the whole national production of the article or commodity in question. This resulted in giving the monopolist corporation a complete stranglehold over its competitors. In the case of new manufactures, contemplated by the statute, the grants were similarly abused by granting patents on a mere title without disclosure of the nature of the manufacture and then investing the patentee with a right of surveillance over all producers who might be suspected of infringing. This was in accordance with the prevailing practice of the time. The custom was merely to state the subject matter of the invention in general terms in the patent itself.[33] The difficulty with this practice lay in the fact that it was open to the patentee to charge infringement where anything was done which fell within the general description of his patent; and under the system of search and supervision authorized under the Stuarts this naturally led to many injustices.[34] The right of search and seizure given to the patentee for the protection of his patent was so widely exercised, in combination with the lack of clear definition of the limits of the monopoly, that a patentee could, almost at pleasure, restrict competition

[30]2 Jo. H.C. 11.

[31]2 Jo. H.C. 13.

[32]2 Jo. H.C. 19.

[33]Reference may be had to the smalt patents of 3 Jac. I to Twynhoe and of 6 Jac. I and 16 Jac. I to Baker, to the patent of Dudley of Feb. 22, 1622, for making iron, and Mansell's glass patent of May 22, 1624. Cf. 1 W.P.C. 9 et seq.

[34]The practice of enrolling descriptive specifications, designed not only to delimit the monopoly but to put the public in full possession of the invention, so that its use and method would be publicly known at the expiration of the period for which it was granted, seems only to have arisen early in the eighteenth century. Parliament in 1670 (22 & 23 Car. II) when extending the life of the patent granted to Howard and Watson required a specification to be enrolled. In 1712 John Nasmith enrolled a specification of his patent in the Court of Chancery. In 1730, a proviso in the patent voided the grant if a specification was not subsequently enrolled. Liardet v. Johnson (1778) 1 W.P.C. 53, decided that one of the conditions of validity of a patent was whether the specification was sufficient to work the invention. But patents continued to be granted on a title only, subject to the obligation of enrolling a specification within six months thereafter, until 1852, when the practice of enrolling a specification with the application was first established. 15-16 Vict., c. 83.

of either a domestic or imported character. And, although the statute had forbidden the grant of monopolies to individuals, they were still granted in defiance of its terms, as e.g., a monopoly for glass granted in 1634. These naturally called forth some agitation in Parliament. Thus, in the Long Parliament, Bagshaw, the member for Southwark said that: "Better laws could not have been made than the Statute of Monopolies against Projectors, and the Petition of Right against the infringers of liberties; and yet, as if the law had been the author of them, there hath been, within these few years, more monopolies and infringement of liberties, than have been in any age since the Conquest."[35]

A further method of evading the statute arose when the Crown's title over all mines producing gold and silver was used as a basis of monopolistic control over base metal mines in which the precious metals were only an incidental product.

While Coventry must bear the blame for passing these patents under the Great Seal, Noy, the Attorney-General, was responsible for establishing several companies for the purpose of acquiring exclusive privileges. The Statute of Monopolies seemed to secure the public against this type of grievance, but Noy evaded the statute by using the handy tool of corporate structure. For example, he caused a company to be formed for exercising the exclusive right to make soap in accordance with the exception contained in Section 9 of the statute.[36] Every manufacturer was permitted to become a member of the company, known as the Westminster Company of Soap Makers, which paid £8 for every ton of soap made and £10,000 for its charter, in return for which it was entitled to appoint searchers and exercise a sort of inquisition over the trade. Later, the King revoked this patent, and granted a like charter to a new corporation under the name of the London Company of Soap Makers.[37] Noy did not, however, as some writers suggest, devise this means of evading the statute.

[35]2 Parl. Hist. 650.

[36]Proclamation June 28, 1632, reciting letters patent Jan. 20, 1630-1. Rush. II 136, 187. Proclamation Jan. 26, 1633-4, Rot. Pat. p. 6. n. 16. d. Steele Proc. no. 1668. It will be recalled that this was one of the grievances complained of by Pym in his speech to the House during the sitting of the Short Parliament, April 17, 1640. See ante 129.

[37]Proclamation Dec. 28, 1637, Rush. II 617; Rot. Pat. p. 15. n. 6. d. Steele Proc. no. 1759. See also S.P. Dom. Car. I, ccccxlix, 36.

He merely made use of an existing circumstance. Section 9 of the Statute of Monopolies, excepting corporations from the declaration forbidding monopolies, was in full harmony with legal opinion of the time.[38]

The institution of the corporate monopoly of soap making was followed by the creation of a similar company of starch makers,[39] and a great variety of other grants,[40] until monopolies, in transgression or evasion of the Statute, became as common as they had been under Elizabeth and James. When the weight of public odium caused by this diverse list of monopolies began to be felt,[41] a considerable number of the grants was revoked by proclamation. This proclamation,[42] dated April 9, 1639, and obviously prepared in conformity with an order-in-council of March 31, 1639, directing its preparation, is of particular interest not only

[38]Cf. Co. 3 Inst. 185; Hayes et al. v. Harding et al. (1656) Hardres 53. The Statute of Monopolies, it is to be noted, expressly preserved corporate rights and franchises. The City of London, therefore, still has in theory exclusive rights of market within seven miles of the city boundary. (Great Eastern Railway Co. v. Goldsmid (1884) 9 A.C. 927.) Nor has the statute any effect on ancient franchises existing by grant or prescription, such as a ferry, a bridge, or a market with the attendant tolls. (Letton v. Goodden (1886) L.R. 2 Eq. 123.) Coke, in his explanation of the statute (Co. 3 Inst. 182) pointed out that this provision was included for the reason that the city of London, and other cities and boroughs, had some privileges for buying and selling by acts of Parliament. For example, he noted the statute of 1 & 2 Philip and Mary which gave a privilege to cities, boroughs, towns corporate, and market towns, for the sale by retail of certain wares and merchandise.

[39]May 16, 1622; Steele Proc. no. 1330; July 5, 1629. See Rush. II 13, Dec. 26, 1638; Aug. 3, 1661, Steele Proc. nos. 1793 and 3317.

[40]Cf. Proceedings in the Long Parliament, post 140.

[41]Cf. S.P. Dom. Car. I, cccci, 59, November 11, 1638. Resolution of the Committee of Council of War: "It is very requisite that before any levies of men be made for an army some course may be taken for taking off all such projects as yield his Majesty no considerable profit and are grievous to his subjects, as particularly concerning . . . sole exportation of butter, sealing of reels, imposition on iron . . . sealing butter casks, sealing buttons . . . sealing linen and bone lace, of all which the Lords resolved to speak with the King for better preparing the hearts and affections of his Majesty's subjects to serve his Majesty in a business of so great importance."

[42]Hallam, *Constitutional History of England*, II, 10. Rush: III 915. Rot. Pat. p. 23. n. 9. d.; 915; Steele Proc. no. 1800. S.P. Dom. Car. I, ccccxviii, 41, April 23, 1639.

in that it continued the method of approach of the King's predecessors in stating that the grants had been made upon the basis of false suggestion, but also for the reason that it contained two provisions which are met for the first time. The first declared that among the grants which were not thereafter to be put in execution were "all patents for new inventions not put in practice within three years next after the date of the said grants." The second provision with which we are concerned related to the growing abuse of corporations. It provided that among the grants not to be put into execution were "the several grants of incorporation made unto hatband-makers, gutstring-makers, spectacle-makers, comb-makers, tobacco-pipe-makers, butchers and horners." These grants were to be recalled by *quo warranto* or *scire facias* unless surrendered; and the patentees were forbidden to put them in execution.

Apparently the question of monopolies was causing considerable agitation on the political scene for Rushworth, after quoting the text of the King's proclamation of April 15, 1639, revoking many of the monopolies, continued in these words: "This Proclamation gave great Satisfaction to the King's Subjects in the North, and much more in the South: for these Projects and Monopolies had been grievous to the People, who cast out Words of an Indisposition to march in the Army whilst these Burdens were upon the People."

In order to "look a few days beyond the time limited to this second part [of his history], and to let the Reader understand what an ill favour such Patents and Monopolies granted by the King, had amongst the People of better Rank," Rushworth anticipated his chronological order by quoting the speech made in the Long Parliament by Culpeper.[43]

The practice of using the exception contained in Section 9 of the Statute of Monopolies to grant monopolies to corporations called forth an indignant exclamation from Culpeper when, speaking of the "monopolisers" to the Long Parliament, he said: "These are the leeches that have sucked the commonwealth so hard, that it is become almost hectical. And some of these are ashamed of their right names; they have a vizard to hide the brand made by that good law in the last Parliament of King James; they shelter themselves under the name of a corporation; they make bye-laws

[43]Rush. III 917; see also 2 Jo. H.C. 24.

which serve their turn to squeeze us and fill their purses."[44]

The danger inherent in the principle of permitting grants of exclusive privilege to corporations while denying them to individuals was pointed out by Bacon during the debate on monopolies in 1601.[45] But the theory that an exclusive grant to a city, borough, or town or to a corporation, company, or fellowship of any art, trade, occupation, or mystery, or to any companies or societies of merchants within the realm did not constitute a monopoly was too deeply ingrained in the thought processes of the times to be easily eradicated.[46] So we have the Statute of Monopolies[47] specifically providing that it should not affect the liberties and powers of such bodies, which should continue of force and effect as they were before the Act. If, therefore, as was plain at the time, corporations had legal power to hold and exercise monopolies without offending against the law, either common or statutory, such a position offered a fertile field for the continuation of the policy of regulating and supervising trade which had, as far as individuals were concerned, been taken away by the statute of 1624.

Thus, between the date of the accession of Charles I and the sitting of the Long Parliament, the device of using corporations as patentees was freely resorted to. But the granting of monopolies to corporations under the exception contained in the Statute of Monopolies was by no means merely for the purpose of raising revenue. The use of corporations as a means of regulating trade and supervising the quality of production dates back to time immemorial, as we have seen. The guilds were used as a means of protecting artisans within the towns, of enforcing industrial legislation, and of maintaining the quality of manufacture, particularly by the use of standards of apprenticeship training. The theory of search, supervision, and sealing by way of police regulatory powers was an inherent part of guild and company structure

[44]2 Parl. Hist. 656; Rush. III 917.

[45]"If her Majesty make a Patent (or, as we term it, a Monopoly), unto any of her Servants, that we must go, and cry out against; but if she grant it to a number of Burgesses or a corporation, that must stand, and that forsooth is no Monopoly." D'Ewes 645. Prothero, *Constitutional Documents*, 112.

[46]In East India Company v. Sandys (1684) 10 St. Tr. 371 at 434 Pollexfen, for the defendant, argued unsuccessfully that the proviso of the Statute of Monopolies relating to corporations did not "extend to any letters patent after the act of parliament made, but only the letters patent before."

[47]S. 9.

from the earliest times. It was only a natural continuation of such a system of trade regulation when Charles I began to use corporations as the repositories of monopoly grants. It is, however, significant to note that patents, during the time of the first Stuarts, usually contained provisions, or at the least recitals, providing for the production of good quality merchandise. The basic theory of the regulatory powers contained in the Stuart patents was that such powers were necessary for the maintenance of quality, and that no person could be more interested in quality than the patentee.

It was not only newly formed corporations which obtained privileges relative to trade regulation. Under Elizabeth, the wardens of the London Haberdashers were given a right of search with regard to the overseeing of hats and caps.[48] The Companies of the Curriers, Saddlers, and Shoemakers, were given authority to regulate the conditions of work and the quality of the goods produced by all artisans working on leather.[49] Many new companies were formed under Elizabeth and the Stuarts which had monopolistic powers relative to trade regulation and quality of merchandise.[50] These companies were concerned with a great number of commodities of everyday use. No useful purpose would be served by endeavouring to discuss their history[51] or the economic basis of their propriety and expediency.[52] That they caused oppression and raised antagonism is not to be denied: that they were created solely for mercenary and improper reasons cannot be accepted. They were part and parcel of the prevailing theory that trade and industry should be regulated by government action. The grant to a corporation of the monopoly of the manufacture and sale of a commodity was then believed to be the

[48]8 Eliz., c. 11.

[49]5 Eliz., c. 8.

[50]See, e.g., the Cutlers' Company of Sheffield, 21 Jac. I, c. 31; the Brickmakers' Company, Proclamation Nov. 7, 1622. The East India Company was erected by Queen Elizabeth, Dec. 31, 43 Eliz. and renewed to them and successors, May 13, 7 Jac. with prohibition to all others to trade there and confirmed Apr. 3, 13 Car. 2. Cf. East India Company v. Sandys (1684) 10 St. Tr. 371 at 479 per Sawyer, A.-G., *arguendo.*

[51]This has already been authoritatively done by Dr. Hyde Price, *English Patents of Monopoly.*

[52]In East India Company v. Sandys (1684) 10 St. Tr. 371 at 410 Finch, the Solicitor-General, speaking of the company said, after discussing patents for new inventions:

most efficient and expedient manner of ensuring a constant domestic supply; the appointment of overseers and searchers not only had precedent but was felt to be the proper method of maintaining quality; and behind this regulatory system lay the whole weight of the powers of enforcement wielded by the Council and the Star Chamber.

We shall see[53] that the monopolies granted to corporations covered a great variety of commodities, as the protests during the Long Parliament demonstrate. The same condition existed in the time of Elizabeth.[54] If we take one example, we can form an idea of the manner in which corporations were used as the means of controlling trade and regulating quality by the use of the monopoly system. The example we shall consider is the starch monopoly.

The first patent for the manufacture of starch was granted by Elizabeth to Young on April 15, 1588. It was assigned to Sir John Pakington in 1594, and reissued May 20, 1598. The grant was for the making of starch "only upon bran of wheat." Its manufacture was not looked upon with great favour[55] as it was regarded as an unnecessary luxury. But, as it had not been previously manufactured in England, it occupied the position of a new industry, and therefore much could be said in favour of controlling its manufacture. However, the commodity had been introduced shortly before by the Grocers' Company; and, having a large sale of it, that Company naturally came into conflict with

"*A fortiori* therefore in this case, what is of much greater consequence to the nation is a point of trade, than any little slight invention of a particular thing, must be allowed to be good; then I say, sure if the first patent be not a monopoly, then neither can this patent be a monopoly; for there is no law that hath declared how long such a trade as this is may be inclosed, as the statute of 21 king James has set limits for, as new inventions.

"And again, this company is for the advantage and benefit of the nation, which a monopoly can never be: and that it is for the benefit of the nation, appears by the statute of the 14th of this king, cap. 24, which recites it to be of great advantage to the public, and for the encouragement of the public trade and navigation. Here then is both the judgment of the parliament concerning companies of this kind, and an encouragement of this company by the whole parliament."

[53]Cf. post 142.

[54]See ante 71, 78.

[55]Proclamations of James I, August 23, 1607, and July 5, 1608.

the patentee, who claimed the right to seize and destroy all foreign starch. But the price of grain in the summer of 1596, owing to the poor yield, rose so high that Elizabeth, by proclamation of July 31, 1596,[56] strictly forbade the making of starch, in order that grain might be conserved and prices maintained. Obviously the patentee had not confined himself only to the use of bran. However, Elizabeth reissued the starch monopoly two years later to Pakington, the consideration, apart from an annual rent of £40, being the suppression of the manufacture of starch from wheat, the patentee again being confined to the use of "bran of wheat." In 1601, Mr. Martin, in the Commons, inveighed against the fact that he represented "a country that groaneth and languisheth under the burden of monstrous and unconscionable Substitutes to the Monopolitans of Starch . . . . "[57] There is evidence that the agents of the patentee vigorously prosecuted infringers of the patent.[58] Citing this type of abuse as reason for the action, Elizabeth revoked a considerable number of monopoly grants, among them that for starch, by proclamation of November 28, 1601.[59] In 1607 James issued a proclamation stating that great mischief had arisen from Elizabeth's proclamation revoking the monopoly, and ordered that all domestic manufacture of starch should cease.[60] The Starchmaker's Company was then incorporated.[61] The Company was given the monopoly of manufacturing starch: commissioners were appointed for the supervision of the manufacture, and impositions were laid upon foreign starch.[62] The Grocers' Company protested strongly against the monopoly held by the Starchmakers' Company, and, in 1610, after the matter had been brought up in Parliament,[63] it was suspended and all domestic manufacture forbidden.[64] It was found impossible to enforce the prohibition, however, and in 1619 a commission was formed to license manufacture by those who were already doing so in defiance of the prohibition. In 1622, the Starchmakers'

[56]Cunningham, *English Industry and Commerce*, II, 93.

[57]D'Ewes 646.

[58]Hatfield MSS., IV, 261.

[59]See ante 77.

[60]Aug. 23, 1607. Rot. Pat. p. 26. m. 20. d. Steele Proc. no. 1046.

[61]S.P. Docq. Oct. 21, Dec. 23, 1607; March 14, 1608.

[62]Cunningham, *English Industry and Commerce*, II, 305.

[63]See 95; and cf. Hallam, *Constitutional History of England*, I, 305.

[64]Cf. Debate on Grievances, 1620, 1 Parl. Hist. 1205.

Company was re-incorporated, the licensees forming a new company, notwithstanding the protests of the Grocers' Company. Charles I gave the Company exclusive power to manufacture starch, and appointed a surveyor of starch to regulate the manufacture.[65]

On November 23, 1640, a petition of the Grocers' Company was read in the Commons "against a number of Monopolies against Grocers wheerein verie manye Monopolies besides soape, starch and other particulars."[66] The petition was referred to the Committee for Grievances.[67] The monopoly of starch held by the Starchmakers' Company seems to have escaped recall by the proclamation of April 9, 1639, but it did not survive the attack made in the Long Parliament.

The principle that grants of monopoly were good if made to corporations was of long standing and died hard. It had been advanced as early as 1601 when it found its place in a saving section of the bill against monopolies proposed in that year. During the debate Bacon had pointed out the inconsistency embodied in the principle.[68] But, despite the obvious inconsistency, the principle continued to be an accepted part of legal thought on the subject, The Statute of Monopolies itself, by the provisions of Section 9, gave colour to the view of the contemporary lawyers that what they were doing was in strict compliance with the law. But the members of the Commons had made up their minds that monopolies, whether in individual or corporate ownership, had to go. The temper of the Long Parliament was not conducive to the making of nice distinctions or tolerant of legal hair-splitting. In an atmosphere that engendered so much heat it is fortunate that sufficient good sense remained to preserve the patent of invention as the sole brand from the burning.

[65]Cunningham, *English Industry and Commerce*, II, 305; Rush. II 13, 839, 884. For a short history of the starch patents see chap. VI, n. 24.

[66]D'Ewes 54.

[67]2 Jo. H.C. 34. In D'Ewes's notes the starch monopoly is stated as being held by a Mr. Mutis. D'Ewes, ed. Notestein, 540.

[68]"The bill is very injurious and ridiculous; injurious, in that it taketh or rather sweepeth away her Majesty's prerogative; and ridiculous, in that there is a proviso, that this statute shall not extend to grants made to corporations; that is a gull to sweeten the bill withal; it is only to make fools fond." Prothero, *Constitutional Documents*, 114.

XI. DECLINE OF THE MONOPOLY SYSTEM

DURING the sitting of the Long Parliament it is apparent, from the reports contained in the contemporary *Journals*,[1] that the feeling of the House ran almost unanimously against monopolies. When Parliament opened on November 3, 1640, a committee for grievances was immediately proposed.[2] So numerous were the complaints and petitions touching upon all manner of grievances that the whole House was divided and subdivided into more than forty committees to hear and examine them.[3] So serious a view of the matter was taken that a committee on monopolies was set up,[4] and the House voted that grievances arising out of monopolies should be sent to that committee alone.[5] Many petitions were received by the House[6] and by the King,[7] among them being those which attacked the monopolies concerning gunpowder and saltpetre,[8] the grants being revoked and the holders thereof punished.[9] The complaints laid before the Com-

[1]D'Ewes, ed. Notestein, 14, 68, 224, 299; Rush. IV 19 et seq.

[2]Rush. IV 19; S.P. Dom. Car. I, ccccIxxi, 76, Nov. 16, 1640.

[3]D'Ewes 68; Rush. IV 28; George, Lord Digby, speaking in the House, of grievances in the West, recited as one of his main heads: "The multitude of monopolies." Rush. III 1337.

[4]D'Ewes 42, 174, 300.

[5]D'Ewes 312.

[6]D'Ewes 5, 16, 54, 174; 2 Parl. Hist. 542.

[7]Thus, on March 26, 1640, a petition to the Mayor and Council of Newcastle-upon-Tyne was made, complaining of "What burdens the intrenching upon the freedom of the subjects by monopolies of soap, salt, coal, tobacco, starch, and many other such like are palpable, together with the new great impost on wine, lead, and all other commodities." S.P. Dom. Car. I, ccccxlix, 36, March 30, 1640.

On July 11, 1640, the Grand Jury impanelled to serve at the assizes of Berks. presented a petition to the King asking redress of: "The infinite number of monopolies upon everything almost that the countryman has to buy." S.P. Dom. Car. I, cccclix, 77, July 11, 1640; ccccIxiii, 33, August 4, 1640.

On September 24, 1640, the citizens of London petitioned the King for redress of grievances, among them being, "The multitude of monopolies, patents, and warrants whereby trade is decayed." S.P. Dom. Car. I, ccccIxviii, 29.

[8]D'Ewes 299.

[9]D'Ewes 444, 456.

mittee touched upon the subject of improper profit to the patentees only occasionally,[10] the real grievance seeming to be the manner in which searches were conducted and the insolence of the agents of the patentees.[11] The holding of patents of monopoly and the arbitrary and illegal manner of operating them were, as we shall see, among the charges levelled at Strafford in his impeachment,[12] and one of the members of the House went so far as to move that the "Statute of Monopolies might be made a felony or Praemunire at least."[13]

But the Long Parliament was not content merely to receive petitions against monopolies and to cancel the patents. On November 9, 1640 during the debate on Culpeper's speech, it was moved in the House that "every Projector Monopolizer in all respects might bee disabled to sett in this howse."[14] It was thereupon "ordered that all projectors, monopolizers, Promotors, or Advisers of them should be made incapable of setting in this howse."[15] It is, however, important to note that when the motion was put to the House it was resolved upon the question "That the word 'unlawful' should be joined to the word 'Monopolist'."[16] It will be observed, therefore, that monopolies were not, *per se*, regarded as unlawful. The agitation occurring all through this period was not against all monopolies, many of which entirely escaped criticism, but only against those which offended the law.

[10] D'Ewes 14, 190, 351, 357.

[11] D'Ewes 190, 299, 444.

[12] D'Ewes 60 n., and see post 146.

[13] D'Ewes 12 n.; cf. Peyton, f. 5: "That they might suffer death or imprisonment that infringe the statute of monopolies and petition of right."

[14] D'Ewes 19; 2 Jo. H.C. 24; Rush. IV 37.

[15] D'Ewes 20, 531. "That all Projectors and Monopolists whatsoever; or that have any share, or lately have had any share, in any monopolies; or that do receive, or lately have received any benefit from any Monopoly or Project; or that have procured any warrant or command from the restraint or molesting of any that have refused to conform themselves to any such Proclamations or Projects; are disabled, by order of this house, to sit here in this house; and, if any man here knows any Monopolist, that he shall nominate him; That any member of this house, that is a monopolist or projector, shall repair to Mr. Speaker, that a new warrant may issue forth; or otherwise, that he shall be dealt with as with a stranger, that hath no power to sit here." 2 Parl. Hist. 651 and 653; cf. D'Ewes 361; D'Ewes, ed. Coates, 57; 2 Jo. H.C. 24, S.P. Dom. Car. I. cccclxxi, November 9, 1640.

[16] 2 Parl. Hist. 651; 2 Jo. H.C. 24.

The parliamentary agitation against the monopolies must be read with this point constantly in mind.[17]

The patent for sea coal was complained of in the House on November 12.[18] Within the next few days complaints were made against the patents for wines, salt, tobacco, raw hides, calf skins, grocers' commodities, pins, lighthouses, and others.[19] The tobacco monopoly was ordered to be brought forthwith into the House for examination on November 26 and the referees to whom the legality of the patent was referred were ordered to attend the committee at the same time. The same disposition was made of the patents for the sole trade to Guinea, the sole importing of redwood, for the making of copperas stone, and the making of beads and beaugles.[20] Those concerned in the patents were ordered to withdraw from the House until the matter was disposed of.[21] The patents for lighthouses, engrossing wills, for glasses, writing the King's letters and bills at York, for lobsters and salmon, for lampreys, and for lists and shreds, were condemned by the Council after being referred to it by the Commons, leaving those for dispensing with the statute of tillage, for the sole printing on linen cloth, for importation of logwood, for sole importation and garbling of tobacco, and for making farthing tokens, for further consideration and debate.[22] The following January, upon vote called by the Speaker, the holders of the monopolies of sea coal, tobacco, bone lace, and soap were declared to have forfeited their seats; and writs were ordered for a new election to each of the boroughs for which they served.[23] The House held that no monopolizer should remain in the House while his case was being debated[24] and not only the referees and projectors were to be

[17]See, e.g., the speech of Lord Digby in the Commons when he pointed out that the law provided a remedy against those "who have raised mountains of monopolies." 2 Parl. Hist. 665.

[18]Rush. IV 41, 52.

[19]Rush. IV 52-7 *passim*.

[20]Bugles.

[21]Rush. IV 53.

[22]S.P. Dom. Car. I, cccclxxii, 16, November 23, 1640.

[23]D'Ewes 267, 357; 2 Parl. Hist. 707. Rushworth gives this list as the "monopolies of coal, tobacco, bone-lace, the sole using of wine-cask, and marking of butter-firkins." Rush. IV 150.

[24]D'Ewes 308; Scobell, *Memorials*, 71.

punished by disqualification but also the lawyers who drew up the patents.[25]

On May 26, 1641, the imposition on wines, complained of by Culpeper in his speech, was declared illegal[26] and, on August 17, the letters patent for the making of soap granted to Palmer and others on December 17, 1631 and to the Soap Makers of Westminster dated January 20, 1631-2, were declared to be monopolies and illegal in their creation. The proclamation of June, 1632, giving the Westminster Company power of search and seizure was declared to be against the law, the decrees of the Star Chamber regulating the soap-making trade were set aside, the prosecutions in the Star Chamber for infringement of the Company's grants were ordered to be reversed and those joining in the company or having any share or stock in it were classed as delinquents and ordered to make restitution to all who had been hindered in their trade or had any of their goods seized.[27] So ended the soap monopoly.

On November 7, Pym, in a vigorous speech, attacked the Council and the Court of Star Chamber for their part in upholding monopolies and the growing custom of creating and enforcing monopolies by proclamations. Three aspects of the subject were assailed by him:

> Monopolies countenanced by the council-table, and the clause in their patents of monopolies, commanding the Justices of the Peace to assist them; whereby the great abilities of that honourable Board, receive a stain by such matters of so mean a report in the estimation of the law, so ill in the apprehension of the people.
>
> The High Court of Star Chamber, called in the Parliament Rolls ***Magnum Concilium***, to which the Parliaments were wont to refer such matters as they had not time to determine: a court erected against oppression; a court of councils, and a court of justice; now an instrument of erecting and defending monopolies, to set a face of publick good on things pernicious.

---

[25] D'Ewes 531; "That the whole consideration of all monopolies (except those of salt, soap and leather) be referred to a committee, to consider who were the authors of the several patents and grants for monopolies, and of all others that have had any hand in the procuring or concealing of any patent or grant, or have received any money or gift from any of them. And have power to enquire after all grants of patents; all proclamations, commissions, contracts, assignments, or any other thing that may have any relation, or concern any patent, or any grant of any monopoly or project." Rush. IV 165. On Nov. 9, 1641, the House called for a list of all patents issued since 1625. Cf. 2 Jo. H.C. 199.

[26] Rush. IV 277.

[27] Rush. IV 377-8.

The great and most eminent power of the King in Edicts and Proclamations, called *Leges Temporis*, used heretofore to encounter with sudden and unexpected danger, till the Great Council of the King could be called, hath of late been exercised for enjoining and maintaining monopolies.[28]

---

[28]2 Parl. Hist. 642; Rush. IV 23.

In the version of the speech discovered by Forster in the British Museum (cf. 129, n. 29) the passage is given as follows:

"The ninth general head was—that the authority and wisdom of the council table have been applied to the contriving and managing of several monopolies, and other great grievances. The institution of the council-table was much for the advantage and security of the subject, to avoid surreptitious and precipitate courts in the great affairs of the kingdom. But by law an oath should be taken by all those of the King's Council, in which, amongst other things it is expressed that they should for no cause forbear to do right to all the King's people. If such an oath be not now taken, he wished it might be brought into use again.

"It was the honor of that table, to be, as it were, incorporated with the King; his royal power and greatness did shine most conspicuously in their actions and in their counsels. We have heard of projectors and referees heretofore; and what opinion and relish they have found in this House is not unknown. But that any such thing should be acted by the council-table which might give strength and countenance to monopolies, as it hath not been used till now of late, so it cannot be apprehended without the just grief of the honest subject, and encouragement of those who are ill affected. He remembered that *in tertio* of this king, a noble gentleman, then a very worthy member of the Commons' House, now a great lord and eminent counsellor of State, did in this place declare an opinion concerning that clause used to be inserted in patents of monopoly, whereby justices of peace are commanded to assist the patentees; and that he urged it to be a great dishonor to those gentlemen which are in commission to be so meanly employed—with how much more reason may we, in jealousy of the honor of the council-table, humbly desire that their precious time, their great abilities, designed to the public care and service of the kingdom, may not receive such a stain, such a diminution as to be employed in matters of so ill report, in the estimation of the law; of so ill effect in the apprehension of the people!

"The tenth head of civil grievances was comprised in the high court of star chamber, which some think succeeded that which in the parliament rolls is called *magnum concilium*, and to which parliaments were wont so often to refer those important matters which they had no time to determine. But now this court, which in the late restoration or erection of it in Henry VII's time, was especially designed to restrain the oppression of great men, and to remove the obstructions and impediments of the law—this, which is both a court of counsel and a court of justice—hath been made an instrument of erecting and defending monopolies and other grievances; to set a face of right upon those things which are unlawful in their own nature; a face of public good upon such as are pernicious in their use and execution. The soap-patent and divers other evidences thereof may be given, so well known as not to require a particular relation. And as if this were not enough, this court hath lately intermeddled with the ship money! divers sheriffs have been questioned for not levying and collecting such sums as their

As a consequence, on July 3, 1641,[29] a bill was presented abolishing the Court of Star Chamber and was duly passed two days later.[30] On June 23, 1641, the Ten Propositions of the Commons relating to the state of the kingdom were presented;[31] and the third head petitioned the King "to remove such evil councillors, against whom there may be any just exceptions." The petition then went on to say that while the ill effects produced by these ill counsels might have "decayed," "those of another kind and allay had much prospered, of late, amongst us; as matters of Monopolies, of Projects, and new Inventions."[32] Coincidental with all the agitation concerning monopolies, the House was strenuously engaged in pressing the impeachment and attainder of Strafford, and, as some of the articles of the accusation made against him were concerned with alleged abuse of monopoly in his conduct of affairs in Ireland, it is proposed to consider the conduct of the case briefly.

---

counties have been charged with; and if this beginning be not prevented, the star chamber will become a court of revenue, and it shall be made crime not to collect or pay such taxes as the State shall require!

"The eleventh head of civil grievance was now come to. He said, he was gone very high, yet he must go a little higher. That great and most eminent power of the King, of making edicts and proclamations, which are said to be *leges temporis*, and by means of which our princes have used to encounter with such sudden and unexpected danger, as would not endure so much delay, as assembling the great council of the kingdom—this, which is one of the most glorious beams of majesty, most rigorous in commanding reverence and subjection, hath, to our unspeakable grief, been often exercised of late for the enjoining and maintaining sundry monopolies and other grants; exceeding burdensome and prejudicial to the people."

The "projectors" referred to in the above passage were those undertaking monopolies. The "referees" were the law officers appointed by the Crown to decide all legal questions arising in regard to monopolies. It will be recalled that, in 1621, Buckingham threw the blame of all irregularities in the matter of monopolies on the "referees," and, on motion of Cranfield, a parliamentary inquiry was made into their conduct. Cf. Gardiner, *History of England*, IV, 48; Church, *Bacon*, 128.

[29]16 Car. I, c. 10; cf. 2 Parl. Hist. 853; 2 Jo. H.C. 197.

[30]17 Car. I, c. 10; Gardiner, *Constitutional Documents*, 176; 2 Parl. Hist. 853.

[31]2 Parl. Hist. 846; 2 Jo. H.C. 183.

[32]2 Parl. Hist. 842.

XII. THE EARL OF STRAFFORD AND MONOPOLIES IN IRELAND

AT the trial of Thomas Wentworth, Earl of Strafford which opened in Westminster Hall on March 22, 1640-1, several of the articles of the Commons in maintenance of their accusation charging him with high treason, were concerned with his being engaged in monopolistic practices. These articles charged that, while Lord Deputy of Ireland, he restrained the export of pipe-staves without his licence, and raised large sums in return for export licences; that he exercised monopolies in tobacco, starch, iron-pots, glasses, tobacco pipes, and several other commodities, as well as in flax, one of the principal and native commodities of Ireland.[1] Strafford was accused of high treason at the opening of the session of Parliament, November 6, 1640, and was immediately arrested.[2]

According to the evidence adduced against Strafford, he exercised "a monopoly of the sole trade of tobacco, of more gain to the parties interested therein, than the King's whole revenue in Ireland."[3] The duty charged on tobacco was exorbitant, ships were forbidden to land their cargo without paying it, and many persons were heavily sentenced for evading the monopoly. The Commons of Ireland protested: "That the tobacco bought at the low rate, is sold at excessive rates, whereby thousands of His Majesty's subjects are destroyed, and most part of the coin of this Kingdom ingrossed into particular hands; insomuch, that the profits arising thereby, surmount His Majesty's revenue, certain or casual, within this Kingdom, and yet His Majesty

[1]Rush. VIII 6; S.P. Dom. Car. I, cccclxxix, 85, 86. These Articles together with Strafford's oral defence and John Glyn's reply for the prosecution will be found in Appendix XIII, 347 ff. The whole of Volume VIII of the Rushworth Collection is taken up with the trial of the Earl of Strafford. The proceedings relating to monopoly based on Article XII may be examined at Rush. VIII 401-15. The proceedings based on Article XIII appear at Rush. VIII 416-25. Article XI was not proceeded with. Rush. VIII 252.

[2]Rush. VIII 3; 2 Jo. H.C. 21.

[3]Remonstrance of the Irish Commons, Rush. VIII 7; 2 Jo. H.C. 32.

receives very little profit by the same."[4] An earlier remonstrance addressed to Strafford by the Commons had numbered amongst its grievances "the proclamation for the sole emption and uttering of tobacco, which is bought at very low rates, and uttered at high and excessive rates," and "the universal and unlawful encreasing of monopolies, to the advantage of a few, the disprofit of His Majesty, and impoverishment of his people."[5]

Strafford defended on the ground that the Irish Commons had petitioned him to impose the duties for revenue purposes[6] and that the King had specifically instructed him by letter to impose duties on tobacco.[7] He further showed that the prohibition against planting tobacco in Ireland was on the same principle as the course which had been taken in England, and that the licensing of its importation was with the advice and approval of the Council. He further showed that the licensing of the monopoly under the terms of which the grantees of the sole importation paid an annual sum over and above the customs duties, brought profit not to him but to the King, and that it resulted in ample importation of good quality tobacco at reasonable prices.[8] In his written answers to the accusation he stated that, although he was a partner in the monopoly by allowance of the King, he had made no profit out of it.[9]

The charge under Article XIII concerned the proclamation issued by Strafford enjoining the people to work flax into yarn in a way wherein it was alleged they were unskilful. The buying of any linen yarn otherwise made was prohibited and considerable quantities were seized as being in contravention of the proclamations.[10]

To these accusations Strafford answered that the intention of the proclamations was good and the power lawfully executed. The Council had approved and signed the proclamations, thus placing him in the position of a viceroy who acted on the advice of his Council. But his strongest defence was that in which he

[4]Rush. VIII 405.

[5]Rush. VIII 12. See also the opening speech of Maynard for the prosecution, Rush. VIII 402.

[6]Rush. VIII 25, 406.

[7]Rush. VIII 25, 407.

[8]Rush. VIII 409.

[9]Rush. VIII 25.

[10]Rush. VIII 416, 420.

showed that what he endeavoured to do by his proclamations was to discourage the trade of wool growing in Ireland for in this lay a grave competitive danger to the English wool trade. By setting up the trade of linen cloth his intention was to eliminate the conflict with the wool trade in England.

Strafford's written defence to Article XIII of the accusation is worthy of inclusion in full. It reads as follows:

He endeavoured to advance the manufacture of Linnen rather than of Woollen-Cloth, which might prejudice that Trade here; he bought Flax-seed in the Low Countries, and sold it at the same Rate to such as desired it, they making their Cloaths not above a foot broad, and winding 8 or 10 threads from several Bottoms together; the contrary was twined; their Flax, formerly not above a Foot, became a Yard in length, and that soil is fit to bear it, and the people love such easie works; He hath set up many Looms, made much Cloth, and sold it to the loss of some Thousands of pounds; but when the State saw the Natives would not change their old Courses for new and better, the Proclamation was declined. What he did was for the Publick Good, and had nothing from them that was not fully paid for.[11] As to the abuses of the officers in enforcing the proclamations he disclaimed responsibility.[12]

When it fell to Strafford to speak in his own defence it is obvious to one who reads the proceedings that, on these points of the accusation at least, he made a very telling and wholly adequate defence. As to Article XI, concerning pipe-staves he stated that it was well that the prosecution had waived the article for the truth was that if it had been proceeded with it would have appeared that while the Crown made £1,500 profit he had incurred a loss of £400.[13] As he pointed out in regard to "the business of the tobacco," this was certainly "not applicable to treason in any kind." He asked his judges to bear in mind that "it was the petition of the Commons House of Ireland that the grant of impost on the tobacco should be taken in and converted to the King's use, so that whatever was done, was pursuing their intention and desire." He stressed the point that what he had done was no different from what had been done in England.[14] But his most telling argument was that "at the worst, it is but a Monopoly, and a Monopoly of the best condition, because it was begun by

[11]Rush. VIII 25.

[12]Rush. VIII 421, 652; see Strafford's oral defence in Appendix XIV, 349.

[13]Rush. VIII 652.

[14]See, e.g., Proclamation of Aug. 9, 1627; Rot. Pat. 16. m. 21. d. Steele Proc. no. 1516.

a Parliament. I have seen many Monopolies question'd in Parliament, and many overthrown in Parliament, but, I never heard a Monopoly charged for a Treason."[15]

The attitude of the Commons toward the charges made against Strafford is shown by the words of counsel in reply who pointed out that Strafford was defending on the basis that "here is no Treason, though something tending to Oppression, and so at this rate, he can never want an Answer, for if this be not (in this particular) as high and wilful an overthrow of the Fundamental Rules and Justice of the Kingdom, as can be imagined, I appeal to your Lordships: and that it is wherwith he is Charged, not as if this singly would amount to Treason."[16]

What the Commons were trying to do was to set up a principle of cumulative treason. Even if the evidence on all the charges had been legally sufficient, it appeared doubtful whether the crime of treason could be established. As soon as that became evident, the method of attack was changed and the Commons proceeded by way of Bill of Attainder. The Bill was duly passed by the Commons[17] and was sent on to the Lords who assented to it on May 7, 1641.[18]

The proceedings were of course, politically inspired, and, although a bill was later passed reversing Strafford's attainder, it is a blot on history that charges of such an unsubstantial nature as those concerning his dealing in monopolies, should have played their part in bringing a man of Strafford's position and accomplishments to the block. Even had those charges been fully proved, it is difficult to see how the fact of being concerned in monopolies and the imposition of special charges and licence fees on tobacco and other commodities should serve to subject a man to attainder and the loss of his head. While one may censure the men of Parliament, shortly to become the Regicides, for voting the death of a man for charges they did not understand in law but considered only as instruments of political destruction, the serious student of

[15]Rush. VIII 652. The verbatim defence of Strafford to the articles of accusation concerned with monopolies will be found in Appendix XIV, 349. Following Strafford's defence appears the summing up of the evidence on these articles by Glyn for the prosecution.

[16]Rush. VIII 423.

[17]2 Jo. H.C. 125, April 21, 1641.

[18]Rush. VIII 755; 2 Jo. H.C. 140.

history must be impressed in the most unfavourable manner with the action of the judges. When the accusation was under consideration, the Lords requested the opinion of the judges as to whether some of the Articles amounted to treason. The judges returned the evasive answer that they were of opinion "upon all which their Lordships had voted to be proved, that the Earl of Strafford doth deserve to undergo the pains and forfeitures of high treason by law." On May 1, 1641, the King came to the House of Lords and addressed a joint session of both Houses saying that, while Strafford might be guilty of misdemeanour, yet "that in my Conscience, I cannot Condemn him of High-Treason."[19] The members of the Commons, much disturbed by this message, immediately decided to discover a plot for Strafford's escape and an attack by the French on the coast at Portsmouth. Popular tumult ensued and the inevitable result followed. On May 9, the King called his Privy Council together and, in the presence of some of the judges, propounded several scruples to them concerning the bill for the execution of Strafford. Apparently the judges had little difficulty in squaring their views of legal principle with the dictates of political expediency, for after some discussion the King gave order for signing the bill.[20] Charles made a last effort to save Strafford on the day before that set for his execution by writing in his own hand a letter addressed to the Lords which he delivered himself, urging them to approve a reprieve and to substitute life imprisonment for the death penalty.[21] The Lords, however, would have none of it. After deliberating the matter they sent a delegation to the King with the hypocritical message that they could not agree without danger to him, his consort, and children. The King weakly assented to the bill and three days later Strafford was executed on Tower Hill.[22] "The execution of Strafford," observed Lord Russell,[23] "casts a stain upon all parties in the State. The House of Commons were instigated by passion; the House of Lords acted from fear; and Charles from some motive or other, which, at all events, was not the right one. The admission of the mob to overawe the deliberations of Parliament was a sure sign that law was about to be subverted."

[19]Rush. VIII 734; 2 Jo. H.C. 131. The date is wrongly given in Rushworth as May 1, 1640.

[20]Rush. VIII 755.

[21]Rush. VIII 758.

[22]Rush. VIII 759, May 12, 1641.

[23]*English Government and Constitution*, 66.

XIII. EVOLUTION OF THE PATENT OF INVENTION

THE Long Parliament was not, apparently, under the necessity of concerning itself for any considerable length of time with the question of monopolies. They were no longer a great issue because the attacks on the monopolists were resulting in the virtual disappearance of the industrial monopolies. The order of the House of November 9, 1640, that no monopolizer or projector should sit in the House was having its effect, and those who had had any part in the monopolies were regarded with disfavour by the parliamentarians.[1] The abolition of the Star Chamber eliminated what was probably the greatest objection to monopolies by automatically forcing any question of their adjudication into the courts of common law.

Then, too, the proceedings against the Earl of Strafford on his impeachment for high treason and the subsequent debates on the Bill of Attainder occupied much of the time of the House. It is probable that the use, for the first and, happily, the only time in history of charges of being concerned in the exercise of monopolies as the basis of an accusation of high treason, had a painfully restraining effect on the conduct of most persons who were in any way concerned with monopolies and exclusive privileges.

The Grand Remonstrance, presented by Parliament to Charles on December 1, 1641, contained several references to impositions, monopolies, and control of trade, which showed that these improper means of raising revenue without the control of Parliament constituted grievances which were seriously troubling the Commons.[2]

[1]D'Ewes, ed. Coates, xxvii.

[2] "18. Tonnage and Poundage hath been received without colour or pretence of law; many other heavy impositions continued against law, and some so unreasonable that the sum of the charge exceeds the value of the goods."

"27. The monopolies of soap, salt, wine, leather, sea-coal, and in a manner of all things of most common and necessary use.

"28. The restraint of the liberties of the subjects in their . . . trades. . . .

"29. Their vexation and oppression by purveyors, clerks of the market and saltpetre men."

12

Scotland had not been free of agitation concerning monopolies and, in the same year, 1641, an act of Charles I, known as the Scotch Act of Monopolies, after reciting the hurt and prejudice occasioned by monopolies such as "the gifts for selling tobacco," "the patent of the leather," "the patent of the pearling," "the patent of the pearl," and "the patent of armoury," annulled and rescinded all such grants and ordained that "the same, and all other patents of that nature, purchased or to be purchased for the benefit of particular persons, in prejudice of the public, should cease and be ineffectual in all times coming." Prior to that statute, patents in Scotland had been issued as an exercise of the Crown prerogative based on immemorial custom as in England. The abuse of monopolies was apparently as prevalent in Scotland as in England although little appears in contemporary literature on the subject. It is obvious that this statute was modeled on the English Statute of Monopolies. It was repealed, along with all other statutes passed by the Scottish Parliament during the troubled times of Charles I, by the general rescissory act of 1661.

"36. Merchants prohibited to unlade their goods in such ports as were for their own advantage, and forced to bring them to those places which were much for the advantage of the monopolisers and projectors.

"37. The Court of Star Chamber hath abounded in extravagant censures, not only for the maintenance and improvement of monopolies and their unlawful taxes. . . ."

After reciting the calling of a Parliament on November 3, 1641, the Remonstrance continued with a recitation of the matters accomplished by the Parliament, among them the following:

"115. The monopolies are all suppressed, whereof some few did prejudice the subject, about £1,000,000 yearly.

"116. The soap £100,000.

"117. The wine, £300,000.

"118. The leather must needs exceed both, and salt could be no less than that.

"119. Besides the inferior monopolies, which, if they could be exactly computed, would make up a great sum.

"120. That which is more beneficial than all this is, that the root of these evils is taken away, which was the arbitrary power pretended to be in His Majesty of taxing the subject, or charging their estates, without consent of Parliament, which is now declared to be against law by the judgment of both Houses, and likewise by an Act of Parliament."

"141. The setting of some good courses . . . for the advancing of native commodities, increase of our manufactures, and well balancing of trade. . . ."

Cf. 2 Jo. H.C. 307 et seq.

The Scotch Act of Monopolies of 1641 is not, therefore, a part of the statute law of Scotland,[3] although it is usual to refer to it in discussing the Scottish law of patents. It is generally regarded as declaratory of the old law, under which grants of this nature were issued on the same conditions and on the same principles as in England.

Although the practice of granting improper patents of monopoly to corporations did not cease as a result of the strictures in the Long Parliament, the government and the Crown gradually began to exercise care to grant monopolies only for such purposes as would not cause an outburst of popular feeling.[4] Such clamours were, of course, almost inevitable when monopolies controlled and regulated the common necessaries of life such as soap and salt,[5] although it is noteworthy that monopolies of foreign trade which did not touch the people directly or closely[6] were considered quite proper.[7] But the Long Parliament, arrogating to itself a

[3]Cf. McAndrews v. The Solicitors of Edinburgh (1833) 11 S.D. and B. 812; 1 W.P.C. 34 n.

[4]Cunningham, *English Industry and Commerce*, II, 168.

[5]Cf. 1 Parl. Hist. I, 1205; Strafford's Letters, I, 193; Gardiner, *History of England*, VIII, 285. The effect of the popular distaste for monopolies, evidenced all through the seventeenth century by the publication of pamphlets attacking monopolists and projectors, must not be overlooked as a factor in this new trend of official attitude. Levy, *Monopoly and Competition*, 44 et seq., gives extracts from some of these pamphlets illustrating the virulence of the attacks and the depth of the antagonism toward monopolies. Dr. Levy himself makes a spirited attack on monopolies in Chapter III of his work and quite conclusively proves what it would be idle to deny, that monopolies, *in their working and in their effects*, were most harmful to the people and hurtful to trade. He is, however, not on sure ground when he endeavours to trace what might have been the course of English trade and industry if there had been no monopolies. Such an *ex post facto* view presupposes a progress that might well have diverged in a direction quite different from that assumed by Dr. Levy.

Some of the pamphlets published in opposition to monopolies were: *The Projector's Downfall*, 1642; *A True Discovery of the Projectors' Wine Project*, 1641; *A Short and True Relation Concerning the Soap Business*, 1641; A. Wilkins, *The Sope Patentees' Petition Opened*, 1646; J. Davies, *An Answer to Those Printed Papers*, 1641; R. Gardiner, *England's Grievances Discovered in Relation to the Coal Trade*, 1655; *A Looking Glass for Sope Patenters*, 1646; and *The Tinners' Grievances*, 1697.

[6]E.g., the charter to the East India Company.

[7]See East India Company v. Sandys (1684) 10 St. Tr. 371 at 530, in which it was held that "both by the law of nations and by the common law of England, the regulation, restraint and government of foreign trade is reckoned *inter jura*

jurisdiction which had previously been denied by the Crown, called in and cancelled those of the existing patents which gave offence. By gradual degrees, the theory grew up that trade and commerce are best left unhampered. The improper use of monopoly regulation fell into disuse, leaving only those monopolies covered by the grant of patents for new devices as contemplated by the Statute of James. Most of the monopolies having been declared void by the Long Parliament in 1640, and the Bill of Rights in 1689 having ended the claim of the Crown to override the law,[8] monopolies by patents were gradually relegated to a position of slight political importance. Although there is little record of the relative number of monopolies, it is apparent that after 1640 their number decreased rapidly. Is is not safe, however, to assume that, because the question of monopolies did not occupy the attention of Parliament, it had become a dead issue. Murmurings were still heard. Thus on August 23, 1653,[9] a petition

---

regalia, i.e., is in the power of the king; and it is his undoubted prerogative, and is not abridged or controlled by any Act of Parliament now in force." Foreign trade was therefore a matter which was prohibited to the King's subjects until such time as it had been "opened" by act of Parliament or by licence of the King. It was held by Jefferies, L.C.J., that, as a necessary consequence of these powers of the King, he could set up societies with exclusive rights to trade. These could not be called monopolies for a monopoly is a grant whereby persons are restricted of some freedom which they formerly possessed, or are hindered in their lawful trade (*ibid.*, 542). But in view of the fact that there was previously no liberty to trade with the Indies the charter could not be said to create a monopoly (*ibid.*, 542-3). On the ground of public policy and natural equity (*ibid.*, 538-9, 546-7) the East India Company retained its exclusive right to trade, long after similar rights, formerly enjoyed by other companies, had disappeared.

A transcript of relevant parts of the judgment in this case will be found in Appendix XVI, 353.

See also Merchant Adventurers v. Rebow (1686) Comb. 53; 3 Mod. 126; Rogers v. Rajendro Dutt et al. (1860) 13 Moo. P.C. 209 at 217.

In Merchant Adventurers v. Rebow (1686) 3 Mod. 126, the decision in East India Co. v. Sandys was distinguished. The principle set forth in the Merchant Adventurers case was that the King cannot by his charter grant to a society of merchants the exclusive privilege of trading to particular places, and in particular articles, unless he is previously authorized by Parliament so to do. In the East India Case the charter was granted for trade with infidels: in the Merchant Adventurers Case the trade was with the continent of Europe.

[8]Cf. Bill of Rights, Dec. 16, 1689, s. 2, Adams and Stephens, *Select Documents*, 462; Stubbs, *Select Charters*, 523.

[9]S.P. Dom. Aug. 23, 1653, xxxix, 68.

was presented from a number of merchants and soap boilers complaining of the monopoly enjoyed by Sir Edward Bromfield and his Company, with particular reference to their activities of searching and raising of prices. Evidently the old method of guarding the possession of monopolies by staying actions brought upon them in the common law courts had not ceased during the Interregnum for, after reciting the Statute of Monopolies, the petition proceeded to state that "the patentees of England have been the caterpillars of the commonwealth and by obstructing our proceedings at law have incurred the penalties of the Statute of Praemunire. We beg an Act that from henceforth no execution of judgment upon any action grounded on the statute against monopolies made 21 Jas. shall be stayed or superseded by any writ of error or supersedeas thereupon, any law to the contrary notwithstanding, and that we may enjoy the benefit of the law, without interruption by the Commissioners of Indemnity."[10]

In the middle years of the seventeenth century there appear a few vague references to monopolies, in particular some petitions complaining of the monopoly of the postal service.[11] Petitions for special grants involving exclusive privileges were carefully scrutinized,[12] and although an occasional pamphlet appeared on the subject[13] it is obvious, from the paucity of material that is

[10]Action was evidently taken on this petition for an entry of the same date indicates that the Committee of Indemnity was ordered to certify why they had stopped proceedings at law. S.P. Dom. Aug. 23, 1653, xxxix, 69.

[11]See, e.g., the petition of the Mayor and Aldermen of Norwich to the Protector, S.P. Dom. March 13, 1653-4, lxvii, 71. "Having bought our liberties at vast expense of blood and treasure we hope not again to be troubled with distasteful monopolies, but to have liberty to convey our letters freely."

[12]See petition to the Protector for the export of calf-skins, July 21, 1554. The Committee of Council apparently recommended its refusal on the ground that they "think the petitioners aim at getting money and setting up a monopoly." S.P. Dom. lxxiii, 39.

A petition of February 19, 1655, for the sole transport of coal to France, on payment of double customs bears a holograph reference by the Protector: "We desire the council to consider the petition, and whether the same be a monopoly, and so prejudicial to the liberty of the people; or whether it may not lawfully be granted, to the advancement of the public revenue, upon the reasons and grounds annexed." S.P. Dom. Feb. 27, 1654-5, xciv, 103.

[13]See, e.g., *Vox et Lacrimae Anglorum; or the True Englishmen's Complaints to their Representatives in Parliament, Humbly Tendered to their Serious Consideration at their Next Sitting,* praying, among other things, for "the putting down of monopolies." S.P. Dom. Car. II Feb. 6, 1668.

discovered on research, that the issue was no longer a live one. After the Restoration the Crown found itself much hindered in the exercise of its prerogative by the growing strength of Parliament.[14] During the Commonwealth the patent system was virtually suspended and at the Restoration, Charles II agreed to submit all applications of a mechanical or philosophical nature to the examination of the Royal Society.[15] From that time forward, patentees for industrial purposes are no longer heard of except for new inventions and companies created by statute with powers for

[14]Macaulay, *History of England*, 209; Cunningham, *English Industry and Commerce*, II, 201, 205.

Thus when it was proposed, after the Restoration in 1664, to renew the pin monopoly which had been set up in the time of Charles I (cf. S.P. Dom. Car. I, cccc, 87; cccii, 122; Privy Council Register, March 18, 1640, xvii, pt. I, fo. 376), although the plan received the support of Charles II (S.P. Dom. Car. II, lxxix, 120; xci, 95) it was felt necessary to have the arrangement confirmed by Parliament. The bill met with vigorous opposition (Hist. MSS. Commission, *Seventh Report*, 179) and the opinion of the times toward monopolies may be gathered from the fact that at a meeting of the wiredrawers, who opposed the bill, one of the members remarked that the last King had lost his head by granting such patents (cf. S.P. Dom. Car. II, xciii, 60, 61). After the bill was dropped, attempts were made, without success, to promote the scheme before the Privy Council (Hist. MSS. Commission, *Ninth Report*, 451).

[15]During this period the tendency was for patent privileges to be granted by act of Parliament rather than by the more usual method. See, e.g., the statutes relative to Buck's Invention, 1651, c. 2, referred to in Scobell's *Collections of Acts and Ordinances during the Commonwealth* and reprinted in 1 W.P.C. 35.

15 Car. II, c. 12 (1663): Marquis of Worcester for a steam engine.

22 & 23 Car. II (1670): Howard and Watson for sheathing vessels with thin sheets of lead instead of copper.

9 & 10 Wm. III, c. 43 (1697): Act for the better encouragement of the Royal Lustring Company.

10 & 11 Wm. III, c. 31 (1699): Thomas Savery for a new invention for raising water and occasioning motion to all sorts of mill-work by the impellent forces of fire. This was the first steam engine which was actually applied to do work.

11 & 12 Anne, st. 2, c. 15: An Act for providing a public reward for such person or persons as shall discover the longitude at sea.

5 Geo. I, c. 8 (1732): Lombe's patent of Sept. 9, 1719, for engines for making silk, extended.

12 Geo. II, c. 23: Joanna Stephens for the discovery of a medicine.

16 Geo. II, c. 25 (1743): Elwick for an engine.

22 Geo. II, c. 53 (1748): An Act vesting in Pownoll's children an invention which he did not live to complete.

24 Geo. II, c. 28 (1750): Michael Menzies for a machine for conveying coals.

regulating some branch of trade.[16] The free exercise of the prerogative, although preserved in terms by the later statutes relating to patents for inventions[17] was, to all intents and purposes, restrained within the limitations of the Statute of Monopolies by the Bill of Rights of 1689, Section II of which enacted that "no disposition by *non obstante* of or to any statute or any part thereof shall be allowed." Thus the claim of the Crown to dispense with the law and by the exercise of its prerogative to grant monopolies either in evasion or in direct defiance of the statute was finally abrogated and the policy of industrial supervision was left generally to Parliament. The introduction of the excise completely transformed the method of collecting the revenue. The monopoly scheme of regulating, encouraging, and stimulating trade now changed into the policy of accomplishing the same results by tariff, while leaving industry free, within the protected area, to work out its salvation according to its own principles and theories. The policy of refusing to grant charters or letters patent in respect of matters within the mischief of the Statute of Monopolies may be said to have become fixed after the decision in *East India Co.* v. *Sandys*.[18]

The Statute of Monopolies, although it took some time before it became fully effective, is a landmark in the history of law. Although nothing more than a declaratory act, it crystallized the whole concept of the modern patent system into one compendious whole. It stated the basic foundation of the patent systems of most of the civilized countries of the world, and has had a profound effect on the development of industry and the useful arts. While other jurisdictions have, in the statutory establishment of their own patent systems, departed from its wording, they have not departed from its principles to any extent; and it is a significant fact that in England, where it was born, it still remains, despite the considerable number of statutes which have since been passed relating to patents, the base and foundation of this branch of the law. Just as the Statute of Monopolies did not disturb the exercise of the Crown prerogative in the granting of patents, but declared in statutory form only the limitations for such grants which had been established by the common law, so the present

[16]Cunningham, *English Industry and Commerce*, II, 205.
[17]Cf. Patents, etc. Act, 22 & 23 Geo. V, c. 32, s. 97.
[18](1684) 10 St. Tr. 371.

Imperial Patents and Designs Act[19] provides that nothing in the Act shall take away, abridge, or prejudicially affect the prerogative of the Crown in relation to the granting of any letters patent or to the withholding of a grant thereof. And the section of the Act which defines an invention[20] provides that an invention "means any manner of new manufacture the subject of letters patent and grant of privilege within section 6 of the Statute of Monopolies." Any statute which has remained for over three centuries as the basic foundation of a continuing legal concept must take its place with the great enunciations of the world's legal principles.[21]

[19]22 & 23 Geo. V, c. 32, s. 97.

[20]S. 93.

[21]The Statute of Monopolies is still in force and effect *ex proprio vigore*. The Province of Ontario has re-enacted the statute in similar terms and it will now be found as c. 323 of R.S.O. 1897 in the Appendix, volume IV of R.S.O. 1937. Cf. Fox, "Abuse of Monopoly" (1945) 23 Can. Bar Rev., 353.

XIV. ANALYSIS OF THE MONOPOLY SYSTEM

THE judgment of history has almost universally condemned the monopolies. They have been regarded by most of the modern writers whether in the field of law, of history, or of economics, as constituting unwarranted interferences with the liberty of the subject and with his freedom of trade. They have been viewed as the means of oppressing the poor, of raising the prices of commodities, of hampering industry and retarding the growth of a sound economic policy of industrial and commercial expansion. In the face of such sweeping condemnation it needs a full amount of resolution to assert a contrary view. But discretion must not bar the road of history, and prudence has no part to play in the formation of historical judgment. Evidence is the only sure footing; and that must be sifted with caution. From the same evidence, conclusions diametrically opposed may be arrived at with complete honesty, as the records of our appellate courts all too clearly show. But the doctrine of *stare decisis*, while it may make good law, will make bad history, if the conclusions or judgments based upon the facts of history are followed as precedents without independent study and consideration.

It would seem that there are, in the main, two classes of judgment already delivered concerning the monopolies, the one contemporary and the other modern. The contemporary judgment laboured under the disadvantage of having to bear with the abuses and oppressions attendant upon the monopolies without having the benefit of the all-embracing view of the ultimate purpose of the monopolies. That judgment suffered from lack of perspective. If a man went short of a commodity for a time, if he had to pay more for it, if his house were searched in the supervision of the monopoly, his anger and annoyance would tend to strip him of the calmness of judgment necessary to appraise the original reason for the existence of the monopoly and the end it might have been designed, *by the grantor*, to accomplish. Monopolies touched almost everyone in his daily life and his daily needs. It is not surprising that the irritations engendered by them affected an appraisal of their worth.

The modern judgment has been formed on the basis of two considerations. In the first place, modern opinion is prone to found itself on the contemporary judgment, and to follow it without inquiring whether any other factor should be considered. In the second place, we are apt to confuse our judgment of the propriety and efficacy of a monopoly system for those times with a judgment of its expediency and utility today. Because a system would not be fitting or proper for our economy today is not to say that it would not be fitting and proper in an earlier day. The world progresses, and not only do economic theories change but the factors on which they are based change or pass away. Now that we have something that the men of the sixteenth and seventeenth centuries did not and could not have, namely, the perspective of history, the duty devolves upon us of assessing the fitness and usefulness of the monopoly system, not as an individualized problem of personal impact but as a national policy deliberately set up as a motive force and inherent factor in a planned system of economy. If we do that, the judgment of today on any question which agitated the contemporary minds of past centuries may well be different from what it then was.

It is suggested that the approach to the problem has heretofore been from the wrong angle. The questions for decision should not be whether the monopolies were in themselves good or bad; whether they were abused or not; or whether they did or did not occasion oppression, extortion, and resentment. Those questions have been answered long since. It would seem that the proper approach lies in an examination of the intent behind the establishment of the system, and the effect upon legal institutions and thought occasioned by the operation and breakdown of the monopoly policy in its broader aspects, and its resurgence, in its narrow and proper sphere, from the ashes of failure to ultimate success, as one of the great contributing factors to industrial and scientific development. The questions for decision are whether the monopoly system was a reasonable and expedient system for the times in which it operated; whether it was designed and instituted from proper or improper motives; whether it should bear the odium that has surrounded it for centuries past; and whether we can, from considering and answering these questions, draw any principles and concepts which will serve us usefully today and in the future.

The value of the monopoly system from an economic standpoint has already been assessed completely and fully,[1] and from those assessments one conclusion is inescapable. In their operation, some of the monopolies laid a grievous weight on the people, tending rather to shorten supply than to increase it and to enhance prices unduly to the great hurt of the subject. The charge has been made also that quality suffered, and that, upon every consideration, monopolies and the monopoly system were wholly bad. The evidence is clear that in their operation, some were hurtful, and that, throughout the seventeenth century, they occasioned so much public mischief and oppression that the clamour against them both in Parliament and in public was fully justified.

But monopolies and the monopoly system were touched with some redeeming qualities. Not all monopolies were bad, and it cannot be accepted that the system itself was wholly subject to condemnation. The monopoly system received its great trial through a testing period now centuries past. Much must be forgiven the economists of those early days who were endeavouring to establish sound bases for commerce and industry in a rapidly changing and expanding economy. They were groping for a desideratum. If they groped in the dark, it was their misfortune but not their fault. If they made errors, our present experience may enable us to censure, and at the same time, condone.

In all the attacks on monopolies the force is directed against the monopolies themselves and against their holders. Their effects in operation are used as the evidence upon which to condemn them. Upon the basis of their operation the attacks must succeed, for the evidence is too circumstantial and too cogent to argue otherwise. But the submission is made that such an attack is to some extent misdirected. The focus of inquiry and analysis should be upon the motive underlying the monopoly system, the reasons for establishing it in the beginning, and the persistence in adhering to a systematic monopoly policy on a national scale even after so much opposition to its operation had developed.

[1]Cf. Levy, *Monopoly and Competition;* Cunningham, *English Industry and Commerce;* Macaulay, Gardiner, *inter alia.*

Emphasis in this investigation should be maintained on the germination from the mass of the monopoly theory, of the seed of inventive and industrial encouragement, into the full flower of the modern patent system. Only from such an inquiry can we obtain an objective view of the propriety of the monopoly system, and, coupled with the judgment of the effects of the operation of the monopolies, draw some instruction for future service.

First, let us examine the contemporary legal opinion as to the validity and legality of monopolies. In the first place, we have considered at some length the *Case of Monopolies.*[2] Even Dodderidge, arguing as counsel for the defendant, admitted that monopolies were legal if the subjects derived benefit from them, or if they were necessary for the peace and safety of the realm, and the judgment proceeded generally on the basis that the monopoly of playing cards, declared illegal by the judgment, was not of benefit to all subjects, but only to one.

Sir Edward Coke, one of the leading figures in the attack on Mompesson and Michell in 1621, and a proponent of the Statute of Monopolies, passed three years later, had this to say on the subject:[3] "The King can prohibit or license *mala prohibita* and can restrain matters of pleasure and this for the public good although it may involve damage to private persons."[4] Furthermore, in defining a monopoly,[5] Coke was careful to include only those grants by virtue of which any person or persons "are sought to be restrained of any freedom or liberty that they had before, or hindered in their lawful trade." Any grant, therefore, which fell outside that definition was not, in Coke's view, a monopoly. Thus a grant which restrained the making or sale of a new manufacture could not be a restraint of any freedom or liberty which persons had had before, nor could it hinder them in their lawful trade. So, in the *Great Case of Monopolies*[6] Sir George Treby, afterwards Lord Chief Justice, in his argument for the defendant stated the prevailing view when he said "The nature of a monopoly consists in restraining a common right; it appropriates to one, or a few, what others had the lawful use of before."

[2](1602) 11 Co. Rep. 84; see ante 87.

[3]Co. 3 Inst. 181.

[4]Case of Monopolies (1602) Moore K.B. 671; 11 Co. Rep. 84.

[5]See ante 8.

[6]East India Co. v. Sandys (1684) 10 St. Tr. 371 at 386.

Bacon's views on monopolies may be gathered from a number of sources. When he was Attorney-General the patent for inns was brought to him, and, unwilling to accept the responsibility of settling the legal question himself, he asked that three of the judges might be associated with him in the inquiry. The result was a unanimous report in favour of the plan. The question of its general policy was then submitted to Suffolk, Montague, Winwood, Lake, and Serjeant Finch, and these men, differing from one another in character and in politics, concurred in recommending the adoption of the scheme.[7] As we have seen, the patents which caused the greatest agitation were those with respect to inns and alehouses and for gold and silver thread. If all these differing temperaments agreed on the propriety of the monopoly with respect to inns, it would need cogent evidence to show that the premises upon which they based their judgments were false. Obviously, the scheme proposed by the patent was an excellent one,[8] with much to be said in its favour, had it not been for the

[7]Gardiner, *History of England*, IV, 3.

[8]There were obviously, at that time, grave inconveniences to be apprehended in handing over the unrestrained management of local affairs to the local authorities. In the actions of the justices of the peace there was sure to be irregularity. This conflict between the central government and the local authorities is to be met with constantly during this period and it is evident on which side Bacon's sympathies lay. While the patent itself contains the only general statement on the government's views with respect to inns, nevertheless a quotation from a letter written by the King, long before the patent in question, will show something of the opinion of the times. In 1608 he wrote:

"Being informed of the excessive numbers of ale-houses, victualling and tippling houses within our realm, and of the great abuse in granting licenses for the same, and in setting them up and putting them down at pleasure upon suit and means made without due regard either to the number or the quality of persons so licensed, and that not without more charge to them than is warrantable, although the matter may seem to concern the meanest of our subjects, yet, inasmuch as we are answerable to God for toleration of disorders and vices, whether it be in great or small, specially where the care of our inferior and subordinate ministers appeareth to be wanting, we have thought good by the advice of our Privy Council to take a course for a reformation in this behalf." (The King to the Mayor and Justices of Southampton, March 3, 1608. Cott. MSS. Titus, B. III, fo. 1.)

The preamble to the patent for inns gives the ostensible reasons for its issue in the following terms:

"Forasmuch," it runs, "as great disorders groweth by the abuse of innes in this our realme, and where we are informed that sithence the fifte yeare of the

part played in its execution by human nature. In like measure, the gold and silver patent had the laudable object of preserving intact the country's bullion rather than having it dissipated in the making of thread and lace. Even if it were based on a false economic theory, the underlying motive was that of benefitting the subjects of the realm.[9] In recommending these patents which

---

raigne of our predecessor Edward the Sixte, late Kinge of England, dyvers and sondry persons have taken uppon them of their owne heade and without anie lawful authority to keepe innes, or houses in the nature of innes, which weare not innes before that tyme; whereby they have incurred the daunger of lawe, and are by the due course of the lawes of this our realme to be suppressed and putt downe from keeping of a common hostery or inne, and yett, nevertheles, mannie of the said persons are meete and convenient to keepe innes and dwell in howses and places fitt for itt; of whom many, knowing the daunger, have made suite for our grace and licence, and the reste itt is like will be desirous of the like grace and safetie; and because the authority of Justices of the Peace extendeth not to the licencing of innes and common hosteries, and the Justices of Assize by reason of theire other manyfolde ymployments and the shorte time whereunto they are confyned in theire circuitts cannot have leizure to take sufficient information whoe may be fitt persons for such licences to be granted to them; Wee therefore, &c." (Commission to Mompesson and others, March 3, 1617, Pat. Roll., 14 Jac. I. part 22.)

Following this preamble, the patent granted to Sir Gyles Mompesson, Gyles Bridges, and James Thurburne, authority to survey all the inns in the kingdom, and to inform themselves of the due keeping of the assizes of bread and horsemeat, and to treat with such as desired to keep inns, being men of substance and honest life, and thereupon to draw up a licence with a yearly rent reserved to the Crown. This licence was to be under the hand of Mompesson, and at least one other commissioner, and under the seal of the office. It was to be presented to the Justices of Assize, or, if it referred to a place to which they did not come, to the Chief Justice. Unless the Justices declared that the proposed innkeeper was a person of ill-fame, they were bound to sign the licence. The justices were to have 5*s.* for each signature. The rents were to go to the King, excepting that each commissioner was to have £100 a year for his trouble, with an additional £100 to Mompesson as receiver of the rents and fines.

[9]In his comment "On Four Letters from Lord Bacon to Christian IV, King of Denmark" (1867) 41 Archaeologia, 219 at 265, S. R. Gardiner observes: "The bulk of the gold and silver thread used in England during the first years of James's reign was imported from the Continent. Fowle and Dyke discovered the method of the foreign manufacture or learned it from others, and at great cost introduced it into England. It then appeared that a manufacture had been previously carried on by a different method, but only on a very small scale. It was by the energy of Fowle and Dyke alone, that a competition with the foreign manufacturers was rendered possible, and, in consideration of this, the sole right of making the article by any method whatever was conceded to them. Experi-

later caused so much agitation and contributed in some measure to his fall, Bacon was acting in full conformity with the best legal opinion of his time. Not only did the judges agree with the patent for inns as above mentioned, but Coke, who was more likely to be opposed to Bacon, stated his opinion that the patent was good.[10] Bacon's views were those of his time, particularly those on the doctrine of prerogative, which was inextricably bound up with any question touching patents. And those views, which were generally shared, neither ceased nor were materially altered in current acceptance by Bacon's fall from power.

Even at the time of the Long Parliament, Peyton[11] laid down this definition: "Patents are Lawfull which are nott *ad Damnum Populi*, and where it is good for the buyer and seller,"[12] and Coke,[13] in 1620, noted that some patents were good in law, if ill in execution. In the *Great Case of Monopolies*[14] Jefferies, L.C.J., expressed the prevailing view when he said: "Now if the subjects of England had not, before this grant, a freedom and liberty to trade to the Indies against the king's royal pleasure, the charter at the bar will be no monopoly within that rule."[15]

The second point of consideration is whether, in the grant and operation of these patents of monopoly, the Crown acted for the good of the realm or from motives of personal gain. The grant of patents was established as a settled policy in the reign of Elizabeth

---

ence has taught us that it is impolitic to make such wide concessions. But is it necessary to accuse of dishonesty the statesmen of all parties, including men of such different character as Ellesmere, Suffolk, and Bacon, because they held that the grant ought to be given to those who had really benefited the country by meeting foreign competition?"

Nor must it be forgotten, in connection with the patent of 1616, that Yelverton afterwards affirmed that for seventeen months, "Ellesmere stopped it; . . . but afterward, and upon proof it was a new invention, he passed it." (Notes of Yelverton's speech, House of Lords MS.) Cf. Gardiner (1867) 41 Archaeologia, 219 at 241. Cf. chap. VIII, note 79 for a fuller discussion.

[10]Proceedings and Debates, I, 65; Gardiner, *History of England*, 4; see also Vin. Abr. 437, Article Inns, s. 9; Bulst., I, 109; Bac. Abr., tit. Monopoly.

[11]F. 66.

[12]Cf. D'Ewes, ed. Notestein, 248.

[13]1 Parl. Hist. 1193.

[14]East India Company v. Sandys (1684) 10 St. Tr. 371 at 542; Skin. 132.

[15]Jefferies was here referring to the definition of illegal monopoly given by Coke in 3 Inst. 181, cited 8.

and the system was continued at an increasing rate during the reigns of James I and Charles I up to the Long Parliament in 1641, a period of almost a century. If the evidence shows that the Crown enriched itself materially by its grants during that time, it would constitute grave and weighty evidence in favour of the suggestion that the Crown was acting largely from pecuniary motives. If, on the other hand, the Crown received little financial return, the conclusion is practically irresistible that some motive other than pecuniary considerations lay back of the systematic policy. Gardiner[16] states that "a careful examination of these grants will convince us that they were not open to the charges which are habitually brought against them. They were not made with the object of filling the Exchequer. They were not made, primarily at least, with the object of filling the pockets of the courtiers." An examination of the royal profit from a number of the grants accentuates this statement. Cunningham[17] points out that the monopoly of the foreign market in wool granted by Edward III in 1337 resulted in very little gain to the King, probably because all the profit went to the factors.[18] The monopoly for the working of the alum deposits, set up as a government undertaking by a patent of 1607, and specially exempted from the Statute of Monopolies,[19] cost James I thousands of pounds instead of bringing him any revenue; and over the two reigns of James I and Charles I the operation did not return to the Crown a pittance of the investment.[20]

The exchequer was not greatly enriched by the returns from the monopolies. In the debate on the glass patent,[21] when it was declared to be a grievance, Coke reported to the House that £1,000 per annum had been reserved to the King, yet nothing had been paid.[22] The patents for inns and for alehouses and the monopoly of gold and silver thread engineered by the Buckingham group in the time of James I resulted in little return to the Crown.

[16]*History of England*, IV, 6.

[17]Cunningham, *English Industry and Commerce*, I, 325.

[18]Longman, *Edward III*, I, 117.

[19]21 Jac. I, c. 3, s. 11.

[20]Price, *English Patents of Monopoly*, 82 et seq.; Lansdowne MSS., clii.

[21]1 Jo. H.C. 622, May 16, 1621.

[22]By a special proviso this patent was excepted out of the Statute of Monopolies, s. 13. Cf. S. P. Dom. Add. Car. I, dxxi, 148.

Bacon, writing to Buckingham in 1620, advised him to give up the patents on the ground that in themselves they bore "no great fruit" and it would be better to "take the thanks for ceasing them than the note for maintaining them." From the whole number of the obnoxious patents, Gardiner states[23] that the Exchequer received less than £900 a year. It cannot be shown that a single penny found its way into Buckingham's pocket. Sir Edward Villiers received a pension out of the patent for gold and silver thread, but the pension was nothing more than a fair dividend on the money he had actually invested. Christopher Villiers, although entitled by the patent to a pension, never received more than £150 during the whole existence of the monopoly. He received an uncertain sum out of the patent for alehouses. Lord Purbeck, the remaining Villiers brother, received nothing.[24] The subsidy for the new draperies yielded the Crown only £100 annually.

The policy of Charles I, of setting a fee on each unit of sale and openly selling privileges to the highest bidder, improved the revenue to a certain extent, but an assessment of the result is shown by the following statement: "Projects of all kinds, many ridiculous, many scandalous, all very grievous, were set on foot; the envy and reproach of which came to the king, the profit to other men, insomuch as of £200,000 drawn from the subject by these ways in a year, scarce £1500 came to the king's use and account."[25]

[23]*History of England*, IV, 21.

[24]Gardiner, in a foot-note, at 21, gives an estimate of the total royal return from all the patents of £1,883 of which £1,000 came from the glass patent. S.P. Dom. cx, 35. The latter sum, however, should not have been reckoned, as it was paid out again in a pension to Bowes. Price, at 32, shows that Gardiner has over-estimated the revenue to the Exchequer and gives authority to show that hardly £50 was derived from the true monopoly rents.

[25]Clarendon, *History of the Rebellion*, bk. I, 148. Charles was more fortunate than his predecessors in obtaining revenue from the monopolies, but his gain was only a pittance of the total. Price (*English Patents of Monopoly*, 43) points out that, shortly before the Civil War, the wine licences brought in £30,000 a year, tobacco £13,050, soap £30,825, cards and dice £750, and a modest rent from the alum industry. Bearing in mind that the royal revenues were expected to bear the expense of all the burdens of state, including the army and navy, these sums seem paltry enough when regarded as the beginnings of our present excise tax. All that was needed to make the process respectable and legitimate was to remove the authority for levying the impost from the Crown to Parliament and to change the name from "monopoly" to "excise." Pym, speaking in the Commons on November 7, 1640, on the subject of grievances, said: "In monopolies and such

The cloth working project assigned to the new Company of Merchant Adventurers by patent in 1615,[26] an attempt to "develop the resources of the realm and render it economically independent,"[27] ended in complete failure and without any return to the King. Although it is true that James was looking for means of raising money after he dismissed Parliament in 1614, his need is not to be taken as the only motive for granting the patent. Of course, the Crown hoped to get revenue out of some of its monopoly grants, for which it can hardly be censured. Royalty must live the same as commoners; and the charges against the royal revenue were by no means light. If a monopoly could be made the means of increasing the revenue, it was a reasonable expedient.[28]

In the case of the salt monopoly, Charles I was pursuing an entirely proper economic policy. All salt had formerly been

---

like, the third part comes not to his majesty's coffers, as to instance in that of Wines. The King hath only £30,000 per ann. upon them, whereas the Wines, in the gains by the Patent, come to £80,000 at the first, from the time of their arrival; and being drawn, come to £230,000 per ann. and the same proportion holds in all other monopolies; hereby it appears, how much the subject is damnified, and how little the king gains." 2 Parl. Hist. 551; see also Rush. IV 23.

According to the version of this speech, discovered by Forster in the British Museum (cf. 129, n. 29; 144, n. 28) Pym spoke as follows: "The King, for instance, hath reserved upon the monopoly of wines thirty thousand pounds rent a year; the vintner pays forty shillings a ton, which comes to ninety thousand pounds; the price upon the subject by retail is increased two-pence a quart, which comes to eight pounds a ton, and for forty-five thousand tons brought in yearly, amounts to three hundred and sixty thousand pounds; which is three hundred and thirty thousand pounds loss to the kingdom, above the King's rent! Other monopolies also, as that of soap have been very chargeable to the kingdom and brought very little treasure into his Majesty's coffers. Thus it is that the law provides for that revenue of the crown which is natural and proper, that it may be safely collected and brought to account; but this illegal revenue, being without any such provision, is left to hazard and much uncertainty, either not to be retained, or not duly accounted of."

During the Long Parliament Sir John Clotworthy noted that "upon monopolie Tobacco business a great grievance a great losse to the Kingdome and small profitt to the King." D'Ewes, ed. Notestein, 14. Peyton (f. 6) elaborates this: "Tobacco, engrossed by one Mr. Carpenter, and Mr. Little who pay the King £2,000 per annum, yields to them their rent to the King and all other charges deducted £100,000 per annum." See also Hume, *History of England*, chap. LIII.

[26]Gardiner, *History of England*, II, 387.

[27]Cunningham, *English Industry and Commerce*, II, 294.

[28]Cf. S. P. Dom. 1635-6, pref., viii; Strafford's Letters and Despatches, ed. Knowler, I, 193; Cunningham, *English Industry and Commerce*, II, 288.

imported, and there could be no question of the desirability of introducing the manufacture into England, rather than depending for its continued supply upon foreigners. The payment to the Crown in return for the monopoly could hardly be complained of in view of the loss of revenue from the diminution of customs duty owing to the commodity being no longer imported.[29] That the use of monopolies was recognized as a legitimate means of raising revenue may be seen by the fact that in the Long Parliament in 1640, a member moved "to consider of the King's revenue and to make reparation for Monopolies, shipp-monie, and other things taken away."[30]

In assessing the place which the monopoly system occupies in history—whether it is to be subjected to opprobrium and disfavour on the one hand or to praise and a just appreciation of its merits on the other—no factor is so important for consideration as the motive which actuated the making of the grants and the setting up of the monopolies complained of. We have discussed at length the character of Elizabeth, her constant care for the welfare of her subjects and the safety of the realm, her desire to make the country strong and self-sufficient. Nowhere is this more evident than in the monopolies granted by her in respect of the manufacture of ordnance and gunpowder. At the beginning of her reign there was a frightening need for ordnance.[31] Supplies of saltpetre and sulphur for gunpowder, and of iron and copper for ordnance could only be procured through ports controlled by prospective enemies. By 1591 English cannon were acknowledged to be the best in Europe, and even the Spaniards tried to buy them.[32] The monopoly for the making of iron in 1575[33] was granted as being "of a service done

[29]In speaking of the patent for gold and silver thread, Gardiner observes: "Part of the profit expected was derived from an equivalent for the customs duty lost by restriction of importation. The duty upon foreign gold and silver thread had been 3*s*. 4*d*. a pound. And this custom had been farmed in the early part of the reign for £200 a year. The 3*s*. 4*d*. was now imposed upon all the gold and silver thread manufactured in England, and it was probably hoped that the sum raised would far exceed that which had been obtained by the import duty." S. R. Gardiner, "On Four Letters from Lord Bacon to Christian IV, King of Denmark" (1867) 41 Archaeologia, 219 at 264.

[30]D'Ewes, ed. Notestein, 146.

[31]S.P. Dom. Eliz. vii, 5, Oct. 4, 1559.

[32]S.P. Dom. Eliz. ccxliv, 116.

[33]Pat. Roll. 17 Eliz., Feb. 14.

greatly to our honour and the benefit of our realme." Despite the contemporary and subsequent protests concerning the patents for sulphur in 1565 and for saltpetre in 1561 and 1587[34] the necessity for their supply was greater than any inconvenience. Thus in the debate on monopolies in 1601, Cecil said to the House: "There is another Patent for Saltpeter, that hath been both accused and slandered; It digs in every man's House, it annoys the Inhabitant, and generally troubleth the Subject: For this I beseech you be contented. Yet I know I am to blame to desire it, it being condemned by you *in foro Conscientiae*: but I assure you it should be fully sifted and tryed *in foro judicii*. Her Majesty means to take this Patent unto her Self, and advise with her Council touching the same. For I must tell you the Kingdom is not so well furnished with Powder now as it should be."[35] Not only was the House satisfied with this explanation but the monopoly was expressly excepted by the Statute of Monopolies[36] and was not set aside until 1641.[37] It was again revived for two years during the Civil War.[38]

In principle little distinction can be drawn between the sulphur and saltpetre monopolies of the Elizabethan and Stuart periods and the monopolistic control of atomic energy at the present time. In the last analysis, the presently existing control is exercised for the same purpose as the monopoly respecting gunpowder over three centuries ago, namely, the instinct of self-preservation. There does not exist today one person capable of answering adequately and perfectly the question of whether the monopolistic control of atomic energy by the present holders of the secret is for the good or ill of mankind. Only history can answer that question. For it must not be overlooked that atomic energy *may* have beneficial as well as destructive qualities and uses, and the withholding of those benefits from the mass of mankind *may*, so long as they are withheld, stay the march of progress. Nor is high-mindedness the criterion by which this decision will ultimately be judged. No

[34]Foed., xiii, 650; S.P. Dom. Eliz. xvi, March 30, 1561.

[35]D'Ewes 653. The "saltpetre men" were not however permitted to do as they pleased. Cf. Attorney-General v. Tirrette and Shelton (1597) Hawarde, 76, where two of them were fined and imprisoned for abuse of authority.

[36]Sec. 10; see also Proclamation of James I, January 16, 1623, appointing a sworn proof-master for testing the quality of the gunpowder made with the saltpetre.

[37]16 Car. I, c. 21.

[38]Cunningham, *English Industry and Commerce*, II, 61.

one can question the patriotism and spirit of Burleigh who was responsible for the foundation of the saltpetre monopoly, and yet that was acknowledged to be the worst and most irksome of all. The present monopolizers *may* be condemned by the historians of the future for their monopolistic practices, just as some historians today condemn the earlier monopolists. What must be remembered is that each age, in general, conducts its affairs as seems best, according to the knowledge and experience available, and *ex post facto* judgment is not always just.

The soap monopoly, granted to the London Company of Soap Makers by Charles I in 1631, has been characterized as one of the worst. Of its successor, granted to the Westminster Company, Price says[39] that "whatever may be said in justification of other monopolies of the period, opinion is unanimous in condemning this one." Dr. Price's stricture is, of course, applicable not so much to the monopoly itself as to the manner in which it was abused. Cunningham, to whom Price refers for this unanimous condemnation, is on the contrary, not only other than condemnatory of the monopoly but careful to point out the propriety and expediency of its grant. He says: "In attempting to interfere with the manufacture of soap the government was on more delicate ground, as the industry had been practised in the country from time immemorial. Under existing conditions, however, the supply was inadequate, and the country was forced to pay largely for the importation, not only of materials for the manufacture, but of the soap itself. There seemed to be a good case for interference." Nor must it be forgotten that the Court of Exchequer, after litigation running over a number of years, held the grant to be good.[40] The maintenance of a proper supply of necessary commodities can hardly be condemned as a motive force for the grant of monopoly patents, and monopoly is usually the best way of ensuring adequate supply, as any manufacturer will readily testify.[41]

[39]*English Patents of Monopoly*, 123.

[40]See post 184.

[41]Thus, in Re Brownie Wireless Co. Ltd. (1929) 46 R.P.C. 457 at 474 per Luxmore, L.J.: "It is admitted that a patentee is entitled to work his invention either by himself or his licensees; he may limit the number of his licensees, and he may select such licensee at his own free will and pleasure, subject only to this, that he must not abuse his monopoly rights. If the patent is in fact being worked in such a way that the public demand is being supplied to an adequate extent and

We have already seen[42] that Elizabeth's policy was one of establishing trade and industry within the realm. Burleigh, the master mind of the reign, had the systematic policy constantly in mind of establishing a permanent supply of all things necessary for the life of the kingdom and its people. He encouraged English merchants to seize every opportunity to push trade. His desire to develop the mining industry for the purpose of ensuring a domestic supply of ordnance[43] was only one example of his insistence upon the fostering of domestic industries. He was anxious to make England economically independent; and he pursued as a deliberate policy the granting of patents for new enterprises and industries. The effect of monopoly upon an existing trade was carefully examined, the policy being designed either to promote new inventions and processes or to introduce new ones into the realm and to protect them on that ground, even if they were well known beyond the seas. The patents for glass, salt, and starch were all based on this policy. Elizabeth and her adviser, Burleigh, were actuated practically entirely by considerations of patriotism—the establishment of new industries, the stimulation of old or weak industries, the development of new inventions and processes, the maintenance of a constant supply of commodities of good and proper quality, and the systematic fostering of a policy of self-sufficiency for the realm.

The governments of James I and Charles I had ideals no less high. They were actuated by motives not of fiscal policy but of

---

on reasonable terms, no one can complain, and public interest does not in such circumstances require that a particular manufacturer who desires to manufacture and sell the patented article should be granted a licence so to do. Indeed, the public interest may itself require that the number of licensees shall be limited, because it may well be that the public interest is best served by ensuring a steady supply of the patented article by preventing the flooding of the market, and a drastic reduction of price by wholesale competition."

When incorporated in 1631 the Company of Soapmakers of Westminster was prepared to deliver wholesale, and promised the Crown to supply 5,000 tons of soap yearly. Cf. Levy, *Monopoly and Competition*, 6.

Observations like those of Lord Justice Luxmoore, quoted above, are of much weight in considering the importance to be attached to statements concerning "existing abuses of monopoly power" such as are contained in the Report of the McGregor Commission on *Canada and International Cartels*, October 10, 1945.

[42]Ante 80.

[43]See ante 66, 67, 169.

sound trade development. If pecuniary profit from the monopolies flowed into the royal revenues in addition, that should merely have entitled the Crown and its ministers to greater credit as being astute men of business. But so much has popular, ill-informed clamour warped judgment on this point that it has become necessary to show that the royal revenues were barely enriched at all from the monopolies. It should not be a ground for condemning the monopolies if they had been profitable. In modern times, it is no criticism of any of the many government monopolies to say that they are operated profitably. Indeed, it is hoped and expected that they will be; and governments take every opportunity to boast of the fact. Apparently it all depends on who gets the credit. The Crown, operating the earlier monopolies with little if any profit, has received little but odium for its "greed and rapacity." A modern democracy, operating monopolies far more extensive than any of the seventeenth century, receives nothing but praise for succeeding in doing what the Crown hoped to do three centuries earlier.

In assessing the effect of the monopoly policy in the time of the Stuarts, it is important not to overlook the underlying motives. James has been accused of rapacity and unscrupulous disregard of the welfare of his people and of the convenience and furtherance of trade and industry in his handling of the monopolies. What is the evidence on which this charge is based? A careful and authoritative writer has stated:[44]

> The English Government under James I and Charles I attempted to realise a very high idea of duty with regard to the internal condition of the realm . . . in the earlier part of the seventeenth century the Stuart kings endeavoured to maintain positive standards of what appeared good and fair. They were not content to put down abuses, but aimed at so ordering the economic life of the country that every man should have opportunities of practising his calling, and that he might be able to count on obtaining the necessaries of life at reasonable prices and of good quality.

The Stuarts tried to do two things which were mutually inconsistent and hence irreconcilable: to introduce improvements

[44]Cunningham, *English Industry and Commerce*, II, 285.

So also, Unwin, no friend of the monopoly system, says: "The idea of protecting the interests of the poorer industrial classes was a real motive of Stuart policy. . . . The records of the Privy Council during the period when Charles governed without a Parliament leave no doubt as to the sincere desire of the King or of his ministers to promote the interests of the working classes." *Industrial Organization*, 143.

in the arts and industry and to render each person's position stable and secure. Positive security is impossible except in Utopia, and is probably quite undesirable in any other place and time. Constant interference with business life flowing from national regulation and supervision was entirely repugnant to the Englishman's idea of liberty. The citizen's desire was then, as now, to be allowed to buy and sell with as little interference and regimentation as possible. He wanted economic freedom unless it could clearly be shown that interference was proper in his own or the national interest; and it is significant that agitation developed primarily against those on whom had been conferred some special privilege to interfere in private business transactions and supervise and regulate the conduct of business affairs.

The only defence against the attack on patents was that they tended to promote the general good. While this was mainly true of the industrial patents, it was not true of many of the others and in no way relieved the gravity of the charges of oppression with respect to their enforcement and supervision. During the debate on monopolies in 1601 it is clear that the attack was not so much on the monopolies themselves as on the methods used by the agents or substitutes of those who were the actual patentees. Thus, during the debate in the House, Mr. Martin said: "I do speak for a town that grieves and pines, for a Country that groaneth and languisheth under the burthen of monstrous and unconscionable Substitutes to the Monopolitans of Starch, Tinn, Fish, Cloth, Oyl, Vinegar, Salt, and I know not what, nay what not? The principallest commodities both of my Town and Country are ingrossed into the hand of those blood-suckers of the Commonwealth."[45]

So, during the same debate, Mr. Spicer of Warwick said that: "I speak not, Mr. Speaker, neither repining at her Majesties Prerogative, or misliking the reasons of her Grants; but out of grief of heart, to see the Town wherein I serve pester'd and continually vext by the Substitutes and Vicegerents of these Monopolitans, who are ever ill-disposed and affected Members. . . . The Substitutes for Aquavitae and Vinegar came not long since to the Town where I serve, and presently stayed sale of both these Commodities; unless the Sellers would compound with them,

[45]D'Ewes 645.

they must presently to the Council-Table."[46]

When Cecil gave his undertaking to the House to carry out the Queen's message of November 25, 1601, and to revoke or suspend monopolies, he made particular point of the letters of assistance from the Privy Council supporting the monopolies. In stating that these should be revoked and no more granted, he put his finger on the crucial point of the agitation when, in speaking of these letters, he said, "But to whom do they repair with these letters? To some outhouse, to some desolate widow, to some simple cottage, or poor, ignorant people, who rather than they would be troubled and undo themselves by coming up hither, will give anything in reason for these caterpillars' satisfaction."[47]

The same thing is evident in the proceedings against Mompesson and Michell in 1621. The patent for the control of inns had been originally designed for the accomplishment of a worthy and necessary object, the control of innkeepers, and the supervision of the quality and price of the food they served to the public. The patent was issued as the result of a project of Mompesson and two others,[48] but it soon became apparent that the scheme was unworkable. No scale of charges was set by the patent, with the result that it was to the patentees' benefit to sell as many licences as they could and to charge as high a fee as possible for them. But the oppressions of Mompesson, into whose pocket went most of the fees rather than into the Exchequer, were as nothing compared with those of his agents.[49] The right of search and supervision was prostituted from its purpose of proper regulation into a means of harsh and unceasing oppression, and it was not until the impeachment of Mompesson and Michell in 1621 that innkeepers received any relief.

The patent for the supervision of alehouses, granted to Almon and Dixon in 1618, furnishes another example of abuse by agents or substitutes. By an act of 1552,[50] alehouse keepers were required to be licensed by the justices of the peace. Owing to constant complaints of drunkenness and the resort of undesirable characters to the alehouses, it was felt desirable for their control to pass into

[46]D'Ewes 644.
[47]1 Parl. Hist. 635; D'Ewes 652.
[48]Pat. Roll., 14 Jac. I, pt. 22; Bacon's *Works*, ed. Montague, XII, 486.
[49]1 Parl. Hist. 1192.
[50]5 & 6 Edw. VI, c. 25.

the royal hands. Accordingly the recognizances for good conduct to be given by the keepers to the justices of the peace were immediately to be certified into the King's Bench. Almon and Dixon were appointed by patent to supervise and control the conduct of the alehouse keepers. There can be no question but that many abuses were rife in the conduct of the alehouses. The act of 1 Jac. I, c. 9, illustrates the deplorable conditions by stating that it was designed to put down "inordinate haunting and tippling in Innes and Ale-houses" and that "the true and principall uses of ale-houses" are for the relief of wayfarers and not for the "entertainment of lewde and idle people."[51] The act and the patent granted to Almon and Dixon were unworkable because of the character of the parochial officers delegated to supervise their execution. But behind these nominal patentees, certain of the members of the court, among them Christopher Villiers, half-brother of the Duke of Buckingham, exercised the real power. They cared nothing for supervision and regulation, but made a regular practice of extorting fines and compounding with alehouse keepers who were enabled to break the law with impunity. The laudable object of the patent was to restrict the number of alehouses, and to promote a reasonable degree of temperance. Unfortunately, it did not have the desired result, but gave rise to scandalous exactions and abuses. But the motive behind the patent was good: it was in its execution by venal officials that abuses arose.

In both of these cases, that of the patent for inns and that respecting alehouses, the name of Sir Francis Michell has an unsavoury repute. He was charged with having abused his powers as a magistrate by using them in support of the oppressions and iniquities complained of. The patents were subjected to severe attack during the debate on grievances in 1620, both Noy and Coke speaking strongly against them. Another member stated that, instead of reforming abuses, the patents merely raised the reckonings on the poor traveller, and, instead of restraining the number of innkeepers, on the contrary, increased them. "Every poor man that taketh in but a horse on a market day is presently sent up to Westminster and sued, unless he compound with these patentees."[52] There could be no question of Michell's guilt, and,

[51]See also 4 Jac. I, c. 5; 21 Jac. I, c. 7.

[52]1 Parl. Hist. 1194.

on May 4, 1621, Parliament sentenced him to fine, imprisonment, forfeiture of office, and degradation from knighthood.[53] The patents for inns and alehouses were cancelled by a proclamation of James dated March 30, 1621,[54] and the patent for alehouses was further condemned by the Commons in its session of April 21, notwithstanding the fact that it had been previously cancelled by proclamation.[55]

There is much confusion as to the conduct of persons holding monopolies; and any blameworthy conduct on their part has reflected against the monopolies themselves with no inquiry as to whether there is any connection between them. This situation is well illustrated in the case of the grant of a patent in 1616 to Bassano and Vaudrey[56] on the ground that they had discovered and perfected a method of keeping fish alive in boats, thereby enabling them to bring fresh salmon and lobsters from Ireland. The application for the grant was supported by the Fish-mongers' Company, and the patent was thereupon granted to Bassano and Vaudrey giving them the sole right of bringing into the realm fish from such rivers and seas as had not theretofore supplied fish to the London market. Instead of establishing fisheries in Ireland, however, the agents of the patentees laid in wait for fishermen at the mouth of the Thames, and forced them to hand over their catch for a mere fraction of the price to which they would normally be entitled. The patent itself seems of a somewhat unusual nature to a modern reader, but it had its advantages for the times in which it was granted. There was much indignation aroused by the action of the patentees' agents, and the patent is sometimes cited as an example of the abuse that arose from the grant of improper monopolies.[57] To take such an attitude is to confuse the issue, for the actions of the agents of the patentees should be distinguished from the objects of the patent. These actions were nothing more than simple robbery and extortion by way of piracy. As well might a monopoly patent be stigmatized

[53]Jo. H.L. III, 89, 95, 108.

[54]Jo. H.L. III, 73.

[55]Jo. H.C. I, 586.

[56]Jan. 27, 1615-16, Pat. Roll., 13 Jac. I, pt. 16; Proceedings and Debates, I, 295. The patent was held to be a grievance by the House of Commons, April 25, 1621. Cf. 1 Jo. H.C. 591.

[57]Gardiner, *History of England*, IV, 8.

as odious and unclean because its owner was a member of the fraternity of Hounslow Heath. The offences of the person must be kept separate and distinct from the offences flowing from the patent system. As Noy pointed out in the course of the debate in 1620, "There are some patents that in themselves are good and lawful, but abused by the patentees in the execution of them, who perform not the trust reposed in them from his Majesty."[58] So also, in the final putting down of grievances by way of monopoly by the Long Parliament, it is quite apparent that the agitation was not so much against the monopolies themselves as against the searchers and substitutes who oppressed the subject with their illegal excesses of authority.[59]

There is, it is felt, little need to justify those monopolies which were granted in consideration of the setting up of new manufactures based upon inventions made within the realm or introduced from abroad. We have already considered them at some length. Every encouragement was constantly given to those interested in and capable of introducing and practising new arts, processes, and manufactures. The grants of this type during the reign of Elizabeth have been collected and summarized by Hulme.[60] They cover a wide variety of subject matter including the making of white soap, saltpetre, dredging machines, machines for draining marshes, sulphur, Spanish leather, ovens and furnaces, salt, grinding machines, glass, frisadoes, knife hafts, earthen pots, grinding mills, sailcloth, drinking glasses, trumpets, train oil, armour, starch, writing paper, flasks, mathematical instruments, and instruments of war, and processes for tempering iron, saving fuel, calendering cloth, manufacturing iron, steel, and lead, and refining coal. We need not concern ourselves further at this stage with this type of patent monopoly other than to point out that there never has been, until the present time, any criticism of this type of exclusive privilege. It was always recognized at

[58]1 Parl. Hist. 1192.

[59]See also Coke's opinion, 1 Parl. Hist. 1193. In the session of 1620-1 the House, in enquiring into the various patents, made a distinction between those that were unlawful *in origine* or *in executione*. Even though a patent was held void "in the Original" the holder of such patent was not put out of the House if there was "no Offence in the Execution." See, e.g., 1 Jo. H.C. 566.

[60]Hulme (1909) 3 A.A.L.H., 117; see also Fairman, "Early English Inventions" (1885) 12 Antiquary, 1 et seq.

common law as a proper subject for a prerogative grant, and the Statute of Monopolies made no change in this conception.[61]

Nor can it be said that the monopoly grants made by the early Stuarts were all of an objectionable character. One of the first acts of the reign of James I with regard to monopolies was the revocation of the patents for tin in response to complaints concerning them.[62] The subject matter of those grants made by royal proclamation during the reigns of James I and Charles I shows a considerable preponderance of mechanical and commercial substance over those grants which can be considered of a harmful, monopolistic type. The catalogue of patents issued for new inventions demonstrates the continuation of a fixed policy of encouraging and stimulating both new and old manufactures. Among those matters of manufacturing techniques which were protected by grants during this period were the manufacture of smalt,[63] pumping engines,[64] hard wax,[65] the manufacture of glass according to a new process using coal instead of wood, the great waste of timber being a matter of serious concern,[66] the making of white and red lead,[67] machines for the boulting and dressing of meale,[68] rape-seed oil for use in cloth making,[69] cast iron pots, kettles and pans,[70] leaden seals,[71] blue paper,[72] as well

[61]During the debate in the Commons on the examination of the patent for gold and silver thread, Coke expressed his opinion that the prohibition of importation of gold and silver thread was against the law, whereupon the Solicitor-General said: "If this a Manufacture newly invented, it may have a Patent of Privilege for some few Years." One of the members added that the patent was improper because it was prejudicial to the silk men and other ancient trades, saying that no longer time of privilege should be allowed than was necessary to instruct others in the manufacture. Another member expressed the opinion that the patent constituted a grievance because it was "not a new, but an old, Invention." 1 Jo. H.C. 543, March 7, 1620-1.

[62]Rot. Pat. p. 3. m. 13. Steele Proc. no. 955.

[63]Feb. 4, 1608-9: Steele Proc. no. 1072.

[64]Sept. 21, 1612: Steele Proc. no. 1124.

[65]Feb. 3, 1618-19: Steele Proc. no. 1239.

[66]May 23, 1615: Rot. Pat. p. 5. n. 1.; Steele Proc. no. 1164; Feb. 25, 1619-20: Steele Proc. no. 1273. See also Rot. Pat. p. 30. n. 7. d. Steele Proc. no. 1707.

[67]Oct. 5, 1622: Rot. Pat. p. 3. n. 32; Steele Proc. no. 1337.

[68]July 31, 1623: Steele Proc. no. 1360.

[69]Dec. 18, 1624: Steele Proc. no. 1390.

[70]Oct. 19, 1635: Steele Proc. no. 1708.

[71]Jan. 17, 1637-8: Steele Proc. no. 1761.

[72]July 20, 1666: Rot. Pat. p. 5. n. 5. d; Steele Proc. no. 3466.

as methods for the steeping of grain,[73] the printing of linen cloth,[74] the saving of fuel and lessening of smoke,[75] and for the construction of kilns for the drying of malt and hops.[76] The proclamations relative to the prohibition of the import of alum,[77] the manufacture of saltpetre,[78] and gunpowder,[79] were designedly made with the object of giving work to the people and ensuring an adequate supply of war material. Even the much derided patents for the manufacture of gold and silver thread[80] show an endeavour on their face to protect the purchaser from faulty workmanship, and the final grant, after the Mompesson affair, to the Company of Gold Wire Drawers of London[81] indicates that protection of the public and not royal revenue was the motivating force behind the monopoly. Of course, monopolies were granted which seem to us now to be improper as e.g., monopolies of playing cards and dice,[82] tobacco pipes,[83] the repairing of arms,[84] and for printing on one side of paper only[85] but, on balance, a fair observation is that

[73]June 5, 1613: Rot. Pat. p. 30. n. 18; Steele Proc. no. 1130.

[74]Oct. 25, 1619: Steele Proc. no. 1260.

[75]June 25, 1634: Rot. Pat. p. 16. n. 2. d; Steele Proc. no. 1679.

[76]Feb. 8, 1637-8: Rot. Pat. p. 15, n. 5. d; Steele Proc. no. 1762.

[77]June 19, 1609: Rot. Pat. p. 2. m. 3; Steele Proc. no. 1082; March 16, 1617-18: Rot. Pat. p. 11. m. 14. d; Steele Proc. no. 1207.

[78]Jan. 13, 1589-90: Steele Proc. no. 820; Jan. 1626-7; Rot. Pat. p. 4. m. 11. d; Steele Proc. no. 1499.

[79]Jan. 16, 1622-3: Rot. Pat. p. 16. n. 18. d; Steele Proc. no. 1346.

[80]March 22, 1617-18: Rot. Pat. 16 Jac. I, p. 12. m. 29. d; Steele Proc. no. 1208 Oct. 10, 1619: Steele Proc. no. 1258.

[81]June 16, 1623: Rot. Pat. p. 10. m. 4. d; Steele Proc. no. 1359.

[82]July 21, 1615: Steele Proc. no. 1169; May 15, 1637: Rot. Pat. p. 15. n. 17. d. Steele Proc. no. 1747. Monopolies of this type were justified because they were for "vain and unnecessary commodities." S.P. Dom. Car. I, ccccli, 110, April, 1640.

[83]May 27, 1620: Rot. Pat. p. 19. m. 18. d; Steele Proc. no. 1282.

[84]July 11, 1620: Rot. Pat. p. 14. n. 21; Steele Proc. no. 1284.

[85]1620: Steele Proc. no. 1261. In the Cholmondeley Papers, Historical Manuscript Commission, *Fifth Report*, 355, appears the following note:

"Folio, seven leaves [13 written pages], A.D. 1620, endorsed. *My Collection of Monopoly Patents*. There are particulars of 96, all in the reign of James I. One dated 30 Oct., 13 James I, is to Roger Wood and Thomas Symcott for 30 years of the sole imprinting of all briefs and other things upon one side, except Proclamations and other things granted by Patent. Another is for the making and selling a back skreen for the ease of the back. Another is to Don Diego de Sarmiento de Acunas, Earl of Gondomar, and his heirs, to carry out of England

the great majority of monopolies were granted with the object of improving the conduct of manufacture and the condition of the people. An impartial view is materially assisted by the following observations of Gardiner: "It would, unfortunately, be impossible to give here even a general idea of the nature of the forty or fifty grants recalled in 1621. I can only state that my impression, after an examination of them as they stand upon the patent rolls, is that, though they are full of faults according to the ideas of the present day, and not without grave errors leading to abuses which speedily recoiled upon their authors, these grants are, taken as a whole, an expression of a definite commercial policy, bearing frequently the impress of Bacon's mind, and by no means the mere makeshift contrivances for extracting money from the purses of the subjects which it has now for two centuries and a half been the fashion to represent them."[86]

The great trading monopolies, which were set up in Tudor and Stuart times, have also come in for their share of opprobrium having been attacked as the means of debarring the rest of England from trading with three-fourths of the known world and as being the chief cause of the decline in England's foreign trade in the eighteenth century. That they were free from objection cannot be asserted, but that they constituted the only likely and probable method of achieving success in the extension of England's foreign trade at the time of their formation is too obvious to admit of question. A number of these exclusive trading companies were incorporated by royal authority, among them being the Muscovy Company of 1553, the Eastland Company of 1579, the Company of Merchant Adventurers, the Guinea Company, and the Virginia Company. Those that called forth the most opposition were the Turkey Company incorporated in 1581 with the exclusive right to trade in Africa and certain parts of Asia, amalgamated with the Venice Company in 1592 under the name of the Levant Company; the East India Company, originally incorporated in

---

yearly six horses, six hawks, and 12 dogs without any taxation or imposition. Another is for making a stone to imitate marble."

A summary of a number of the grants made in the reigns of Elizabeth and of James I up to 1617 appears in an article entitled "Early English Inventions" by T. Ordish Fairman in (1885) 12 Antiquary, 1, 61, 113.

[86]Gardiner, "On Four Letters from Lord Bacon to Christian IV, King of Denmark" (1867) 41 Archaeologia, 219 at 226.

1600 with a monopoly of trade from the Cape of Good Hope to Japan; the Hudson's Bay Company, chartered in 1670 with the monopoly of trade in large areas around Hudson Bay; and the South Sea Company, chartered in 1711 with a monopoly of trade in the southern part of the western hemisphere. Of these, the last named failed in 1720, the Levant Company was still trading in the eighteenth century, the East India Company was absorbed by the Crown on the establishment of British rule in India, and only the Hudson's Bay Company, shorn of its monopoly, remains in existence at the present time.

Among the motivating forces behind the patent grants which must not be left unconsidered was the desire for the maintenance of quality. The establishing of high and proper standards of quality had always been a function of the guilds,[87] and in pursuit of their duty of maintaining those standards many ordinances were enacted by the guilds for the regulation and supervision of the various trades and the journeymen and apprentices working in them. Quality could only be maintained if men who were properly skilled in the trade were appointed to supervise, with a right of search into all that was done by the craftsmen. They had to see to the quality of the materials as well as the skill of the workmen. The right of search and supervision amounted, in effect, to a police system.[88] This system, based as it was upon an ordered policy, transferred itself naturally from the guilds to the industrial monopoly system. The early patents almost all contained recitals to the effect that they were granted for the purpose of ensuring not only proper supply but also the proper quality of the commodity which was the subject of the monopoly. Thus, the smalt patent to Twynphoe *et al.*[89] recited the undertaking of

[87]See ante 36, 135.

[88]Cunningham, *English Industry and Commerce*, I, 342.

[89]17 July, 3 Jac. I; cf. 1 W.P.C. 9.

The basis of grant for patents of this type is aptly illustrated by further recitals in the patent to Twynhoe and his associates: "Whereby not only great profit and commodity is very likely to ensue to many our loving subjects, but also divers of our poor people, for their relief and comfort, shall be continually set on work and employed in and about the making, working and compounding of the said blue stuff; and fit it is that they, the said [patentees], should receive some convenient recompense and reward, as well for their great labour, charges and expenses, in attaining to the skill and art of making, working and compounding of the said blue stuff, as for the common good, which by their good endeavours shall thereby ensue to the whole realm." Cf. 1 W.P.C. 9.

the patentees to make within England "a certain blue stuff called smalt . . . and which shall be as good, perfect, and merchantable, as the same or like stuff called smalt, made, wrought and compounded in the parts beyond the seas, and brought into this realm, are or usually have been, and in such quantity and proportion as shall be sufficient for the use and employment of our loving subjects." The patent to Baker[90] recited the undertaking of the patentee "to make sufficient quantity of the said smalt to serve for the use of this our kingdom, and to serve the same with smalt as good and as cheap as the like brought from beyond the seas."[91] The glass patent to Mansell,[92] as a consideration for the grant, recited that "the glass made by the said Sir Robert Mansell was perfectly good, clear, and merchantable, or rather better glass than formerly was made with wood."

The soap monopoly, formed during the later years of James I[93] and continued by Charles I, was quite clearly undertaken with a desire to supply the country with an improved grade of soap.[94] The records of the City of London show that a trial was held on April 6, 1624,[95] as a result of which a committee of aldermen issued a report on the quality of the soap being made. It is probable that Charles regarded his part in the soap monopoly as being for the benefit of both the public at large and the Crown; and on this

Nor is it without significance that by this time it had become the general practice to insert in letters patent a proviso first met with in a grant of 1593, that if the grant should be found hurtful or prejudicial to the subjects or to the state, and should be so certified by the Privy Council, it should from thenceforth be void and of none effect. See, e.g., the patent to Twynhoe et al., 1 W.P.C. at 10.

[90]6 Jac. I, Feb. 4; cf. 1 W.P.C. 11.

[91]See also patent to Baker, 16 Jac. I, Feb. 16; cf. 1 W.P.C. 12.

[92]21 Jac. I, May 22; cf. 1 W.P.C. 17.

[93]20 Jac. I, Feb. 23, 1623.

[94]The interest in the quality of soap is apparent from the fact that the proclamation of June 28, 1632 (Rush. II 136, 143, 187), provided for the appointment of an assay office and an assay master who was required to report to the Court twice annually on the quality of the soap. The proclamation commanded that only good material be used, such material to be only pure olive oil and rape oil, and that no soap should be sold except such as was marked good and serviceable by the deputies of the Society of Soap Makers. The patentees, in obtaining their patent, undertook to make good soap and to sell it for not more than 3*d.* per pound which, as the patent recited, was cheaper than theretofore. See also Decree of Star Chamber, Aug. 23, 1633. Rush. II 189; Rush. III appendix, 60, 109.

[95]Cf. Price, *English Patents of Monopoly*, 119.

basis his actions were not only plausible but perfectly defensible.[96] That he took a sincere interest in the quality of the product is apparent from the fact that he erected an office for the assay of soap by giving the Company of Soap Makers of Westminster[97] powers of search over other manufacturers.[98] When the London Company of Soap Makers was incorporated to succeed to the monopoly of the Westminster Company, it ran into litigation extending over a number of years and culminating in a judgment of the Court of Exchequer in 1656. The report of the case recites that the King, by letters patent of May 22, 1637[99] for preventing and reforming of abuses in the trade of soap making, and the better government of that trade, had incorporated a company of soap makers who paid to the King for the charter the sum of £43,000 besides 6*d*. a ton impost upon the soap made by its members. The plaintiffs were of the company, but the defendants were not, and had not served an apprenticeship of seven years in the art of soap making as required by an ordinance of the company. It was held that the patent was not within the statute against monopolies. The judgment is interesting as showing that this monopoly, reviled generally as being of the most irksome kind, was nevertheless of sufficient merit to call forth the following expression from the judge who upheld its validity:

> I know very well that common and vulgar judgments run high against all such patents and condemn them before they understand them, as being contrary to the liberty of the subject and the freedom of trade; but they that consider them better are not so hasty in their censures; for certainly upon a serious consideration, all such patents and by-laws as tend most to the well regulating and ordering of trades and the better management of them, so that the benefits of them may be derived to the greater part of the people, with a prejudice to some particular persons, have always been allowed by the law, but patents which tend to the engrossing of trade, merchandise, and manufacture, though never so small value, into one or a few hands only, have always been held unreasonable and unwarrantable.[100]

---

[96]Cunningham, *English Industry and Commerce*, II, 290.

[97]Patent Jan. 20, 1631-2; cf. Rush. II 136.

[98]Proclamation June 28, 1632; cf. Rush. II 187.

[99]Cf. Proclamation December 28, 1637. Rot. Pat. p. 15. n. 7. d. Steele Proc. no. 1759, reciting patent of May 22, 1637.

[100]Hayes et al. v. Harding et al. (1656), Hardres 53. Bacon, in his *Abridgement*, under the title Monopoly, said on this point: "Also it seems to be the better opinion, that the king may grant to particular persons the sole use of some particular employments where an unrestricted liberty might be of dangerous consequence to the public." Cf. Mod. 256; 3 Keb. 792; 3 Mod. 75.

Both James and Charles made constant efforts to maintain the quality of English manufactures, to assess prices, regulate wages, and supervise trades.[101] They set up an elaborate system of search and supervision depending upon the co-operation of central and local authorities. All this was swept away by the Civil War. As pointed out by Cunningham,[102] the elaborate system of search, which the earlier Stuarts had instituted, fell to pieces, and the government abandoned the attempt to exercise an effective supervision over the quality of goods.

Examples could be multiplied showing the efforts made, by the use of the monopoly system, to regulate and supervise quality and standards of manufacture. That the efforts did not entirely succeed is traceable not to any fault inherent in the system itself but to qualities of mind residing in the instruments chosen to exercise the supervision. The proof of the efforts of the Tudors and the early Stuarts to maintain quality lies in the fact that, when their system of supervision and search broke down after the outbreak of the Civil War, the quality of English workmanship suffered a severe relapse and was the subject of general complaint and petition.[103] If competition, the use of trade marks, industrial pride, and self-interest, are today among the controlling factors in the maintenance of quality (which they obviously are), an earlier day needed supervision and search to accomplish the same purposes in an industrial system the policies and practices of which had not yet crystallized into rules and doctrines of appropriate commercial policy and honest industrial usage. Just as the alnager was a necessary supervisor of quality in the cloth trade,[104] so the creation of an office and the conferring upon an individual of the responsibility of detecting poor workmanship was a proper and reasonable expedient to apply to the constituent elements of an expanding industrialism. The monopoly system offered a natural field within which the creation of such supervisory offices could function with success. This was the basis upon which the Stuarts proceeded. That it failed of its purposes was not a fault of the monopolies but of the venality and rapacity of those who

[101]Cunningham, *English Industry and Commerce*, II, 203.

[102]*Ibid.*, 203.

[103]*Ibid.*, 204.

[104]See ante 40.

were appointed to the offices of search and supervision.[105]

A reading of the parliamentary journals and records of the proceedings goes far to indicate that the greatest antagonism displayed against the monopolies was not so much in respect to their existence but, as we have already shown,[106] to the manner in which they were supervised. In examining and considering the complaints and grievances aired from time to time concerning the monopolies, it should not be overlooked that many of them provoked no adverse criticism. Elizabeth's policy of trade regulation was based on the laudable aim of introducing new arts and industries and stimulating old. James's policy, dictated not only by changing times and changing conditions on the Continent, and the removal of the threat to England's safety by invasion, but by the considerable increase in crafts provided by the stimulation injected into industry by the monopoly system, was on the contrary one of maintaining established trade and the quality of production. For the monopoly policy of Elizabeth and Cecil had done its work, and had done it well. Industry had expanded and new trades and arts had multiplied at an amazing rate. James conceived his function to be even more the maintenance of quality than the introduction of new arts; and in this policy he was followed by Charles. To that end the stress was laid on supervision and inspection. There was ample precedent for this procedure in the cloth trade where, from time immemorial, the alnager had inspected, measured, and sealed the cloth offered for sale, so that no person should be deceived by

[105]"The chief object which James and Charles set before themselves in regard to the industry of the country was not the introduction of new forms of skill; they were much more occupied in providing for the supervision of the existing industries, so that the wares produced might be of good quality. This was of first importance with regard to goods manufactured for export; according to common consent, the best means of promoting commerce lay in maintaining the reputation of English cloth in foreign markets. So far as articles produced for home consumption were concerned, there was a strong tradition for inspecting them minutely and carefully. The organization of craft gilds, and the whole machinery of the assize of bread and ale, had been primarily concerned with caring for the interest of the consumer, in every town and village. Under the Stuarts, strenuous efforts were made to organize a system of industrial supervision on national lines, and thus to maintain a high standard of quality for goods of every kind, manufactured for sale either at home or abroad." Cunningham, *English Industry and Commerce*, II, 296.

[106]At 131, 141, 174.

buying inferior cloth.[107] Adopting the same system, officials were appointed for the supervision of the trade in tin,[108] lead, iron,[109] the manufacture of silk,[110] the supply of coal, the management of alehouses,[111] and other matters of everyday commerce.

The use of corporations as a means of evading the prohibitions of the Statute of Monopolies has already been discussed.[112] But these corporations had their precedents in the associations, fraternities, and guilds which, from time immemorial, had been incorporated for the express purpose of regulating trade and supervising quality. As an incident of the police regulatory power went the right of search, which right is evident in some of the early charters.[113] With Charles, however, the procedure was a combination of supervision by the companies and by officials appointed by the government. In the case of the soap monopoly Charles endeavoured to maintain the quality of the product by giving to the patentee company a right of search with respect to other manufacturers.[114]

A storm of indignation arose over the actions of the searchers which culminated in the explosion of Sir John Culpeper in the Long Parliament in 1641. When Culpeper spoke of the "monopolies and polers of the people," it was not the existence of monopolies he was quarrelling with so much as the fact that "they have marked and sealed us from head to foot." It was the searching and supervision that irritated him and his contemporaries so much. When Charles's government ended, with it went the system of national supervision of industry.[115] No doubt this occasioned some injury to English trade and some deterioration in quality, for the

[107]See the proclamation of James, Sept. 16, 1605, which recited a proclamation of Elizabeth appointing an alnager for drapery, July 13, 1594.

[108]Cf. 1 Parl. Hist. 928.

[109]Proclamation, July 29, 1637.

[110]Proclamations of 1606, 1632, and 1639.

[111]1 Jac. I, c. 9; 4 Jac. I, c. 5; 21 Jac. I, c. 7; cf. Foed., XVII, 236.

[112]See ante 131, 132.

[113]E.g., the statute 8 Eliz., c. 11 gave the wardens of the London Haberdashers a right of search in respect of hats and caps. The statute 5 Eliz., c. 8 gave a similar right of search with respect to leather to the Companies of the Curriers Saddlers, and Shoemakers. The statute of 18 Eliz., c. 15 conferred a right of search on the wardens of the Goldsmiths' Company to ensure that plate which bore their mark was of the proper quality.

[114]Proclamation June 26, 1632.

[115]Cunningham, *English Industry and Commerce*, II, 285, 311.

temptation to reduce quality upon the collapse of all systematic searching and inspection must have been almost irresistible. The balance, however, was no doubt restored by manufacturing pride combined with the growing conception of the use and value of trade marks already well established in the cloth and cutlery trades.[116]

From the above discussion certain conclusions may be drawn with relation to the monopoly policy of Elizabeth and the early Stuarts. These conclusions may be summarized as follows:

(1) The grant of the industrial monopolies, under the systematic policy of national industrial expansion and encouragement, together with the recognized system of trade regulation and supervision, was in harmony with contemporary legal opinion.

(2) The financial returns to the Crown were at the most negligible, and, while it may be admitted that fiscal policy and the hope of raising revenue were contributing factors, they were not the main nor even an important motivating force in the grant of monopolies. Had the policy stemmed from cupidity and avariciousness it could not possibly have endured for a century, but would have been abandoned when it was seen to be practically useless as a means of raising revenue.

(3) The motives for the monopoly policy were generally laudable, and were by no means subject to the condemnation levelled at them either presently or contemporaneously. These motives were:

- (*a*) The maintenance of adequate supplies of commodities necessary for the welfare of the people.
- (*b*) The rendering of the realm self-sufficient and independent of supply from foreign countries.
- (*c*) The maintenance of quality of manufactured goods.
- (*d*) The promotion of trade and the expansion of industry by the introduction of new arts, processes and inventions arising either within the realm or by introduction from abroad, this policy being designed to encourage new industries and to stimulate old and failing industries.

(4) The policy of search and supervision attached to the principle of the maintenance of quality of manufactured goods

[116]Fox, *Canadian Law of Trade Marks*, 6.

was in itself a good and proper objective, but the venality and corruption of those appointed for the purpose defeated the object sought. The monopolies themselves were not what provoked the adverse criticism so much as the actions of the searchers and agents of the patentees.

The final conclusion must, therefore, be that it was not the monopolies which were bad, but only their abuse.[117] The monopoly policy of the sixteenth and seventeenth centuries was based on sound and legitimate economic principles and was a sincere effort to further new industries and arts. The patents issued in pursuance of that policy were, in general, designed to promote laudable objects, but were perverted in operation. The patent system, as a system based on a preconceived national policy, has, subject to the abuses attendant upon the operation of the individual monopolies, a long and honourable tradition. It may be compared, in a sense, to the refinement of the precious metals. Out of a block of rock and dirt much dross must be carved and refined away before the clear and shining core of gold can ever meet the eye. So, the dross of abuse and impropriety in the monopoly system had to be refined in the furnace of experience before the gold of the present patent system emerged to take its place as the greatest contributory factor to modern industrial progress. A full and impartial examination of history will show that the present attacks on the validity of the patent system cannot be sustained by the appeal to the past which is usually made. The iniquities of the past, so glibly spoken of as counterparts to the abuses of the present, disappear under the light shed by the commercial and industrial advantages which accrued from the system, just as the so-called abuses of patents today, thrashed over and over in speech and in print, appear, from a full, impartial study and reasoned judgment, to be but a mite in the scale against the benefits accruing from a patent system properly administered.

[117]Cf. Wigmore, "The Public Interest in a Sound Patent System" (1943) 195 Journal of Commerce (no. 15082, March 11), 24.

XV. THE FUTURE OF THE PATENT OF INVENTION

THE foregoing history of the law relating to monopolies by patents has, it is submitted, more than an antiquarian interest. It sheds light on the vital question of the reason for the existence of monopolies and of the necessity for a patent system. That system as we see it in operation today, is not the result of inspired thinking, but is a dictate of historical necessity. Nothing can prove that statement as simply and as effectively as a study of the causative factors which originally operated to call the system into being. There is, on the American continent particularly, a tendency to believe that the patent system sprang full-born, like Pallas Athene from the forehead of Zeus, when in the United States the framers of the Constitution incorporated the provision[1] investing Congress with the power to enact the necessary legislation "to promote the progress of science and useful arts, by securing for limited times to authors and inventors the exclusive right to their respective writings and discoveries." So too, in Canada, the Supreme Court has pointed out that the basis of grant in Canada rests upon an express statutory limitation not by any means identical with the prerogative basis as in England.[2] Such views are, however, open to question. The statutory enactments, it is submitted, are nothing more than the modern expression and acceptance of rights long since established and rendered necessary in a civilized state by the exigencies of human existence. In the United States the constitutional provision was nothing more than an instance of the delegation to the central government of one of the powers which the states already possessed, and which they had theretofore used for the purpose of granting patents to their own citizens as an exercise of the prerogative power formerly held by the Crown but, since the Revolution, asserted to reside in the people of the individual states. In Canada, the argument, as advanced by Mr. Justice Idington, that the basis for grant of

[1]Art. I, s. 8, c. 8.

[2]Electric Fireproofing Co. of Canada v. Electric Fireproofing Co. (1909) 43 S.C.R. 182 at 186 per Idington, J.

patent is one of statutory limitation, as distinct from Crown prerogative, and that widely divergent results have flowed from such distinction, overlooks the fact that, upon the adherence of Canada to the British Crown, the common law of England became the law of the country, and that the right to grant patents for inventions by the exercise of the prerogative was an integral part of the common law and had been recognized as such by the imperial Parliament in the Statute of Monopolies in 1624. This fact, considered in the light of the Quebec Act of 1774,[3] and the Constitutional Act of 1791,[4] raises considerable doubt as to the validity of Mr. Justice Idington's statement, and seems to indicate that the grant of patents in Canada is also founded on prerogative right, which was merged into the statutory right upon enactment, but not thereby extinguished. The study of the history and causes of the rise and development of the patent system, becomes, therefore, as Mr. Justice Holmes has pointed out,[5] a matter of necessity.

The patent systems of Great Britain, Canada, and the United States exhibit certain basic differences which might usefully be discussed. The reasons for the existence of these differences lie embedded in the memorials of industrial and constitutional history. We have already discussed[6] the backward position of England in the Middle Ages so far as the industrial arts were concerned. Compared with other countries the trade and commerce of the island kingdom were in an undeveloped condition undergoing a process of tardy growth in response to a combination of factors which eventually enabled the country to emerge as the great industrial centre of the world. The policy, stimulated by the religious wars of the seventeenth century on the Continent, of inviting foreign workmen to bring, under protection, their skills and dexterities to the building up of new and improved domestic industries, caused an influx of crafts to England which, coupled with the encouragement of local inventors and improvers, caused, by the time of the Stuarts, a reversal of the earlier position, and placed England in the industrial lead. In the eighteenth century the increased use of coal, urged on by the problems attendant on

[3]14 Geo. III, c. 83.

[4]31 Geo. III, c. 31.

[5]Holmes, *Collected Legal Papers*, 138. "Historic continuity with the past is not a duty, it is only a necessity."

[6]At 30, 61.

deforestation, combined with the invention and development of the steam engine, enabled England to maintain her pre-eminent position in the industrial and technical arts, at least until, during the nineteenth century, the centre of industrial production shifted across the Atlantic.

We have also seen[7] that this industrial development, assisted as it was by a considered and vigorous policy of encouraging industrial expansion by the use of paternalistic and compensatory protective measures, found a field of the type necessary for its existence in the securely integrated area of England under the control of a monarchy with sufficient strength and purpose to ensure its maintenance and continuity. To these factors, the constitutional history of England supplied the final causative force. Whereas in the continental countries the grant of monopoly rights by prerogative power continued unchecked, thereby in large measure precluding technical and industrial advance, England, alone of the European countries, had a Parliament strong and active enough to abridge the royal prerogative and restrain it within the limits which had been set by the common law. Whereas in other countries the promulgation of a patent law was accomplished as a legislative act reflecting the changing spirit of the times and springing into being as a full-fledged expression of that spirit, the patent law of England is but the present acceptance of a system which developed slowly out of the mass of trial and experience, disclosing in its philosophy the stigmata of its history. Thus the patent law of England, which antedated by a century and a half its statutory counterpart across the Atlantic, is still based upon an exercise of the royal prerogative.[8] Patents are therefore not the inalienable right of the English inventor but rather an act of grace and expediency on the part of the Crown. This principle has been adhered to in other parts of the Empire with the exception of Canada.

In the United States, on the contrary, the framers of the Constitution provided for the necessary legislation by investing Congress with the power of "securing for limited times to authors and inventors the exclusive right to their writings and discoveries." Based upon this constitutional provision, Congress has enacted

[7]At 27, 81.

[8]Patents and Designs Act, 1907, 7 Edw. VII, c. 29 amended by 9 & 10 Geo. V, c. 80, s. 97.

legislation which provides that, subject to certain conditions, the inventor may obtain a patent for his invention. Thus the right to obtain a patent is here expressed as being no longer a matter of grace or expediency but a right to which, upon fulfilment of the prescribed conditions, any person is entitled. It is not without significance that this new principle implying a duty on the part of the state to protect the intangible and incorporeal as well as the physical property of its people should have come into being in the same period that saw the American and French Revolutions. The law of France owes its similar theory of a grant as of right to the same spiritual causes and it is, therefore, of some consequence to note that, among the first acts of the representative legislatures of the two new republics, was the promulgation of a patent law at almost coincidental dates, the United States in 1790 and France in 1791. From the ideological factor inherent in each of these statutes most of the countries of the world, with the exception of the British Empire and Russia, have proceeded to enact patent laws based on the fundamental right of the individual to be protected in the fruits of his mental labour.

The patent law of Canada has taken a somewhat middle course, combining in its provisions some of the principles of the British law with those of the American. I have already suggested that, at least in its origin, the right to grant patents in Canada was a continuation of the prerogative power as it was exercised in Great Britain. I do not think there can be any serious question as to the validity of that opinion, and, although diligent search has failed to unearth any evidence of grants of patents for inventions having been made in Canada prior to 1792,[9] it is obvious

[9]A search in the Public Archives of Canada discloses that the earliest Canadian grant of exclusive privilege with respect to new inventions was in the form of an act or ordinance of 1792. This was a private act, being c. 7 of the statutes of that year, but it seems probable, from the use of the word "ordinance" in its title, that it was an order of the governor and council of Lower Canada, and not a legislative act in the modern sense. The Archives reveal a memorial dated October 22, 1795, addressed to "His Excellency Guy Lord Dorchester, Captain General and Commander in Chief of the Province of Lower Canada," begging "your Excellency's Patent" for "the exclusive right of making bricks" by means of a machine "lately discovered for the making of brick." The *Journals* of the Legislative Council of the Province of Lower Canada for the years 1816 to 1819 contain a number of petitions for the grant of exclusive privileges for newly invented devices. All these entries tend to show conclusively that in its origin, the patent system of Canada was founded on an exercise of the Crown prerogative, which was later merged in the statutory enactments.

that, according to constitutional practice, the prerogative right to do so could hardly be questioned when the provinces and territories were in the colonial stage of their development. But at any rate, when the decision was made to give statutory effect to the law of patents in Canada the first Act on the subject, the Statute of Lower Canada of 1823,[10] proceeded on the principle expressed in the Patent Act of the United States. This Act was duplicated in Upper Canada in 1826[11] and when, by virtue of the jurisdiction conferred upon it by the British North America Act, 1867,[12] the Parliament of Canada proceeded, in 1869, to pass a Patent Act applicable to the whole Dominion[13] it modelled it upon the existing United States Act of 1836, the operative granting section being in almost identical terms with that of the United States, providing that an inventor, upon certain conditions "may obtain a patent" for his invention. It is therefore proper to say that the prerogative right of granting patents in Canada has now been merged into the statutory system[14] and that the inventor no longer rests his claim on grace or expediency but is entitled to his patent *ex debito justitiae*. Canada probably constitutes the nearest approach of any country to the adoption of the

---

The Archives disclose no grants of this type under the French régime, the probable reason being that the sparsely settled nature of the country did not conduce to serious invention or the seeking of monopolies for any that might have been made. This explanation is, of course, highly speculative in character, but is the best that can be advanced until research discloses whether any further records exist.

The Archives of the Province of Ontario yield little or no assistance. The early records of the Province are incomplete and widely scattered due to several reasons: (1) At first it was the practice of the governors at the expiration of their term of office to take the records with them; (2) on two occasions the provincial records have been destroyed by fire; and (3) with the frequent change of the site of the capital, there was difficulty keeping the records intact.

The only record obtainable in the Province of Ontario prior to the passing of the Patent Act of 1826 appears to be an entry in the *Journals* of the House of Assembly of Upper Canada, March 6, 1811, to the effect that a bill to encourage useful arts and inventions in the Province was that day read for the first time. There is no record extant of what happened to the bill thereafter.

[10]4 Geo. IV, c. 25.

[11]7 Geo. IV, c. 5.

[12]30 & 31 Vic., c. 3, s. 91 (2).

[13]32-3 Vic., c. 11.

[14]Cf. Attorney-General for New South Wales v. Butterworth & Co. (Australia) Ltd. (1938) N.S.W.R. 195.

patent system of the United States at least so far as statutory framework is concerned.

There are, of course, numerous points of similarity and of dissimilarity between the patent systems of Great Britain, the United States, and Canada, the meticulous comparison and contrast of which would contribute little to the present discussion and has already been adequately done.[15] In general, the British system is designed to serve the national interest, while the system of the United States is designed to give denizens an advantage. The Canadian system, on the other hand, takes a somewhat middle course, being designed neither in the national interest nor in that of denizens. In the United Kingdom the grant must be obtained quickly while in Canada and the United States it may be long delayed. In Great Britain the only lawful patentee is the person who first makes the invention publicly known there by filing a specification. In the United States the only lawful patentee is the person who has conceived the invention, has been diligent in its development, and has not used it commercially in the United States for more than a year before he files a specification. In Canada the lawful patentee is the person who first reduced the invention to practical shape anywhere in the world provided he has not kept it secret, and who files a specification within two years of its first commercial use in Canada. But there is one principle upon which the United States system on the one hand, and the British and Canadian systems on the other, exhibit a fundamental difference. Under the American system the patentee within his domain is czar. The law does not require the inventor to manufacture his invention in order to sustain his patent. He may refuse to exploit his patent, he may practise it or grant licences for its use; he may "secrete" his patent and his invention and refuse either to manufacture or to permit others to manufacture without in any way endangering the validity of his patent.[16] Against such a situation the public is powerless to do anything except await the expiration of the term for which the patent has been granted. Under the British and Canadian systems the

[15]See Vojáček, *A Survey of the Principal National Patent Systems;* Biggar, *Canadian Patent Law.*

[16]American Lecithin Co. v. Warfield Co. (1939) 37 USPQ 177; 42 USPQ 180; 43 USPQ 520; B. B. Chemical Co. v. Ellis (1940) 45 USPQ 418; Berry v. Bohn Aluminum & Brass Corp. (1939) 43 USPQ 132; Hartford-Empire Co. v United States (1944) 323 U.S. 386 at 432.

principle is in complete antithesis. Under both these systems, patents are granted subject to certain conditions, and abuse of monopoly calls forth specified remedies which are available to the public. The Canadian Patent Act contains the declaration of the basis of grant of patents that "it shall be taken that patents for new inventions shall so far as possible be worked on a commercial scale in Canada without undue delay."[17] A similar provision appears in the British Act.[18] Both statutes contain definitive provisions[19] for controlling and prohibiting abuse of monopoly and, in a proper case, for punishing such abuse by revocation of any patent concerned. The comprehensive nature of these provisions is apparent from the declaration that the following acts constitute abuse of monopoly:

(1) Failure to make or to work the patented invention.

(2) Importation to the detriment of home manufacture.

(3) Failure to meet the demand to an adequate extent and on reasonable terms.

(4) Prejudicing, contrary to public interest, the country's trade or industry, or that of particular concerns by refusing a reasonable licence to others.

(5) Attaching unfair conditions to the acquisition, use, or working of the patented article or process.

(6) Using a patent for a process to prejudice the manufacture, use, or sale of materials used in that process.

In Canada the Commissioner of Patents[20] has power at any time after the issue of a patent to require the patentee to provide evidence as to whether a patented invention is being worked within Canada on a commercial scale, and if not, why such is not being done. At any time after three years from the issue of a patent, any person may, alleging abuse of exclusive rights as above mentioned, apply to the Commissioner for a compulsory licence permitting that person to make and use the invention. Upon such an application the Commissioner has power to order the grant of a compulsory licence, either exclusive or non-exclusive, upon such royalty as he shall decide is fair and reasonable, one of the principles being that he shall endeavour to secure the

[17]S. 65 (3).

[18]S. 27.

[19]Canadian Patent Act, ss. 64-71; British Patents Act, s. 27.

[20]In Great Britain the Comptroller.

widest possible use of the invention in Canada consistent with the patentee deriving a reasonable advantage from his patent rights. In a proper case the Commissioner has power to order the revocation of the patent. The British Act contains similar provisions, the Canadian sections having been copied from the British.

It is obvious that this fundamental antithesis is based in the industrial and constitutional history of the countries concerned. The deep opposition engendered by abuses of monopoly privileges in the Tudor and Stuart era, while it did not find statutory expression until fairly recent times, left so marked an impression on the development of the law that, once patents again became numerous with the advances in invention and the industrial arts, the deep-seated feelings evoked by historical memories made such provisions not only a legal but a practical necessity. From those memories the people of the new republic of the United States felt themselves free, or, at any rate, capable of coping with them without placing any restraint on the inalienable right of the inventor to be protected in the enjoyment of the fruits of his genius. Whether opinion considers the American or the British and Canadian system to be the more proper, divergent results have flowed from the adoption of each, results which are having a marked effect on the public attitude toward patents and will doubtless continue to have an increasingly important bearing on the public acceptance of, or antagonism to, the patent system.

The necessity for a study and appreciation of historical continuity with the past is well exemplified by the many attacks which are presently being made on patents and the patent system. The name of Mr. Thurman Arnold, has, in the United States, become so synonymous with this type of attack that the mere mention of his name tends not only to suggest the subject but to include a large measure of the essence of the quality and nature of the arguments presently being advanced for the abolition of the system. Mr. Arnold's thesis can be summed up in one sentence which he himself wrote:[21] "The principa smoke screens under which domestic and international cartels have cloaked their activities are patent laws"—and to Mr. Arnold cartels are anathema—abuses to be destroyed root and branch. The final report of the United States Temporary National Economic Committee

[21]Arnold, "The Abuse of Patents" (1942) 170 Atlantic Monthly.

relating to enforcement of anti-trust laws and proposed changes in the patent laws had this to say:

> No one can read the testimony developed before this committee on patents without coming to a realization that in many important segments of our economy the privilege accorded by the patent monopoly has been shamefully abused. It is there revealed in striking fashion that the privilege given has not been used, as was intended by the framers of the constitution and by the Congress, "to promote the progress of science and the useful arts," but rather for purposes completely at variance with that high ideal. It has been used as a device to control whole industries, to suppress competition, to restrict output, to enhance prices, to suppress inventions, and to discourage inventiveness.

In 1942 the Justice Department of the United States sponsored Senate Bill 2303 before the Senate Committee on Patents. This bill provided that: "The President may grant a license to any person under any patent or patents in respect to such manufacture, use, or sale upon such terms and for such period of time as the President may prescribe." Such a bill, granting such unlimited authority without any attempt at definition of its exercise, was not only "packed with dynamite for the destruction of the patent system"[22] but, had it passed, would have rung the death-knell of the patent system there and then. As one authoritative American writer has expressed it, there is "a persistent attempt under the guise of anti-monopoly control to create the public impression that there is something fundamentally wrong with our patent laws, with the purpose of so amending those laws as to completely emasculate and destroy the patent system."[23]

Until recently, the attack in Canada and Great Britain has not been so severe or so harsh. This is probably due to the fact that both countries have had in operation for a considerable number of years a system of compulsory licensing of patents which is designed to eliminate any real abuse of monopoly rights. The statutory enactments setting up this system[24] are based expressly on the principle "that patents for new inventions are granted not only to encourage invention but to secure that new inventions shall so far as possible be worked on a commercial scale . . . without undue delay." While such provisions naturally tend to soften the vigour and vehemence of attacks on patents

[22]Barnett, *Patent Property and the Anti-Monopoly Laws*, 393.

[23]*Ibid.*, 398.

[24]Canada, Patent Act, s. 65 (3); Great Britain, Patents and Designs Act, s. 27 (2).

and the patent systems in those countries which have provided for compulsory licensing, there is not wanting evidence of ill-informed antagonism to patents as being examples of improper monopolies. Thus, in the Report of the McGregor Commission on *Canada and International Cartels*, appears a number of statements which demonstrate an attitude of antagonism toward patents which, it can only be charitably inferred, is due to lack of practical contact and experience with them in the commercial field. Thus, one of the criticisms levelled at the patent system is in the following words: "The patent-holder thus has in effect a monopoly which protects him from competition from within the country and a sort of private tariff wall which protects him from competition from outside the country."[25]

The only rejoinder to such a statement is an admission of complete agreement with it. Not only is it a fact, but that is the whole purpose and intent behind the Patent Act as enacted by the Parliament of Canada. It is also the purpose and intent of the patent statutes of every other country in the world. It states succinctly and accurately the purpose for which a patent is and has always been designed, namely, to give adequate and proper protection and reward to an inventor in return for the benefit he confers upon the people at large. The proper criticism of the quoted remark is that, while it states an undisputed fact, the choice of language and the method of expression carry with them the innuendo of an impropriety which is totally lacking in practice.

The Report contains a further statement of the same type:[26] "British, Canadian and United States patent laws are thus used

[25]See McGregor Report, 46.

[26]See *ibid.*, 49. Probably the best answer to the present attack on patents and cartels is supplied by a quotation from the *Second Interim Report* of the British Board of Trade Committee on the Patents and Designs Act, April, 1946, 6, para. 25:

"It is easy to overestimate the part played by patents in creating and maintaining cartels, whether national or international. Several of the most important monopolies in this country exist with little or no help from patents, and it seems likely that, even where patents do form an important element in cartel arrangements, these arrangements could be re-constituted upon some other basis, even if patents were totally abolished. Where firms find it convenient and profitable to work together in regulating output and fixing prices, or where one or a few powerful firms desire to dominate smaller rivals, they will make use of whatever means come to hand to cement their agreements. Patents are often an available

for the purpose of ensuring that trading in that industry is strictly confined to national compartments. In those situations the foreign patents operate to prevent Canadian export trade."

The author of the Report evidently felt it quite improper for a foreign inventor or patentee to restrain any Canadian from infringing his patent by shipping Canadian-made goods into the foreign country in which such patentee holds a patent. Apparently Canadians should be able to infringe patents with impunity, providing they are foreign patents.

So, too, among the modern trends which endeavour to make capital out of the ever-popular device of using monopolies and patents as the whipping-boy, there must not be overlooked the public utterances of the hungry aspirants to public office who promise the abolition of all private monopolies in return for a single, gigantic monopoly to be held by the state. The danger is that the confused thinking of a considerable number of people may be influenced by these attacks on monopolies because—and here is the crucial fact that ought to be emphasized more often—unless monopolies are analysed and examined not only on a scientific but on a historical basis, the attack upon their propriety may seem to be sound and reasonable. It is only when they are so scrutinized that the true facts emerge, and that monopolies by patents, far from constituting a detriment to humanity and a handicap to progress, are seen to be one of the greatest assets to the development of civilization yet devised by the mind of man.

It is hoped that a perusal of the history of the development of monopolies and patents, as discussed in these pages, will already have demonstrated, to a discerning reader, the necessity and propriety of their existence. The protection of the inventor is demanded not alone by natural justice but equally on grounds of economic expediency. For the purpose of emphasizing the point it may be well to repeat the famous statement of Daniel Webster when, in 1852, he summarized the patentee's rights:

> The Constitution does not attempt to *give* an inventor a right to his invention, or to an author a right to his literary productions. No such thing. But the Constitution *recognizes* an original, pre-existing, inherent right of property in the invention, and authorizes Congress to secure to inventors the enjoyment of

---

means, but they are not the only one. No conceivable reform of the patent system, nor even its total abolition would, by itself, solve the problem of monopoly in modern industry."

that right. But the right existed before the Constitution and above the Constitution, and is, as a natural right, more clear than that which a man can assert in almost any other kind of property. What a man earns by thought, study and care, is as much his own, as what he obtains by his hands. It is said that by the natural law, the son has no right to inherit the estate of his father—or to take it by devise. But the natural law gives a man a right to his own acquisitions, as in the case of securing a quadruped, a bird, or a fish by his skill, industry, or perseverance. Invention, as a right of property, stands higher than inheritance or devise, because *it is personal earning.* It is more like acquisitions by the original right of nature. In all these there is an effort of mind as well as muscular strength.

Upon acknowledged principles, rights acquired by invention stand on plainer principles of natural law than most other rights of property. Blackstone, and every other able writer on public law, thus regards this natural right and asserts man's title to his own invention or earnings.

The right of an inventor to his invention is no monopoly. It is no monopoly in any other sense than as a man's own house is a monopoly. A monopoly, as it was understood in the ancient law, was a grant of the right to buy, sell, or carry on some particular trade, conferred on one of the king's subjects to the exclusion of all the rest. Such a monopoly is unjust. But a man's right to his own invention is a very different matter. It is no more a monopoly for him to possess that, than to possess his own homestead.

But there is one remarkable difference in the two cases, which is this, that property in a man's own invention presents the only case where he is made to pay for the exclusive enjoyment of his own. For by law the permission so to enjoy the invention for a certain number of years is granted, on the condition that, at the expiration of the patent, the invention shall belong to the public. Not so with houses; not so with lands; nothing is paid for them, except the usual amount of taxation; but for the right to use his own, which the natural law gives him, the inventor as we have just seen, pays an enormous price. Yet there is a clamor out of doors, calculated to debauch the public mind.[27]

The courts have been no less emphatic. Thus, the Supreme Court of the United States has said:[28]

The patent for an invention is not a conveyance of something which the Government owns. It does not convey that which, but for the conveyance, the Government could use and dispose of as it sees fit, and to which no one save the Government has any right or title except for the conveyance. But for the patent the thing patented is open to the use of any one. Were it not for this patent any one would have the right to manufacture and use the Berliner transmitter. It was not something which belonged to the Government before Berliner invented it. . . . It conveyed to Berliner, so far as respects rights in the instrument itself, nothing that he did not have theretofore. The only effect of it was to restrain others from manufacturing and using that which he invented. After

[27]*The Writings and Speeches of Daniel Webster*, XV, 438, 439.

[28]United States v. American Bell Telephone Co. (1897) 167 U.S. 224 at 238 per Brewer, J.

his invention he could have kept the discovery secret to himself. He need not have disclosed it to any.one. But in order to induce him to make that invention public, to give all a share in the benefits resulting from such an invention, Congress, by its legislation, made in pursuance of the Constitution, has guaranteed to him an exclusive right to it for a limited time; and the purpose of the patent is to protect him in this monopoly, not to give him a use which, save for the patent, he did not have before, but only to separate to him an exclusive use. The Government parted with nothing by the patent. It lost no property. Its possessions were not diminished. The patentee, so far as a personal use is concerned, received nothing which he did not have without the patent, and the monopoly which he did receive was only for a few years.

What seems to be forgotten by the modern destroyers of useful institutions is that a patent constitutes a contract. It is a bargain between the inventor and the state,[29] and is a bargain founded on good and valuable consideration. The consideration for the grant is twofold; first, there must be a new and useful invention, and secondly, the inventor must present to the public a sufficient description of the invention with sufficiently complete and accurate details as will enable a workman, skilled in the art to which the invention relates, to construct or use that invention when the period of the monopoly has expired.[30] This synallagmatic feature in the grant of a patent has been lost sight of in the attacks on the patent system. It should never be forgotten that, while the patentee may obtain the right to exclude others from exercising his invention, those others—the public—get something they never had before. During the term of the patent they obtain this new improvement and advantage from the patentee: at the conclusion of the term it falls into the public domain. The patent system therefore provides a never-ending stream of new and useful amenities and improvements to enrich the public domain.

The patent monopoly does not, as is commonly and popularly supposed, operate by a process of subtraction. It takes nothing away from the public, but only adds to the common store. A patent does not grant to the patentee the right to make and sell the subject of his patent. That right he had before his patent, quite independent and apart from any government grant. The right to make, use, and sell an invention is a common law right,

[29]Cf. Harmar v. Playne (1807) 14 Ves. 130; 11 East 101; Dav. P.C. 311.

[30]B.V.D. Co. Ltd. v. Canadian Celanese Ltd. (1936) Ex. C.R. 139; (1937) S.C.R. 221, 441; Western Electric Co. Inc. et al. v. Baldwin International Radio Co. of Canada (1934) S.C.R. 570; Badische Anilin und Soda Fabrik v. Thomson (1904) 21 R.P.C. 473.

and has so been held in numerous cases.[31] All the state grants by a patent is the incident of the right to exclude others—not from something they previously enjoyed and had in possession—but from something that is newly discovered and invented and will, in due time, be presented to them as part of the pool of common enjoyment. The patentee receives nothing from the law which he did not have before. The only effect of the patent is to restrain others from encroaching upon the private property of the patentee—property which is his by the highest possible title of natural right.[32]

Where did this property come from? The state parted with nothing by the patent. The patentee, in effect, received nothing which he did not have without the patent. Even the right of exclusive use which is given by the patent operates only for a short term.[33] This short term is little enough compensation for the labour, toil, and expense of making inventions. Obviously, therefore, a property which is acquired by a patentee, which was never previously known to or enjoyed by the public, and which constitutes a contribution to progress in science and the useful arts, can have only one origin. Its origin is in production,[34] and there could hardly be a higher title. Nowhere has this been better expressed than in the Third Report of the National Patent Planning Commission in 1945: "One further fact should be emphasized. The property represented in a patent is unique. The invention safeguarded by the patent is something that has been brought from the realm of ideality to the sphere of actuality and utility. But for the inventor's success in converting mere

[31] See, e.g., Crown Die & Tool Co. v. Nye Tool & Machine Works (1923) 261 U.S. 24, 36; L. L. Brown Paper Co. v. Hydroloid Inc. (1939) 44 USPQ 655.

[32] Bloomer v. McQuewan (1852) 55 U.S. 539, 549; Continental Paper Bag Co. v. Eastern Paper Bag Co. (1908) 210 U.S. 405; United States v. American Bell Telephone Co. (1897) 167 U.S. 224; Motion Picture Patents Co. v. Universal Film Mfg. Co. (1917) 243 U.S. 502, 510.

[33] Cf. United States v. American Bell Telephone Co. (1897) 167 U.S. 224 at 239.

[34] Jefferys v. Boosey (1854) 4 H.L.C. 815 at 867 per Erle, J.

The French Revolutionaries recognized the principle when, in the preamble to the Patent Law of January 7, 1791, they observed: "L'Assemblée nationale, considerant que toute idée nouvelle, dont la manifestation ou le développement peut devenir utile à la société, appartient primitivement à celui qui l'a conçue, et que ce serait attaquer les droits de l'homme dans leur essence, que de ne pas regarder une découverte industrielle comme la propriété de son auteur . . . décrète ce qui suit."

potentiality to materiality the world would have been deprived of a benefit whether great or small; whether a telephone, an airplane, a radio, or a useful but simple latchet for a shoe."

Patents are monopolies. As such they owe no apology. Unfortunately, many minds are ready to accept catchwords, particularly of the destructive type, without stopping to inquire whether there is any justification for the proposed destruction or any truth in the application of the word. There is nothing inherently wrong with monopoly, and in practice most monopolies have a profoundly beneficial effect on the economies of business and production. True, they may be abused, but that does not condemn their existence. The suggestion that abolition and destruction is the only remedy to cure a system which is subject to abuse is to confuse cause and effect. Every species of property known to the law is the subject of abuse, but no one suggests that property generally should be abolished. Granted that the socialists propose to abolish *private* property, the answer to that is that the proposals have been made since the time of Plato and More, and, though many such plans were tried, none have proved successful.

Once it is admitted that property—private property—is an acceptable and proper incident of law and of human life, then the argument against monopolies fails. For every property constitutes monopoly, and everything that we own creates a monopoly. Those rights of property have usually been acquired by purchase—a right which the moralists will agree is hardly as high a right as arises from production. John Stuart Mill, the great moralist of the nineteenth century, summed up the position by saying that "it would be a gross immorality in the law to set everybody free to use a person's work without his consent and without giving him an equivalent." Jeremy Bentham was no less emphatic when, in his *Manual of Political Economy*, he said: "With respect to a great number of inventions in the arts, an exclusive privilege is absolutely necessary, in order that what is sown may be reaped. In new inventions, protection against imitators is not less necessary than in established manufactures protection against thieves. He who has no hope that he shall reap, will not take the trouble to sow. But that which one man has invented, all the world can imitate."

The period of protection accorded to a patent is relatively short. Whereas ownership of property generally is on a perpetual basis, the period accorded to industrial and intellectual property is limited. Even among the various classes of this last type of property there is a wide variance. A patent grants protection for seventeen years only; a trade mark may endure indefinitely; and copyright, whether for a work of genius or a mere scribble or daub, lasts for the life of its author and fifty years after his death.[35]

Nor is the obtaining of the grant of a patent a simple and easy matter. An inventor may, whether by a "flash of genius"[36] or after years of patient research, the application of deep learning and scientific knowledge, and the expenditure of considerable sums of money in experimentation, discover and disclose to the world a contribution which may be the means of raising the general standard of living or of providing a useful and agreeable addition to the amenities and luxuries of life. In order to obtain a patent he is required to convince the examining staff of the Patent Office that what he has provided is new, is useful, is properly described and claimed in his patent, and, in addition, that it possesses an inherent quality which distinguishes it as a thing invented rather than something which has been produced by mere mechanical skill. Unhappily, neither the legislature, nor the courts, nor the examiners of the Patent Office, nor anyone else has ever supplied a definition of this quality called invention. It has been interpreted differently in hundreds of decisions by the courts of this continent and those of Great Britain and is characterized by a variety of names ranging from "invention," "inventive ingenuity," and "subject matter" to "flash of genius."

Even after the grant of a patent, the patentee may have to defend its worth in court proceedings where he must again prove

[35]See the Revised Berne Convention; Fox, *Canadian Law of Copyright*, 654. In the United States the term is twenty-eight years with a right of renewal for a further like term.

Cf. Shaw, *Everybody's Political What's What*, 99: "Shakespeare made comparatively no social changes: Watt and Stephenson made the industrial revolution. One would have thought that if any difference were to be made between the inventors and authors, the inventors would be given the better terms. Yet the author's copyright lasts for his life and fifty years, the inventor's patent fourteen years from its registration."

[36]Cf. Cuno Engineering Corporation v. The Automatic Devices Corporation (1941) 51 USPQ 272.

those facts if he is to maintain his rights. And even if the courts hold in his favour, after proceedings the expense of which have on many occasions been characterized as scandalous,[37] he is all too often met with the necessity of justifying the existence and possession of his property and of defending it against attacks from the modern witch-hunters who see in any form of monopoly none of the beneficial qualities but only the odious characteristics which arose from the early abuses.

I venture to suggest that there are three economic advantages to be secured by the functioning of a sound patent system. There is nothing new contained in their enumeration, and although they have formed the basis of innumerable arguments *ad invidiam* and called forth vehement statements of corresponding disadvantages and counter-proposals, I nevertheless feel that they constitute inescapable justification of the patent monopoly. These three economic advantages may be summed up in the words incentive, secret process, and foreign attraction. A word of explanation may not be amiss. When Willes, J. in his admirable observations in the case of *Millar* v. *Taylor*[38] gave a justification of the existence of copyright, he might, with equal facility and justice, have applied his words to patents. In general, inventions are not the result of inspiration or genius, but are the practical embodiment of monumental patience, colossal energy, and the expenditure of substantial sums of money. The hope of reward by securing to the inventor a limited monopoly, free from competition and piracy, can act only as an incentive to spur the imagination in originating new ideas and to maintain the tedious and laborious effort necessary to turn the imaginative concept into a device of practical application. Nor can the incentive to the venturing of capital in promoting and developing the perfection and marketing of new devices be overlooked in this connection. If the investor is to find that the venture and risk of his money is to result in giving him no advantage over those who have incurred no risk but, like the servile flock of imitators, wait only to reap where they have not

[37]Cf. "Patent Injustice" by K. E. Shelley, K.C. (1942-3), 61 Transactions of the Chartered Institute of Patent Agents, 17; Potts, "The Definition of Invention in Patent Law" (1944) 7 Mod. L. R., 113; Third Report of U.S. National Patent Planning Commission, pt. 7, para. 4.

[38](1769) 4 Burr. 2303 at 2335.

sown, it is doubtful whether the entrepreneur would ever embark on the enterprise of making new devices available to the public.

The patent monopoly is granted not only because of the invention or discovery involved but equally for its disclosure to the public on the expiration of its term. If the monopoly incentive is removed, there can obviously be little, if any, incentive to make a public disclosure with the inevitable result that many worthwhile improvements in the technology, and contributions to the amenities, of our industrial and personal life, which are the subjects of processes and methods of manufacture, will be driven into a corner where they will be kept as secret processes. The restraint upon the progress of the arts by such a situation is obvious. The danger of loss of the secret by the death of its possessor may retard progress for a considerable time until it is rediscovered. The payment of exorbitant wages and the meticulous carrying on of continuous precautions in order that the secret may be preserved will necessarily result in higher prices being paid by the public for the product.

Finally, if reasonable monopoly compensation is not given to the inventor he will go elsewhere with his invention. When, in the time of Elizabeth, the inventor of the stocking frame took his invention to France in return for a patent rather than publishing it freely in England where a patent had been refused him, he was merely obeying the impulse of self-interest and the dictates of human nature. The history of the last three and a half centuries has disclosed nothing to indicate that humanity would be more unselfish today; and little, if anything, in the moral views prevalent at the present time would seem to suggest a progression to a more liberal and altruistic attitude. Nor is there any reason why an inventor should be expected to donate his work to the common pool, so long as he must find himself the only one called upon to exercise benevolence and generosity.

The reproach of monopoly should, therefore, be met by the justification of monopoly. Industrial and social improvement has been furthered in all countries which have a soundly based and properly functioning patent system. Lawyers, inventors, and industrialists should not shirk the obligation of upholding and defending from unjust attack a system which is obviously a fair and proper system and has served for so many years to play an important part in the enrichment of human progress. Patents should not be numbered among the bad and harmful monopolies for, in that unpleasant company, they have no place. There should be no apathetic indifference on the part of those who ought to be the champions and defenders of the system, but rather more of the courage to express themselves fearlessly and forcefully in defending the legitimacy of monopoly privileges by patents which has been evidenced by the judges and treatise writers of earlier times. Before permanent damage is done to the patent system, the public should receive proper enlightenment on a problem which is of high importance. The economic history of any country will show conclusively that a strong and efficiently working patent system has been coincidental and coterminous with the relative progress and development of that country scientifically and industrially. If then, the economic past has so demonstrably been dependent on a strong patent system, how much more dependent is the economic future and prosperity of any country upon a clear understanding of those historical factors which created the necessity for a patent system and dictate its uninterrupted continuance.

Part Two

INVENTION & THE PATENT LAW

XVI. INTRODUCTION: THE PROBLEM STATED

IMPROVEMENT in the patent system is long overdue. The lack of attention to those of its doctrines which lead to abuses and injustices has already called forth the suggestion that perhaps the patent system is outworn.[1] Such a suggestion is disturbing for, as an American jurist recently pointed out,[2] "there seems still to be room for some kind of patent monopoly which, through hope of rewards to be gained through such a monopoly, will induce venturesome investors to risk large sums needed to bring to the commercially useful stage those new ideas which require immense expenditures for that purpose." The necessity for revision of the patent system, which is just as apparent in Canada and Great Britain as it is in the United States, is indicated by the letter which the President of the United States addressed, on April 17, 1942, to the Chairman of the Senate Committee on Patents: "The problem you are studying is vital. Patents are the key to our technology; technology is the key to our production; production is the key to victory. I trust that your Committee will . . . help the government to formulate a wise patent policy to guide us through that victory for democracy which we all so devoutly wish."

Why is a revision of the patent system so necessary? Why is it that men of such long experience and sound judgment as Judge Learned Hand suggest that the patent system may be outworn? Why is it that there is, at the present time, a veritable flood of discussion and writing relative to patents and the patent system, some of it constructive, much of it destructive, particularly in the United States? These are weighty questions which urgently require constructive answers. That the patent system is in danger no one can doubt who has followed at all closely the tenor of the attacks which are presently being levelled against it. That it needs amendment cannot be denied by a sincere student of the law on the one hand and the practical man of business on the other.

[1]Hand, J., in Dewey & Almy Chemical Co. v. Mimex Co. (1942) 52 USPQ 138. Debates of the Senate of Canada, July 25, 1946. *Globe and Mail,* Toronto, July 26, 1946, 23.

[2]Picard v. United Aircraft Corp. (1942) 53 USPQ 563 at 572 per Frank, J.

That its destruction would be a tragedy no honest person can doubt, for, whatever its failings and shortcomings, it has been one of the greatest of all those elements which have contributed toward the expansion of industry and the development of science and the useful arts.

This is intended, therefore, not as a general enquiry into the sufficiency and propriety of the patent system so much as an attempt to indicate one point—and that, in the opinion of the writer, a major one—at which the patent system has broken down and has failed to serve adequately the ends for which it was designed, namely the promotion of science and the useful arts (to borrow a phrase from the United States' Constitution), the general development and progress of industry, the introduction of new manufactures, and the furtherance of new trades (to use the original expressions upon which the system was based).

The point at which trouble has arisen and at which the patent system has partially failed arises from the growth of the doctrine of invention. The system of granting patents other than for mischievous monopolies was in the beginning based upon a reward to the person who introduced or brought into being a new manufacture, or, in other words, to the inventor of a new manufacture within the country. In its origin that was a simple formula but, with the progress of three centuries and more, it has degenerated into a complicated doctrine whereby the subject of the patent, the thing which is to be protected, must, before a valid patent can be granted in respect thereof, be possessed of a mystical, indefinable quality known as invention. From that doctrine much evil has resulted. The submission is made that it was not a necessary incident of the law of patent grant at the time the system was instituted and has been merely the outgrowth of that unhappy element of legal development known as judicial legislation.[3] If it had never found its way into the law, we should have had a much more satisfactory and workable system and should not be facing some of the absurdities to which a slavish adherence to false doctrine has driven us today.

[3]See per Lord Monboddo in Brown v. Annandale (1842) 1 W.P.C. 433 at 452 n.: "I regard not arguments *ab incommodo*; we must judge according to law, not conveniency. If there are such evil consequences from patents, why, let the king grant none such, or let the legislature regulate them." Cf. Bacon, *Essays: Of Judicature:* "Judges ought to remember that their office is *jus dicere* and not *jus dare*; to interpret law, and not to make law or give law."

In order to demonstrate the principle involved, it will be necessary to trace the history of this branch of the law of patents from earliest times. It will also be of assistance to discuss the laws of other countries on the subject. This is done only as it may serve to assist in an understanding of the development of the law of Canada on the subject and in an effort to discover some solution to our difficulties. It would not, of course, be proper for me to attempt an exposition of any system of law other than that of Canada, and it would be presumptuous in the extreme to offer suggestions to lawyers of other countries with reference to possible improvements in their laws. If I have borrowed from the jurisprudence of other systems, particularly that of the United States, and if at times I have appeared critical of some decisions and principles, it is in no measure designed or intended to give offence but only to offer comparisons and illustrations of our own system. The three countries, Canada, Great Britain, and the United States each has a system of patent law the main principles of which operate on parallel lines. In the nature of things there is far more activity in the law relating to patents in the two larger jurisdictions than in Canada and the smaller country is of necessity obliged to use much of the material from the larger countries for the exposition and illustration of its own system.

XVII. DOCTRINAL TRENDS IN THE CONCEPT OF INVENTION: A COMPARATIVE AND HISTORICAL VIEW

I. England

THE foundation of the patent systems of Canada, Great Britain, and the United States was the common law of England as expressed and declared in the Statute of Monopolies, 1624.[1] It is often assumed that the Statute itself was the basic foundation but an examination of its terms will show it to be nothing more than a declaratory act. It is necessary, therefore, to ascertain what was the common law to which the statute gave effect. We have already considered the historical incidents which led to the solidification of the common law principles into statutory form in the reign of James I. These principles appear from an examination of three of the decided cases and a consideration of the terms of the statute itself.

In general, monopolies were void at common law unless for the common good. Any patent creating a monopoly was subject to being declared void unless it fell within certain particular exceptions under which it could be held to be for the good of the subjects of the realm generally. One of these exceptions was that it was granted in respect of the introduction of a new trade or industry or for an engine tending to the furtherance of a new trade or industry. That, shortly, was the effect of the decisions which we shall now examine and of the statute which incorporated their principles in its terms.

The first of these cases is that of *Davenant* v. *Hurdis*[2] heard in the Court of King's Bench in 1599. The action, which was one of trespass for the breach of a by-law, was brought by the plaintiff against the defendant for breaking into his dwelling in London and taking a cloth of the value of £20. The plaintiff had been admitted a member of the Society of Merchant Tailors of London, a corporation which, by charter, had power to make ordinances for the government of its affairs and members. The Charter granting

[1]21 Jac. I, c. 3.

[2](1599) Moore K.B. 576, often referred to as the Merchant Tailors' Case. See the synopsis of this case in Appendix I, 311.

those powers had been confirmed by Parliament. The plaintiff had agreed to abide by the ordinances of the company, one of which provided that no member of the company should put out more than half his cloths to be dressed by other than brothers of the company, on pain of fine. It was alleged that the plaintiff had put out twenty broad cloths to be dressed by one who was not a member of the company and had not put an equal quantity to be dressed by a brother as required. The defendant was thereupon required to distrain for penalty. It was held[3] that the by-law made a monopoly: and that a prohibition of such a nature, confining the sole trade or traffic to a company, or a person, and excluding all others, was contrary to law.[4]

It is apparent from the judgment in this case that the common law had by that time taken the settled view that monopolies were void unless they contained some element contributing to the general good. The important point of the case is that an ordinance which created a monopoly was held to be void even though done under the authority conferred by charter, the terms of which charter had been confirmed by Parliament. It remained only to hold void a monopoly expressly created by royal charter and such a case followed close on the heels of the *Merchant Tailors' Case.*

In 1603 there was heard in the same court the famous case of *Darcy* v. *Allin*[5] better known as the *Case of Monopolies.* Queen Elizabeth had, in 1598, made a grant to the plaintiff of the sole right of importing and selling playing cards within the realm. The grant was made in consideration of the fact, as therein stated, that many, who should be occupied in husbandry, were employed in making cards, by reason of which card playing was becoming more frequent, especially among servants, apprentices, and poor artificers. The grant commanded that no person other than the grantee should bring any cards or buy, sell, or make any cards, within the realm, under penalty of fine and imprisonment. The case was exhaustively argued and an elaborate judgment delivered

[3]Trin. 42 Eliz.

[4]"Mes al darraign fuit adjudge Trin. 42 Eli. ove le pl'; Sur le corps del matter, quia le by-law est de faire monopoly; et prescription de tiel nature d'inducer sole trade ou traffique al un company, ou un pson, et dexcluder touts autres est encounter le ley, per touts les Justices Popham, Gawdy, Clentch et Fenner."

[5](1602) 11 Co. Rep. 84b; Moore K.B. 671. See the analysis of this case contained in Appendix IV, 318.

which declared that the grant was void as being against the common law and divers acts of Parliament relating to the freedom of trade. The Court held, in terms, that the grant was void because it was a monopoly and stated that the grant of the sole right of making or selling a commodity was against the common law and the benefit of the subject.

The judgment in the *Case of Monopolies* did not, as is popularly supposed, contain any exception relative to patents for new manufactures. The well-known extract on this subject is taken from the argument of Fuller, counsel for the defendant. This extract, which laid down the principle of the common law upon which the modern patent system is based is as follows:

"Now therefore I will shew you how the Judges have heretofore allowed of monopoly patents which is that where any man by his own charge and industry or by his own wit or invention doth bring any new trade into the Realm or any Engine tending to the furtherance of a trade that never was used before and that for the good of the Realm; that in such cases the King may grant to him a monopoly patent for some reasonable time, until the subjects may learn the same, in consideration of the good that he doth bring by his Invention to the Commonwealth; otherwise not."[6] This passage, as pointed out by Mr. Gordon in his exhaustive and scholarly analysis of the judgment in the *Case of Monopolies*,[7] has formed the foundation of our modern theory of patents not only throughout the British Commonwealth and the United States of America but most of the civilized world. But it was not, as mistakenly stated by judicial authority and most of the text-book writers, a part of the judgment. It was merely a submission by counsel. Thus, in Webster's *Patent Cases*,[8] published in 1844, the writer gave a summary of the report by Coke and Noy, followed by an extract, in quotation marks, from Noy,[9] without indicating to whom the quotation is to be attributed. This part is not quoted by Abbott in his report of the case.[10] A substantially similar passage was employed by the Court of

[6]See Noy at 182. Bacon and Coke were of the same opinion. See D'Ewes 644; Holdsworth, *History of English Law*, IV, 351.

[7]Gordon, *Monopolies by Patents*, 219.

[8]At 1.

[9]At 178, see 1 W.P.C. 5.

[10]Cf. Abbott, *American and English Patent Cases*, I, 1.

King's Bench in 1615 in the *Cloth Workers of Ipswich Case.*[11] The quotation was cited and adopted by Tindal, C.J., in *Crane* v. *Price,*[12] prefaced with the obviously erroneous statement that, "The case of monopolies states the law to be that . . . . "

It would not be amiss, at this point in our chronological restatement of the common law, to make mention of the Declaration of James I published in 1610 and known as the *Book of Bounty*. This Declaration, which has been stated by no less an authority than Coke[13] to have influenced the enactment of the Statute of Monopolies fourteen years later, was an exposition by the King of the extent to which he proposed to exercise his prerogative in the granting of patents.[14]

Next in chronological order occurred the *Cloth Workers of Ipswich Case.*[15] That was an action for a penalty brought by the masters and wardens of the Cloth Workers or Tailors of Ipswich. The declaration alleged that the King had incorporated the plaintiffs and had granted them a charter by which no person might exercise the art or trade of a cloth worker or tailor within the town, unless he had first served an apprenticeship; and that the defendant had exercised the trade in violation of this charter. It was held by the Court that the ordinance was unlawful; and it was agreed by the Court that the King might make corporations and grant to them that they might made ordinances for the ordering

[11](1615) Godb. R. 252. See post 218.

[12](1842) 1 W.P.C. 411.

[13]Co. 3 Inst. 182.

[14]11 Co. Rep. 88 d. The *Book of Bounty* was published in facsimile form in 1897. Page 13 contains "A memorial of Those Speciall things for which Wee expressly command that no Suitor presume to move Us, being matters either contrary to Our lawes, or such principall Profits of Our Crowne, and setled Revenue, as are fit to be wholly reserved to Our Owne use, until Our Estate be repaired.

"Things contrary to our Lawes.

1. Monopolies.
2. Graunts of the benefite of any Penal Lawes, or of power to dispence with the Lawe, or compound for the forfeiture."

Pages 17 and 21 contain: "A Memorial of Those Suits wherein We are contented to bee moved by Our Servants and Subiects, and to reward them according to the particular merit of the Suitor."

"9. Proiects of new invention, so they be not contrary to the Law, nor mischievous to the State, by raising prices of commodities at home, or hurt of trade, or otherwise inconvenient."

[15](1615) Godb. R. 252.

and government of any trade, but thereby they could not make a monopoly, for that was to take away free trade which is the birthright of every subject.[16] The Court further went on to refer to a case in 2 Henry V, c. 5, "a case in debt upon a bond, upon condition that one should not use his trade of a dyer in the town where the plaintiff did inhabit for one year; and there said that the obligation was void because the condition was against the law."[17] It was resolved that although such clause was contained in the King's letters patent, yet it was void. But where it is either by prescription or by custom confirmed by Parliament, there such an ordinance may be good, *quia consuetudo legalis plus valet quam concessio regalis.* The Court pointed out that grants of this type were expressly against the Statute of 9 Edw. III, c. 1, and referred to the charter granted by King Henry VIII to the physicians of London which had the same clause in it but pointed out that if it had not been confirmed by act of Parliament, made 33 Henry VIII, it would have been void. The Court, however, then proceeded to enunciate the principles which attached to monopolies or grants of privilege at common law in the following terms:

> But if a man hath brought in a new invention and a new trade within the kingdom, in peril of his life, and consumption of his estate and stock, etc., or if a man hath made a new discovery of anything, in such cases the King, of his grace and favour, in recompense of his costs and travail, may grant by charter unto him, that he only shall use such a trade or traffic for a certain time, because at first the people of the kingdom are ignorant, and have not the knowledge or skill to use it; but when that patent is expired, the King cannot make a new grant thereof, for when the trade has become common, and others have been bound apprentices in the same trade, there is no reason why such should be forbidden to use it.

These three cases and the expressions contained therein, together with the statement in the *Book of Bounty*, all had their effect on the framers of the Statute of Monopolies in 1624. By its terms[18] all monopolies, grants, licences, and charters for the sole

[16]"At common law no man could be prohibited from working in any lawful trade, for the law abhors idleness . . . and therefore the common law abhors all monopolies which prohibit any from working in any lawful trade and that appears in 2 H. V, 5 B."

[17]Sometimes known as the Case of John the Dyer, Year Book, 2 H. V, 5B. Sir John Hull, in delivering judgment holding the bond against the common law, added, "and by God, if the plaintiff was here he should go to prison till he paid a fine to the king."

[18]Cf. s. 1 of the Statute.

buying, selling, making, working, or using of any thing within the realm, or of any other monopolies were declared to be utterly void and of none effect, and in no wise to be put in use or execution. The statute did, however, contain certain exceptions to this general prohibition, the important one for our present purposes being that contained in Section 6, which reads as follows:

> Provided also and be it declared and enacted, that any declaration before mentioned shall not extend to any letters patents and grants of privilege for the term of fourteen years or under hereafter to be made of the sole working or making of any manner of new manufactures within this realm, to the true and first inventor and inventors of such manufactures, which others at the time of making such letters patents and grants shall not use, so as also they be not contrary to the law, nor mischievous to the State, by raising prices of commodities at home, or hurt of trade, or generally inconvenient: The said fourteen years to be accounted from the date of the first letters patent, or grant of such privilege hereafter to be made, but that the same shall be of such force as they should be if this Act had never been made, and of none other.

It is of importance to note that, although the section speaks of the "true and first inventor and inventors" it makes no use of the word "invention."[19] The subject matter of letters patent and grants of privilege which were expressly excepted from the operation of the Statute of Monopolies was defined as being "any manner of new manufactures within this realm."[20] This is by no means an expression synonymous with the modern concept of the word "invention." While a number of statutes has since been passed in England dealing with the subject of patents for invention, these have dealt mainly with the machinery for the grant and enforcement of patents, and the question as to whether the grant is one which might legally be made is still ordinarily determined by the above quoted section of the Statute of Monopolies.[21] That section still forms the basis of grant of the English patent law and, although in form it merely declares that certain grants of the sole privilege of working shall have the force they

[19]Although James's *Book of Bounty*, 21, para. 9, did mention "projects of new invention."

[20]In examining the process by which the clear meaning of this expression has broken down it is proposed to show that the judges have neglected to follow that concept of "our system of law in which precedents are authoritative and in which therefore, it has been said, the judge is 'a slave to the past and a despot for the future'." In re Cementation Co's Applications (1945) 62 R.P.C. 151, at 153 per Evershed, J.

[21]Patents and Designs Act, s. 93.

formerly had, it was in fact, and has always been treated by the judges as being declaratory as to what grants of this kind were and are legal.[22] In England, patents are still granted as an exercise of the royal prerogative[23] which is expressly preserved by Section 97 of the Patents Act. So far as Canada is concerned, while the basis of grant originally rested in the royal prerogative, it may be said that Parliament, by the use of the terms employed in the enactment of our patent legislation, has given to an inventor the right to a patent upon the terms and conditions specified.

Reduced to its most simple verbiage, the Statute of Monopolies declared all letters patent invalid except those for new manufactures. The question in each case, therefore, to be determined is whether the subject matter of the patent falls within the definition of the term "manufacture" and if so, whether it is a *new* manufacture. The question of novelty, that is, whether that which is claimed to be done has been done before or not, is solely a question of fact, while the question of whether the subject matter constitutes a manufacture, is a mixed question of both law and fact.[24]

The exception from the prohibition contained in the statute is not in favour of inventions but is in favour of any manner of new manufactures, to "the true and first inventor and inventors of such manufactures." But there has gradually developed a judicial interpretation, which has been reflected in statutory draftsmanship, that the expression "new manufacture" is synonymous and interchangeable with the word "invention."[25] And, unfortunately, that transposition of meaning has occurred without any understanding of the significance which could be and has later, become, attached to it.

What was originally meant by the term "manufacture?" Let us look at some of the early decisions. The first of these cases is *Boulton* v. *Bull*[26] in the course of which Eyre, C.J., commenting on the meaning of the term "manufacture," said as follows:

---

[22]Australian Gold Recovery Company v. Lakeview Consols Co. (1901) 18 R.P.C. 114; Feather v. The Queen (1865) 6 B. & S. 275; cf. Co. 3 Inst. 85.

[23]Von Heyden v. Neustadt (1880) 14 Ch. D. 230.

[24]Walton v. Potter (1841) 1 W.P.C. 597 at 601; Cornish v. Keene (1835) 1 W.P.C. 501 at 517; Losh v. Hague (1838) 1 W.P.C. 200 at 205; Hill v. Evans (1862) 31 L.J. Ch. 457; Lyon v. Goddard (1894) 11 R.P.C. 354.

[25]Cf. Cornish v. Keene (1835) 1 W.P.C. 508 and see post 222.

[26](1795) 2 H. Bl. 463; Dav. P.C. 162; 3 Ves. 140.

It was admitted in the argument at the bar that the word "manufacture" in the statute was of extensive signification; that it applied not only to things made but to the practice of making, to principles carried into practice in a new manner, to new results of principles carried into practice. Let us pursue this admission. Under things made, we may class, in the first place, new compositions of things, such as manufactures in the most ordinary sense of the word; secondly, all mechanical inventions, whether made to produce old or new effects, for a new piece of mechanism is certainly a thing made. Under the practice of making we may class all new artificial manners of operating with the hand, or with instruments in common use, new processes in any art producing effects useful to the public.

Eyre, C.J., also noted in his judgment that: "In the case of *Edgebury* v. *Stephens*[27] the words 'new devices' are substituted and used as synonymous with the words 'new manufacture'."

In *Hornblower* v. *Boulton*[28] Lord Kenyon, C.J., speaking of the word "manufacture" used the words, "'Manufacture,' which I understand to be something made by the hands of man."

In *Cornish* v. *Keene*[29] it was held that the word "manufacture" had a very wide and extended meaning and might be interpreted "invention." Upon motion for a new trial,[30] Tindal, C.J., said: "The first objection is that the invention is not the subject-matter of a patent. . . . The question therefore, as to this point, is does it come under the description of 'any manner of new manufacture' which are the terms employed in the Statute of James. That it is a manufacture can admit of no doubt; it is a vendible article produced by the hand of man."[31]

In *Ralston* v. *Smith*[32] Lord Westbury, L.C., said: "Your Lordships are well aware that by the large interpretation given to the word 'manufacture' it not only comprehends productions, but it also comprehends the means of producing them. Therefore, in addition to the thing produced, it will comprehend a new machine, or a new combination of machinery; it will comprehend a new process, or an improvement of an old process. But, if we look at this patent, I think there is no such improvement as amounts to a new manufacture."

[27]Cf. 1 W.P.C. 35.

[28](1799) Dav. P.C. 221; 8 T.R. 95; see also Rex v. Wheeler (1819) 2 B. & Ald. 345 per Abbott, C.J.

[29](1835) 1 W.P.C. 508.

[30]1 W.P.C. at 517.

[31]See also Morgan v. Seaward (1835) 2 M. & W. 544; 1 W.P.C. 167 per Parke, 73.

[32](1865) 11 H.L.C. 223 at 243.

The last sentence by Lord Westbury is arresting—"such improvement as amounts to a new manufacture." There is a plain definition. A "new manufacture" is an "improvement" in those things which make up the sum total of man's necessities and utilities.

From these cases we may extract a definition. A "manufacture" is "something made by the hand of man." A "new manufacture" is an "improvement" in those things that are made by the hand of man. The manufacture may be an article, vendible as such, an engine or instrument to be employed either in the making of an article or for a useful purpose, or a process. If it shows improvement—if it shows a step forward—then it is new and is within the statute. On the authority of *Cornish* v. *Keene*[33] an invention is proper subject matter of a patent if it comes under the description of a new, vendible, man-made product.

Now those definitions constitute something quite apart from our modern conception of invention. Hedged about as it now is with all the negative rules which the ingenuity of judicial opinion has been able to contrive over a considerable number of decades, the use of the words "inventor" and "inventors" in the Statute of Monopolies constituted a temptation to occupants of the Bench to indulge in loose thinking and strained construction. It was a great temptation and an easy transition from "first inventor of a new manufacture" to read "first inventor of a new invention." So we find as early as the year 1795 Eyre, C.J., in commenting on the meaning of the term "manufacture" in *Boulton* v. *Bull*[34] in the passage quoted above, using the term "mechanical inventions" as being included within the expression "manufacture." This confusion of "manufacture" with "invention" was materially assisted in 1835 by Tindal, C.J., in *Cornish* v. *Keene*[35] where he said: "The main question is whether this No. 3 which is the principal subject of the patent was or was not in use in England at the time of granting these letters patent. Was it or was it not, in the language of the Act of Parliament, such a manufacture (which has a very wide and extended meaning—you may call it almost invention), was it or was it not such an invention, at the time of making the letters patent, as was current in use."

[33](1835) 1 W.P.C. 517.
[34](1795) 2 Henry Bl. 463; Dav. P.C. 162; 3 Ves. 140.
[35](1835) 1 W.P.C. 508.

It is, however, of much importance to scrutinize carefully two things in this quotation. In the first place, Tindal, C. J., did not use the terms "manufacture" and "invention" as completely synonymous. Secondly, he was not discussing patentability from the standpoint of subject matter at all. He was discussing patentability entirely from the viewpoint of novelty and if his words are examined closely, it will be seen that he was relating them entirely to the wording of the Statute of Monopolies, except that he fell into the error of using the word "invention" as almost synonymous with "manufacture." Tindal, C.J., was not there using the word "invention" as having any mystical meaning such as it has today. He was using it in its plain meaning as it was used at the time of the passing of the Statute of Monopolies and before it had become glossed by modern misunderstanding. That is clear from the fact that to him an invention was proper subject matter of a patent if it fell within the description of "any manner of new manufacture."[36]

What did the word "invention" mean at the time the principles of the common law were established and at the time they were crystallized in the Statute of Monopolies? Let us, first of all, examine the definitions which are given by various standard dictionaries of the words "inventor" and "invention," and let us then consider their derivation and the probable meaning of the use of the word "inventor" in the Statute of Monopolies according to the understanding of the word at the time it was used and not as it has become surrounded with a superficial incrustation of meaning after upwards of three hundred years' use.

The Oxford Dictionary[37] gives the prevailing sense of the meaning of the word "inventor" as being: "One who devises or produces something new (as an instrument, an art, etc.) by original contrivance; the originator of a previously unknown method of doing something; 'the first finder-out'."

But that is the presently prevailing sense of the word, influenced as it has been, by the trend of judicial decision. The essential point is to understand what the word meant in 1624, at the time of the passing of the Statute of Monopolies. The word is derived from the Latin "*inventor,*" from "*invenire,*" to come upon. The Oxford Dictionary gives the obsolete meaning of the word as:

[36]See ante 221.

[37]1933, V, 453.

"One who finds out, a discoverer (whether by chance, or by investigation and effort)." That is the meaning which was intended by the Statute and the decisions on the point of accidental discovery as basis for letters patent bear out the statement.[38] As late as 1881, Bramwell, L.J., used the expression "found it out, which I take to be equivalent to invention."[39]

[38]See post 229, 252.

[39]Hayward v. Hamilton (1879-81) Griff. P.C. 115.

In the examples given in the Oxford Dictionary appear the following:

1509, Barclay, *Shyp of Folys* 7 b (8a), "Esculapius which was the fyrst inuentour of Phesyke";

1546, Langley, *Pol. Verg. de Invent.* I, xvii, "The inventours of Herbes medicinable";

1726, Freind, *Hist. Med.* II, 315 "Dr. Willis, the first inventor of the nervous system."

Under the dated meaning of the word "invention" the Oxford Dictionary gives the following illuminating examples:

1531 Elyot, *Gov.* I, xxvi "They that write of the firste inventions of things have good cause to suppose Lucifer to be the first inventour of dice playinge."

1604 Jas. I, *Counterbl.* (Arb.) 99 "The first invention of Tobacco taking."

1651 Hobbes, *Leviath.* I, iv, 12, "The Invention of Printing . . . compared with the invention of Letters."

An illuminating discussion on this point is included in the U.S. Senate Report of April 2, 1930, on the bill to provide for plant patents: "At the time of the adoption of the Constitution the term 'inventor' was used in two senses. In the first place the inventor was a discoverer, one who finds or finds out. In the second place an inventor was one who created something new. All the dictionaries at the time of the framing of the Constitution recognized that 'inventor' included the finder out or discoverer as well as the creator of something new. Thus Sheridan in 1790 defined 'inventor' as 'a finder out of something new' and, 'invention' as 'discovery.' Kersey in 1708 defined 'invention' as 'the act of inventing, or finding,' and Martin in 1754 defined 'to invent' as 'to find out or discover.' The word 'discover' or 'discovery' is given as an equivalent by Cocker in 1715 and 1724, Ash in 1775, Perry in 1795, Entick in 1786, Fenning in 1771, and Barclay in 1841. 'To find' or 'find out' or 'finding' as a synonym of invent or inventor, was noted by Rider in 1617, Holyroke in 1649, Coles in 1724, Johnson in 1824, Kendrick in 1773, Martin in 1754, Kersey in 1708, Sheridan in 1790, Ash in 1775, Cocker in 1715 and 1724, Entick in 1786 and 1791, Fenning in 1771, and Coxe in 1813.

"The distinction between discovering or finding out on the one hand and creating or producing on the other hand, being recognized in the dictionaries current at the time of the framing of the Constitution, it is reasonable to suppose the framers of the Constitution attributed to the term 'inventor' the then customary meaning. That they did not ignore the meaning of inventor as 'a discoverer or finder out' is furthermore indicated by the fact that in the Constitution itself the framers referred to the productions of inventors as 'discoveries.'

Now the Statute of Monopolies was passed in the reign of James I and its enactment was much influenced by James's *Book of Bounty*, which speaks of "projects of new invention." To a King who also used the word "invention" as applicable to the first taking of tobacco the meaning was obviously plain.[40] It was no doubt equally plain to the members of Parliament who enacted the statute. They certainly had no thoughts in their minds of nice questions of any "impalpable something that distinguishes things invented from things otherwise arrived at," of "obviousness," of "inventive ingenuity or mechanical skill," or of "flash of creative genius," which bedevil the modern patentee and lawyer.

Bacon, who in 1601 spoke at length in the debate on monopolies in Parliament, may be taken to have had some knowledge of the current meaning to be attached to the word "invention." In his *Advancement of Learning* published in 1605, he spoke of finding "among the heathen the inventors of new arts, such as Ceres, Bacchus and Apollo." Again he compared the invention of the ship with that of letters. Yet again he stated that, "It were desirable that there should be a calendar or inventory made of all the inventions whereof man is possessed, with a note of useful things not yet invented." And finally, in discussing the intellectual arts he used the word "invention" as synonymous with inquiry. This contemporary meaning of the word, in its broadest aspect, was the meaning which was obviously used by the framers of the Statute of James.

Webster's New International Dictionary also gives as obsolete the form of the verb "invent" as meaning "to come upon, to meet or to find" and again as "to originate, found or establish." The modern definition of Webster is "to discover as by study or inquiry, to find out; to devise; to contrive or produce for the first time;—

"With the development of the patent laws and modern industry the meaning of the word 'inventor' as a creator of something new became the prevailing use and, while both meanings of inventor are still recognized in such modern dictionaries as Murray's New English Dictionary, Webster's New International Dictionary, and the Century Dictionary and Encyclopedia, the meaning of inventor as 'a finder out or discoverer' is now considered obsolete or archaic. However, it seems to the committee that the meaning to be attached to the term 'inventor' as used in the Constitution must be the meaning in general use at the time of the framing of the Constitution rather than the meaning prevailing in present-day usage."

[40]See n. 39.

applied commonly to the discovery of some serviceable mode, instrument or machine."

It is noteworthy that Webster also defines the word "invent" as being synonymous with "discover" and "find out." Here again there are no barnacles of confused thought. The meaning is plain and clear as it was when the statute was passed. To endeavour to create a legal, artificial meaning of the word for purposes of the patent law is to disregard entirely the clear meaning of the legislature in enacting the statute— and how many times, in works on the construction of statutes, are we not invited to look to the intention of the legislature and the meaning which was intended by that body to be placed on words and the sense in which they are used. To suggest that the modern interpretation placed upon the word by the courts was the meaning intended by the legislature which enacted the statute is to disregard the history of the meaning of the word. The modern interpretation is nothing but a sophistical gloss which has overgrown the word after more than three centuries of judicial law making.

While it is quite true that the *Book of Bounty* and some of the letters patent which were expressly continued by Section 5 of the Statute of Monopolies used the word "invention,"[41] the exact meaning then placed upon the use of the word "invention" must not be lost sight of. Thus, in Dudley's patent the recital stated that Dudley had "found out the mystery, art, way and means of smelting iron ewre [ore] and of making the same into cast works or bars with sea coals or pit coals in furnaces with bellows, of as good condition as hath been heretofore made of charcoals; a work and *invention* not formerly performed by any within this our kingdom of England." So far as appears from the letters patent, the invention was simply the substitution of pit coal for wood or charcoal. In Mansell's glass patent the expression "all profitable and beneficial devices, projects and inventions" was used. In the granting part of the letters patent, the grant was to "use, exercise, practice, set up and put in use, the art, feat, and mystery, of melting and making of all manner of drinking glasses, etc." It is obvious, from a study of the available technical material of the day, that glass made in a different manner, or iron made with

[41]See, e.g., Dudley's Patent, 19 Jac. I, Feb. 22, 1622; cf. 1 W.P.C. 14; Mansell's Glass Patent, 21 Jac. I, May 22; cf. 1 W.P.C. 17.

a new fuel,[42] were substantially and really new things; that each of these was a new manufacture. If the sense of the word "new manufacture" is considered as being synonymous with "art, feat, mystery, discovery," then we have a clear understanding of that which was contemplated by the exception contained in Section 6 of the Statute of Monopolies.

It is, therefore, suggested that, at the time of the Statute of Monopolies, the word "inventor" was used as synonymous with "discoverer" or "the first finder-out." The submission now made, and which we shall proceed to discuss, is that there is no justification in the terms of the Statute of Monopolies for the presence of the ingredient of invention or subject matter, as it is used in the modern sense, in a patent in order to make it valid. The Statute of Monopolies made only two amendments to the common law—the one relating to the trial of disputes concerning patents by the courts of common law, and the other setting the term at fourteen years. The consideration for the grant remained unchanged. At common law there was required as consideration the introduction of a new manufacture; the true and first inventor meant, at common law, not only the first person who discovered a new process but also a person who brought into England a process or machine not previously worked in England.[43] In these requirements the statute made no change: they remained as before. The present requirement of inventive ingenuity is simply a refinement which has been added to the patent law by the courts as the history of patent litigation has developed. There is no justification in the Statute itself and there is no justification in the meaning of the word as it was used at the time of the Statute. Thus, as late as 1778,[44] we have Lord Mansfield using the following expression: "Inventions are of various kinds; some depend on the result of figuring, others on mechanism, etc.; others depend on no reason, no theory but a lucky discovery; water tabbies[45] were discovered by a man spitting on the floor."

In 1785, Buller, C.J., in charging the jury in *Rex* v. *Arkwright*[46] on the question of invention, had the following to say: "As to

[42]Cf. Dudley's Patent, 1 W.P.C. 14.

[43]Hulme (1900) 16 L.Q.R., 55; (1909) 3 A.A.L.H., 139-41; Holdsworth, *History of English Law*, III, 354.

[44]Liardet v. Johnson (1778) Bull. N.P. 76; 1 W.P.C. 53.

[45]Waved or watered taffeta.

[46](1785) 1 W.P.C. 64, at 71.

the other points, there are two; first, whether it is a new invention; . . . if there be any thing material and new which is an improvement of the trade, that will be sufficient to support a patent."

On this point Webster, writing in 1844, made the following note:[47]

The dictum of the learned Judge seems to present an admirable test of the sufficiency of an invention to support letters patent. The improvement of the particular trade is the principle upon which the policy of such limited monopolies rested, and in many cases the materiality and importance of the change can only be judged by the effect on the result, which effect is tested by the improvement in the trade in the commercial sense of the term, that is, by the production of the article as good in quality at a cheaper rate, or of a better quality at the same rate, or both these partially combined. Thus the latter words "improvement of the trade," define and explain the preceding, and the utility of the invention as ascertained by this result becomes, in cases of this kind, the real test. In other cases, as when some particular instrument or machine is the subject of the patent, the same test is indirectly applicable. This view is suggested by the Court of Exchequer in their elaborate judgment in the case of *Morgan* v. *Seaward*. Parke, B.; "On a review of the cases, it may be doubted whether the question of utility is anything more than a compendious mode introduced in comparatively modern times of deciding the question whether the patent be void under the Statute of Monopolies."[48] So that whenever utility is proved to exist in any great degree, sufficiency of invention to support a patent may be presumed; and if such invention be any manner of manufacture, and new, and the specification be sufficient, the letters patent for such invention will be valid in law.[49]

The reference by Lord Mansfield to water tabbies in the case of *Liardet* v. *Johnson*[50] was cited by Buller, J., in *Boulton & Watt* v. *Bull*[51] where he said: "The case of water tabbies which has often been mentioned in Westminster Hall may afford some illustrations of the subject. The invention first owed its rise to the accident of a man spitting on a floor cloth which changed its colour from whence he reasoned on the effect of intermixing water with oil or colours and found out how to make water tabbies and had his patent for water tabbies only."

Our viewpoint is borne out further by the words of Buller, J., in *Boulton & Watt* v. *Bull*.[52] He there observed, in discussing the exception contained in Section 6 of the Statute of Monopolies,

[47]1 W.P.C. 71 n.

[48]2 M. & W. 563.

[49]To the same effect see Morgan v. Seaward (1835) 1 W.P.C. 167 at 197 n.

[50](1778) Bull. N.P. 76; 1 W.P.C. 53.

[51](1795) 2 H. Bl. 463 at 487.

[52]Supra.

that "whether the manufacture be with or without principle, produced by accident or by art, is immaterial."[53] In *Hayward* v. *Hamilton*[54] Bramwell, L.J., said: "Why has it never been done before? Why, because nobody has found it out, which I take to be equivalent to invention." In *Huddart* v. *Grimshaw*[55] which concerned Huddart's patent for the making of cables and cordage, we find Lord Ellenborough, C.J., charging the jury as follows:

> In inventions of this sort, and every other through the medium of mechanism, there are some materials which are common, and cannot be supposed to be appropriated in the terms of any patent. There are common elementary materials to work with in machinery, but it is the adoption of those materials to the execution of any particular purpose, that constitutes the invention; and if the application of them be new, if the combination in its nature be essentially new, if it be productive of a new end, and beneficial to the public, it is that species of invention which, protected by the King's Patent, ought to continue to the person the sole right of vending.

It is significant to note that in the above remarks of Lord Ellenborough there is not one word of that quality which we now call subject matter or invention in its limited sense. What Lord Ellenborough stated to the jury may be put shortly as "if this device provides a mechanism which produces a result useful to the public; if it was not known before but on the contrary originated as the idea of the patentee, then it is a new manufacture within the statute and the patentee has a good patent."

That the view here advanced is on sound ground is substantiated by the fact that the practice in England always has been, and still is, to grant patents on communications from abroad. At common law the basic theory for the grant of patents was the stimulation and improvement of domestic trade and manufacturing and patents were granted for the introduction of new trades and improvements, whether by original discovery or by importing the knowledge. In the early smalt patents granted before the statute,[56] smalt was well known and in constant use within the kingdom but the method of its manufacture was unknown or at least not practised therein. The grantees, therefore, were held to be the introducers of a new trade into the realm. This theory

[53]See also Crane v. Price (1842) 4 M. & G. 580 per Tindal,C.J., cited post 231; Hayward v. Hamilton (1879-81) Griff. P.C. 115 per Bramwell, L.J.

[54](1879-81) Griff. P.C. 115.

[55](1803) 1 W.P.C. 85 at 86.

[56]See 1 W.P.C., 8 n., 9 et seq.

was undisturbed by the Statute of Monopolies and although some writers, as e.g., Webster,[57] seemed to think that grants to first importers would have been void after the statute if the courts had not interpreted the expression "true and first inventor" used in the statute to include an importer, it is hardly seen how the courts could have done anything else. The meaning of the expression obviously included an importer in the minds of the framers of the statute and the courts followed the meaning intended by Parliament and as it was laid down in the earlier cases.

The words "true and first inventor" in the Statute of Monopolies then were intended to include not only the first originator of a device but also the true and first importer into the realm. This is obvious from a reading of the early cases decided under the common law. Thus Hasting's patent of 1567[58] for the making of frisadoes appears to have been granted in consideration of the patentee's having imported the skill of manufacturing them from abroad. In *Matthey's Case*[59] the patent for knives with bone hafts was granted because the first use of them was brought from beyond seas. Again in the *Cloth Workers of Ipswich Case*[60] both inventors and importers were regarded as proper grantees of patents.[61]

After the Statute of Monopolies, the case of *Edgebury* v. *Stephens*[62] held that "if the invention be new in England, a patent may be granted though the thing was practised beyond sea before; for the statute speaks of new manufactures within this realm; so that if it be new here, it is within the statute; for the act intended to encourage new devices useful to the kingdom, and whether learned by travel or by study it is the same thing."[63] A modern expression of this view was stated by Jessel, M. R., in *Plimpton* v. *Malcolmson*:[64]

Shortly after the passing of the statute, the question arose whether a man could be called a first and true inventor who, in the popular sense, had never invented

[57]Cf. 1 W.P.C. 8 n.

[58]Noy 183.

[59]Noy 183.

[60](1615) Godb. 252.

[61]Cf. the words of the judgment quoted ante 218.

[62](1693) 1 W.P.C. 35.

[63]See also Lombe's Patent (1719) 1 W.P.C. 38 and the recitals contained in various grants and Statutes granting patents summarized in 1 W.P.C. 38-40 and notes. Cf. also Boulton v. Bull (1795) 2 H. Bl. 463 at 491 per Eyre, C.J.

[64](1876) 3 Ch. D. 555.

anything, but who having learned abroad (that is, out of the realm, in a foreign country . . .) that somebody else had invented something, quietly copied the invention, and brought it over to this country, and then took out a patent. As I said before, in the popular sense he had invented nothing. But it was decided, and now, therefore, is the legal sense and meaning of the statute, that he was a first and true inventor within the statute.[65]

The meaning of the expression "true and first inventor" has therefore not been perverted in Great Britain by judicial interpretation, for patents are still granted to the first introducer from abroad even though he may have had no part in originating the idea. Hence it is all the more strange to follow the manner in which the meaning of the similar term "invention" has been perverted by judicial interpretation.

In the year 1842 Tindal, C. J., in *Crane* v. *Price et al.*[66] said: "There are numerous instances of patents which have been granted, where the invention consisted in no more than in the use of things already known, and acting with them in a manner already known, and producing effects already known, but producing those effects so as to be more economically or beneficially enjoyed by the public. It will be sufficient to refer to a few instances, some of which patents have failed on other grounds, but none on the ground that the invention itself was not the subject of a patent."

In his note[67] to this remark by Tindal, C.J., Mr. Webster stated that "it may be observed, that no case is reported or men-

[65]See also Lewis v. Marling (1818) 1 W.P.C. 488 at 492, 496; Renard v. Levinstein (1864-5) 10 L.T.N.S. 177; Marsden v. Saville Street Foundry and Engineering Co. (1878) 3 Ex. D. 203, per Jessel, M.R.; Wirth's Patent (1879) 12 Ch. D. 303; Avery's Patent (1887) 36 Ch. D. 307 at 316; Moser v. Marsden (1893) 10 R.P.C. 350 at 359; Von Krogh's Application (1932) 49 R.P.C. 417.

[66]1 W.P.C. 377 at 409.

[67]Cf. 1 W.P.C. 409 n. John Dyer Collier, in his *Essay on the Law of Patents*, chap. IX, discusses the nature and extent of letters patent for inventions, under such headings as, "What is a New Manufacture?"; "Who is the First Inventor?"; and "What is the Patent Which is Contrary to the Law, or Mischievous to the State?" In all the discussion there is not one use of such words as subject matter, inventiveness, inventive ingenuity, mechanical skill, genius, obviousness, or words of any similar import. The entire discussion proceeds on proof of whether a device is new and whether it is material and useful, i.e., in the words of Buller, J., in Rex v. Arkwright, that "if there be any thing material and new, which is an improvement of the trade, that will be sufficient to support a patent." The word inventor is used throughout as synonymous with discoverer, and the word invention as synonymous with manufacture. The mystical concept of

tioned in any of the books in which a patent has failed, simply on the ground of the invention not being the subject matter of letters patent; some other ground, as want of novelty, or defect of specification, having been the real cause of failure."

One who has read at all carefully the judgments of the courts in England for the first two hundred odd years following the Statute of Monopolies must be impressed with the fact that all of them were concerned with defences such as a denial of infringement or a denial of validity based upon one of three things, first, a lack of novelty, secondly, a lack of utility, and thirdly, and even more generally, insufficiency of the specification. Until the time of *Crane* v. *Price*, there is no reported instance, as Mr. Webster observed, and as Tindal, C.J., pointed out, in which a patent had been declared invalid for want of invention or subject matter.[68] The defence of lack of subject matter was raised in *Hall* v. *Jarvis et al.*[69] when counsel for the defendants said: "The process is not new—fire, and even flame, having been applied to similar purposes before the plaintiff's invention: the mere doing by means of other kinds of flame, cannot be the subject matter of a patent." But the defence was not even considered, the jury intimating that they did not require any observations in reply and Abbott, C.J., charging them that there could be no doubt their verdict must pass against the defendants.[70]

The question received some passing attention in the case of *Losh* v. *Hague*[71] where Lord Abinger, in charging the jury, said:

---

subject matter or inventive ingenuity found no place in the law at the time Collier wrote his work.

To the same effect see Chitty, *Prerogatives of the Crown*, chap. X, sec. II, 176 ff.

[68]Upon careful examination the cases of Brunton v. Hawkes (1820) 4 B. & Ald. 541; Saunders v. Aston (1832) 3 B. & Ald. 881; Kay v. Marshall (1841) 5 Bing. N.C. 491, will show that in the Brunton case the defence was lack of novelty, in the Saunders, or button case, the plaintiff failed because his real invention had not been properly claimed, and in Kay's case the real defect was not in the subject matter but in the subject matter as disclosed on the face of the letters patent and in the specification. Thus, in Hill v. Thompson (1817) 1 W.P.C. 235 at 237 Lord Eldon, L.C., appears to have approved a judge's charge in which the only points submitted to the jury were novelty, utility, and the sufficiency of the specification.

[69](1822) 1 W.P.C. 100 at 102.

[70]See also Neilson v. Harford et al. (1841) 1 W.P.C. 16 n.

[71](1838) 1 W.P.C. 200 at 204.

"I observe one of the pleas states, that the improvements are something trifling and insignificant. If that is the improvement you will consider whether it is worth a patent or not." In the result, however, the jury found in favour of the defendant on the issue that the plaintiff was not the true and first inventor. The reason for raising this defence in the early days of patent litigation was that the original consideration for the grant of a monopoly was not the disclosure of the patentee's secret but the furtherance of trade.[72] For that reason, small improvements upon existing processes were not regarded as fit subjects of a grant.[73] It will be recalled that, in its origin, the patent system was not evoked as a system of rewards for inventive acts but rather as a system for encouraging the setting up of new manufactures. Unless, therefore, the content of a monopoly grant disclosed that which resulted in the bringing into the realm or the setting up of a new process, technique, or apparatus with the consequent employment of additional workmen or a contribution to the policy of self-sufficiency of the realm, there was not sufficient consideration for the grant. Unless this somewhat fine distinction is kept clearly in mind, it is difficult to distinguish the precise meaning and application of the doctrine of some of the early decisions. Thus in *Matthey's Patent*[74] the patent was for knives with bone hafts and plates of latten which the patentee had brought from beyond seas. "Yet nevertheless, when the wardens of the company of cutlers did show . . . that they did use to make knives before, though not with such hafts, that such a light difference or invention should be no cause to restrain them, whereupon he could never have benefit of this patent, although he laboured very greatly therein."[75] But in his notes to the reference in *Darcy v. Allin* to *Matthey's Patent*, Webster[76] pointed out that one of the conditions of validity was that "the subject matter must be such

[72]Hulme (1897) 13 L.Q.R., 313-14.

[73]Holdsworth, *History of English Law*, IV, 351.

[74]Temp. Eliz. ref. to in 1 W.P.C. 6.

[75]Cf. also Bircot's Case, ref. to in 1 W.P.C. 31 n., Co. 3 Inst. 181, where Coke said of this case that it was held in the Exchequer Chamber (E.T. 15, E. 4) that "such a privilege as is consonant to law, must be substantially and newly invented; but if the substance was *in esse* before, and a new addition thereunto, though that addition made the former more profitable, yet is it not a new manufacture in law . . . it is much easier to add than to invent."

[76]1 W.P.C. 7.

as in the result leads to a new trade or manufacture." The defence, therefore, had no relation to the modern defence of lack of invention or obviousness. It was merely a defence alleging that the contribution was not large enough to make a new manufacture.

The matter was first fully stated by Tindal, C.J., in *Crane* v. *Price*[77] as follows:

> It was objected, in the course of the argument, that the quality or degree of invention was so small, that it could not become the subject matter of a patent; that a person who could procure a license to use the hot air blast under Neilson's Patent, had a full right to apply that blast to coal of any nature whatever, whether bituminous or stone coal. But we think, if it were necessary to consider the labour, pains, and expense, incurred by the plaintiff, in bringing his discovery to perfection, that there is evidence in this cause, that the expense was considerable and the experiments numerous. But in point of law, the labour of thought, or experiments, and the expenditure of money, are not the essential grounds of consideration on which the question, whether the invention is or is not the subject matter of a patent, ought to depend. For if the monopoly be new and useful to the public, it is not material whether it be the result of long experiments and profound research, or whether by some sudden and lucky thought, or mere accidental discovery.
>
> The Case of Monopolies[78] states the law to be, that where a man, by his own charge or industry, or by his own wit or invention, brings a new trade into the realm, or any engine tending to the furtherance of a new trade that never was used before, and it was for the good of the realm, that the King may grant him the monopoly of a patent for a reasonable time. If the combination now under consideration be, as we think it is, a manufacture within the Statute of James, there was abundant evidence in the cause, that it had been the great object and desideratum, before the granting of the patent, to smelt iron stone by means of anthracite coal, and that it had never been done before; there was no evidence on the part of the defendants to meet that which the plaintiff brought forward. These considerations, therefore, enable us to direct, that the verdict ought to be entered for the plaintiff on the third issue; that it was a new manufacture—new as to the public use and exercise thereof within England and Wales.

Until 1835, therefore, the principles of the common law as expressed in the Statute of Monopolies were still effective. No case had as yet arisen in which a patent had been declared invalid for lack of subject matter. Subject matter was quite definitely understood as being "any manner of new manufacture." The institution of doctrinal trends to defeat patents had not yet crept into the law courts.

[77]1 W.P.C. at 410.

[78](1602) 11 Co. Rep. 84; Noy 173.

But although judgment went for the plaintiff in *Crane* v. *Price*, a new idea had been injected into the law of patents. The defence had been received by the court and considered in its charge to the jury. From then on it was merely a matter of time until a jury or a court would be found which would hold that the subject matter of a particular patent was not of sufficient significance to be dignified by the grant of letters patent. A reading of the decisions in the English courts during the next half-century demonstrates a considerable amount of confused thinking. Gradually there grew up the theory that in order for a patent to have proper subject matter, the invention which it disclosed must be such as would have required an inventive act of the mind to have produced it. But, alongside that theory we have the clear expression from the judges that a patent might be valid if such an act of inventive ingenuity had not in fact taken place. Thus we have it plainly held both before and subsequent to the decision in *Crane* v. *Price*[79] that an accidental discovery may be good foundation for a patent.[80]

The principle to be extracted from these decisions is therefore the *reductio ad absurdum* that, although no inventive act *in fact* took place, nevertheless the disclosure of the patent must be for something that, *in theory*, required an act of inventive genius or ingenuity to produce it. Attempts were made from time to time to preserve the spirit of the Statute of Monopolies by requiring only that an invention or improvement should be a manufacture and be possessed of novelty, and utility, without examination of the quantitative content of the contribution to science or industry involved in scrutinizing the quality of the act of the mind which produced the improvement. Thus in 1843 Lord Brougham said in the case of *Soames's Patent*:[81]

It is very fit their lordships should guard against the inference being drawn, from the small amount of any step made in improvement, that they are disposed to undervalue that in importance; if a new process is invented, if new machinery is invented, if a new principle is found out and applied so as to become the subject of a patent right, embodied in a manufacture, then, however small it may be in advance of the state of science or of art previous to the period of that step being made, that is no reason whatever for undervaluing the merits of the person who makes a discovery in science or an invention in art, because the whole history of

[79](1842) 1 W.P.C. 377.

[80]See ante 229.

[81](1843) 1 W.P.C. 729 at 735.

science, from the greatest discoveries down to the most unimportant—from the discovery of the system of gravitation itself, and the fractional calculus itself, down to the most trifling step that has ever been made—is one continued illustration of the slow progress by which the human mind makes its advance in discovery; it is hardly perceptible, so little has been made by any one step in advance of the former state of things, because generally you find that just before there was something very nearly the same thing discovered or invented.[82]

But the new theory of inventive ingenuity was apparently attractive for, once promulgated, it quickly gained adherents. So, by the year 1867, just twenty-five years after *Crane* v. *Price*, we have Malins, V.-C., saying, in *White* v. *Toms*:[83] "There is no invention in it. However meritorious as an improvement . . . it is not the subject of a patent."[84]

Nearly twenty years later, this new doctrine was still imperfectly understood for in *Hayward* v. *Hamilton*[85] we find Brett, L.J., saying:

There was a point raised and discussed which for a time did seem to me to present a difficulty, namely, whether although this was new and useful, it could be said to be an invention. Now the difficulty that that proposition presented to me was this: that I did not recollect of myself any case in which, where a thing had been pronounced to be new and useful, the question of whether it was an invention had been ever discussed, or even left to a jury, for instance. It seemed to me in all previous cases it had been taken for granted that if the thing were new and useful there must have been an invention in order to arrive at a thing that can be so described, and I should say that in nine hundred and ninety-nine cases out of a thousand that must be so. I say if the thing is new and useful it is impossible to suppose there is not sufficient to make an invention, but I do not think as a matter of law that could be predicated as an absolute rule of law, because I think it is possible, although a thing were new and useful, it might be, under certain circumstances, that there was no invention in it.

It would seem that this was the point at which confusion entered. The issue of whether a patent discloses a step forward in an art relates solely to the question of novelty. The courts arrived at the dubious conclusion that it related to subject matter. The result is that the content of ideas relating to subject matter became enlarged with the addition of a quality which never should

[82]Compare this reasonable statement with the modern doctrine enunciated by Judge Arnold quoted post 294.

[83](1867) 37 L.J.Ch. 204.

[84]See also Horton v. Mabon (1862-3) 12 C.B.N.S. 437; 16 C.B.N.S. 141; 31 L.J.C.P. 255 per Willes, J. "No doubt a new combination of old machinery or instruments, whereby a new and useful result is attained, may be the subject of a patent; but there must be some invention."

[85](1879-81) Griff. P.C. 115 at 121.

have been included in that content. The true orbit of the idea of subject matter is coterminous with the idea of "manufacture." The sole question on the issue of subject matter should never have been allowed to go farther than an inquiry whether what was disclosed by the patent was a manufacture within the meaning of the Statute of Monopolies. After that inquiry had been decided in the affirmative, there was only one further question to be asked: "Was it new?" The concept of importing into the question for decision a theory of inventive ingenuity which must be present as a quality but not as a *fact*, savours somewhat of the blind man in the dark room looking for the black cat that was not there.

Lord Esher, M. R., tried to stem the tide when he said in *Edison Bell Phonograph Co.* v. *Smith & Young*:[86]

Now, whenever I hear the objection taken to a patent which has been used, which has been bought and sold, which has been therefore treated by men of business, as a useful thing, that it is wanting in subject matter, I look upon it, I confess, with an amused contempt. What is the meaning of want of subject matter? It is not the same thing as want of invention, or rather I should say want of novelty;[87] it is not the same thing as want of utility, but, where you cannot maintain either of these propositions which would be sufficient to destroy the patent, it is something else which someone or other at some time has invented as an idea for destroying patents.

And what is it? It really comes to this, that, although the invention is new—that is, that nobody has thought of it before—although it is useful, yet when you consider it you come to the conclusion that it is so easy, so palpable that everybody who thought for a moment would come to the same conclusion; or, in more homely language, hardly judicial, but rather business-like, it comes to this, it is so easy that any fool could do it. Well, I look, as I say, upon that objection, when all others have failed, generally with amused contempt. It can be made out, but hardly ever, when you find that which I have stated, it is hard to think that people would be buying and selling a thing—and that has been sometimes the whole thing—and yet the objection should be taken that it is wanting in subject matter.

I like Lord Esher's direct ridicule where he terms this type of defence as "something else which someone or other at some time has invented as an idea for destroying patents." For that is what it is. There is no authority for it in the Statute of James under which the previous cases had been decided and it is noteworthy that the idea had grown up by such insensible degrees

[86](1894) 11 R.P.C. at 398.

[87]Consider the importance of this correction by Lord Esher in his own reasoning.

that Lord Esher was no more able to put his finger on its beginning or on its author than has the present writer. Like Topsy, it apparently "just growed up." Bacon's injunction had been forgotten.[88]

A factor which has been generally overlooked but which may well have had a material effect on the growth of this doctrine by the process of judge-made law is that the technicians of the Industrial Revolution created a deep impression upon the courts by their discoveries and improvements. The novel conceptions of Boulton, Watt, Arkwright, Hargreaves, Crompton, Stephenson, and others set a stamp on the quality of subject matter for letters patent which the courts felt should be emulated by all others who brought their patents before them for decision. It is probable that they felt that they were part of a rapidly advancing and improving age—an age of great strides in industries, in mechanisms, in chemistry—and that the criteria of an earlier day were no longer valid and applicable. They confused the advances of an era with the general and steadily-marching, but unspectacular advance of science and the arts, and, in doing so, lost to some extent their senses of perception and proportion. They threw away the yardstick provided them by the Statute of Monopolies, by which they were bound, and using their new-found sense of unity with a spectacular period of scientific advance as a tool, they carved themselves, without authority, a new yardstick designed to measure all advances and improvements against those of the greatest, and to cudgel down the common, painstaking improver whose work has, in all ages, contributed as much to human progress as has the genius. They were somewhat slow in arriving at this conclusion, for it came some time after *Crane* v. *Price*. It took some time for the mechanical advances of the Industrial Revolution to be fully perceived, but when they were, the altered trend of thinking on the question of subject matter became manifest. There is at least a suspicion that the new doctrinal trend on this point has been materially assisted and furthered by the impact on the scientifically untrained mind of the great inventive strides of the present century in the fields of radio communication and location, and electrical and chemical engineering.

The surprising thing about the trend of judicial decision on this point is that not only was the statute of James ever present

[88]See ante 212, n. 3.

to form a basis for decision, but that the Imperial Patents and Designs Act and all its amendments preserved the basis of grant by specific definition and reference to the Statute of Monopolies. That act has continued to include this provision: "'Invention' means any manner of new manufacture the subject of letters patent and grant of privilege within s. 6 of the Statute of Monopolies (that is, the Act of the 21st year of the reign of King James I, c. 3, intituled 'An Act concerning monopolies and dispensations with penal laws and the forfeiture thereof'), and includes an alleged invention."[89]

The trend of judicial decision in England on the question of invention continued to be quite at variance with statutory authority until 1932. Prior to 1883 the proceeding to repeal a patent was by *scire facias*. The grounds upon which a patent might be revoked were those set out in Coke's Fourth Institute[90] as being first, where two patents were granted for the same thing, the first patentee should have a *scire facias* to repeal the second patent; secondly, when a patent was granted on a false suggestion or where the King granted anything which by law he could not grant, then *jure regio*, he should have a *scire facias* to repeal the grant.[91] Proceedings by way of *scire facias* were abolished by the act of 1883,[92] it being provided that a patent could be revoked on petition to the court and that every ground on which a patent might, at the commencement of the act, be repealed by *scire facias* should be available by way of defence to an action for infringement, and should also be a ground of revocation.[93] This was continued with some slight modification in the act of 1907.[94] The legislature did not, however, catch up with the judge-made law on the question of inventive genius until 1932 when the section was amended by adding to the grounds upon which a patent might be revoked an itemized list of sixteen specified grounds of invalidity.[95] The ground we are here concerned with as reason for revocation is:[96]

[89]This definition was continued by the Patents and Designs Act, 1907 (7 Edw. VII, c. 29, s. 93) and by the act of 1932 (22 & 23 Geo. V, c. 32, s. 93).

[90]At 88.

[91]See Sir Oliver Butler's Case (1680) 2 Vent. 334.

[92]S. 26.

[93]S. 26 (3).

[94]7 Edw. VII, c. 29, s. 25.

[95]S. 25 (3).

[96]S. 25 (2) (f).

"that the invention is obvious and does not involve any inventive step having regard to what was known or used prior to the date of the patent."

So, at long last, there was provided statutory authority for the doctrine which the courts had been exercising without authority for nearly a century—a sort of *legitimatio per subsequens matrimonium.* Even though the doctrine is now legitimate in Great Britain, it is suggested that it was rendered so only by subsequent act and the cloud of illegitimacy still hangs about its head. It never should have been born at all, and never would, if its fathers had been careful in their thinking, and it should have been obvious to its draftsman that this provision is repugnant to the definition of invention contained in Section 93 of the same Act.[97]

In reporting to Parliament in 1931, the Departmental Committee on the Patents and Designs Acts[98] considered[99] the definition of "invention" contained in Section 93, together with certain recommendations made to it, and reported against making any change therein. Two paragraphs are of interest.[100]

In support of the third proposal, namely, that there should be a sort of codification of the meaning of "patentable invention" as judicially determined to date, it was contended that obscurity and inconvenience are involved in a reference to such ancient legislation as the Statute of Monopolies and in an examination of a case law extending over several centuries.

But we see grave difficulty in the way of adopting this proposal. The general principles determining what is a patentable invention have been arrived at in a series of judicial decisions which have extended over two or three centuries, and with which there is no quarrel. Not only would any attempt to embody the result of these decisions in a statute prove very difficult and be likely to fail, but the result might be to stereotype the law at the date of the statute, and to deprive the Courts in the future of any elasticity of power of adaptation to changing circumstances such as they have enjoyed in the past. This would, we think, be a retrograde step. Further we have not found that there is any general criticism of the present position in this respect, or any general demand for any such codification as suggested.

It is suggested that, far from its being a retrograde step, it would be a most progressive one to "stereotype the law at the date of the statute." To do so would be to impart some measure of certainty to it, and it is certainty which prospective litigants

[97]Cf. supra 239.

[98]H.M. Stationery Office, Gr. Br. 1931.

[99]At 60.

[100]Paras. 279-80, at 62.

always seek—too often in vain. To deprive the courts of elasticity and power of adaptation to changing circumstances is a most desirable thing in the interests of the litigants, who should be the first concern of the courts, for to deprive them of elasticity is to deprive them of the power of arbitrariness, and to add materially to the predictability of result. The legislature is present to take care of "adaptation to changing circumstances." If this power is to reside in judicial hands why should we trouble to have a legislature? As an eminent American jurist has said, the motto of the courts should be *obsta principiis*.[101]

Peculiarly enough, the committee[102] noted that, in considering the grounds for revocation theretofore existing, legislation by reference to the grounds for revocation by way of *scire facias*[103] was inconvenient, and recommended that the grounds on which a patent can be revoked should be stated directly and exhaustively in the acts, although it recognized that "there may be some difficulty in making an exhaustive enumeration of these grounds." What it did not recognize was that such a recommendation, and more definitely still, at least one of the grounds for revocation which were placed in the act of Parliament, constituted a distinct repugnance to the definition of "invention" contained in Section 93.

The doctrine of "obviousness," however, now had full statutory authority in Great Britain and, like a willing horse, it has been flogged well-nigh to death in the decisions. If any case has been heard in recent years in Great Britain where validity of the patent was in issue, and where the defence of obviousness has not been raised, it has missed the writer's attention.[104]

The attempted definitions of invention or subject matter which go beyond the simple statement that those words equal "manufacture," inevitably lead to trouble and confusion. Apart from such an equation, no definition of either the term invention or subject matter can be given which is applicable to all cases in issue.[105] It may be said that the present practice is to settle the point by

[101]Boyd v. United States (1886) 116 U.S. 616 per Bradley, J.

[102]Paras. 122-4, at 28.

[103]S. 25 (2).

[104]Cf. Mr. Herbert Levinstein in *The Times*, May 26, 1944: "Of those decided in court 90% failed owing to lack of subject matter."

[105]Membri & Garton Ltd. et al. v. Albion Sugar Company Ltd. (1936) 53 R.P.C. 281.

negative rules which operate by a process of exclusion.[106] Where there is a doubt, each case must be considered and judged by its own facts. Thus, Fitzgibbon, L.J., in *Pirrie* v. *York Street Flax Spinning Co.*[107] said: "It is obviously impossible to frame any rule which will serve as a guide to show at once whether any particular instance is one involving invention or not. The authorities are necessarily decisions on particular cases and are useful only as affording some guide to the decision of any particular instance coming under consideration. Each case must be decided on its own merits and with reference to its own special circumstances." That statement is as applicable today as it was before the enactment of the defence of "obviousness" in the 1932 act.

This, however, is nothing more nor less than the measure of equity according to the Chancellor's conscience and the measure of justice according to the length of the Chancellor's foot.[108] Mechanical, chemical, electrical, and scientific advance is to be decided, without any standard other than the individual opinion

[106]Wright & Corson v. Brake Service Ltd. (1925) Ex. C.R. 131; (1926) S.C.R. 434.

[107](1894) 11 R.P.C. 454.

[108]The reference here is to the remark of Selden, *Table Talk*, "Equity is a roguish thing; for law we have a measure. Equity is according to the conscience of him who is Chancellor, and as that is larger or narrower, so is equity. It is all one as if they should make the standard for the measure we call a *foot* 'a chancellor's foot.' What an uncertain measure would this be? One chancellor has a long foot; another a short foot; a third, an indifferent foot; it is the same thing in the chancellor's *conscience*." In discussing the practice of the earlier chancellors judging according to their conscience, Lord Campbell (*Lives of the Lord Chancellors*, I, 12) noted that they "have decided in a very arbitrary manner, and have exposed their jurisdiction to much odium and many sarcasms." But he pointed out that "the preference of individual opinion to rules and precedents has long ceased; 'the doctrine of the court' is to be diligently found out and strictly followed; and the Chancellor sitting in equity is only to be considered a magistrate, to whose tribunal are assigned certain portions of forensic business, to which he is to apply a well-defined system of jurisprudence—being under the control of fixed maxims and prior authorities, as much as the judges of the common law." The only trouble with this statement is that it is at least arguable that the judges of the common law have not been sufficiently under the control of fixed maxims and prior authorities. They are so in theory but too often for stability of principle they are not so in fact. Cf. Frank, *Law and the Modern Mind*, 40 . . . "legislation that is being accomplished by judges"; and Brown (1920) 29 Yale Law Journal, 400—"The ancient fiction that judges never added to, but only applied, pre-existing law, has been long since discredited."

of each particular judge, and, generally speaking, by a judge who knows little, if anything, of any of the arts and sciences.

II. The United States

A recent view in the United States was promulgated by Circuit Judge Frank in *Picard* v. *United Aircraft Corporation*.[109]

"Invention" for patent purposes, has been difficult to define. Efforts to cage the concept in words have proved almost as unsuccessful as attempts verbally to imprison the concept "beautiful." Indeed, when one reads most discussions of "invention" one recalls Kipling's, "It's pretty, but is it Art?" and the aphorism that there is no sense in disputes about matters of taste. Anatole France once said that literary criticism is the adventure of the critic's soul among masterpieces. To the casual observer, judicial patent decisions are the adventures of judges' souls among inventions. For a decision as to whether or not a thing is an invention is a "value" judgment. So are many other judicial judgments in other legal provinces, but "invention" is a peculiarly elusive standard.

In the same case, Judge Learned Hand gave a negative test to the effect that nothing is an invention which is the product of "the slow but inevitable progress . . . through trial and error" and of "the exercise of persistent and intelligent search for improvement." As Judge Frank pointed out; "Obviously, for the intelligent application of such a test, there is needed the judgment of men who are experts in science, since the ordinary man has no means of knowing how any new process or machine was discovered."

The starting point of the American patent system is contained in Article I, Section 8, Clause 8 of the Constitution which invests Congress with the power to enact the necessary laws for the protection of inventions and reads as follows: "The Congress shall have power . . . to promote the progress of science and useful arts by securing for limited times to authors and inventors the exclusive right to their respective writings and discoveries."[110]

The first patent law enacted by Congress pursuant to the power conferred by the Constitution was that of April 10, 1790,[111] which was supplemented and extended by the act of February 21,

[109](1942) 53 USPQ 563 at 569.

[110]As to the power of Congress to enact legislation pertaining to patents, see the decision of the United States Supreme Court in McClurg v. Kingsland (1843) 42 U.S. 202, per Baldwin, J.; for a discussion of authorship of the patent clause in the Constitution see the article by Karl Fenning (1929), Georgetown Law Journal.

[111]1 St. at. L. 109.

1793,[112] the act of April 17, 1800,[113] and the act of February 15, 1819.[114] Subsequent complete revisions were the Patent acts of July 4, 1836[115] and of July 8, 1870.[116] The latter act was confirmed and re-enacted in the revision of 1874.[117] This statute[118] as amended May 23, 1930[119] reads as follows: "Any person who has invented or discovered any new and useful art, machine, manufacture or composition of matter or any new and useful improvement thereof, or who has invented or discovered and asexually reproduced any distinct and new variety of plant, other than a tuber-propagated plant, . . . may . . . obtain a patent therefor."[120]

It is significant to note that the Constitution of the United States authorized the grant of patents only to inventors and discoverers and there can, therefore, be no such case as that which exists in England of the grant of patents on communications from abroad.[121] Thus, in *Livingston* v. *Van Ingen*[122] Kent, C.J., said: "It seems to be admitted that Congress are authorized to grant patents only to the inventor of the useful art. . . There cannot, then, be any aid or encouragement, by means of an exclusive right under the laws of the United States, to importers from abroad of any useful invention or improvement." To the same effect Nelson, J., in *Pitts* v. *Hall*[123] said: "A person, to be entitled to the character of an inventor, within the meaning of the Act of Congress, must himself have conceived the idea embodied in his improvement. It must be the product of his own mind and genius, and not of another's."

The early view of the subject of invention in the United States and the trend of decision may be gathered from the following selection.

[112]1 St. at L. 318.

[113]1 St. at L. 37.

[114]3 St. at L. 481.

[115]5 St. at L. 117.

[116]16 St. at L. 198.

[117]Rev. St. paras. 4883-936.

[118]U.S. Code title 35, s. 31.

[119]46 St. at L. 376.

[120]The reference to a composition of matter was first mentioned in the Statute of February 21, 1793, and the phrase making possible the grant of plant patents was added by the amendment of May 23, 1930. 46 St. at L. 376.

[121]See, e.g., Edgebury v. Stephens (1693) 2 Salk. 447; 1 W.P.C. 35.

[122](1812) 9 Johns. 507 at 583.

[123](1851) 2 Blatch. 229.

Chancellor Kent in his Commentaries[124] said: "The law has no regard to the process of mind by which the invention was accomplished, whether the discovery be by accident or by sudden or by long and laborious thought."

In *Earle* v. *Sawyer*[125] the doctrine stated was that "a combination, if simple and obvious, yet if entirely new, is patentable." Justice Story[126] said: "It is of no consequence whether the thing be simple or complicated, whether it be by accident, or by long, laborious thought or by an instantaneous flash of the mind, that it was first done. The law looks to the fact, and not the process by which it is accomplished."[127]

But this simple view did not long persist. The doctrine of invention as we now know it was propounded in the leading case of *Hotchkiss* v. *Greenwood.*[128] The alleged invention related to door knobs and consisted only in the substitution of material in order to make a previously known type of door knob out of clay and porcelain instead of out of metal as theretofore. In holding the patent invalid for lack of invention, the Supreme Court laid down the doctrine that "unless more ingenuity and skill in applying the old method . . . were required . . than were possessed by an ordinary mechanic acquainted with the business, there was an absence of that degree of skill and ingenuity which constitute essential elements of every invention. In other words, the improvement is the work of the skilful mechanic, not that of the inventor." That definition supplied the standard of inventiveness to be used in judging validity, although, as we shall see, it has been knocked about a bit, and its interpretation and application in some recent cases is causing a great amount of strain if not actual distortion. Some further references may usefully be considered as expository of the principle laid down by the Supreme Court in that case.

[124]2 Kent's Comm. 371.

[125](1825) 4 Mason 1.

[126]Earle v. Sawyer (1825) 4 Mason 1 at 16.

[127]See per Woodbury, J., in Hotchkiss v. Greenwood (1850) 52 U.S. 248 at 269.

[128](1850) 52 U.S. 248. See Carl A. Castellan, "The Shifting Sands of Skill and Ingenuity" (1946) 28 J.P.O.S., 416 at 419: "It appears, therefore, that the judicial trend toward ever higher standards of ingenuity lacks any legislative or constitutional basis. A careful consideration of the matter will show that it was unnecessary and unfortunate ever to have considered ingenuity a factor of a patentable invention."

In *Ransom* v. *The Mayor of New York*[129] Hall, J., said, "Invention in the sense of the patent law, is the finding out, contriving, devising, or creating something new and useful, which did not exist before, by an operation of the intellect." In 1885 in *Rosenwasser* v. *Berry*[130] Colt, J., said, "Not every improvement is invention; but to entitle a thing to protection it must be the product of some exercise of the inventive faculties, and it must involve something more than what is obvious to persons skilled in the art to which it relates." In 1886, Dwyer, J., said in *May* v. *County of Fond du Lac*,[131] "To be patentable, a thing must not only be new and useful, but must amount to an invention or discovery." Again, in *Smith* v. *Elliott*[132] Woodruff, J., said, "The law, however, gives no monopoly to industry, to wise judgment, or to mere mechanical skill in the use of known means, nor to the product of either if it be not new. These are within the proper field of competition, and are open to all. In general they will in that competition be justly appreciated, and will command their proper remuneration if usefully employed. It is invention of what is new, and not comparative superiority or greater excellence in what was before known, which the law protects as exclusive property, and it is that alone which is secured by patent."

A comparatively modern view may be had from the decision in *Radiator Specialty Co.* v. *Buhot*.[133]

> The question of invention being a question of fact, to be determined, however, by rules of law, we are constrained to hold the patent valid on a fact-finding of invention in its subject matter. In pronouncing this judgment we may observe that, though invention, it is not a great one. Yet, though not the work of genius, it still may be invention. Invention is not always the offspring of genius; for frequently it is the product of plain hard work; not infrequently it arises from accident or carelessness; occasionally it is a happy thought of an ordinary mind; and there have been instances where it is the result of sheer stupidity. It is with the inventive concept, the thing achieved, not with the manner of its achievement or the quality of the mind which gave it birth, that the patent law concerns itself.

This seemingly moderate and reasonable view was, however, promulgated alongside a doctrinal trend which had been pro-

[129](1856) 1 Fisher 252 at 265.
[130](1885) 22 Fed. Rep. 841 at 843.
[131](1886) 27 Fed. Rep. 691 at 695.
[132](1872) 1 O.G. 331 at 332.
[133](1930) 39 F. 2d 373 at 376.

nounced as early as 1880 when the Supreme Court spoke of "a flash of thought" as a vital ingredient of invention.[134]

Such, in general, was the trend of judicial decision in the United States until the holding of the Supreme Court in the case of *Cuno Engineering Corporation* v. *The Automatic Devices Corporation.*[135] In that case Douglas, J., delivering the opinion of the Court, said:[136]

> We may concede that the functions performed by Mead's combination were new and useful. But that does not necessarily make the device patentable. Under the Statute[137] the device must not only be "new and useful," but it must also be an "invention" or "discovery." Since *Hotchkiss* v. *Greenwood,*[138] decided in 1851, it has been recognized that if an improvement is to obtain the privileged position of a patent more ingenuity must be involved than the work of a mechanic skilled in the art. "Perfection of workmanship however much it may increase the convenience, extend the use, or diminish expense, is not patentable."[139] The principle of the Hotchkiss case applied to the adaptation or combination of old or well-known devices for new uses. That is to say the new device, however useful it may be, must reveal the flash of creative genius, not merely the skill of the calling. If it fails, it has not established its right to a private grant on the public domain.
>
> Tested by that principle Mead's device was not patentable. We cannot conclude that his skill in making this contribution reached the level of inventive genius which the Constitution[140] authorizes Congress to reward.

Since the decision in the *Cuno Case* was handed down, a great deal of disputation has been indulged in and a great deal of writing has been published criticizing the decision in no uncertain terms and pointing out the radical and deleterious effect it will have upon the progress of research on this continent.

The great criticism that is now levelled against this doctrine first found expression in 1850 when Woodbury, J., in his dissenting judgment in the Supreme Court in *Hotchkiss* v. *Greenwood*[141] showed that there was no precedent or authority for the distinction between inventive genius and mechanical skill. After setting out the basis of decision in previous English and American cases he said: "It is thus apparent to my mind that the test adopted below for the purpose to which it was applied, and which has just been

[134]Densmore v. Scofield (1880) 102 U.S. 375 at 378.

[135](1941) 51 USPQ 272.

[136]At 275.

[137]35 U.S.C. para. 31, R.S., paras. 48, 86.

[138](1850) 52 U.S. (11 How.) 248, 267.

[139]Reckendorfer v. Faber (1875) 2 Otto (92 U.S.) 347, 356, 357.

[140]Art. 1, para. 8.

[141](1850) 52 U.S. 248 at 270.

sanctioned here, has not the countenance of precedent, either English or American; and, at the same time, it seems open to great looseness or uncertainty in practice." More will be said about this at a later stage in this discussion.

III. Canada

What is the position in Canada? The foundation of our patent law is traced to the statute of Lower Canada of 1823.[142] This Statute granted to inventors of any art, machine, manufacture, or composition of matter invented by them, the exclusive right and liberty of making, constructing, using, and vending to others to be used, the said invention.

In 1826 the act was duplicated in Upper Canada.[143] These two acts were amended and consolidated on various occasions, and were, after Confederation, superseded by the act of 1869,[144] passed by the federal legislature by virtue of the jurisdiction conferred upon it by the British North America Act, 1867,[145] whereby "Patents of invention and discovery" were assigned to the exclusive jurisdiction of the Parliament of Canada. This act, which was modelled upon the then existing Patent Act of the United States of 1836, forms broadly the basis of our subsequent acts. The basis of grant was contained in Section 6 which provided as follows: "Any person . . . having invented or discovered any new and useful art, machine, manufacture, or composition of matter, or any new and useful improvement . . . may . . . obtain a patent granting to such person an exclusive property therein. . . . "

This act was in turn superseded by the act of 1872[146] to which were made amendments in 1903,[147] 1919,[148] and 1921.[149] It was amended and consolidated in 1923[150] and again in 1935[151], which latter act now constitutes the present patent law of Canada, the basis of grant being found in Section 26 which reads as follows: "26.—(1) Subject to the subsequent provisions of this section,

[142] 4 Geo. IV, c. 25.

[143] 7 Geo. IV, c. 5.

[144] 32-3 Vic., c. 11.

[145] S. 91 (22).

[146] 35 Vic., c. 26.

[147] 3 Edw. VII, c. 46.

[148] 10 Geo. V, c. 26; 9 & 10 Geo. V, c. 64.

[149] 11 & 12 Geo. V, c. 44.

[150] 13-14 Geo. V, c. 23.

[151] 25-6 Geo. V, c. 32.

any inventor of an invention . . . may . . . obtain a patent granting to him an exclusive property in such invention."

The interpretation section of the act[152] defines the word "invention" as meaning "any new and useful art, process, machine, manufacture or composition of matter, or any new and useful improvement in any art, process, machine, manufacture or composition of matter."

The words "or discovered" were eliminated in the 1872 revision. The act of 1935, therefore, save that it for the first time attempted a definition of the term "invention" provided for no different basis of grant than that existing after 1872. Indeed, it is obvious that the act did not furnish a definition of the word "invention" of any greater certainty than that contained in the act of 1923 or the previous acts.

Canada in its patent statutes has followed more closely the statutory law of the United States than it has that of England. And yet, the strange spectacle is presented that, while we in Canada have adopted practically *ipsissima verba* the patent statute of the United States, at least in so far as its definition of invention and grant of patents is concerned, we have followed closely the jurisprudence established by decisions in England. It is always difficult to ride two horses at once. The results are sometimes complicated but happily in this instance the courts of Canada have been enabled to straddle the horses with reasonable success, placing one foot firmly on the legislative enactment which follows United States practice and the other on the judicial interpretation by the English courts of the Statute of Monopolies. The result is, of course, not entirely satisfactory. While we in Canada operate under a statute which in its essential provision is *verbatim* the same as that of the United States, practically no American decisions interpreting this section are ever cited in Canadian courts but on the other hand, many decisions of the English courts, and particularly of the House of Lords, are cited which define and interpret the meaning to be placed upon the words "subject matter" and "obviousness" which are used so much in England and which find no place in the Canadian statute.

The first Canadian case that had to be decided on the question of subject matter occurred after the doctrine of invention *versus*

[152]S. 2 (d).

mechanical skill had begun to exercise the courts in England, and had been firmly established in the United States by the decision of the Supreme Court in *Hotchkiss* v. *Greenwood.*[153] While the earliest reported instance of an action brought upon letters patent in Canada is *Van Norman* v. *Leonard*[154] the decision in that case did not turn upon the question of invention or subject matter.

The early Canadian cases[155] followed the earlier English decisions. While the word "invention" was used in those judgments, it was employed, following the wording of the Upper Canada statute, as a word of coextensive significance with the word "manufacture." It was used as a term descriptive of the subject of the patent and not as descriptive of the mental act which called that subject into existence. In those cases, the trend of decision may clearly be seen as approximating the basis employed in England. The defences employed were that the subject of the patent was not a *new* invention, i.e., that it was not a new manufacture, and that it was insufficiently described in the specification. But with the decision of the Upper Canada Court of Common Pleas in *Waterous* v. *Bishop*,[156] the new doctrinal trend introduced in England by such decisions as *Horton* v. *Mabon*[157] and *White* v. *Toms*[158] found its way into Canadian jurisprudence, and we find Hagarty, C.J., citing with approval and following the principle laid down in those cases that "no doubt a new combination of old machinery or instruments whereby a new and useful result is attained may be the subject of a patent; but there must be some invention." Thus, the doctrinal trend of transposing the application of the word "invention" from a physical fact to a mental quality was seized upon as a further judicial method of invalidating patents and the process became complete when, in *Ball* v. *Crompton Corset Co.*,[159] the doctrine was adopted and approved by the Supreme Court of Canada.

153(1850) 52 U.S. 248.

154(1845) 2 U.C.Q.B. 72.

155Smith v. Hall (1861) 21 U.C.Q.B. 122; Huntington v. Lutz (1864) 13 U.C.C.P. 168; Emery v. Iredale (1862) 11 U.C.C.P. 106; Powell v. Begley (1867) 13 Gr. 381; Summers v. Abell (1869) 15 Gr. 532.

156(1870) 20 U.C.C.P. 29.

157(1862-3) 12 C.B.N.S. 437; 16 C.B.N.S. 141; 31 L.J.C.P. 255.

158(1867) 37 L.J.Ch. 204.

159(1887) 13 S.C.R. 469.

The modern Canadian view on the subject of invention may be gathered by an examination of one or two recent cases. Thus, in *Canadian Gypsum Co. Ltd.* v. *Gypsum, Lime and Alabastine, Canada Ltd.*[160] Maclean, J., said:

To support a valid patent there must be something more than a new and useful manufacture, it must have involved somehow the application of the inventive mind; the invention must have required for its evolution some amount of ingenuity to constitute subject-matter, or in other words invention. Fortunately the law does not authorize the granting of a monopoly for everything that is new and useful. The design of the patent law is to reward those who make some substantial discovery or invention which adds to our knowledge and makes a step in advance in the useful arts. If there is no novelty there can of course be no inventive ingenuity, but if there is novelty in the sense required in the law of patents, it must be the product of original thought or inventive skill.

In the Judicial Committee of the Privy Council Lord Dunedin gave a very succinct definition of invention in *Pope Appliance Corporation* v. *Spanish River Pulp and Paper Mills Ltd.*[161] where he said: "After all, what is invention? It is finding out something which has not been found out by other people."

It is obvious, of course, that Lord Dunedin's definition is an over-simplification of the problem as it stood at the date of his judgment unless there is imported into the expression "finding out" some of the meaning which now surrounds the word "invention" rather than that which attaches to the word "discovery."

Maclean, J., put the matter more shortly in *Crosley Radio Corporation* v. *Canadian General Electric Co. Ltd.*[162] when he said: "There is an 'impalpable something' which distinguishes things invented from things otherwise produced."[163]

That is the state in which the law presently stands. In succeeding chapters we shall see some of the results that have followed from this doctrinal trend.

[160](1931) Ex. C.R. 187.

[161](1929) 46 R.P.C. 55.

[162](1935) Ex. C.R. 190. The judgment of the Supreme Court of Canada on appeal, (1936) S.C.R. 551, is a striking illustration of the "value" quality of a decision on the question of invention.

[163]See also Harris v. Brandreth (1925) 42 R.P.C. 471.

XVIII. CROSS-CURRENTS IN JUDICIAL OPINION

IT seems somewhat curious that this doctrine of an impalpable something which distinguishes things invented from things otherwise produced should be propounded in the face of the following doctrine laid down by the Supreme Court of Canada in *Smith* v. *Goldie*.[1] "There have been some most important inventions made by mere accidental discovery, and after being discovered, the great wonder. has been, that what appears after discovery so palpable, had never been discovered before. Such may be said, to some extent of the discovery in this case, but there is no reason why the inventor should not get the benefit of his discovery through its protection as provided by law."

It would be indeed interesting to know what is the "impalpable, distinguishing something" in an accidental discovery that brings it within the doctrine of invention. Where, for example, in an accidental discovery, is the "flash of genius" required by the doctrine of the *Cuno Case* and its Canadian counterparts? Is this merely a perpetuation of the absurdity that, although *in fact* no inventive act took place, the quality of the subject matter of a patent must be such that *in theory* an inventive act was necessary to produce the subject matter? In other words, if the accidental discoverer asks for a patent which required no exercise of the inventive faculty at all for the reason that he did not have to think about the problem, he must nevertheless prove that the subject matter for the patent was such that if he had thought about it, it would require a certain high quality of thought characterized by the expression "inventive ingenuity."

Occasionally a word of warning has been sounded by some courts on this important question. Thus, in *British Westinghouse Electric & Manufacturing Co.* v. *Braulik*,[2] Fletcher Moulton, L.J., had this to say: "I confess that I view with suspicion arguments

[1](1883) 9 S.C.R. 48, per Henry, J.

[2](1910) 27 R.P.C. 209; see also British Celanese Ltd. v. Courtaulds Ltd. (1933) 50 R.P.C. at 269 per Lord Hanworth, M.R.; British Acoustic Films Ltd. v. Poulsen (1936) 53 R.P.C. 221 at 251.

to the effect that a new combination bringing with it new and important consequences in the shape of practical machines, is not an invention, because, when it has once been established, it is easy to show how it might be arrived at by starting from something known, and taking a series of apparently easy steps. This *ex post facto* analysis of invention is unfair to the inventors and in my opinion it is not countenanced by English patent law."

But Lord Justice Fletcher Moulton was unfortunately a voice crying in the wilderness on this point. For some reason or other commercial success has always been regarded with suspicion from the Bench. Thus, Viscount Haldane, L.C., said in *British Thomson-Houston Co. Ltd.* v. *Charlesworth Peebles & Co. et al.*:[3] "It has slowly but surely resulted in a great commercial success. That fact affords the presumption of novelty in discovery. But it does not follow by any means conclusively that the improvement lay in a discovery based on a new invention. It may have consisted in a mere improvement, of however great an order, in the mode of treatment of metal, due to what was no more than increased skill in the mode of preparation, arising from what was no more than improvement in the technical art of the metal worker."[4]

The Canadian view was put by Maclean, J., in *Crosley Radio Corporation* v. *Canadian General Electric Co. Ltd.*[5] where he said: "A favourite form of argument of counsel in supporting invention in a patent is to put the question: Why did not some one else suggest this before? Asking such a question does not necessarily carry one far in deciding whether or not there is invention in any particular case. If it were known that there were a well-defined need and demand for a particular improvement, that the solution had long been sought, and that considerable experimental work had been done in that connection, the question would have some force."

Again, it will be noted how the question of commercial success is looked upon with suspicion and the greatest amount of caution is exercised to preserve meritorious inventions from being held valid. Here again the length of the Chancellor's foot is more

[3](1925) 42 R.P.C. 180 at 195.

[4]To the same effect see the words of Sargent, L.J., in British United Shoe Machinery Co. Ltd. v. Johnson (1925) 42 R.P.C. 243 at 252.

[5](1935) Ex. C.R. 190 at 197; see also (1936) S.C.R. 551.

important than practical improvements to civilization and human living. Romer, L. J., might say in *Woodrow* v. *Long Humphreys & Co.*[6]—"In questions relating to patents it is more than usually necessary to beware of that wisdom that comes after the event . . . . If the thing was so obvious how comes it that it was not thought of before?"—but the note of warning has in general been ignored. This question of commercial success and the judicial attitude towards it is of some importance to our subject. We shall have more to say on it at a later stage.

[6](1934) 51 R.P.C. at 33.

XIX. RESULTS OF JUDICIAL UNCERTAINTY

THE uncertainty of judicial opinion on the question of invention indicates that there is a serious problem to be solved.[1] Uncertainty of judicial opinion is a result of the arbitrary principle of deciding the question without a fixed standard. This arbitrariness is no better illustrated than by an examination of actual occurrences in the decided cases. In the tables below a selection has been made of Canadian, English, and American decisions where the question of the validity of the patent in suit has turned upon invention or no invention, giving the result of the litigation and the number of judges throughout the various courts who have held the patent invalid or valid as the case may be.

I. Canada

The following is a tabulation of all the patent cases in Canada since the establishment of the Supreme Court of Canada at the time of Confederation in 1867, which have been considered by that court, and in which the validity of the patent was in issue on the ground of lack of invention. Those cases which were further appealed to the Privy Council appear in black-face type. In each case the number of judges in each court who ruled in favour of or against the validity of the patent on this ground is clearly shown. If more than one patent was in issue in any case, such

[1]The *Second Interim Report* of the Board of Trade Committee in Great Britain, April, 1946, at 21, observes that there is a "widespread, in fact a universal feeling of dissatisfaction" with the entire conduct of legal proceedings in patent matters. This feeling stems from a number of factors, among which the *Report* notes the high cost of patent litigation, "a very general lack of confidence in the adequacy of the tribunal before which these patent cases come, and a feeling that the Judges charged with the task of deciding patent actions have not the necessary scientific technical knowledge or experience to assess the value of the expert evidence or arrive at sound conclusions where the invention in question involves, as it frequently does, the discussion of highly complex chemical, electrical, mechanical or physical matters."

fact is indicated, together with the result of the judicial vote in each case.

Name of Case	*Citation*	*Court*	*No. of Judges for validity*	*No. of Judges against validity*
Smith v. Goldie	Unreported	Ont. Ct. of Ch.		1
	(1882) 7 Ont. A.R. 628	Ont. C.A.		4
	(1883) 9 S.C.R. 46	S.C.C.	5	
Hunter v. Carrick	(1881) 28 Gr. 489	Ont. Ct. of Ch.	1	
	(1883) 10 Ont. A.R. 449	Ont. C.A.	1	3
	(1884) 11 S.C.R. 300	S.C.C.	4	1
Grip Printing & Publishing Co. of Toronto v. Butterfield	Unreported	Ont. H.C.J.	1	
	(1885) 11 O.A.R. 145	Ont. C.A.		3
	(1885) 11 S.C.R. 291	S.C.C.	5	
Ball v. Crompton	(1885) 9 O.R. 228	Ont. H.C.J.		1
	(1886) 12 O.A.R. 738	Ont. C.A.		4
	(1887) 13 S.C.R. 469	S.C.C.		5
Dansereau v. Bellemare	Unreported	Que. S.C.	1	
	Unreported	Que. Ct. of Q.B.		5
	(1889) 16 S.C.R. 180	S.C.C.	5	
Wisner v. Coulthard	Unreported	Ont. Q.B.		1
	Unreported	Ont. C.A.		4
	(1893) 22 S.C.R. 178	S.C.C.	1	4
Meldrum v. Wilson	(1901) 7 Ex. C.R. 198	Ex. C.C.		1
	Cout. Dig. 1039	S.C.C.		5

Name of Case	*Citation*	*Court*	*No. of Judges for validity*	*No. of Judges against validity*
Copeland-Chatterson v. Paquette	(1906) 10 Ex. C.R. 410	Ex. C.C.		1
	(1906) 38 S.C.R. 451	S.C.C.		5
Clinton Wire Cloth Co. v. Dominion Fence Co.	(1907) 11 Ex. C.R. 103	Ex. C.C.	1	
	(1907) 39 S.C.R. 535	S.C.C.	5	
Dominion Chain Co. v. McKinnon Chain Co.	(1918) 17 Ex. C.R. 255	Ex. C.C.		1
	(1919) 58 S.C.R. 121	S.C.C.	1	4
Durable Electric Appliance Co. Ltd. v. Renfrew Electric Products Ltd.	(1926) 31 O.W.N. 93	S.C.O.	1	
	(1926) 59 O.L.R. 527	S.C.O. App. Div.		5
	(1928) S.C.R. 8	S.C.C.		5
Pope Appliance Corpn. v. Spanish River Pulp & Paper Mills Ltd.	(1927) Ex. C.R. 28	Ex. C.C.		1
	(1928) S.C.R. 20	S.C.C.		5
	(1929) 46 R.P.C. 23	J.C.P.C.	5	
Canadian Raybestos Co. Ltd. v. Brake Service Corpn. Ltd. et al.	(1926) Ex. C.R. 187	Ex. C.C.		1
	(1928) S.C.R. 61	S.C.C.		5
Adams & Westlake Co. et al. v. E. T. Wright Ltd.	(1928) Ex. C.R. 112	Ex. C.C.	1	
	(1929) S.C.R. 81	S.C.C.	5	
Guettler et al. v. Canadian International Paper Co. et al.	(1927) 4 D.L.R. 517	Ex. C.C.		1
	(1928) S.C.R. 438	S.C.C.		5

Name of Case	*Citation*	*Court*	*No. of Judges for validity*	*No. of Judges against validity*
Detroit Rubber Products Inc. v. Republic Rubber Co.	(1927) 4 D.L.R. 744 (1928) S.C.R. 578	Ex. C.C. S.C.C.		1 5
Nieblo Mfg. Co. v. Reid et al.	(1927) 4 D.L.R. 785 (1928) S.C.R. 579	Ex. C.C. S.C.C.		1 5
Canadian General Electric Co. Ltd. v. Fada Radio Ltd.	(1927) Ex. C.R. 134 (1928) S.C.R. 239 (1930) 47 R.P.C. 69	Ex. C.C. S.C.C. J.C.P.C.	1 3	 5
Grissinger v. Victor Talking Machine Co. of Canada Ltd.	(1929) Ex. C.R. 24 (1931) S.C.R. 144	Ex. C.C. S.C.C.		1 5
Mailman et al. v. Gillette Safety Razor Co. of Can. Ltd.	(1932) Ex. C.R. 54 (1932) S.C.R. 724	Ex. C.C. S.C.C.	1 	 5
Gillette Safety Razor Co. of Can. Ltd. v. Pal Blade Corpn. Ltd. et al.	(1932) Ex. C.R. 132 (1933) S.C.R. 142	Ex. C.C. S.C.C.		1 5
Burt Business Forms Ltd. v. Autographic Register Systems Ltd.	(1932) Ex. C.R. 39 (1933) S.C.R. 230	Ex. C.C. S.C.C.		1 5
Lightning Fastener Co. Ltd. v. Colonial Fastener Co. Ltd. et al.	(1932) Ex. C.R. 89 (1933) S.C.R. 363 (1934) 51 R.P.C. 349	Ex. C.C. S.C.C. J.C.P.C.	1 5	 5

Name of Case	*Citation*	*Court*	*No. of Judges for validity*	*No. of Judges against validity*
Lightning Fastener Co. Ltd. v. Colonial Fastener Co. Ltd. et al.	Unreported	Ex. C.C.		1
	(1933) S.C.R. 371	S.C.C.		5
Lightning Fastener Co. Ltd. v. Colonial Fastener Co. Ltd. et al.	(1932) Ex. C.R. 127	Ex. C.C.		1
	(1933) S.C.R. 377	S.C.C.		5
Baldwin International Radio Co. of Can. Ltd. v. Western Electric Co. Inc. et al.	(1933) Ex. C.R. 13	Ex. C.C.	1	
	(1934) S.C.R. 94	S.C.C.	5	
Dominion Mfrers. Ltd. v. Electrolier Mfg. Co. Ltd.	(1933) Ex. C.R. 141	Ex. C.C.	1	
	(1934) S.C.R. 436	S.C.C.	5	
Baldry v. McBain et al.	(1935) 4 D.L.R. 160	Man. C.A.		5
	(1936) 1 D.L.R. 673	S.C.C.		5
Canadian General Electric Co. Ltd. v. Crosley Radio Corpn.	(1935) Ex. C.R. 190	Ex. C.C.		1
	(1936) S.C.R. 551	S.C.C.		5
B.V.D. Co. Ltd. v. Canadian Celanese Ltd.	(1936) Ex. C.R. 139	Ex. C.C.		
Pat. 265, 960			1	
311, 185				1
265, 960	(1937) S.C.R. 221	S.C.C.		5
	(1939) 56 R.P.C. 122	J.C.P.C.	(Anticipation)	5

Name of Case	*Citation*	*Court*	*No. of Judges for validity*	*No. of Judges against validity*
The King, v. Smith Incubator Co. et al.	(1936) Ex. C.R. 105	Ex. C.C.	1	
	(1937) S.C.R. 238	S.C.C.		5
Smith Incubator Co. v. Seiling	(1936) Ex. C.R. 114	Ex. C.C.		1
	(1937) S.C.R. 251	S.C.C.		5
Imperial Tobacco Co. of Canada Ltd. v. Rock City Tobacco Co. Ltd. et al.	(1936) Ex. C.R. 229	Ex. C.C.		1
	(1937) S.C.R. 398	S.C.C.		5
Belding-Corticelli et al. v. Kaufman	(1938) Ex. C.R. 152	Ex. C.C.		1
	(1940) S.C.R. 388	S.C.C.		5
Niagara Wire Weaving Co. Ltd. v. Johnson Wire Works Ltd.	(1939) Ex. C.R. 259	Ex. C.C.		
Pat. 234, 657				1
259, 465				1
332, 216				1
	(1940) S.C.R. 700	S.C.C.		
Pat. 234, 657				5
259, 465				5
332, 216				5
Samson-United of Canada Ltd. et al. v. Canadian Tire Corpn. Ltd.	(1939) Ex. C.R. 277	Ex. C.C.	1	
	(1940) S.C.R. 386	S.C.C.	5	
National Electric Products Corpn. v. Industrial Electric Products Ltd.	(1939) Ex. C.R. 282	Ex. C.C.		1
	(1940) S.C.R. 406	S.C.C.		5

Name of Case	Citation	Court	No. of Judges for validity	No. of Judges against validity
Beck v. United Drug. Co. Ltd. et al.	(1940) 3 D.L.R. 437	Ex. C.C.	1	
	(1941) 1 D.L.R. 99	S.C.C.		5
Northern Electric Co. Ltd. et al. v. Brown's Theatres Ltd.	(1939) 3 D.L.R. 729	Ex. C.C.		
Five patents				
No. 3				1
No. 4			1	
No. 5				1
	(1941) S.C.R. 224	S.C.C.		
No. 3				5
No. 4			5	
Somerville Paper Boxes Ltd. et al. v. Cormier	(1941) Ex. C.R. 49	Ex. C.C.		1
	(1941) 1 D.L.R. 367	S.C.C.		5
Short Milling Co. (Canada) Ltd. v. Weston (Continental Soya Co. Ltd. v. Short Milling)	(1941) Ex. C.R. 69	Ex. C.C.		
Pat. 347, 252			1	
347, 251			1	
345, 532			1	
345, 534			1	
	(1942) 2 Fox. Pat. C. 103	S.C.C.		
Pat. 347, 252			5	
347, 251			5	
345, 532			5	
345, 534			5	

Name of Case	*Citation*	*Court*	*No. of Judges for validity*	*No. of Judges against validity*
Thermionics Ltd. et al. v. Philco Products et al.	(1941) 1 Fox Pat. C. 166	Ex. C.C.		
Pat. 213, 178			1	
265, 517			1	
	(1943) 3 Fox Pat. C. 92	S.C.C.		
Pat. 213, 178			2	3
265, 517			3	2
Fiberglas Canada Ltd. v. Spun Rock Wools Ltd. et al.*	(1942) Ex. C.R. 73	Ex. C.C.	1	
	(1943) S.C.R. 547	S.C.C.	1	4

*Reversed by the Privy Council, February 25, 1947.

The above list shows that, in Canada, since Confederation in 1867, forty-three cases involving the validity of patents in which the question of invention was in issue have been heard in the Supreme Court of Canada. Of these cases the patentee was successful in thirteen, the attack on the validity of the patent succeeded in twenty-eight, and success was divided in two.

The cases involved fifty-one patents. All, as above mentioned, were attacked on the ground of non-invention. Seventeen patents were held valid and thirty-four were held invalid on the ground that they did not show inventive ingenuity.

Four of the cases were appealed to the Judicial Committee of the Privy Council. In three of the cases the judgment of the Supreme Court of Canada was reversed where the patents had been held invalid for lack of invention. The Privy Council in each of these cases restored the judgment of the trial judge which had held the patents valid. In the fourth case the Supreme Court held the patent invalid for lack of invention: the Privy Council held the patent invalid on the ground of anticipation. Leaving, therefore, the judgments of the Privy Council out of consideration for the moment, the score for the Supreme Court of Canada for the whole term of its existence on this question is: valid—fourteen; invalid—thirty-seven.

The point to be gathered from this survey is obvious. Something must be wrong under a patent system where the Supreme Court makes use of such a very different standard of invention than does the Patent Office. The inventor solicits his patent from a department of the government and pays the appropriate fees (plus of course the fees to his attorney). When, however, he starts to litigate his patent and to enforce the monopoly granted to him on his own improvement, he finds that he has at best only a one in three chance of succeeding on the point of invention alone—to say nothing of all the other defences that are raised against him.[2] This seems to be weighting the scales a little too heavily against the inventor. The net result is, of course, that few patentees are willing to litigate their patents and infringements are widespread. In many cases, inventors think so little of patents that they do not bother to apply for them but endeavour to maintain secrecy concerning their inventions and to work them in private on the basis of keeping all the technical knowledge to themselves. The public is thus deprived of many useful inventions and the full and complete knowledge of putting them into practice.

In the period under review[3] when fifty-one patents were brought to the attention of the Supreme Court on the question of invention, 425,701 were issued by the Canadian Patent Office. Certainly only a portion of these was ever worked and developed and a much smaller number was ever infringed. But the number of patents infringed is, and always has been, immeasurably greater than the number of patents which form the basis of infringement actions. It is obvious, therefore, that many patents are being issued for no other purpose than to "paint the devil on the wall." If we are going to continue to issue patents, let us, for the good of progress and advancement in the arts, issue good patents and then sustain them in the courts except upon clear proof of anticipation.

[2]It is no answer to this argument to point out that the Patent Office is not equipped in the same manner as the courts to decide the question of validity by the presence of expert witnesses and all the testimony that can be presented by a defendant who has actively and at great expense searched the prior art for references of anticipation and prior use. That fact is admitted. But we are not here concerning ourselves about *novelty*, which is a question of fact upon which evidence may be adduced, but upon *invention*, which is a value judgment depending not upon evidence but upon judicial appreciation.

[3]1867-1944.

The survey above given is also of interest as showing something of the impossibility of eliminating judicial arbitrariness in deciding the question of invention without the use of a fixed and defined standard. These figures show the effect of "value judgments" based upon insufficient scientific and technical knowledge. Of the four cases which reached the Privy Council the Supreme Court's opinion was overruled in three. In the fourth, the Privy Council's judgment proceeded on other grounds. Of the forty-three cases heard by the Supreme Court the judgment of the lower court was overruled in eleven cases and in part in a twelfth case.

In only twenty-seven of the cases was there unanimity of opinion throughout the courts on the question of the presence or absence of invention. In sixteen of the cases there were differences in the views of the judges on this point. They all had the same evidence and the same facts before them. Yet in those sixteen cases different "values" were placed on the mystical concept of invention.

But the startling point is that in this short list of forty-three cases there were three where the final judgment was the result of the opinions on this point of only a minority of the judges who heard and determined them. Thus in *Smith* v. *Goldie*, five judges were for validity while six were against validity. In the final result the patent was held valid on a judicial vote of five to one.

In *Pope Appliance* v. *Spanish River Pulp & Paper Mills* five were for validity; six for invalidity: final result, valid five to none.

In *Canadian General Electric Co.* v. *Fada Radio* four were for validity; five for invalidity: final result, valid three to none.

One other case is worthy of note—*Lightning Fastener Co. Ltd.* v. *Colonial Fastener Co. Ltd.* For validity six; for invalidity five: final result, valid five to none. In this case the trial judge held the patent valid; the Supreme Court unanimously (five to none) held it invalid; the Privy Council, equally unanimously (five to none) restored the judgment of the trial judge and held it valid. That is probably as good an illustration as could be desired of hoping to be on the receiving end of the final judicial guess.

A further calculation has been made of the fate accorded to patents in Canada during the present century. The final result of those actions for infringement in all the courts of Canada in which the validity of the patent was clearly in issue during the years 1901-44 may be summarized as follows. There were 149 actions involving a total of 174 patents. In forty-seven of these actions success went to the plaintiff, the patent being held valid; in seventy-two the plaintiff lost on the ground of invalidity of the patent sued upon; in twenty-four the defendant won on the ground of non-infringement; and in six success was divided—as to two of these actions one patent was held valid and infringed and the second sued upon was held not infringed; as to three of them one patent was held valid and the second invalid; as to one of them three patents held invalid and one invalid in part.

As to the patents sued upon the score for and against validity was as follows: Valid fifty-three; invalid eighty-eight.

II. The United States

The trend of decision in the United States has been indicated by Judge Frank in a foot-note to his opinion in *Picard* v. *United Aircraft Corporation.*[4] Frank, J., summarizes the record of the Supreme Court of the United States as follows: May 24, 1927, to May 24, 1937, three patents held valid, sixteen held invalid.

The results of patent litigation have been further summarized by the Honourable Evan A. Evans[5] as follows (only those cases are here noted in which the validity of the patent was in issue).

Results of Patent Litigation in Circuit Courts of Appeals

(October, 1936, to March, 1941)

Number of Cases	*Patents held valid*	*Patents held invalid*	*Patents held partly valid and partly invalid*
371	86	250	35

Judge Evans summarizes the experience of patents before the Supreme Court of the United States in the following table, prepared according to five-year periods.

[4](1942) 53 USPQ 563 at 569; see 297. The Temporary National Economic Committee issued in 1941 its monograph no. 31, *Patents and Free Enterprise*, which showed that, in the period 1930 to 1939 the question of validity was in issue before the United States Supreme Court in thirty cases involving twenty-seven separate patent claims. Of the twenty-seven, only one was held valid and infringed, two were held not infringed, and twenty-four were held invalid.

[5]Of the U.S. Circuit Court of Appeals, 7th Circuit. Cf. article by Judge Evans, "Disposition of Patent Cases by the Courts" (1942) 24 J.P.O.S., 19.

Results of Patent Litigation before the Supreme Court of the United States

Years	*Total number of opinions*	*Patents held valid*	*Patents held invalid*	*Patents held not infringed*
1900-05	9	2	3	4
1906-10	7	3	1	3
1911-15	4	4	0	0
1916-20	16	5	9	2
1921-25	14	3	8	3
1926-30	12	3	5	4
1931-35	14	3	11	0
1936-40	15	0	13	2
Summary:				
1900-40	91	23	50	18
1941-45	18	3	10	5

These figures are supplemented by others from Judge Evans's own circuit, for the period October, 1936, to March, 1941, in which he shows that of seventy-four cases in which the validity of the patent was in issue, eighteen were held valid; three partly valid and partly invalid; and fifty-three invalid.

III. Great Britain

An examination has also been made in the Reports of Patent Cases[6] from the commencement of that series of reports in 1884 until the end of 1944, a period of sixty-one years, of those cases which were finally decided by the House of Lords, the final court of appeal for actions originating in Great Britain. Only those cases which were decided on the issue of invention are discussed and the results are here tabulated.

Name of Case	*Citation*	*Court*	*No. of Judges for validity*	*No. of Judges against validity*
British Dynamite Co. v. Krebs	(1875) Goodeve P.C. 88	H.C.J.	1	
	(1875) Goodeve P.C. 89	C.A.		3
	(1879) 13 R.P.C. 190	H.L.	4	

[6]Great Britain.

Name of Case	*Citation*	*Court*	*No. of Judges for validity*	*No. of Judges against validity*
Thomson v. American Braided Wire Co.	(1887) 4 R.P.C. 316	H.C.J.		1
	(1888) 5 R.P.C. 113	C.A.	3	
	(1889) 6 R.P.C. 518	H.L.		5
Morgan v. Windover	(1887) 4 R.P.C. 417	H.C.J.	1	
	(1888) 5 R.P.C. 295	C.A.	3	
	(1890) 7 R.P.C. 131	H.L.		4
In re Gaulard and Gibbs' Patent	(1888) 5 R.P.C. 525	H.C.J.		1
	(1889) 6 R.P.C. 215	C.A.		3
	(1890) 7 R.P.C. 637	H.L.	1	2
Vickers v. Siddell	(1888) 5 R.P.C. 81	H.C.J.	1	
	(1888) 5 R.P.C. 416	C.A.	3	
	(1890) 7 R.P.C. 292	H.L.	4	
Longbottom v. Shaw	(1888) 5 R.P.C. 497	H.C.J.		1
	(1889) 6 R.P.C. 143	C.A.		3
	(1891) 8 R.P.C. 333	H.L.		5
Boyd v. Horrocks	(1888) 5 R.P.C. 557	Ch. Lancs.	1	
	(1889) 6 R.P.C. 152	C.A.	3	
	(1892) 9 R.P.C. 77	H.L.	4	

Name of Case	*Citation*	*Court*	*No. of Judges for validity*	*No. of Judges against validity*
Goddard v. Lyon	(1893) 10 R.P.C. 121	H.C.J.	1	
	(1893) 10 R.P.C. 334	C.A.	3	
	(1894) 11 R.P.C. 355	H.L.	4	
Moser v. Marsden	(1893) 10 R.P.C. 205	Ch. Lancs.		1
	(1893) 10 R.P.C. 350	C.A.	3	
	(1896) 13 R.P.C. 24	H.L.	4	
Deeley v. Perkes	(1895) 12 R.P.C. 65	H.C.J.		1
	(1895) 12 R.P.C. 192	C.A. Claim 1		3
		Claim 2	3	
	(1896) 13 R.P.C. 581	H.L. Claim 1		4
		Claim 2	4	
Riekmann v. Thierry	(1895) 12 R.P.C. 412	H.C.J.	1	
	(1895) 12 R.P.C. 543	C.A.	3	
	(1897) 14 R.P.C. 105	H.L.	1	3
Dredge v. Parnell	(1898) 15 R.P.C. 84	H.C.J.		1
	(1898) 15 R.P.C. 88	C.A.	1	2
	(1899) 16 R.P.C. 625	H.L.		4
Acetylene Illuminating Co. Ltd. v. United Alkali Co. Ltd.	(1902) 19 R.P.C. 232	H C.J.		1
	(1903) 20 R.P.C. 161	C.A.		3
	(1905) 22 R.P.C. 145	H.L.		3

Name of Case	*Citation*	*Court*	*No. of Judges for validity*	*No. of Judges against validity*
In the Matter of Klaber's Patent	(1905) 22 R.P.C. 1	H.C.J.		1
	(1905) 22 R.P.C. 405	C.A.		3
	(1906) 23 R.P.C. 461	H.L.		5
Haskell Golf Ball Co. Ltd. v. Hutchison (No. 2)	(1905) 22 R.P.C. 478	H.C.J.		1
	(1906) 23 R.P.C. 301	C.A.	1	2
	(1908) 25 R.P.C. 194	H.L.		4
Arnot v. Dunlop Pneumatic Tyre Co. Ltd.	(1905) 22 R.P.C. 105	Ct. of Sess. Scotland	1	
	(1905) 22 R.P.C. 472	Ct. of Sess. Scotland Inner House		3
	(1908) 25 R.P.C. 309	H.L.		3
British Vacuum Cleaner Co. Ltd. v. London & S.W. Ry. Co.	(1910) 27 R.P.C. 649	H.C.J.	1	
	(1911) 28 R.P.C. 77	C.A.	2	1
	(1912) 29 R.P.C. 309	H.L.	7	
Pugh v. Riley Cycle Co. Ltd.	(1913) 30 R.P.C. 32	H.C.J.	1	
	(1913) 30 R.P.C. 514	C.A.	3	
	(1914) 31 R.P.C. 267	H.L.		4
Osram Lamp Works Ltd. v. Pope's Electric Lamp Co. Ltd.	(1915) 32 R.P.C. 538	H.C.J.		1
	(1916) 33 R.P.C. 29	C.A.		3
	(1917) 34 R.P.C. 369	H.L.	4	1

Name of Case	*Citation*	*Court*	*No. of Judges for validity*	*No. of Judges against validity*
British United Shoe Machinery Co. Ltd. v. Standard Rotary Machine Co. Ltd.	(1916) 33 R.P.C. 221	H.C.J.		1
	(1916) 33 R.P.C. 373	C.A.		3
	(1918) 35 R.P.C. 33	H.L.		5
British Thomson-Houston Co. Ltd. v. Duram Ltd.	(1917) 34 R.P.C. 117	H.C.J.		1
	(1917) 34 R.P.C. 148	C.A.		3
	(1918) 35 R.P.C. 161	H.L.	1	3
Bonnard v. London General Omnibus Co. Ltd.	(1919) 36 R.P.C. 279	H.C.J.		1
	(1919) 36 R.P.C. 307	C.A.	3	
	(1921) 38 R.P.C. 1	H.L.		5
Aktiengesellschatt für Autogene Aluminium Schweissung v. London Aluminium Co. Ltd. (No. 2)	(1920) 37 R.P.C. 153	H.C.J.	1	
	(1921) 38 R.P.C. 163	C.A.	2	1
	(1922) 39 R.P.C. 296	H.L.	5	
Hale v. Coombes	(1923) 40 R.P.C. 283	H.C.J.		
	Pat. A			1
	Pat. B			1
	Pat. C		1	
	Pat. D			1
	(1924) 41 R.P.C. 112	C.A.		
	Pat. B		3	
	Pat. C		3	
	(1925) 42 R.P.C. 328	H.L.		
	Pat. B		2	1

Name of Case	*Citation*	*Court*	*No. of Judges for validity*	*No. of Judges against validity*
British Celanese Ltd. v. Courtaulds Ltd.	(1933) 50 R.P.C. 63	H.C.J.		1
	(1933) 50 R.P.C. 259	C.A.		3
	(1935) 52 R.P.C. 171	H.L.		3
Mullard Radio Valve Co. Ltd. v. Philco Radio Co. Ltd. et al.	(1934) 51 R.P.C. 333	H.C.J.		1
	(1935) 52 R.P.C. 261	C.A.		3
	(1936) 53 R.P.C. 323	H.L.		4
Electric & Musical Instruments Ltd. et al v. Lissen Ltd. et al.	(1937) 54 R.P.C. 5	H.C.J.	1	
	(1937) 54 R.P.C. 307	C.A.		3
	(1939) 56 R.P.C. 23	H.L.	2	3
Non-Drip Measure Co. Ltd. v. Stranger's Ltd. et al.	(1942) 59 R.P.C. 1	H.C.J.	1	
	(1942) 59 R.P.C. 18	C.A.		3
	(1943) 60 R.P.C. 135	H.L.	4	

From the above survey it will be seen that from the year 1884 until the end of 1944—a period of sixty-one years—twenty-eight cases involving the question of invention—or subject matter as it is termed in England—were decided by the House of Lords. Of these, ten decisions held that there was proper subject matter and seventeen that there was not. In one case, success was divided—one claim being valid and one invalid. Counting that as a victory the score is eleven valid; seventeen invalid.

Here again, the arbitrariness of judgment is apparent—although not so much as on the other side of the Atlantic. But in *Morgan* v. *Windover* it is noticeable that a unanimous House of four opinions held the patent invalid as lacking in subject matter after an equal number of judicial opinions had held it a meritorious invention.

In *Osram Lamp Works Ltd.* v. *Pope's Electric Lamp Co. Ltd.*, the patent was held valid by a vote of four to one. Four judges had earlier held the patent to be lacking in subject matter and so—on a show of judicial hands—the patent was upheld by a minority.

In *Pugh* v. *Riley Cycle Co. Ltd.* the patent was held invalid by a unanimous House of four, although the same number of judges had earlier held it to be valid.

In *Electric and Musical Instruments Ltd.* v. *Lissen Ltd. et al.* the patent was declared invalid by the House dividing on the narrow margin of three to two.

On the whole, however, the results of the decisions in the House of Lords appear to be fairly consistent.

A survey has also been made of the results of decisions in all the English courts where the validity of the patent came into question from the year 1887 to the end of 1944. These figures are summarized from the Reports of Patent Cases and include all applications to the courts, whether by way of action for infringement, petition for revocation or petition for extension. These consist of all the decisions of all the courts before which patents were litigated. Where, therefore, a case went to the Court of Appeal there will be two decisions and if to the House of Lords, three. It will, therefore, be understood that it is the number of individual decisions on the question of validity that we are regarding and not the number of patents that are held good or bad. The proportion of patents held good or bad respectively will, however, compare roughly with the percentage of decisions.

Results of Patent Litigation in English Courts, 1887-1944

Period	*Number of decisions*	*Number holding patent valid*	*Number holding patent invalid*
1887-1890	87	40	47
1891-1900	275	123	152
1901-1910	250	120	130
1911-1920	110	47	63
1921-1930	104	56	48
1931-1940	85	31	54
1941-1944	14	5	9
Summary: 1887-1944	925	422	503

Again, not as bad as across the Atlantic, but the startling fact is inescapable. Only a small number of the patents issued is litigated and of that small number more than half are held invalid by the courts.

XX. RECENT SUGGESTIONS FOR IMPROVEMENT

THERE is, therefore, a serious problem to be considered. So long as we have this mystical concept known as invention which is to be judged and determined by the individual perceptions and standards of particular judges without reference to any defined standard, just so long will we be lacking any possibility of certainty or predictability of the basis upon which judgments in patent actions can be rendered. Such a situation is intolerable to prospective litigants and if a remedy with any possible prospect of workable success can be predicated, no delay should occur before it is made effective and a new system given a reasonable trial. Several suggestions have lately been made to remedy the situation and they all merit examination and consideration.

One suggestion recently made by the late Mr. Harold E. Potts, a member of the Chartered Institute of Patent Agents, London,[1] has been based upon the theory of graduated validity. Mr. Potts stated the problem by saying that "although there are insensible gradations between unpatentable improvements and patentable inventions, we must in practice treat them differently." He started with a quotation from Mr. Justice Oliver Wendell Holmes:

> When he has discovered that a difference is a difference of degree, that distinguished extremes have between them a penumbra in which one gradually shades into the other, a tyro thinks to puzzle you by asking where you are going to draw the line, and an advocate of more experience will show the arbitrariness of the lines proposed by putting cases very near it on one side or the other. But the theory of the law is that such lines exist, because the theory of the law as to any possible conduct is that it is either lawful or unlawful. As that difference has no gradation about it, when applied to shades of conduct that are very near each other, it has an arbitrary look. We like to disguise the arbitrariness, we like to save ourselves the trouble of nice and doubtful discrimination.[2]

Mr. Potts pointed out the classical resolution of this dilemma which has been adopted in British law by using the doctrine of the scintilla of inventive ingenuity and he quoted on this point from the decision of Tomlin, J., in *Samuel Parkes & Co. Ltd.* v.

[1]See Potts, "Invention in Patent Law" (1944) 7 Mod. L. Rev., 113.

[2]*Collected Legal Papers*, 233.

Cocker Bros. Ltd.[3] "Nobody, however, has told me, and I do not suppose anybody ever will tell me, what is the precise characteristic or quality the presence of which distinguishes invention from a workshop improvement. Day is day, and night is night, but who shall tell where day ends or night begins. . . . It is, I think, practically impossible to say there is not that scintilla of invention necessary to support the patent."[4]

The solution suggested by Mr. Potts is a broadening of judicial discretion in the boundary line cases. In his view, under the present system there are many cases where given improvement falls clearly inside or outside the line; these cases can be decided as heretofore. But where a case falls near the border line, within the penumbra between light and darkness, he suggested that, in an infringement action, the court should have power to grant a limited relief with discretion as to costs and other conditions. His suggestion was that no injunction would be granted against infringement but the defendant would be entitled to continue user of the patent on payment of a moderate royalty assessed by the court to be commensurate with the contribution made to the art. The clearcut cases would be adjudicated valid or invalid as hitherto; border-line cases would be adjudicated as having a validity graduated in accordance with the evidence. In effect these border line cases would be placed under conditions similar to those obtaining in patents endorsed "licences of right" and royalty could be made either nominal or substantial depending on the amount of novelty and utility in the case while all the relevant factors would also receive consideration.

Mr. Potts's theory of graduated validity applied to border line cases of invention has the unfortunate result of allowing further scope for judicial discretion. Very few judges have

[3](1929) 46 R.P.C. at 248.

[4]To the same effect see the following cases: American Braided Wire Co. v. Thomson (1889) 6 R.P.C. 518; Patent Exploitation Ltd. v. Siemens Bros. & Co. Ltd. (1904) 21 R.P.C. 549; Gramophone & Typewriter, Ltd. v. Ullman (1906) 23 R.P.C. 260, 752; Hickton's Patent Syndicate v. Patents & Machine Improvement Co. Ltd. (1909) 26 R.P.C. 61, 339; Fox v. Astrachans Ltd. (1910) 27 R.P.C. 377; Turner v. Bowman (1925) 42 R.P.C. 40; Rheostatic Co. Ltd. v. Robert McLaren & Co. Ltd. (1936) 53 R.P.C. 109 at 117; Wright & Corson v. Brake Service Ltd. (1925) Ex. C.R. 131; (1926) S.C.R. 434; Crosley Radio Corpn. v. Canadian General Electric Co. Ltd. (1935) Ex. C.R. 190; (1936) S.C.R. 551; King v. Smith Incubator Co. et al. (1936) Ex. C.R. 105; (1937) S.C.R. 238.

scientific and technical knowledge. It is not too much to say that they grasp only with extreme difficulty the principles embodied in many of the inventions contained in the patents which come before them for decision. The fear might well be expressed that the graduated theory of Mr. Potts would provide merely a retreat to easy decisions by judges either unskilled through inability, or unwilling through a sense of fatigue engendered by the length of most patent suits, to examine the evidence, the prior art, and the science sufficiently to make an all-embracing and adequate judgment.

Mr. Potts's suggestion is, in a measure, a variation of the solution sometimes advanced that there should be two types of patent, as e.g., the patent for inventions and the petty patents or Gebrauchsmuster of the German system. Mr. Potts solved the difficulty presented to the inventor and his attorney of deciding whether to apply for full protection or only a petty patent by allowing the decision to be made *ex post facto* by the court. To that extent the suggestion is unacceptable. We do not want to increase the discretion of the courts: we want rather to increase predictability of result.

Judge Frank in *Picard* v. *United Aircraft Corporation*[5] made the suggestion, based upon the theory of necessity of investment rather than invention, that there should be a classification of patentable devices into two categories: (1) "gadget" patents and those for contrivances which require for their development relatively small expenditures, and (2) those which require the investment of relatively large sums to bring them to practical fruition.[6] As to the first category, Judge Frank suggested that they might be granted only a very brief period of patent monopoly, and as to the second category, that they might be made subject to the compulsory licensing system such as that which obtains in England.[7]

It is submitted, with the greatest respect to Judge Frank, that it would be highly improper to distinguish between the relative time of protection to be accorded to patents on the basis of the expense necessary to develop them. This is, indeed, against

[5](1942) 53 USPQ 563 at 574.

[6]Cf. Woodward, "A Reconsideration of the Patent System as a Problem of Administrative Law" (1942) 55 Harv. L. Rev., 950 at 967, 969, 977.

[7]Such a system is also in operation in Canada.

all modern thinking. But apart from that, some of the best and most useful inventions can be manufactured with a minimum of capital: some requiring large capital expenditures for plant and equipment contribute only moderate, step-by-step advances in technical progress. It is felt that this proposal is based upon a faulty hypothesis. As for the suggestion that the compulsory licensing system be invoked in the United States, I have no desire to exercise the presumption of telling the learned patent profession of the United States that the Canadian and British patent systems are superior to theirs. I merely point out that the compulsory licence system has worked with great satisfaction to all parties, including the public interest, both in Canada and in England. But, if it is adopted, it should be adopted with reference to all patents and not to any one class set off by arbitrary decision. Nor should such licences be granted merely for the asking or as of right. They should be granted only in case of abuse of monopoly rights as provided in the Canadian and British systems, which are discussed a little later.[8] Otherwise there would be justification for Judge Frank's expressed fear that "a provision for universal compulsory licenses . . . may tend to frighten off extensive investment in new patents which will induce competition." If my friends in the United States will not object to such a suggestion coming from a neighbour, may I say that I believe the adoption of such a system might preclude, or at least take the sting out of, a great many of the attacks which are currently being made on the patent system. There could then be no suggestion that the patent system was being used as a vehicle to block progress and prevent improvement by buying up patents and "putting them in mothballs."[9]

A different form of argument has recently been advanced which calls to mind the words of Viscount Haldane, L.C., in the *British Thomson-Houston Case* above mentioned[10] and those of Maclean, J., in the *Crosley Radio Case*—[11] in particular that part of Mr. Justice

[8]At 300.

[9]See Picard v. United Aircraft Corporation (1942) 53 USPQ 563 at 575 per Frank, J., and see n. 27 at 574 *ibid.*

[10]British Thomson-Houston Co. Ltd. v. Charlesworth Peebles & Co. et al. (1925) 42 R.P.C. 180 at 195, see ante 253.

[11]Crosley Radio Corpn. v. Canadian General Electric Co. Ltd. (1935) Ex. C.R. 190 at 197, see ante 253.

Maclean's reasoning which states that the asking of the question, why did not some one else suggest this before, might have some force if it were known that there was a well-defined need and demand for a particular improvement, that the solution had long been sought, and that considerable experimental work had been done in that connection. The argument recently advanced[12] is that if necessity be the mother of invention a want rather soon supplied does convincingly point to obviousness to one skilled in that art or denies the exercise of invention. If, on the one hand, a problem has remained unsolved or a clear improvement has not been conceived during a period of several years prior to the date of filing of the solving or improving application for a patent, the applicant would be entitled to the benefit of a strong presumption that invention was required to make the discovery. If, on the other hand, the solving or improving application had been filed within a time to be fixed by defining the word "recent," from and after the existence of the need, obviousness and not invention would be rightly presumed.

The criticism of that point of view is again that it leaves too much to judicial discretion. It creates only a presumption. We have now the presumption of validity and invention in favour of patents which supply a long-felt want,[13] for whatever good it may be in practical working, and the suggestion made by the last mentioned writer serves only to put a term or a limitation upon the exercise of judicial discretion. As Judge Learned Hand remarked in *Condenser Corporation of America* v. *Micamold Radio Corporation*:[14] "Lapse of time alone is no test of the difficulty of taking a last step," although it may, in some cases have a considerable effect.[15] Nor can it be seen that this limitation, so long as

[12]Muller " 'Invention' Crux" (1942) 24 J.P.O.S., 795.

[13]American Braided Wire Co. v. Thomson (1888) 5 R.P.C. 125; British Vacuum Cleaner Co. Ltd. v. Suction Cleaners Ltd. (1904) 21 R.P.C. 312; Patent Exploitation Ltd. v. Siemens Bros. & Co. Ltd. (1904) 21 R.P.C. 548; British United Shoe Machinery Co. Ltd. v. Lambert Howarth & Sons Ltd. et al. (1927) 44 R.P.C. at 524; Wood et al. v. Gowshall Ltd. (1937) 54 R.P.C. 39; Howaldt Ltd. v. Condrup Ltd. (1937) 54 R.P.C. 121; General Engineering Co. of Ontario v. Dominion Cotton Mills and Stoker Co. (1899-1902) 6 Ex. C.R. 309; 31 S.C.R. 75; (1902) A.C. 570; Adams & Westlake Co. et al. v. E. T. Wright Ltd. (1928) Ex. C.R. 112; (1929) S.C.R. 81.

[14](1944) 63 USPQ 244 at 245.

[15]In re Shortell (1944) 61 USPQ 362; see also Schering Corporation v. Gilbert et al. (1946) 68 USPQ 84.

the discretion exists, will be for the good either of the patentee or of the public. It certainly has no place alongside the "flash of genius" doctrine laid down in the *Cuno Case*, for a flash of genius may arrive without chronological significance. The flash of genius is not limited by the operation of time and the statement of Mr. Muller that "a want rather soon supplied does convincingly point to obviousness to one skilled and active in that art or denies the exercise of invention" is completely contrary to the flash of genius idea enunciated by Mr. Justice Douglas. Unfortunately, the trouble with all epigrammatic formulae is that they are splendid as epigrams but prove in practice to be unhappy formulae for the solution of difficulties, legal or otherwise. The flash of genius doctrine is an excellent example of an epigrammatic formula. It constitutes an over-simplification of a complex problem and the resounding protests that have arisen since its enunciation demonstrate quite clearly that it is quite unacceptable as a formula for the resolution of those difficulties.

Other suggestions have favoured the transference of the decision on the question of invention from the judicial to the administrative branch of government. Thus, it has been suggested in the United States that a patent commission be set up, ranking with the Circuit Courts of Appeals in prestige, to pass on questions involving validity and scope of patents,[16] and also that an administrative agency be set up or the Department of Justice empowered to bring actions in court to cancel or recall patents or parts of their claims.[17] Then again, the solution has been suggested as lying in the giving to the Patent Office of the power to entertain proceedings directed to obtaining the cancellation of issued patents comparable to the opposition proceedings in Great Britain.[18] The proposal made is that the United States Patent Office be authorized to hold cancellation proceedings at any time during the life of a patent upon the motion of any interested party.

The United States National Resources Planning Board has already suggested its reform in its report:[19] "The issuance of

[16]Rice, "A Constructive Patent Law" (1939) 16 N.Y.U. Law Q. Rev., 179.

[17]Woodward, "A Reconstruction of the Patent System as a Problem in Administrative Law" (1942) 55 Harv. L. Rev., 950.

[18]Zitver, "Judicial Review of 'Invention' and a Proposed Alternative" (1943) 25 J.P.O.S., 318.

[19]National Resources Planning Board, *National Resources Development, Report for 1943*, pt. I, *Post War Plan and Program*, 1943, 28.

many unmerited patents might be forestalled by the publication of applications to make possible the challenge of patents on grounds that might otherwise be unknown to the patent office."

This suggestion was made upon the basis of eliminating a great deal of the crushing expense which attaches to patent litigation.[20] This cost is increased by the almost inevitable attack on the validity of the patent for "lack of invention" and on this point long and technical expert evidence is called to explain scientific matters to a non-technical judge. Under the proposal made it was suggested that the legislation would provide that all pending litigation involving a given patent be suspended until the termination of the cancellation proceedings.

This, of course, is not to attack the problem but only to change the forum. It is an amelioration in degree only of an almost impossible condition for the average patent owner.

The report of the United States National Patent Planning Commission[21] observed that:

the most serious weakness in the present patent system is the lack of a uniform test or standard for determining whether the particular contribution of an inventor merits the award of the patent grant. . . . There is an ever-widening gulf between the decisions of the Patent Office in granting patents and decisions of the Courts who pass upon their validity. It would be highly desirable and a great step forward if patents could be issued with a greater assurance that their validity would be upheld by the Courts. No other feature of our law is more destructive to the purpose of the patent system than this existing uncertainty as to the validity of a patent. . . . There should be a uniformity in the grant and treatment of patents. The present confusion threatens the usefulness of the whole patent system and calls for an immediate and effective remedy.

It is inconsistent with sound national policy to continue to grant patents with existing uncertainty as to their validity, and unfair to the inventors of this country and to manufacturers and investors who have proceeded on the basis of a protected security in the form of a patent issued to them by the Federal Government.

The Commission therefore recommends the enactment of a declaration of policy that patentability shall be determined objectively by the nature of the contribution to the advancement of the art, and not subjectively by the nature of the process by which the invention may have been accomplished. [The National Patent Planning Commission then proceeded to point out that] the

[20]See "Patent Injustice" by K. E. Shelley, K.C. (1942-3) 61 Transactions of the Chartered Institute of Patent Agents, 17; Potts, "The Definition of Invention in Patent Law" (1944) 7 Mod. L. Rev., 113. *Second Interim Report* of the British Board of Trade Committee, April, 1946, 21, quoted in chap. XIX, n. 1.

[21](1943) 25 J.P.O.S., 445 at 462.

provision of a definitive yardstick for determining the existence of an invention is not alone sufficient. There must also be some assurance of a uniform application of the yardstick. . . .

The Commission therefore recommends that whenever the validity of a patent is attacked in an infringement suit before a District Court, the court shall certify the record to the Patent Office for a report on the validity of the patent. The report of the Patent Office as to the effect of the court record upon the validity of the patent shall be advisory only.

As pointed out by Mr. Nathan Heard[22] the recommendations above made were obviously intended to nullify the flash of genius theory at present maintained by many of the courts and in this respect are praiseworthy. Mr. Heard criticized the proposal as being both unwise and unconstitutional. As he pointed out, the Constitution of the United States limits the patent privilege to the "inventor," and statutes repeatedly use the term "invention," and even the proposed test itself employs the latter term. Mere novelty and utility, no matter how great the contribution to the advance of the art, cannot alone constitute invention; there still must be present something additional. Mr. Heard suggested that the declaration of policy by the National Patent Planning Commission be changed to read: "That patentability shall be determined primarily objectively by the nature of the contribution to the advancement of the art and secondarily, subjectively by the nature of the process by which the patent may be accomplished."

This would mean, he submitted, that Congress declares that "the progress of science and useful arts" is to be considered by the Court as more important than the quality of invention but does not attempt to eliminate the requirement that invention must still be present. He submitted that no declaration can prevent the courts from considering the question of invention in view of the provisions of the Constitution above mentioned. With that view any student of the American Constitution must be forced to agree, if he accepts also the present meaning of the word "invention" which has arisen through judicial interpretation. Once the original meaning of the word, at the time of the framing of the Constitution, is accepted as that which was intended by the first Congress, any constitutional difficulty disappears. But it should be pointed out that there are no constitutional limitations

[22]Heard, "Uniform Standard of Invention" (1943) 25 J.P.O.S., 676; see also Schramm, "Patent Laws and the Chemist" (1945) March, Chemical and Engineering News, 537.

or questions standing in the way of statutory revision and amendment in Canada and the rest of the British Empire.

This attempt by the National Patent Planning Commission to create a scale for patentable invention may be the beginning of a new era in patent thinking[23] and the suggestion of the Commission of certifying the record in an infringement suit to the Patent Office for a report on the validity of the patent would tend to supplement both the courts and the Patent Office whereby their joint efforts would produce better decisions, particularly so where both were guided by a national policy requiring the measuring of inventions by the "functional test" which awards the grant of a patent for things which advance the art. On this point Mr. Woodling pointed out that "generally, a judge lacks engineering knowledge and experience. On the other hand, substantially all of the examiners have had basic training in engineering." Another writer expressed the opinion that: "If patent decisions could be kept in line with a national policy which charts a course, the Patent Office and the Courts would be brought closer together in their views, eliminating a great deal of the current criticism that the Patent Office is more lenient in granting patents than the Courts are in sustaining them."[24]

Then there is the solution proposed by Judge Frank in *Picard* v. *United Aircraft Corporation*[25] which has recently received the strongest support,[26] that the Court, in deciding on the question of invention, should consult with thoroughly disinterested scientists.[27] This suggestion is a weighty one. It brings in the practice used so long in the Admiralty Courts of importing assessors or advisers to assist the Court on technical matters.

[23]See Woodling, "What's a Good Yardstick for Patentability" (1944) 26 J.P.O.S., 320.

[24]Cf. "Standard of Invention" (1944) 26 J.P.O.S., 439.

[25](1942) 53 USPQ 563.

[26]*The Second Interim Report* of the British Board of Trade Committee, April, 1946, recommends that, in addition to appointing judges to hear patent actions who possess technical or scientific qualifications (p. 22) a scientific assistant should sit on all occasions with the special judge or judges appointed to try patent actions, unless such assistance is unnecessary (p. 25). The function of such an assistant "would not be to assist in the trial of matters in issue, but to elucidate the technical aspects of the case. The essential qualification of the proposed scientific assistant should be an expert knowledge of the art involved" (p. 26).

[27]See also Parke-Davis v. H. K. Mulford Co. (1911) 189 F. 95 at 115 per Hand, J.

Of all the suggestions made so far, it is unquestionably the best, and one which this writer has urged on previous occasions.[28] It would very definitely be a step in the right direction but it would not completely solve the question. The criticism which can validly be levelled at it is that it would be questionable whether the combination of full scientific knowledge of the art in issue in any given case with complete disinterestedness could ever exist. Would not complete scientific knowledge indicate too close a connection with the minutiae of the progress of the art in its commercial as well as its scientific aspects to permit of thorough disinterestedness?

None of these suggestions unfortunately strikes at the root of the trouble. None of them presents a solution of the difficulty. All of them leave the matter in the hands either of judges without technical and scientific training or of such judges jointly with technically trained men acting in an advisory capacity only. They still leave the matter open to the arbitrariness of decision which must *ex necessitate* be an accompanying factor of the absence of exact rule and definition.[29] In other words, we hark back again to the Chancellor's conscience and the length of his foot. Nowhere perhaps has this been better expressed than in a recent article by an anonymous contributor in the *Journal* of the Patent Office Society:[30]

> I suggest we will always have these periodical swings for and against patentability. When a Court gets too liberal it runs into criticisms from the Bar and its fellow jurists in other Circuits and a reaction occurs. When it gets too

[28]See *Proceedings* of Canadian Patent Institute, 1939, 15. See also *Memoranda* on Patent Law Reform, by Trade Marks, Patents and Designs Federation, Limited, and by Joint Chemical Committee of Association of British Chemical Manufacturers et al., submitted to the British Board of Trade, 1945.

[29]The "flash of creative genius" theory enunciated by the Supreme Court inevitably leads one to a recollection of the words of Judge Hutcheson, who, speaking of the force of imagination used by judges in rendering decisions said (Frank, *Law and the Modern Mind*, 103): "And brooding over the cause, waits for the feeling, the hunch—that intuitive flash of understanding that makes the jump spark connection between question and decision and at the point where the path is darkest for the judicial feet, sets its light along the way." Perhaps the "flash of creative genius" was a necessary sequel to the flash of judicial genius—the "intuitive flash of understanding." But it does seem a pity that the aleatory nature of judicial decision should be reflected as a *sine qua non* in the process of scientific fruition and the definition of patentability.

[30](1944) 26 J.P.O.S., 619.

narrow, it is charged with making the patent system a fraud on inventors and with completely failing in its duty as the final machinery of the patent system. Then it starts to swing the other way. The swing is likely to be accompanied by a change of personnel. Sometimes an individual judge suddenly realizes that he is going too far one way or the other and tries to move in the opposite direction. I think there is no use in having either the Patent Office or the Bar try to keep up with these necessarily personal and temporary fluctuations. Most of us who have practised for any length of time get a pretty good feeling about what ought to be patented. It is as impossible to define in words as our aesthetic standards, yet our notions are, I think, fairly definite. I have known Courts to be more liberal than I would be, and I have in more cases known them to be less liberal. But I am sure few of the Courts have intended to say anything new about invention. They were simply trying to apply orthodox rules in the manner dictated by their own personal views as to the ability of the skilled mechanic acquainted with the business.

XXI. PROPOSED SOLUTION OF THE PROBLEM

BEFORE venturing to advance his own suggestion for attacking the problem, the writer believes it would be of value to consider the provisions of the law of France on the subject, for an examination of that system is necessary for a complete understanding of the remedy proposed.

The present law of France is the law of July 5, 1844.[1] The first title of that law constitutes in itself a compendium of the basis of patent grant in France as applicable at the present day and merits our consideration. It reads as follows:

Article Premier.—Toute nouvelle découverte ou invention, dans tous les genres d'industrie, confère à son auteur, sous les conditions et pour les temps ci-après déterminés, le droit exclusif d'exploiter à son profit ladite découverte ou invention.

Ce droit est constaté par des titres délivrés par le Gouvernement, sous le nom de brevets d'invention.

Article 2.—Seront considérées comme inventions ou découvertes nouvelles:

L'invention de nouveaux produits industriels;

L'invention de nouveaux moyens ou l'application nouvelle de moyens connus, pour l'obtention d'un résultat ou d'un produit industriel.

Article 3.—Ne sont pas susceptibles d'être brevetés:

1° Les compositions pharmaceutiques ou remèdes de toute espèce, lesdits objets demeurant soumis aux lois et règlements spéciaux sur la matière et notamment au décret du 18 août 1810 relatifs aux remèdes secrets;

2° Les plans et combinaisons de credit ou de finances.

According to the French law on the question of subject matter[2] the following will be considered as inventions or discoveries:

(1) The invention of new industrial products.

(2) The invention of new means or the new application of known means, for the obtaining of an industrial result or product.

In discussing this definition of patentability Casalonga[3] says: "De cette définition il résulte que l'on peut breveter une découverte

[1]As amended by the laws of May 31, 1856, July 9, 1901, April 7, 1902, August 11, 1903, April 13, 1908, December 26, 1908, June 26, 1920, January 1, 1922, April 7, 1927.

[2]Loi du 5 juillet, 1844, Art. 2.

[3]Casalonga, *Traité de la brevetabilité*, 75.

ou une invention consistant en un moyen nouveau permettant d'obtenir un résultat industriel. On peut également protéger un produit nouveau à condition qu'il soit industriel.

"En conséquence, deux caractéristiques essentielles indespensables pour la brevetabilité: la nouveauté de l'objet ou du moyen et le caractère industriel de cet objet et du résultat ou du but poursuivi."

Under the French system, therefore, there is an almost, if not complete, lack of any requirement of invention as it is understood in the Anglo-Saxon countries. The term "invention" is used by the French as being synonymous with "discovery." Certainly they do not use the word in the mystical sense in which we employ it. To the French, a plain, realistic statement is sufficient—an invention or discovery is something that is new and is of an industrial character.

The danger inherent in any system which attempts to examine into the mystical concept of invention is pointed out by Casalonga.[4] In discussing the provision of the Belgian law which requires that type of originality which is designated as the unforeseen or unexpected—"l'imprevu, l'inattendu"[5] he states: "Cette notion d'imprévu est assez diffuse et tout à fait relative, comme le remarque M. Vander Haeghen.[6] La prévision des résultats, obtenus par une modification apportée à un objet determiné, est fonction, en effect, dans de larges proportions, des connaissances techniques et scientifiques du juge ainsi que de son état d'esprit; c'est ce qui, à notre avis, rend dangereuse l'utilisation de ce critère, pourtant très ingénieux et susceptible de rendre parfois de grands services."

The French are indeed fortunate to have escaped a system which, as M. Casalonga says, depends on the scientific and technical knowledge of the judge as well as on his state of mind. And if he is, as it is submitted that he is, quite correct in pointing out the danger inherent in such a criterion, how right he has been proved by the unsatisfactory trend of decision on the question of invention in the Anglo-Saxon countries.

The most striking difference between the French law and that of the English-speaking countries lies in the divergent emphasis

[4] *Ibid.*, 226.

[5] Cf. Potts, *Patent and Chemical Research*, 131.

[6] *Le Droit intellectuel*, no. 230.

on the quality of invention. If in France the patent covers a new industrial product, or new means, or a new application of old means to obtain an industrial product or result, the question whether the advance involves invention becomes of very minor importance, if indeed it does not disappear.[7] In those countries which require the presence of invention as an ingredient of patentability, if courts attempt to answer the question as to whether invention is or is not present, arbitrariness is almost inevitable. Thus, after discussing the requirements for patentability in various other countries, M. Casalonga[8] says:

> La différence essentielle, présentée par tous ces critères avec la notion française de brevetabilité, consiste dans leur manque d'objectivité: l'utilité, l'ingéniosité, le progrès techniques, la caractère imprévu du résultat et l'originalité sont autant d'éléments subjectifs, laissés a l'arbitraire du magistrat.
>
> En France, au contraire, il suffit qu'il y ait un résultat industriel quel qu'il soit ou, plus exactement, un effet technique dans le sens où nous l'entendons.
>
> Peu importe la nature de l'effet technique obtenu: il peut être meilleur ou plus mauvais, cela n'influe en rien sur la brevetabilité de l'invention. Peu importent également le mérite de l'invention, son originalité, la grandeur de l'effort créateur développé par l'inventeur et l'importance ou la valeur de son idée inventive.

The writer's suggestion is a radical one but he believes it to be sound. It may be simply stated as the complete elimination from the content of qualities which are required for the validity of letters patent of that ingredient known as invention, thereby eliminating the application of orthodox rules by judges "dictated by their own personal view" of what does or does not constitute invention. In other words, the suggestion is now made that to this extent we adopt the view of the French law. So long as the subject matter of a patent constitutes a new industrial product or new means, or a new application of known means, for the obtaining of an industrial result, or an industrial product, the subject matter should be patentable.

In the United States, the decision in the Supreme Court in *Hotchkiss* v. *Greenwood*[9] set the new standard. But it is submitted that Woodbury, J., in his dissenting judgment placed his finger on the spot when he said:[10]

[7]Biggar (1941) 4 University of Toronto Law Journal, 197.

[8]*Traité de la brevetabilité*, 226.

[9](1850) 52 U.S. 248.

[10]At 268.

Now, on the point as to the invention being patentable, the direction virtually was to consider it not so, if an ordinary mechanic could have made or devised it; whereas in my view the true test of its being patentable was, if the invention was new, and better and cheaper than what preceded it. . . . Then, if they become convinced that the knob in this case, by its material, or form inside, or combination with the shank, was in truth better and cheaper than what had preceded it for this purpose, it would surely be an improvement. It would be neither frivolous nor useless, and, under all the circumstances, it is manifest that the skill necessary to construct it, on which both the court below and the court here rely, is an immaterial inquiry, or it is entirely subordinate to the question, whether the invention was not cheaper and better. Thus, some valuable discoveries are accidental rather than the result of much ingenuity, and some happy ones are made without the exercise of great skill, which are in themselves both novel and useful. Such are entitled to protection by a patent, because they improve or increase the power, convenience, and wealth of the community.

The kernel of this thought was presented by Webster in his note to the decision of *Rex* v. *Arkwright*[11] where he advanced the opinion that "whenever utility is proved to exist in any great degree, sufficiency of invention to support a patent may be presumed; and if such invention be any manner of new manufacture, and new, and the specification be sufficient, the letters patent for such invention will be valid in law." Lord Esher, in the *Edison Bell Phonograph Case*,[12] converged this principle to its proper focus when he poured ridicule on the attempt to defeat a patent, when all else had failed, by saying that it lacked subject matter, or, as we say on the American continent, that it did not display inventive ingenuity or the flash of genius, notwithstanding that the material covered by the patent had been bought and sold and therefore treated by men of business as a useful thing The experience and hardheadedness of the common business man receives little respect from the courts, but it is entitled to the highest respect, for this is the yardstick by which the decision is made as to whether, as a matter of practical business, there is a new and useful improvement or not—whether an alleged invention shall live or die.

This experience of men of business in the patent field ought to be the inflexible guiding principle of the doctrine of commercial success, so long as the theory of inventive ingenuity remains as a concept of the law of patents. Many judicial pronouncements have been made in connection with that doctrine from the extreme that it

[11](1785) 1 W.P.C. 71 n.
[12]Ante 237.

should control the entire decision on the question of subject matter, invention or no invention,[13] to the other extreme that, if anything at all, it is only one of the many factors to be taken into consideration in weighing the question.[14] In practice, the decision of men of business ought to be conclusive. So long as we are going to be bedevilled with this doctrine of subject matter, invention, inventive ingenuity, flash of genius, or whatever name is used to designate it, let us approach it realistically. The best possible evidence of invention and improvement lies in the fact that men of business use the device—and among those men of business do not let us lose sight of the defendant. For if a man of business thinks enough of a device or a process not only to use it, but to run the risk of an action for infringement and, *a fortiori*, if he goes to the trouble and expense of defending the action, he pays the alleged invention a tribute and respect which ought not to be swept aside so lightly, so cavalierly, so thoughtlessly as it so often is by a judge, exercising a legally and not a scientifically or industrially trained mind, by the operation of a sophisticated and hypothetical doctrine composed of a group of negative rules that are used in place of a positive definition. We had the positive definition once upon a time but unfortunately we lost it. Now we have nothing but a number of "personal views" of what constitutes invention, the number seemingly limited only by the number of judges.[15] Lord Camden once

[13]Prentice Mfg. Co. v. Kenny et al. (1931) Ex. C.R. 24 per Audette, J.: "As a test of the difference between success and failure the evidence discloses that the plaintiff's device—notwithstanding the large field of the prior art—has proved a great success commercially. . . . The general adoption of the improvement, with increased productivity, is a strong evidence of its novelty and usefulness and would seem to have advanced the art." Cf. Hinks & Son v. Safety Lighting Co. (1876) 4 Ch. D. 607 at 615 per Jessel, M.R.; Samuel Parkes & Co. Ltd. v. Cocker Bros. Ltd. (1929) 46 R.P.C. 241 at 248 per Tomlin, J.

[14]Longbottom v. Shaw (1891) 8 R.P.C. 333 at 336 per Lord Herschell; Wildey & White's Mfg. Co. Ltd. v. Freeman and Letrik Ltd. (1931) 48 R.P.C. 405 at 414 per Maugham, L.J.; Bergeon v. De Kermor Electric Heating Co. Ltd. (1927) Ex. C.R. 181; Detroit Rubber Products Inc. v. Republic Rubber Co. (1928) Ex. C.R. 29; (1928) S.C.R. 578; Guettler et al. v. Can. International Paper Co. et al. (1928) S.C.R. 438; Burt Business Forms Ltd. v. Autographic Register Systems Ltd. (1932) Ex. C.R. 39; (1933) S.C.R. 230.

[15]Cf. (1944) 14 Fortnightly Law Journal, 138; cf. also Picard v. United Aircraft Corp. (1942) 53 USPQ 563 at 569 per Frank, J., "For a decision as to whether or not a thing is an invention is a 'value' judgment."

said: "The discretion of a judge is the law of tyrants: it is always unknown; it is different in different men; it is casual, and depends upon constitution, temper and passion. In the best, it is oftentimes caprice; in the worst it is every vice, folly, and passion, to which human nature is liable."[16] In commenting on Lord Camden's remarks Peters, J., in *Ex parte Chase*[17] said:

It may be extreme, but every practitioner of experience knows that it is not without truth. . . . Moreover, it cannot safely be denied that mere judicial discretion is sometimes very much interfered with by prejudice, which may be swayed and controlled by the merest trifles such as the toothache, the rheumatism, the gout, or a fit of indigestion, or even through the very means by which indigestion is sought to be avoided . . . the uncertain security of a power so uncontrollable and liable to error as mere judicial discretion—a power that may

---

These value judgments based upon discretion or the personal feelings and perceptions of individuals as to what constitutes invention have contained more judicial obscurity and vagueness than any other doctrine of law. Here are some examples of the *vox et praeterea nihil* engendered by the judicial effort to capture the *ignis fatuus.*

"Whether there is or is not invention such as will support a patent is a question of fact and degree." Riekmann v. Thierry (1897) 14 R.P.C. 105 per Halsbury, L.C.

"It is difficult, almost impossible, to express in apposite language what exactly constitutes a sufficient invention to justify the court in upholding a patent." Wood v. Raphael (1897) 14 R.P.C. 496 per Lindley, L.J.

"It is a difficult thing to say whether there is that amount of invention about a patent that will support it." Dredge v. Parnell (1898) 15 R.P.C. 84 per Rigby, L.J.

"It is obviously impossible to frame any rule which will serve as a guide to show at once whether any particular instance is one involving invention or not." Pirrie v. York St. Flax Spinning Co. (1894) 11 R.P.C. 454 per Fitzgibbon, L.J.

"Nobody, however, has told me and I do not suppose anybody ever will tell me, what is the precise characteristic or quality the presence of which distinguishes invention from a workshop improvement." Parkes v. Cocker (1929) 46 R.P.C. 241 per Tomlin, J.

"The question here is one of fact whether having regard to the condition of the art there is sufficient invention in that which the patentee claims to justify the granting of a patent. . . . There must be a substantial exercise of the inventive power or inventive genius, though it may in cases be very slight." Canadian General Electric Co. Ltd. v. Fada (1930) 47 R.P.C. 69 per Lord Warrington.

"There is an 'impalpable something' which distinguishes things invented from things otherwise produced." Crosley Radio Corpn. v. Canadian General Electric Co. Ltd. (1935) Ex. C.R. 190 per Maclean, J.

[16]Cf. Campbell, *Lives of the Lord Chancellors*, 13.

[17]43 Alabama, 303.

possibly be misdirected by a fit of temporary sickness, a mint julep, or the smell or look of a peculiar overcoat, or things more trivial than those.[18]

So long as we have that impalpable something which distinguishes things invented from things otherwise produced, as mentioned by Mr. Justice Maclean in *Crosley Radio Corporation* v. *Canadian General Electric Co. Ltd.*[19] just that long shall we have a continuation of vagueness and uncertainty in the administration of justice. It is, I venture to think, no improper criticism of the Bench to suggest that, in the ever-widening field of research and the constantly broadening and expanding territory of technical and scientific investigation and advance, no occupant of the Bench can adequately decide the issue of invention with respect to more than a small percentage of the patents brought before him for adjudication. This thought has already been expressed much more forcefully and with much more authority by Frank, J., in *Picard* v. *United Aircraft Corporation*:[20]

It is clear that very few men on the bench can qualify as scientific experts—as Judge Hand provocatively suggested in *Parke-Davis* v. *H. K. Mulford Co.*;[21] "I cannot stop without calling attention to the extraordinary condition of the law which makes it possible for a man without any knowledge of even the rudiments of chemistry to pass on such questions as these. The inordinate expense of time is the least of the resulting evils, for only a trained chemist is really

[18]Cf. Yntema, 37 Yale Law Journal, 468: "Of the many things which have been said of the mystery of the judicial process, the most salient is that decision is reached after an emotive experience in which principles and logic play a secondary part." See also Mercoid Corp. v. Mid-Continent Investment Co. (1944) 60 USPQ 21 at 28 per Black, J.

[19](1935) Ex. C.R. 190.

[20](1942) 53 USPQ 563 at 570. *The Second Interim Report* of the British Board of Trade Committee, April, 1946, 21 ff., does not mince words on this subject. An extract from the *Report* on this subject has already been quoted in chap. XIX, n. 1. The *Report* speaks plainly of the universal feeling of dissatisfaction owing to the very general lack of confidence in the adequacy of available tribunals, the disadvantages of being required to occupy considerable time "in instructing the Judge in the elements of the technology with which the invention is concerned, in order that the specification can be made intelligible to him," and of "entrusting the decision of such cases to Judges who have had no previous scientific training, however learned and eminent they may be as exponents of the law." The *Report* points out that a judge with no background of scientific knowledge is himself at a disadvantage and, where he has had no experience at the patent bar before his appointment, much time is consumed in familiarizing him with the principles of patent law and citing authorities with which all practitioners in patent litigation are thoroughly familiar.

[21](1911) 189 F. 95 at 115.

capable of passing upon such facts, e.g., in this case, the chemical character of Von Furth's so-called 'zinc compound' or the presence of inactive organic substances. . . . How long we shall continue to blunder along without the aid of unpartisan and authoritative scientific assistance in the administration of justice, no one knows; but all fair persons not conventionalized by provincial legal habits of mind ought, I should think, unite to effect some such advance." Little has happened in the intervening thirty years since that case was decided to justify a different view today.

The flash of genius doctrine of the *Cuno Case* is a direct attack and assault upon scientific research. To deny that statement is to admit a lack of knowledge of the conduct of modern research. Thomas Edison has many times been hailed as the greatest genius and greatest inventor of the age. On the doctrine of the *Cuno Case* he probably was not an inventor at all and as to genius possessed only a very little of the quality required by Mr. Justice Douglas for he himself stated that "Genius is 2% inspiration and 98% perspiration." Under those circumstances the "flash of genius" in Edison's case would probably have been drowned in good, honest sweat, and on his own statement, his patents should have been held invalid.

That this matter has for some years past been of some concern may be gathered from the 1931 Report of the British Departmental Committee on the Patents and Designs Acts:[22]

In the Report of the Committee of the British Science Guild it was stated that there is a fear in the minds of some research workers that the validity of patents for research inventions may be imperilled by the circumstances of their origin, and that whether this fear is warranted or not, it should, if possible, be removed. It was suggested, therefore, that the Courts in deciding upon the presence of subject matter in any particular instance, ought to give very favourable consideration to an alleged invention which has arisen from prolonged and meritorious research work even on a laboratory scale.

The evidence given in support of this suggestion was somewhat unconvincing. It transpired, during our examination of the representatives of the British Science Guild who gave evidence before us, that the views expressed on this subject in the Report of the Committee of the British Science Guild were far from being unanimous, the majority of the Committee apparently holding the view that the Court, so far from criticising an invention because it had originated from systematic research, would be inclined to be benevolent to it for that reason.

We are of opinion that the view last stated is the correct one, and that the Courts are favourably impressed by the circumstances of an invention being the result of systematic research, and that there is no foundation for the fear which was stated to exist in the minds of some research workers. . . . In any case

[22]H.M. Stationery Office, Gr. Br. 1931, paras. 308-10, at 68-9.

however, the suggestion made in the Report of the British Science Guild is not, in our view, a practical one, being in the nature of a recommendation to the Court, and hardly suitable for statutory enactment.

The criticism is inescapable that, if it is proper to insert in a statute an exhaustive list of grounds of invalidity of a patent,[23] it is equally proper to insert this particular reason in a list of grounds for validity either as one of an exhaustive list or by way of exception to the first mentioned list.

The Committee was not impressed by the fear of the British Science Guild, but that Guild was, after all, closely anticipating the trend of decision and has been proved right by the decision in the *Cuno Case.* The fact that the actual decision occurred in the Supreme Court of the United States does not derogate from the view expressed by the Guild because on questions of patent law the trend of decision in the English-speaking countries has marched side by side for a century or more. The *Cuno Case* is a threat to systematic research. It must inevitably result in setting aside many patents painstakingly arrived at as the cumulation of effort sustained over a long period, and possibly by a large number of workers. Modern research is not carried on by the Edison or the old-fashioned inventor mentioned in the judgments who works and keeps his secrets "locked in his closet." Research supplies the product after minute experimentations and slow, step-by-step advances, by a number of people working in close co-operation. There is probably no place in that entire chain of production where one can place a finger and say—"There entered genius. There was 'the flash of genius'." The decision in the *Cuno Case* shows that the British Science Guild was right in entertaining fear and the Committee was wrong in paying so little attention to its view.

In 1942 Judge Learned Hand in *Picard* v. *United Aircraft Corporation*[24] said, in speaking of a patent for lubricating systems for internal combustion engines: "Unless we are to mistake for invention the slow but inevitable progress of an industry through trial and error, and confer a monopoly merely upon the exercise of persistent and intelligent search for improvement, there was no invention in this."

[23]S. 25 (2) and see ante 239.
[24](1942) 53 USPQ 563 at 567.

In concurring in this judgment, Judge Frank thought it desirable, while bowing to Judge Hand's superior wisdom, to emphasize the "startling implications of Judge Hand's negative test of invention" and "to point out where we are heading, by recognizing these implications."

The extent to which this doctrine has been carried will be seen by an examination of the words of Arnold, J. in *Potts* v. *Coe, Commissioner of Patents*[25] that:

a discovery which is the result of step-by-step experimentation does not rise to the level of invention. . . . Furthermore, though the discovery may appear to be a startling innovation, actually it is frequently the product of years of research by many men who come and go, who consult each other and the employees of other corporations with which their own employer has affiliations and agreements. The result is a gradual advance in scientific knowledge made possible because large funds have been spent on research—not an invention. . . . We do not deny that patentable invention may exist in a case where a corporation seeks a patent on the work of one of its employees who has been engaged in organized research. But the essential nature of corporate research makes such a situation unusual. . . . In the first place; the incentive to invent supplied by the patent law will not work in organized research because it destroys team work and co-operation. If one man or even a small group is competing with the others to be prior in invention, joint experimentation on a large scale becomes impossible. This has been pointed out over and over again by men familiar with successful research. It might be said that only in a very poorly organized research laboratory is individual invention at all likely.

And so, finally, we have the argument reduced *ad absurdum*. The bigger the problem, the greater the organization, the wider the field of research necessary in solving the problem, the less is the likelihood of obtaining a valid patent. It does not matter how great the result, how beneficial to mankind, no valid patent can, as a rule, be granted if the discovery is the result of organized research. The patent law, says the Court, is designed to encourage and stimulate only the lone, competing individual with little, if any facilities for research at his command, or, at the most, the "very poorly organized research laboratory." Is it any wonder that in 1931 the members of the British Science Guild were perturbed? If they are not now entirely preoccupied with thoughts of war and its aftermath, one may be permitted to speculate on their present reflections and apprehensions.

It is significant, too, that the District of Columbia Court of Appeals, in delivering the above judgment, quoted from a memo-

[25](1944) 62 USPQ 331 at 333.

randum of Dr. F. B. Jewett, a research director of the Bell Telephone System[26] to the effect that: "Organized industrial research has done infinitely more than change the relation of inventors to society and enlarge their opportunities, however. It has opened up whole areas for application of science in which the lone inventor never had and never can operate. These areas are those in which the problems are so complicated and the processes of their solution so involved and expensive, that they can be attacked successfully only by teams of men, each a specialist in a limited field and part of an organization provided with large funds and many facilities."

It is true that independent inventors like Henry Kaiser and Edsel Ford have repudiated the notion that corporate research is so expensive that the financing of research would stop if corporations were not offered a monopoly on the improvements for which they spend their funds.[27] But such statements, despite the prominence and importance of their makers, do not constitute the last word. In the first place, they are opinions of two men only, and can be met by contrary opinions expressed by others.[28] In the second place, even if research did not stop, it would certainly be curtailed. In the third place, it would inevitably lead to the shutting up of some processes into the secret class, a condition to which modern industry does not desire to be forced and which would result in a material slowing-down and hampering of progress. In the fourth place, if we do not need patents as bait for inventors we may still need them as a lure to investors.[29] In the fifth place, there is the question of justice. The social system of today

[26]See Jewett, "The Relation of Research and Invention to Economic Conditions" (1939) 21 J.P.O.S., 195 at 201.

[27]*Hearings*, Temporary National Economic Committee, Investigation of Concentration of Economic Power, pt. 2, 272; *Hearings*, Subcommittee of the Committee on Military Affairs, U.S. Senate, 77th Cong. 2nd Sess. (1942) on S. 2721, I, 234.

[28]"The inventor has . . . always . . . refused to work without sufficient offer of reward, just as everybody else does." Schramm, "Patent Laws and the Chemist" (1945) March 25, Chemical and Engineering News, 537.

[29]Cf. Picard v. United Aircraft Corporation (1942) 53 USPQ 563 at 573 per Frank, J. "The controversy between the defenders and assailants of our patent system may be about a false issue—the stimulus to invention. The real issue may be the stimulus to investment"; cf. also National Resources Committee, *Technological Trends and National Policy*, 39-66.

seems to be quite definitely "one law for the rich, another for the poor." In this day of the "common man" the great should receive nothing and the humble everything. Whatever the legal mind may say about it, that thought is the force which directs the type of thinking that will grant valid patents only to the lone, competitive inventor of the "very poorly equipped research laboratory" while denying them to the large corporations which have well-equipped, expensively-operated and, therefore, efficiently-run research laboratories.

Judge Hand adopted the same standard of invention in the negative rule he expressed in the *Picard Case.*[30] And in commenting on that yardstick for invention Judge Frank pointed out in the same case[31] the startling implication to be derived from such a yardstick, that if judges rely on thoroughly disinterested scientific experts who are fully aware of what is going on in the scientific world to advise them as Judge Hand suggests,[32] the result will be that those experts will report that today only a very small fraction of mechanical or chemical novelties are anything more than what has been yielded "through trial and error" and the "exercise of persistent and intelligent search for improvement." It is therefore highly likely that only an infinitesimal percentage of so-called inventions will be patentable under Judge Hand's test if informedly applied. For, as Judge Frank pointed out,[33] there are still brilliant and striking flashes of intellect which create startling inventions which would not otherwise be made for perhaps a generation. But inventions of this type are few and far between, and they are insignificant in number compared to the nearly 100,000 patents now issued annually in the United States. Before the modern large-scale research laboratories and scientific techniques were developed, it was correct to say that the "discoveries" of men like Edison resulted from creative genius. The area open for discoveries thus made has become severely restricted and as Kaempffert says[34] "It is not difficult to predict the effect

[30]See ante 243, 293.

[31]At 571.

[32]See ante 291.

[33]Referring to the *Report* on the Relation of the Patent System to the Stimulation of New Industries, published in the T.N.E.C. Hearings (Jan. 16-20, 1939), 1139.

[34]Kaempffert, *Invention and Society,* 30; cf. Picard v. United Aircraft Corporation (1942) 53 USPQ 563 at 571.

of industrial group research on invention. As organized invention and discovery gain momentum, the revolutionist [type of inventor] will have no chance in an explored field. Possibly Edison may be the last of the great heroes of invention."

As Judge Frank pungently pointed out:[35] "If all that be true, then, perhaps, with exceedingly few exceptions, it will only be to the untrained eye of a member of the judiciary (i.e. to a scientific amateur) that anything will appear to be an invention. If Judge Hand's yardstick is applied, a valid patent will, usually, be a function of judicial scientific ignorance, . . . it is intolerable that the public interest should be at the mercy of the haphazard scientific information of judges."

The expression of such an unusual sentiment from the Bench can do nothing but call forth deep respect and admiration. Such a courageous admission of the natural and honourable limitations of the judicial mind, is stimulating and encouraging to the progress of legal thought.

The result is obvious. "If we adhere to a patent system founded on the notion of giving rewards to inventors, and, if at the same time, we streamline that system, we shall discover that there will be but the tiniest handful of persons entitled to such rewards. As Judge Hand recently remarked in another case, 'Perhaps the [patent] system is outworn'."[36]

The trend of decision in the United States was clearly indicated by Circuit Judge Learned Hand in *Picard* v. *United Aircraft Corporation*:[37] "We cannot, moreover, ignore the fact that the Supreme Court, whose word is final, has for a decade or more shown an increasing disposition to raise the standard of originality necessary for a patent. In this we recognize 'a pronounced new doctrinal trend,' which it is our 'duty, cautiously to be sure, to follow, not to resist'."[38]

[35]At 571. See also per Thomas, J., in Sbicca-Del Mac. Inc. v. Milius Shoe Co. (1944) 63 USPQ 249 at 254: "In invention what constitutes the 'flash of genius' that is more than the 'skill of an ordinary mechanic acquainted with the business' must still be determined without the aid of any statutory or judicial definition in each particular case, and sometimes by judges without ordinary skill in the particular art."

[36]Dewey & Almy Chemical Co. v. Mimex Co. (1942) 124 F. 2d. 986, 990; 52 USPQ 138, 143; Frank, J., Picard v. United Aircraft Corp., supra, at 572.

[37](1942) 53 USPQ 563 at 567.

[38]Perkins v. Endicott Johnson Company (1942) 128 F. 2d. 208.

In delivering judgment in the same case, Frank, J., concurred because, as he said, he was "reluctantly compelled to join in their experienced interpretation of that 'doctrinal trend' to which Judge Hand refers and which, at least since 1928, has spelled itself out in Supreme Court decisions sustaining a very small percentage of patents."

In a foot-note to that part of his judgment, Judge Frank added the following trenchant information:[39]

> That trend is not (as some commentators imply) due to the presence on the Supreme Court of Justices appointed by President Franklin D. Roosevelt. No such appointee sat in that court before May 24, 1937. Yet, in the ten-year period ending with that date, the Supreme Court, as I compute it, held 17 patents invalid and 2 valid. One patent held twice valid in 1935 was denied validity by the same Justices in 1937. In *Bassick Mfg. Co.* v. *R. M. Hollingsworth Co.*[40] the patentee had won 299 victories in the lower courts, but the Supreme Court held the patent invalid except as to narrow claims which were not infringed; perhaps, in a limited sense, that was a decision for validity; on that basis, the score for that decade is 16 (invalid) to 3 (valid).

A number of attempts have been made to reconcile the "flash of genius" doctrine of the *Cuno Case* and the "trial and error" doctrine of the *Picard Case* with the original doctrine laid down in *Hotchkiss* v. *Greenwood*.[41] Thus, in *In re Shortell*[42] Lenroot, J., in the Court of Customs and Patent Appeals concluded that all that is intended by these judicial statements is that "the thing patented must involve more than the skill of the art to which it relates." In quoting Judge Lenroot's opinion with approval, Thomas, J., in *Sbicca-Del Mac. Inc.* v. *Milius Shoe Co.*[43] said of the two cases considered by Judge Lenroot: "It is not believed that they were intended to be amendments of the law," and the standard of originality and skill stated in *Hotchkiss* v. *Greenwood* has not been raised by these decisions.[44]

[39]At 569.

[40](1936) 298 U.S. 415; 29 USPQ 311.

[41](1850) 52 U.S. 248 at 266.

[42](1944) 61 USPQ 362 at 367.

[43](1944) 63 USPQ 249 at 254.

[44]See also Goodyear v. Ray-O-Vac. (1944) 321 U.S. 275; 60 USPQ 386; Bellavance v. Frank Morrow Co. Inc. (1944) 60 USPQ 311; 61 USPQ 1, 542.

The furore of protest raised by the decision in the Cuno case caused the Supreme Court to attempt a disclaimer in Sinclair & Carroll Co. Inc. v. Interchemical Corp. (1945) 65 USPQ 297, by saying "It is not concerned with the quality of the inventor's mind, but with the quality of his product."

Those expressions appear to be based on sophisticated reasoning. A more straightforward method was used by Evans, J., in *Chicago Steel Foundry Co.* v. *Burnside Steel Foundry Co.*[45] when he refused to follow the doctrine of the *Cuno Case* in these forceful terms:

> The test of "flash of genius" has been applied to curtain the field of patentable discovery and to eliminate from the protection of patents, all products (even though they came from the superior mind of genius) which were, nevertheless, the product of prolonged study and step by step advance. In short, it would eliminate nearly all the advances in history, in science, and in the field of mechanics. All that would be left are the products and processes which come to a genius, only occasionally as flashes. Only a matured child prodigy (if there is any such thing) is capable of experiencing such flashes. . . .
>
> The test of a "flash of genius" should be rejected not only because it is incapable of acceptable definition but because it injects into the statute something not appearing therein. The Federal decisions covering a century contain many to the effect that *it is the fact of accomplishment,*—novelty appearing, rather than the method of accomplishment with which judicial inquiry is concerned. . . .
>
> Nowhere in the statute can be found any words which require, or permit us to inquire into the quality of mind or the activity of the mind of the inventor to determine the patentability of his products or processes. Congress was interested in protecting the product of the mind,—not in whether it came as a flash to the mind, or as a happy thought, or by long painstaking search and experiment.

The final paragraph above reproduced might well be studied and digested by those who persist in requiring a "display of inventive ingenuity" before holding an improvement to be an invention.

Perhaps the yardstick has not been changed, although a plain reading of the words of the various judgments seems to

---

As so ably pointed out by Harry C. Duft in an article discussing this decision in (1945) 27 J.P.O.S., 779: "When all of the Court's findings in regard to the product are considered . . . it is impossible to find the slightest suggestion that the quality of the product found anything wanting. The Court having found the product good proceeded to examine the quality of mind required to produce the product. . . . The result is wholly at variance with the avowed purpose. It does not reward the advance in the art: it attempts to base the award on the quality of the mind of the inventor. Many inventions have been the result of sheer stupidity; others have been made through accident. According to the language of the decision, such inventions are patentable. According to the result of the decision, such inventions are not patentable. . . . Every one of the objective tests applied by the Court were favorable to the patentee, so it turned to the subject who made the invention and retraced the steps by which he arrived at the admittedly new and useful object. The Court denied that his mental processes during the discovery were not sufficiently abstruse."

[45]See (1943) 25 J.P.O.S., 141.

indicate quite clearly that it has. But of one thing there can be no doubt. The application of the yardstick has changed and is in process of further change and the result is the same as if the yardstick or standard itself had been changed. In a similar manner, the adherence to the outmoded doctrine of invention, whether defined as a flash of genius or otherwise, is not only to deny to the inventor his reward but is to deny to the public a large part of that incentive and spur which goads the ordinary worker, unfired by the divine spark of genius, to the production of better engines and instruments for human living.

It may be said in criticism of the present suggestion that such a course would open up a large field of exploitation of the public by the industrial and mechanical enterprisers. The answer to that lies in the compulsory licensing system. Both the Canadian and British Patent Acts[46] provide full safeguards for the grant of compulsory licences upon terms to be approved by the responsible head of the respective patent offices in cases of abuse of monopoly rights. Shortly stated, these cases of abuse may be summarized as being (1) if the patented invention is not being worked within the country on a commercial scale and no satisfactory reason can be given for such non-working; (2) if such working is being prevented or hindered by importation from abroad of the patented article by the patentee or persons claiming under him; (3) if the demand for the patented article in the country is not being met to an adequate extent and on reasonable terms; (4) if by reason of the refusal of the patentee to grant a licence or licences upon reasonable terms, the trade or industry of the country or the trade or industry of any person or classes of persons trading in the country, or the establishment of any new trade or industry in the country, is prejudiced and it is in the public interest that a licence or licences should be granted; (5) if any trade or industry in the country, or any person or class of persons engaged therein, is unfairly prejudiced by the conditions attached by the patentee to the purchase, hire, licence, or use of the patented article, or to the using or working of the patented process; (6) if it is shown that the existence of the patent, being a patent for an invention relating to a process involving the use of materials not protected

[46]Canada (1935) 25-6 Geo. V, c. 32, ss. 65 to 71; British Patents and Designs Act (1907-32), s. 27.

by the patent, or for an invention relating to a substance produced by such a process, has been utilized by the patentee so as unfairly to prejudice within the country the manufacture, use, or sale of any such material. And it is provided by both the Canadian and the British Patent Acts that in determining whether there has been any abuse of the exclusive rights under a patent, it shall be taken that patents for new inventions are granted not only to encourage invention but to secure that new inventions shall, so far as possible, be worked on a commercial scale within the country without undue delay.

A further protection of the public lies within the remedy suggested itself. The orbit of protection granted by a patent monopoly is coincident and coterminous with the orbit of the subject matter. If the subject matter of a patent, whether it be a great invention called forth by the flash of genius, or whether it be a mere mechanical improvement, decides and dictates the orbit of protection to the patent holder, it dictates also the orbit of exclusion of the public. Let us examine for a moment a judgment of the Supreme Court of the United States, which, through Justice Bradley, delivered an instructive argument on the non-patentability of devices arrived at only by mechanical skill as opposed to invention.[47]

> The process of development in manufacture creates a constant demand for new appliances, which the skill of ordinary head workmen and engineers is generally adequate to devise, and which, indeed, are the natural and proper outgrowth of such development. Each step forward prepares the way for the next, and each is usually taken by spontaneous trials and attempts in a hundred different places. To grant to a single party a monopoly of every slight advance made, except where the exercise of invention somewhat above ordinary mechanical or engineering skill is distinctly shown, is unjust in principle and injurious in its consequences. The design of the patent laws is to reward those who make some substantial discovery or invention which adds to our knowledge and makes a step in advance in the useful arts. Such inventions are worthy of all favor. It is never the object of those laws to grant a monopoly for every trifling device, every shadow of a shade of an idea which would naturally and spontaneously occur to any skilled mechanic or operator in the ordinary process of manufactures. Such an indiscriminate creation of exclusive privileges tends rather to obstruct than to stimulate invention. It creates a class of speculative schemers who make it their business to watch the advancing wave of improvement, and gather its

[47]Atlantic Works v. Brady (1882) 107 U.S. 192 at 199; see also Thompson v. Boisselier (1885) 114 U.S. 1 at 11; Western Electric Co. v. Rochester Tel. Co. (1906) 145 Fed. Rep. 41.

foam in the form of patented monopolies, which enable them to lay a heavy tax upon the industry of the country without contributing anything to the real advancement of the arts. It embarrasses the honest pursuit of business with fears and apprehensions of concealed liens and unknown liabilities to lawsuits and vexatious accountings for profits made in good faith.

Let us examine this statement. The learned judge stated that "such an indiscriminate creation of exclusive privileges tends rather to obstruct than to stimulate invention. It creates . . . it embarrasses." What system was he speaking of? What the learned justice obviously overlooked was that such a system does exist in France, and that it has worked very well—much better, indeed, than has our system—and without the obstruction and inconvenience of which he speaks.

Another point that the learned justice overlooked, as so many learned justices both before and after him, have overlooked, is that the orbit of protection is coterminous only with what is given to the world. Whether there is an invention or a mere useful novelty—a mere mechanical improvement—is really quite beside the point. If it is a mere mechanical step forward, then the orbit of protection and of monopoly is limited to that extent. Why should the "little fellow" not have a monopoly in his "little" improvement? Why should it only be the great and mighty advances in the arts that should receive protection? Is there to be one law for the man of great scientific attainment and another for the humble worker who has little education and no scientific training except his own experience? Those little advances and improvements are as much entitled to a patent monopoly to the extent that they are new and useful as are the greatest inventions of the age. For the great inventions create great monopolies and the little mechanical improvements under such a system would only create little, restricted monopolies, instead of being, as they are at present, the prey of everybody who desires to make use of them.

Consider the case of *Reckendorfer* v. *Faber*[48] which is, so far as the law goes, the American counterpart of the *Sausage Machine Case*[49] on the question of aggregation *versus* combination. The patents were for an article, of which many millions of specimens had been sold, composed of a piece of soft rubber united to one

[48](1875) 92 U.S. 347.

[49]Williams v. Nye (1890) 7 R.P.C. 62.

end of a lead pencil. The Supreme Court called attention to the fact that there was no joint operation performed by the pencil and the rubber, and therefore held the patents to be void for want of invention.

Why such a new and useful device should be denied monopolistic protection by some technical rule of law, will satisfy the abstract lawyer, perhaps, but it has never satisfied anyone else—particularly the man in the street.[50] If the originator of that idea—such a new, useful, and popular idea that ever since its disclosure to the world, almost all the millions of pencils manufactured each year are made in accordance with that disclosure—had been given a monopoly, it would have withdrawn nothing from the public sphere that the public had before, and it would have been a monopoly only in what he had given to the world as a new and useful improvement in a small matter of daily life. The orbit of the monopoly would have been small and restricted. It would not have prevented any person manufacturing lead pencils. It would not have prevented any person manufacturing rubber erasers. It would merely have prevented others from manufacturing, for a reasonable term of years, lead pencils with erasers attached to one end. In the result, the world received a new and useful device. The originator received nothing—it was not an invention. It was only one of those "trifling devices" and one of those "slight advances" that it was not the "design of the patent laws to reward." But it has sold billions, and is today a universally used device.

This viewpoint received support from the words of Judge Learned Hand in *Texas Company* v. *Sinclair Refining Company*:[51]

The patent seems to us another instance of a kind which must become more and more common, as the arts advance in understanding and multiplication of detail, only a corollary of what had gone before, demanding no more than the competent use of knowledge already at hand. Courts have always discouraged efforts to dress up such advances, when exploited by well organized selling, as invention; that discouragement was never more proper than at the present time, at least while the patent law remains as archaic as it is. Perhaps if its presuppositions—now three hundred years old and not in their origins the result of inquiry—were reexamined, it might transpire that pushing a new article into general acceptance is as deserving of reward as its invention, certainly if the test of invention be as

[50]See Dawson, "Notes on the Doctrine of Aggregation" (1944) 26 J.P.O.S., 838 at 845.

[51](1937) 32 USPQ 468 at 471.

factitious and subjective as it now is. But until that day comes, as it probably never will while the system lasts, we must continue to proceed as though we were dealing with actualities.

It is useful to compare the relative protection accorded by patents for invention with the protection accorded by copyright. What is required for a good copyright? Under the International Convention one thing only—that the protected work shall not be copied from a pre-existing work. And even this requirement is almost completely relaxed in the case of compilations and anthologies. It does not matter what is the quality of the writing, or the drawing, or the music. So long as it has originality in the sense that it was not slavishly copied, it is entitled to a copyright which endures for the life of the author and fifty years after his death, in the countries of the Convention.[52] No matter how great and novel an invention or discovery may be, no matter how much time and money is consumed in creating it, no matter how great the benefit it confers on humanity, seventeen years is the limit of the monopoly, at least on the North American continent. Even with that comparison evident, there is no lack of the uninformed and misguided who cry that patents should be abolished[53] and there is no dearth of judges doing their best, under the shackling restraints of the antiquated and misguided theory of invention, to deny them validity when they are granted. It seems not unreasonable to suggest that there should be no difference in principle in the basis of grant as between patents and copyright. If novelty, in

[52]Cf. International Convention, Art. 7(1); Canadian Copyright Act, s. 5; Imperial Copyright Act, s. 3. The United States Copyright Act, 1909, s. 23, provides for a term of twenty-eight years, subject to renewal for a further like term, upon application.

[53]The proper perspective of the patent system is often overlooked, sometimes, it is suggested, wilfully. Judge Frank's words in Picard v. United Aircraft Corp. (1942) 53 USPQ 563 at 573, are worth quoting to bring the subject into proper focus. "To denounce patents merely because they create monopolies is to indulge in superficial thinking. We may still want our society to be fundamentally competitive. But there has seldom been a society in which there have not been some monopolies, i.e., special privileges. The legal and medical professions have their respective guild monopolies. The owner of real estate, strategically located, has a monopoly; so has the owner of a valuable mine; and so have railroad and electric power companies. The problem is not whether there should be monopolies, but, rather, what monopolies there should be, and whether and how much they should be regulated. . . . Monopolies may still be socially useful; they may indeed, as I have said, foster competition."

the sense of originality, is the sole ingredient upon which copyright may subsist, and if quality, literary value, or artistic, musical, or dramatic merit are to be completely disregarded, then inventive ingenuity has no place among the considerations which apply to the grant of patents. It seems somewhat strange that the courts should have evolved the doctrine of invention as a part of the law of patents and have at the same time stoutly maintained that quality and merit, literary, artistic, musical, or dramatic, are immaterial on the question of validity of copyright.[54]

Any yardstick or criterion for the standard of invention, if sound, should be applied to all patents. But, unfortunately it is not. Of the large number of patents that are issued each year, after having satisfied the examiners of the various Patent Offices, who are scientifically trained men, only a meagre handful are ever litigated in the courts. And there, a different standard or criterion is applied by judges who are not scientifically trained. The inventor spends his money to obtain a patent, it is examined, and certified as an invention by Patent Office experts, and experience has demonstrated that he has much less than an even chance that, if he litigates it, the court will agree with the Patent Office on the question of invention. It may be that the standard of inventiveness used by the Patent Office is lower than that employed by the courts. Most patents escape judicial scrutiny since few patents ever get into court. The expense of defending a patent suit is often staggering to the small business man.[55] The result is that a large number of patents which would not stand up in court under the modern doctrinal trend confer, in actual fact, monopolies which are as effective, for all practical purposes, as if they had been held valid. If they are litigated, the chances are that they will be invalidated.

[54]Thus, in Walter v. Lane (1900) A.C. 539, in holding that a reporter was entitled to copyright in his notes of a series of speeches, Halsbury, L.C. said: "That right, in my view, is given by the Statute to the first producer of a book, whether that book be wise or foolish, accurate or inaccurate, of literary merit or of no merit whatever." In the same case Lord Brampton said: "If a person chooses (and many do) to compose and write a volume devoid of the faintest spark of literary or other merit, I see no legal reason why he should not, if he desires, become the first publisher of it and register his copyright, worthless and insignificant as it would be."

[55]Frank, J., Picard v. United Aircraft Corporation (1942) 53 USPQ 563 at 572.

The danger in the patent system is not that patentees abuse the public. The patent system has been the goad and spur to human improvement and has given meagre reward for public benefit. The danger in the patent system lies in the fact that the inventor is abused in that he is often unjustly denied a valid patent.[56] The *Potts Case* is almost the end of the road. What scope is left for patentability? The field of invention is limited only by the march of progress in the arts and sciences. The field of patentability is limited by individual and arbitrary views of what should be accorded the dignity and protection of a patent. The remedy lies in a complete reversal of this situation by statutory enactment clearly providing that the ethereal, impalpable, unrecognizable quality of invention or subject matter need not be an ingredient present in a valid patent. The sooner we take that step, the better for our industrial and scientific future.[57]

[56]An editorial in (1944) 26 J.P.O.S., 850 called attention to the steady decline of applications for patent in the United States which began in 1933. The editorial pointed to the rise of industrial research and the expense and complexity of patent litigation as helping to explain what is happening. Commenting on this editorial in the *New York Times*, October 29, 1944, Mr. Hugo Mock, the well-known patent lawyer of New York, expressed the opinion that one of the reasons for the decline is the nullification of patents by the Supreme Court which is naturally reflected in the decisions of the Circuit Courts of Appeal and Federal District Courts. The conclusion of Mr. Mock's letter shows the view presently held by those who have intelligence of what is going on. Mr. Mock said, "Under these conditions, naturally manufacturers and individuals are loath to apply for patents where the strong possibility exists that after the patents have been granted the courts will invalidate them, so that the main result of the expenditure of time and money by the patentee will be the careful instruction of competitors at the cost of the patentee." In concluding his remarks the editor of the *Journal* of the Patent Office Society (supra) stated that evidently an objective study of the patent system is needed to find out what is wrong with it. Possibly it is outmoded, and possibly new incentives are needed. That there should be less inventive ability in these war years than sixty years ago is simply incredible.

[57]There is some measure of support for the proposal here made in an article by Harry C. Duft in (1945) 27 J.P.O.S., 779 at 783: "Congress could go a long way toward solving this confusion by making it mandatory for the Courts to base their opinions of the validity of patents on the degree of differentiation over the prior art, together with the differentiation in result accomplished. That is something tangible, visible and provable. It is actually the criterion applied by the Patent Office. The degree of genius involved in an invention is an unprovable matter of opinion and could never serve as a satisfactory test of patentability. It involves passing judgment on such a controversial matter as to what constitutes genius or invention in the abstract and can lead only to sophistry.

"There is, however, a practical way of determining the presence of invention and that is by examining the differentiation over the prior art and the differentiation of the result obtained."

Further weight is given to the present proposal by a Memorandum submitted to the British Board of Trade Patents Committee by the Joint Chemical Committee on Patents, May, 1946, pt. II, 29, para. 35-6:

"We consider that every patentable invention is an industrial application (which must, of course, itself have novelty) of the discovery, conscious or unconscious, of an item of new knowledge. If the item of knowledge is in fact new, the invention has subject-matter. In the vast majority of cases this simple statement of the new criterion suffices, but for border-line cases it is necessary to define more closely what is meant by 'new' in relation to the discovery. A piece of knowledge may be formally new and yet so completely deducible from the prior art that the public regards it as already in its possession and does not need to call in the services of an inventor for its ascertainment. If it is known, for example, that all phenols are antiseptics, and that thymol is a phenol, there is no novelty in the discovery merely that thymol is an antiseptic, even though that fact has not previously been stated in so many words. For the determination of novelty the prior art must be regarded as containing not only all published facts, but also every fact which is logically deducible from these without the introduction of an unpublished premise.

"The criterion of subject-matter may therefore be expressed in three short definitions:—

An invention, in order to have subject-matter, must be based upon a discovery.

A discovery is the contribution of some item of new knowledge to the art.

An item of knowledge is new if it is not ascertainable from the prior art, i.e., is not to be found described in the prior art and is not deducible by a strictly syllogistic process of reasoning from data to be found in the prior art.

"In this form the criterion succeeds, in our view, in distinguishing between patentable invention and the results of the exercise of ordinary technical skill, between the inventor who creates and the technician who merely applies his skill to the manipulation of known data."

Among the observations and recommendations of the Joint Chemical Committee appear the following:

"For the application of the new criterion of subject-matter the essential questions to be considered are:

(*a*) What is the discovery on which the invention is based, i.e., what items of new knowledge are necessarily involved in the complete description of the invention?

(*b*) Is the discovery new, i.e., not ascertainable from the prior art?

(*c*) After rejection of such parts of the discovery as are not new, is the invention an industrial application of what is left of the discovery?" (pt. II, 31, para. 40).

"Patentable subject-matter should be defined in the Act as follows:

(*a*) An invention, in order to have patentable subject-matter, must be based upon a discovery;

(*b*) A discovery is the contribution of some item of new knowledge to the art;

(*c*) An item of knowledge is new if it is not ascertainable from the prior art, i.e., is not to be found described in the prior art and is not deducible by a strictly syllogistic process of reasoning from data to be found in the prior art" (pt. II, 32, para. 41).

See also Carl A. Castellan, "The Shifting Sands of Skill and Ingenuity" (1946) 28 J.P.O.S., 416 at 421: "When one creates something really new, he should be entitled to a patent regardless of the degree of skill or ingenuity required for such creation. The mere fact that the product is new proves that it required creativeness and the exercise of this faculty—whether such exercise be great or small—is all that should be required, in addition to novelty as defined by the statute, to constitute invention."

APPENDIXES

I. THE MERCHANT TAILORS' CASE: *DAVENANT* v. *HURDIS**

The action was one of trespass for breach of a by-law brought by the plaintiff against the defendant for breaking into his dwelling in London and taking a cloth of the value of £20. The plaintiff had been admitted a member of the Society of Merchant Tailors of London, and had agreed to abide by the ordinances made by it under its charter. The Company was empowered, by its charter, the grant of which and the privileges and powers therein contained having been confirmed by Parliament,[1] to make ordinances for the better rule and government of the Company, not inconsistent with law and reason. Acting under its charter, the Company made an ordinance "that every brother of the same society who should put any cloth to be dressed by any cloth-worker, not being a brother of the same society, should put one-half of his cloths to some brother of the same society, who exercised the art of a cloth-worker, upon pain of forfeiting ten shillings for every cloth put forth to dressing contrary to the ordinance to be levied by distress or otherwise by the Master and Wardens." The plaintiff, it was averred, had put forth twenty broad-cloths to be dressed by one who was not a member of the Company and did not put out the moiety of the cloths to any brother of the Company by which he forfeited 10*s*. for each of the twenty cloths. The defendant averred that there were other cloth workers able to dress the cloths "as artificially, and for as small wages as any other" and by reason of the plaintiff's action the poor of the company had suffered. The master and wardens had therefore issued a letter under their seal of office instructing the defendant to distrain for the penalty.

The arguments of counsel were exhaustive but we need concern ourselves only with that part of them which relates to our subject. The Attorney-General argued that the by-law was contrary to law, because its effect was to confine the sole trade of dressing cloths to those cloth workers who were free of the Company of Merchant Tailors, and that was to make a monopoly. It made a monopoly because if, for such reason, they could make a by-law to keep the sole trade of cloth dressing of a moiety of cloths to those of the Company of Merchant Tailors, they could make a by-law for all. Thus they could appropriate all cloth dressing solely to members of their company, and inconvenience the public in two respects, first, that they would have no cloths dressed, but only such as the cloth workers desired to dress at their pleasure, and secondly, no other cloth workers would have any work, but would live on relief, which was contrary to the common law, and contrary

*(1599) Moore K.B., 567.

[1] 1 Edw. IV.

to the nature of a by-law: for a by-law is made in furtherance of the public good and the better execution of the laws, and not in utter prejudice of the subjects or for private gain. He cited a number of by-laws made in former times which had been held valid and others which had been held invalid. He then declared that the Civil Law provided that monopolies despoiled everyone of their goods and were against the law. He defined monopoly as derived from the Greek and from the Latin meaning sole sale, and stated that to appropriate the sole sale and exclude others was against the common good, from which he concluded that by-laws made to induce monopolies, such as this one, were void.

For the defendant, Francis Moore confessed that monopolies, in their proper signification, which was *solus vendere*, are against common equity, because from them ensue intolerable mischief, that is to say, the prohibition to people who have no other means of living except by their trade and labour, which they cannot use, because the sole use of that trade is by patent of privilege appointed to another man, his deputies and assigns: also from this follows the enhancing of prices of commodities, because he who has the sole sale can make scarcity at his pleasure; and thirdly, the neglect of the good performance of the work, because no other can furnish the people with the like, but without choice they are constrained to buy that which he alone makes. And if this by-law in question makes a monopoly of this nature, certainly, he argued, it is utterly void. But it seems that it is not a monopoly, because it does not prohibit any cloth worker in England from using his trade, nor does it confine the sole business of cloth dressing to the cloth workers of the Merchant Tailors, because it requires nothing more than the half of the cloths which the drapers, free of the Merchant Tailors, have to be dressed should be sent to the cloth workers of this Company, which is only a handful in respect of all the drapers and cloth workers in the city and towns. And if this by-law should create a monopoly, then all the privileges and customs of the cities and boroughs providing for the exclusion of foreigners, and to restrain the sole trading in the city or borough to freemen therein, should be called monopolies and contrary to the law; from which would follow the decay of all cities and boroughs in the realm, which are a great part of the strength of the realm, and a beneficial part to the Crown in subsidies and fifteenths, and other services, and therefore, have never in any age been disallowed as monopolies contrary to the law and the common law.

It was held[2] by all the justices[3] that the by-law made a monopoly: and that a prohibition of such nature of confining the sole trade or traffic to a company, or a person, and to exclude all others was contrary to the law.[4]

It is apparent from the judgment in this case that the common law had by now taken the settled view that monopolies were void. The important

[2]Trin. 42 Eliz.

[3]Popham, Gawdy, Clench, and Fenner.

[4]"Mes al darraign fuit adjudge Trin. 42 Eli. ove le pl'; Sur le corps del matter, quia le by-law est de faire monopoly; et prescription de tiel nature d'inducer sole trade ou traffique al un company, ou un pson, et dexcluder touts autres est encountre le ley, per touts les Justices Popham, Gawdy, Clench et Fenner."

point of the case is that an ordinance which created a monopoly was held to be void even though done under the authority conferred by charter, the terms of which charter had been confirmed by Parliament. It remained only to hold void a monopoly expressly created by royal charter and such a case followed close on the heels of the *Merchant Tailors' Case.*

II. LIST OF MONOPOLIES IN D'EWES' JOURNAL AT THE TIME OF THE DEBATE ON MONOPOLIES, 1601*

The Committees for the great business of Monopolies and Patents of Priviledge being met, there was shewed amongst them a Note or Catalogue of divers of them, and to whom they were granted, which was as followeth, only altered in some places for Order sake.

To Sir *Henry Nevill* the Patent for Ordnance.

To Sir *Jerom Bowes* the Patent for Glasses.

To *Simon Turner* the Patent for Lists, Shreds and Horns to be transported.

To Sir *Henry Noell* the Patent for Stone Pots and Bottles.

To *Brian Anusley* the Patent for Steel.

To *Eliz. Matthewes* the Patent for Oyl of Blubbers.

To *Richard Drake* a Patent for *Aqua composita & Aquavite.*

To *Michaell Stanhop* a Patent for Spanish Woolls.

To *Thomas Cornwallis* the Licence to keep unlawful Games.

To *William Carr* a Patent for Brewing of Beer to be transported.

To *John Spillman* a Patent to make Paper.

To *Edward Darcie* a Patent for Cards.

To Sir *John Packington* a Patent for Starch.

To Sir *Walter Raleigh* a Patent for Tin.

To *William Wade* Esq; the making of Sulphur, Brimston and Oyl.

To *James Chambers* a Licence for Tanning.

To *William Watkins* and *James Roberts* a Licence to Print Almanacks.

To *Richard Welsh* to Print the History of *Cornelius* and *Tacitus.*

To *John Norden* to Print *Speculum Britanniae.*

To certain Merchants to Traffick.

To *William Allin* to sow six hundred Acres of ground with Oade.

To Mr. *Heyle* to provide Steel beyond the Seas.

To Mr. *Robert Alexander* for Anniseeds.

To *Edward Darcie* a Patent for Steel.

To *Valentine Harris* to sow six hundred Acres with Oade.

To Sir *Henry Singer* touching the Printing of School-Books.

To *Arthur Bassany* a Licence to transport six thousand Calf-Skins.

To *Thomas Morley* to Print Songs in three parts.

To Sir *John Packington* for Starch and Ashes.

To *Thomas Wight* and *Bonnam Norton* to Print Law-Books; and divers others of no great moment touching the transportation of Iron and Tin, the sowing of Hemp and Flax, the gashing of Hydes, the forfeiture of Grigg Mills, the making of Mathematical Instruments, the making of Saltpeter, the Printing of the Psalms of *David*, and touching Fishers Pouldavies and certain Forfeitures.

---

*D'Ewes, 650.

III. A LIST OF MONOPOLIES GRANTED BY QUEEN ELIZABETH*

MONOPOLIES

33° Eliz. A Grant to Reynold Hexton only, and no other, to make flasks, touch boxes (Cartouch Boxes), powder boxes, and bullet boxes, for 15 years.

34° Eliz. A grant to Symon Farmer and John Crafford only, and no other, to transport list and shreds of woollen cloth, and all manner of horns, for 21 years.

35° Eliz. A grant to Bryan Amersley, solely, and no other, to buy and provide steel beyond sea, and sell the same within this realm, for 21 years.

36° Eliz. A grant to Robert Alexander only, and no other, to buy and bring in anneseeds, sumach, &c., for 21 years.

39° Eliz. A grant to John Spilman only, and no other, to buy linen rags, and to make paper.

40° Eliz. A grant to Ede Schets, and his assignees only, and no other, to buy and transport ashes and old shoes, for seven years.

36° Eliz. A grant to   only, and no other, to provide and bring in all Spanish wools for making of felt hats, for 20 years.

34° Eliz. A grant that Sir Jerome Bowes, and no other, shall make glasses for 22 years.

42° Eliz. A grant made to Harding and others only, concerning saltpetre.

41° Eliz. A grant that Brigham and Wimmes shall only have the preemption of tin.

OTHER MONOPOLIES FOR ONE MAN ONLY, AND NO OTHER

To register all writings and assurances between merchants, called policies.
To make spangles, &c.
To print the Psalms of David.
To print Cornelius Tacitus.
To sow woad in certain numbers of shires.
To print grammars, primers, and other school books.
To print the law.
To print all manner of songs in parts.
To make mathematical instruments.
To plainish and hollow silver vessels.

*Lodge, *Illustrations of British History*, III, 6; Talbot Papers, K. fo. 79. Indorsed by the Earl of Shrewsbury, May 25, 1603.

That One Man Only, and No Other

Shall make writs of subpoena in the Chancery. Sir Thomas George.

To write all writs of supplicavit, and supersedeas for the peace and good behaviour, and all pardons of outlawry. George Carew.

To draw leases in possession made by the King. Sir Edward Stafford.

To engross all leases by the great seal.

Licenses and Dispensations

To one man only of the whole penalty of Penal Laws, and power given to license others

8° Eliz. A license to Sir Edward Byer to pardon and dispense with tanning of leather, contrary to the statute of 5° Eliz., and to license any man to be a tanner.

30° Eliz. A patent to Sir Walter Raleigh, to make licences for keeping of taverns, and retailing of wines throughout all England.

31° Eliz. To grant to John Ashley, and Thomas Windebank, to have all forfeitures and penalties for burning of timber trees to make iron, contrary to the Statute of 1° Eliz.

36° Eliz. A licence to Roger Bineon, and others, to take the whole forfeiture of the Statute of 5th and 6th of Edw. VI for the pulling down of gig mills.[1]

37° Eliz. A licence to William Smith only, and no other, to take the benefit of the Statute of 5° Eliz., for gashing of hides, and barking of trees.

38° Eliz. A licence to Thomas Cornewallis only, and no other, to make grants and licences for keeping of gaming houses, and using of unlawful games, contrary to the Statute of 33° H. 8.

39° Eliz. A licence to William Carr, for nine years to authorize and license any person to brew beer to be transported beyond sea.

40° Eliz. A licence to Richard Conisby, to give license for the buying of tin throughout England.

41° Eliz. A licence to Richard Carnithen only, to bring in Irish yarn for seven years.

Impositions

41° Eliz. A grant to Beves Bulmer, to have an imposition of sea cole, paying £6200 rent for 21 years.

36° Eliz. A grant made to John Parker, Esq., to have twelvepence for filing of every bill in Chancery; in respect whereof the subject is to be discharged of payment of any thing for search.

41° Eliz. A licence to trade the Levant seas with currants only, paying £4000 per annum.

Particular Licenses to transport certain numbers of Pelts of sheep skins and lamb skins

[1]Mills so called, for the fulling of woollen cloths.

Certain numbers of woollen cloths
Certain numbers of dickers of calve skins.

New Inventions

Only and no other, so as they were never used in England before.

To inn and drain grounds.
To take water fowl,
To make devises for safe keeping of corn.
To make a device for soldiers to carry necessary provisions.

IV. THE CASE OF MONOPOLIES: *DARCY* v. *ALLIN**

Edward Darcy, a groom of the Privy Chamber to Queen Elizabeth, brought an action on the case against T. Allin, a haberdasher of London for the infringement of letters patent for the sole making and selling of cards. The declaration stated that the Queen, intending that her subjects, being men able to exercise husbandry, should apply themselves thereunto and should not employ themselves in making playing cards, did by her letters patent dated June 13, 30 Eliz., grant to Ralph Bowes, full power, licence, and authority, by himself, his servants, factors, and deputies, to provide and buy in any parts beyond the seas, all such playing cards as he thought good, and to import them into the realm, and to sell and utter them, and that he, his servants, etc., and none others, should have and enjoy the whole trade, traffic, making, and merchandize of all playing cards, within the realm for a period of twelve years. By the same letters patent the Queen charged and commanded that no other person or persons, during the said term, should bring any cards within the realm, nor buy, sell, or offer to be sold, nor should make or cause to be made within the realm any playing cards, upon pain of royal displeasure, "and of such fine and imprisonment as offenders in the case of voluntary contempt deserve." By a further grant, August 11, 40 Eliz., the Queen, by letters patent reciting the former grants to Bowes, granted to the plaintiff, his executors, and administrators, and their deputies, the same privileges, authorities, and other the said premises, for twenty-one years after the end of the former term, rendering to the Queen 100 marks per annum; and further granted to him a seal to mark the cards.

The declaration stated that the former grant to Bowes came to an end on June 30, 42 Eliz., and thereupon the plaintiff caused to be made 4,000 gross of cards for the necessary uses of the subjects, to be sold within the realm, and had expended £5,000 in making them; that the defendant, knowing of the said grant and prohibition in the plaintiff's letters patent, had in March, 44 Eliz., without the Queen's licence, or the plaintiff's, caused to be made at Westminster, eighty gross of playing cards, and had imported another hundred gross, none of which had been made or imported by the plaintiff, or his servants, etc., nor marked with his seal, and had sold them and uttered them to sundry persons unknown, wherefore the plaintiff could not utter his playing cards, *contra formam praedict' literar' patentium, & in contemptum dictae dominae Reginae,* whereby the plaintiff was disabled to pay his farm, to the plaintiff's damage.

The defendant, except as to one-half gross, pleaded not guilty, and, as to that, pleaded that the City of London is an ancient city and that within the same, from time whereof no memory of man is to the contrary, there

*(1602) 11 Co. Rep. 84 b; Moore K. B. 671; Noy 173; 1 W.P.C. 1.

had been a society of Haberdashers and that within the said city there was a custom that every citizen of the said company may buy, sell, and merchandize all things merchantable, within the realm of England; and pleaded that he was *civis et liber homo de civitate et societate illa*, and sold the said half gross of playing cards, being made within the realm, as he lawfully might.

The plaintiff demurred in law and the case was argued before Popham, C.J., and the court by well known counsel of the day. The report by Coke as to counsel engaged in the case is manifestly inaccurate, but it would appear that Coke, the Attorney-General, and Fleming, the Solicitor-General, with Altham as junior, appeared for the plaintiff, while Dodderidge and Fuller with either Dyer, Croke, and possibly Tanfield, appeared for the defendant.

Two general questions were argued at the Bar, arising upon the two distinct grants in the letters patent, namely: (1) If the said grant to the plaintiff of the sole making of cards within the realm was good or not; (2) if the licence or dispensation to have the sole importation of foreign cards granted to the plaintiff was available or not in law.

As to the first question Coke for the plaintiff, argued that the grant of the sole making of playing cards within the realm was good for three reasons.

(1) Because playing cards were not any merchandize, or thing concerning trade of any necessary use, but things of vanity; and the occasion of loss of time, and decrease of the substance of many, the loss of service and work of servants, and therefore it belongs to the Queen who is *parens patriae et paterfamilias totius regni* and *Capitalis Justiciarius Angliae* to take away the great abuse, and to take order for the moderate and convenient use of them.

(2) In matters of recreation and pleasure, the Queen has a prerogative given her by the law to take such order for such moderate use of them as seems good to her.

(3) The Queen in regard of the great abuse of them, and of the cheat put upon her subjects by reason of them, might utterly suppress them, and by consequence without injury done to anyone, might moderate and tolerate them at her pleasure.

As to the second question, Coke argued that the Queen by her prerogative may dispense with a penal law, when the forfeiture is popular, or given to the King, and the forfeiture given by the statute of 3 Edw. IV, c. 4 in case of importation of cards is popular.[1]

On the question of prerogative, Coke cited a wealth of authorities, including a patent for sealing of certain vessels,[2] a patent for the garbling of spices,[3] the patent for printing,[4] the customs and by-laws of cities, boroughs and corporations "which are allowed although contrary to common right and the liberty of the subject," and the patent granted 30 Edw. III for the sole making of the philosopher's stone.[5]

---

[1]The above synopsis of Coke's argument is taken from 11 Co. Rep. 85.

[2]1 Edw. IV.

[3]33 Hen. VIII.

[4]The Charter of the Stationers' Company, which Coke noted was, as well as that for the garbling of spices, "in privilege to this day because they are for the public good."

[5]The synopsis of this part of Coke's argument is taken from Moore K.B. 675.

The Solicitor-General[6] argued that the true power of the Prince is to take effect in these five things: (1) *Imperando honesta;* (2) *Prohibendo injusta;* (3) *Permittendo media;* (4)*Puniendo delicta;* (5)*Munerando benefacta.*

And therefore a patent is void if the King makes it contrary to these five things.

(1) The patent ought not to change the law.

(2) It ought not to be contrary to justice and common right.

(3) It ought not to impose upon the subject a charge without profit.

(4) It ought not to do wrong to the inheritance, liberty, or trade of the subject.

But, nevertheless all general propositions admit particular exceptions. As it respects trades the end of them is *vivere tuto,commode, pacifice, jucunde, honeste et beate* but it appears that the trade of card making is ancillary to the vices of deception by servants of their masters and misemployment of time which ought to be applied to other industries and not to such enormities, therefore the King may prohibit it by patent.[7]

In his argument for the defendant, Dodderidge said that "the case was tender, concerning the prerogative of the Prince and the liberty of the subject and ought to be argued with good caution, for 'he that hews above his hand, chips will fall into his eyes,' and *qui majestatem scrutatur principis opprimetur splendore ejus.* Nevertheless the Princes of this realm have always been content that their patents and grants should be examined by the laws, and so is this our present Queen. In these examinations it had always been held by the judges that the Queen's grants procured contrary to the usual and settled liberty of the subjects are void and those also which tend to their grievance and oppression." The precedents cited by Dodderidge in his argument on this point are interesting. They may be summarized as follows:

(*a*) 2 Hen. V, fo. 5, *Case of John the Dyer*[8] where a bond requiring a craftsman not to practice his trade for a year was held void.

(*b*) 21 Edw. IV, fo. 79, a patent granted of an office of brocage; *semble* void because contrary to reason that the subject should not make a bargain without a broker.

(*c*) 1 Hen. VII, fo. 10, the King caused alum taken from the Florentine factors of the Pope to be restored because otherwise the goods of his merchants in foreign parts could be taken from them.

(*d*) Trin. 41 Eliz. K.B. *Davenant v. Hurdis.*[9]

(*e*) Rot. Parl. 50 Edw. III, nu. 33,[10] the patent to Peachie for the sole selling of sweet wine was held void by Parliament.

---

[6]Cf. Moore K.B. 673.

[7]The idea that card playing was a vice, and hence a proper subject of monopoly regulation, died hard. It is interesting to note that nearly forty years later a brief was prepared for submission to the Grievance Committee of the House of Commons, with respect to the patent of June, 1631, granted to the Company of Cardmakers, justifying the patent and suggesting that it was not a grievance because cards were a vain and unnecessary commodity.

[8]See ante 90.

[9](1599) Moore K.B. 576; 11 Co. Rep. 86; see ante 311.

[10](1376).

Dodderidge agreed that patents of offices and privileges of a fee to be taken for the exercise of them were good and legal because the subjects derive advantage from them; the privilege of sole printing was good for it was necessary for the peace and safety of the realm; also the King can prohibit commerce and traffic with foreigners, and that is proved by Magna Carta, c. 30. Further among the exclusive privileges which are good at law Dodderidge noted

(1) The case of the Archbishop of York in *Registrum Brevium* fo. 105 where he had a custom in his manor of Ripon that none should keep a dye house without his licence, but that was not by patent, and custom can do what a patent cannot do, as 37 Hen. VI, fo. 27 and 37 Hen. VIII.

(2) The case of the Abbot of Westminster in *Registrum Brevium* fo. 107 who claimed that he had a fair by patent for thirty-two days with an express privilege that during that time no one should buy or sell merchandise within a compass of seven miles.

(3) 12 Edw. IV, c. 17, the King can appoint to his subjects certain persons and certain places for obtaining justice.

(4) 40 Edw. III, c. 18, that the King can by his prerogative grant privileges which appear *prima facie* contrary to the common weal, yet are *pro bono publico.*

Dodderidge therefore claimed that the patent was void for these reasons:

(1) The sole power given to Darcy to sell cards without limiting the price would cause great oppression: Thus 27 Ass. Pl. 44,[11] a case of inquest to inquire concerning those offenders who sell at unreasonable prices, and 43 Ass. Pl. a merchant was indicted because, having engrossed a commodity, he sold it at an excessive price.

(2) The language of the patent was contrary to its meaning. It was intended to suppress the multitude of cards yet the liberty to manufacture was not limited.

(3) It took away rights in an ancient trade freely enjoyed, as, e.g., the statute 3 Edw. IV, c. 4[12] which provided that for the advancement of card making in England their importation was forbidden.

The argument of Fuller, for the defendant, is a compendium of instruction on the common law relating to monopolies. It commences at page 174 of Noy's report of the case, and occupies eleven pages. An understanding of the early state of the law is much assisted by a reading of the argument in full, but it may be summarized as follows:

(1) All patents concerning the King and his subjects are to receive exposition and allowance how far they are lawful and how far not by the judges of the law.

(2) That the judges in the exposition of the King's letters patents are to be guided not by the precise letters and words of the letters patents, but by the laws of the realm, the laws of God, and according to the ancient allowance thereof.

[11]Liber Assisarum, 27 Edw. III.

[12](1463).

(3) That the plaintiff's letters patent are contrary to the laws of the realm and of God, hurtful to the commonwealth, and in no part good or allowable.

(4) That the action grounded upon this void patent is no lawful action.

(5) An answer to the cases cited on the plaintiff's behalf.

Fuller gave a number of citations showing the limitations which the common law had placed upon the exercise of the prerogative. The benefit of government, he agreed with the Solicitor-General, was not that the subjects should live safely only but *tute vivere, pacifice vivere, honeste vivere, et jucunde vivere.* Then, attacking the patent in suit, he showed that it was against the common law of the realm, as for example, Magna Carta, c. 29, which provided that freemen should use *libertatibus et liberis consuetudinibus suis,* which was impossible if the plaintiff had a patent to restrain cards, another to restrain tennis play, another hawking and hunting, etc. If, said Fuller, "the Queen cannot to maintain her war, take from the subject 12 d. but by Parliament much less may she take moderate recreation from all subjects which hath continued so long and is so universal. . . . For Commonweals are not made for Kings, but Kings for Commonweals."

Fuller then cited the Statutes of 12 Rich. II, c. 6; 11 Hen. IV, c. 4; and 33 Hen. VIII, c. 9 which restricted gaming and card playing. "If" he said, "in the times of Richard II, Henry IV, and Henry V, it was thought necessary to have several Acts of Parliament to restrain the use of card playing in servants much more is it necessary to have an act of Parliament to restrain all the subjects of the Realm from the moderate use of playing cards and not by Letters Patent alone."

By the patent it was pointed out that the plaintiff had power to bring workmen from beyond the seas to the detriment of domestic workmen and contrary to the statutes of 3 Eliz. 4, c. 4 and 1 Rich. III, c. 12. Before the patent, native born workers were trained during their apprenticeship and supervised by the wardens of the company according to statute 5 Eliz., c. 4, s. 24, but now the plaintiff might work only strangers if he would, which was hurtful to the realm. Cards could, previous to the patent, be sold only at reasonable prices, or else the sellers would be punished as enhancers of merchandise according to statute 27 Eliz., c. 3, and the common law.[13] Yet now Darcy could sell cards at what price he pleased. And where a person by his industry had obtained skill in the trade he might have reaped the fruits thereof. Darcy now had devised means to take such skill away. Such would "discourage men to labour, to be skilful in any art and bring in barbarism and confusion."

Fuller showed that the patent was against the laws of God, that every "man should live by labour, and that he that will not labour, let him not eat."[14] Therefore it was as unlawful to prohibit a man to live by the labour of his own trade, wherein he was brought up as an apprentice, and was lawfully used, as to prohibit him to live by labour. The fact that the

[13]See 27 Ass. Pl. 44 referred to in Dodderidge's Argument, ante 321, n. 11.

[14]2 Thessalonians, c. 3, v. 10.

plaintiff said it was an unnecessary trade was of no weight, because many seemingly unnecessary trades gave much useful employment. He then cited the *Case of John the Dyer.*[15] If, he said, a patent to restrain one man from practising his trade in one town only and for one year only was held void, how much more so this patent, the like of which was not to be found in any case within the realm since the Conquest, which was to restrain men from their trade for twenty-one years and throughout the whole realm.

By statute 9 Edw. III, c. 1 and 25 Edw. III, c. 2, all merchants, strangers as well as denizens, were granted liberty to bring their wares into England and to sell them: therefore this monopoly patent to restrain, or take away that from the subjects, being merchants, which was given unto them by Parliament was not good in law for it was not like the case where the King might dispense with *malum prohibitum*, and it was said in 25 Edw. III, c. 2, that such a charter is hurtful to the King and to his people. So, by the statute of 26 Hen. VIII, c. 10, power was given to the King to restrain or set at liberty traffic beyond the seas for certain countries, which act had been an idle and vain act, if the King by letters patent might have done so much without act.

This was a plain monopoly *cum penes vestrum potestas vendendi fit.* As such it was objectionable and to be distinguished from those exclusive grants given to the various Companies (or guilds) where all members of the craft or Company exercised the privilege. The restriction to one person made this a plain monopoly patent.

Then follows the passage which has laid down the modern principles of patent law:

"Now therefore I will shew you how the Judges have heretofore allowed of monopoly patents which is that where any man by his own charge and industry or by his own wit or invention doth bring any new trade into the Realm or any Engine tending to the furtherance of a trade that never was used before and that for the good of the Realm; that in such cases the King may grant to him a monopoly patent for some reasonable time, until the subjects may learn the same, in consideration of the good that he doth bring by his Invention to the Commonwealth; otherwise not."[16]

[15]2 Hen. V, fo. 5; see ante 90, 320.

[16]See Noy at 182. Bacon and Coke were of the same opinion. See D'Ewes 644; Holdsworth, *History of English Law*, IV, 351.

This passage as pointed out by Mr. Gordon in his exhaustive and scholarly analysis of the judgment in the Case of Monopolies (Gordon, *Monopolies by Patents*, 219) has formed the foundation of our modern theory of patents not only throughout the British Commonwealth and the United States of America but throughout most of the civilized world. But it was not, as mistakenly stated by judicial authority and most of the text-book writers, a part of the judgment. It was merely a submission by counsel. Thus, in Webster's Patent Cases (at 1) published in 1844, the writer gave a summary of the report by Coke and Noy, followed by a further passage, in quotation marks, from Noy (at 178; see 1 W.P.C. 5) without indicating to whom the quotation was to be attributed. This passage is not quoted by Abbott in his report of the case (cf. Abbott, 1 *American and English Patent Cases*, 1). A substantially similar passage was employed by the Court of King's Bench in 1615 in the Cloth Workers of Ipswich Case (1615) Godb. R. 252; see ante 218. The passage was cited and adopted by

After making the submission that we have just discussed, Fuller cited the cases of three patents. The first was the case of Hastings' Patent, granted in 9 Eliz., in consideration that the patentee brought in the skill of making frisadoes as they were made beyond the seas. Upon proof, however, that the subject of the patent had been practised in the realm before the grant of the patent, the defendants were relieved of any punishment or restraint.

Next, Fuller cited the case of Matthey's Patent, granted in the early part of the reign of Elizabeth, for the sole making of knives with bone hafts and plates of latten, on the ground that the patentee brought the first use thereof from beyond seas. When it was shown by the wardens of the Cutlers' Company that they had previously made somewhat similar knives, the patentee was denied any benefit from his patent.

The third case cited by Fuller was the patent to Humphrey of the Tower for the sole and only use of a sieve or instrument for melting lead, on the ground that it was his own invention. The Court of Exchequer Chamber, in an action for infringement, held that if the patentee was not the true and first inventor, he should not have the sole use thereof.

Fuller then discussed the right of free competition, citing several cases, among them the two following:

11 Hen. IV, fo. 47. There was a school of long continuance and another erected a new school in the same town whereby the schoolmaster of the ancient school suffered loss. It was held that there was no right of action. The present case, he argued, was much stronger in that Darcy, who was newly appointed in the art of card making and selling, brought his action against the ancient card seller for hindering his sale.

22 Hen. VI, fo. 14. This was a case of a mill in a town of ancient continuance and another built a mill in the same town and took away some of the ancient mill's customers. This was held to be no wrong, though it was damage, and therefore there was no cause of action.

The argument was further advanced that moderate playing at cards was never thought unlawful or prohibited generally but for servants and in some particular manner for some persons. The patent was not a restraint of card playing but rather an occasion of increase of play, and merely took the trade of making and selling cards from many persons and gave it to one, which was unlawful.

It was held by the court that such a grant as was claimed by the plaintiff was void for two reasons. First, because it was a monopoly, and against the common law; secondly, because it was against divers acts of Parliament. These results may be summarized as follows:

First, the grant was against the common law on four grounds:

(1) All trades, as well mechanical as others, which prevent idleness and exercise men and youth and labour for the maintenance of themselves and

---

Tindal, C.J., in Crane v. Price (1842) 1 W.P.C. 411, who prefaced that part of the above submission beginning with "where any man," and ending with the words "reasonable time," with the obviously erroneous statement that, "The case of monopolies states the law to be that. . . ."

families, and for the increase of their substance, to serve the Queen when occasion shall require, are profitable for the commonwealth and therefore the grant to the plaintiff to have the sole right of making them was against the common law and the benefit and liberty of the subject. On this point the Court cited its own earlier decision of *Davenant* v. *Hurdis*.[17]

(2) The sole trade of any mechanical artifice or any other monopoly is not only a damage and prejudice to those that exercise the same trade, but also to all other subjects, for the end of all these monopolies is for the private gain of the patentees; and therefore there are three inseparable incidents to every monopoly against the commonwealth:

(*a*) That the price of the same commodity will be raised, for he who has the sole selling of any commodity, may and will make the price as he pleases; for every grant made by the King which tends to the charge and prejudice of the subject is void according to 13 Hen. IV, 14b.

(*b*) That after the monopoly granted, the commodity is not so good and merchantable as it was before; for the patentee having the sole trade, regards only his private benefit, and not the commonwealth.

(*c*) It tends to the impoverishment of divers artificers and others, who before, by the labour of their hands in their art or trade had maintained themselves and their families, who will now of necessity be restrained to live in idleness and beggary.

(3) The Queen was deceived in her grant; for the Queen, as by the preamble appears, intended it to be for the weal public, whereas it will be employed for the private gain of the patentee and for the prejudice of the weal public.

(4) The grant was *primae impressionis*, for no such was ever seen to pass by letters patent under the Great Seal before these days; and hence it was a dangerous innovation as well without any precedent or example as authority of law, or reason.

To forbid others to make cards and give the monopoly to one who had no skill was to make the patent utterly void.[18] Playing at cards is a vanity if it is abused, but the making of cards is not a vanity or pleasure but labour and pains. The statutes of 3 Edw. IV, c. 4, and 1 Rich. III, c. 12, prohibited importation of cards in order to sustain the domestic industry. Therefore the Queen could not suppress the making of cards within the realm any more than other articles such as dice, bowls, etc., which are works of labour and art although they serve for pleasure and cannot be suppressed but by Parliament nor a man restrained of exercising any trade but by Parliament.[19] Playing at dice and cards was not prohibited by the common law and was therefore not *malum in se*. Thus, when King Edward III in 39 Edw. III, c. 23, by his proclamation, commanded the exercise of archery and artillery and

[17]Trin. T. 41 Eliz. Rot. 92; Moore K.B. 576. See ante 86, 214 and Appendix I, 311.

[18]See 9 Edw. IV, 5, b.

[19]37 Edw. III, c. 16 and 5 Eliz., c. 4, s. 24.

prohibited the exercise of hand and foot-balls, cockfighting *et alios ludos vanos*, yet no effect followed, until some of them were prohibited by divers acts of Parliament, viz. 12 Rich. II, c. 6; 11 Hen. IV, c. 4; 17 Edw. IV, c. 3; 33 Hen. VIII, c. 9.

Secondly, such a charter of monopoly against the freedom of trade and traffic was against divers acts of Parliament as 9 Edw. III, cc. 1 and 2, which for the advancement of the freedom of trade and traffic extended to all things vendible, notwithstanding any charter of franchise granted to the contrary, or usage, or custom, or judgment given upon such charters, which charters were adjudged by the same Parliament to be of no force or effect.[20]

It was further resolved that the dispositions or licences to have the sole importation and merchandizing of cards without any limitation or stint, notwithstanding the act of 3 Edw. IV, c. 4, was utterly against the law; when the wisdom of Parliament has made an act to restrain *pro bono publico* the importation of many foreign manufacturers to the intent that the subjects of the realm might apply themselves to the making of the said manufactures, and thereby maintain themselves and their families with the labour of their hands, now for a private gain to grant the sole importation of them to one or divers persons notwithstanding the said act, was a monopoly against the common law and against the end and scope of the act itself; and it was pointed out that the effect of the grant was not to maintain and increase the labours of the poor card makers within the realm, but utterly to take away and destroy their trade and labours. The court, on this point, referred to the fact that although Edward III by letters patent granted to one, John Peachie, the sole importation of sweet wine into London, the grant was adjudged void at a Parliament held 50 Edw. III.[21]

---

[20]See also 25 Edw. III, st. 4, c. 2; 27 Edw. III, c. 11; Magna Carta, c. 18, which statutes accord freedom of trade to merchants.

[21]See Rot. Parl. *an.* 50 Edw. III, M. 33; Darcy v. Allin (1602) 1 W.P.C. at 4.

V. THE CASE OF PENAL STATUTES*

Queen Elizabeth made a grant under the Great Seal of the penalty and benefit of a penal statute, with power to dispense with the said statute, and to make a warrant to the Lord Chancellor, or Keeper of the Great Seal, to make as many dispensations, and to whom, he pleased. Upon letters directed to the Judges, they resolved that the said grant was utterly against law.

This term upon letters directed to the Judges to have their resolution concerning the validity of a grant made by Queen Elizabeth, under the Great Seal, of the penalty and benefit of a penal statute, with power to dispense with the said statute, and to make a warrant to the Lord Chancellor, or Keeper of the Great Seal, to make as many dispensations, and to whom he pleased; and on great consideration and deliberation by all the Judges of England, it was resolved, that the said grant was utterly against law. And in this case these points were resolved, that when a statute is made by Parliament for the good of the commonwealth, the King cannot give the penalty, benefit, and dispensation of such Act to any subject; or give power to any subject to dispense with it, and to make a warrant to the Great Seal for licences in such case to be made: for when a statute is made pro bono publico, and the King (as the head of the commonwealth, and the fountain of justice and mercy,) is by the whole realm trusted with it; this confidence and trust is so inseparably joined and annexed to the Royal person of the King in so high a point of sovereignty, that he cannot transfer it to the disposition or power of any private person, or to any private use: for it was committed to the King by all his subjects for the good of the commonwealth. And if he may grant the penalty of one Act, he may grant the penalty of two, and so in infinitum. And such grant of any penal law was never seen in our books, nor before this age was any such grant ever made; but it is true, that the King may (upon some cause moving him in respect of time, place, or person, &c.) make a non obstante to dispense with any particular person, that he shall not incur the penalty of the statute, and therewith agree our books. But the King cannot commit the sword of his justice, or the oil of his mercy, concerning any penal statute to any subject as is aforesaid. It was resolved, that the penalty of an Act of Parliament cannot be levied by any grant of the King, but only according to the purpose and purview of the Act: for the Act which gives the penalty ought to be followed only in the prosecution and levying thereof; and great inconveniences would thereon follow, if penal laws should be transferred to subjects. 1. Justice thereby would be scandalized; for when such forfeitures are granted, or promised to

*(1605) 7 Co. Rep. 36.

be granted before they are recovered, it is the cause of a more violent and undue proceeding. 2. When it is publicly known, that the forfeiture and penalty of the Act is granted, it is a great cause that the Act itself is not executed; for the Judge and jurors, and every other, is thereby discouraged. 3. It will thereupon follow, that no penalty will by any Act of Parliament be given to the King, but limited to such uses with which the King cannot dispense. And hereupon divers who had sued to have the benefit of certain penal laws, were upon this resolution denied. And the certificate of all the Judges of England concerning such grants of penal laws and statutes was in these words: "May it please your lordships, we have (as we are required by your honourable letters of the 21st of October last) conferred and considered amongst ourselves (calling to us His Majesty's counsel learned) of such matters as were thereby referred unto us, and have thereupon, with one consent, resolved for law and conveniency as followeth: 1st. That the prosecution and execution of any penal statute cannot be granted to any, for that the Act being made by the policy and wisdom of the Parliament for the general good of the whole realm, and of trust committed to the King as to the head of justice and of the weal public, the same cannot by law be transferred over to any subject; neither can any penal statute be prosecuted or executed by His Majesty's grant, in other manner or order of proceeding, than by the Act itself is provided and prescribed: neither do we find any such grants to any in former ages: and of late years, upon doubt conceived, that penal laws might be sought to be granted over, some Parliaments have forborn to give forfeitures to the Crown, and have disposed thereof to the relief of the poor, and other charitable uses, which cannot be granted or employed otherwise. We are also of opinion that it is inconvenient, that the forfeitures upon penal laws or others of like nature, should be granted to any, before the same be recovered or vested in His Majesty by due and lawful proceeding; for that in our experience it maketh the more violent and undue proceeding against the subject, to the scandal of justice, and the offence of many. But if by the industry or diligence of any, there accrueth any benefit to His Majesty, after the recovery, such have been rewarded out of the same at the King's good pleasure, &c. Dated 8 November, 1604." And to this letter all the Judges of England set their hands.

VI. LIST OF GRIEVANCES PRESENTED BY THE HOUSE OF COMMONS TO JAMES I IN 1606*

The Judgment of the Lords of the Privie Councelle wth what answeres were fitt to be gyven, and what Course to be holden Concernynge the seueralle grievances presented to his Ma[tie] by the Common House of Parlyament, in order as they are Conceyved in the Instrument Conteyninge the same.

1. Concerninge the pattent graunted to my Lord Davers and S[r] John Gilberte of three partes in foure to be devyded of the yearlie overplus of twoe thousand and eight hundred pownds arysynge of Issues, fynes, amercyam[ts], forfeytures of Recognizances, and the lyke, throughe the Realme.

2. Concernynge a pattend graunted to S[r] Roger Ashton of all fynes, amercyaments and other penalties and forfeytures knowen vnder the name of greene Waxe, growinge from the tenauntes of the Duchie of Lancaster.

3. Touchinge a pattent made to S[r] Henry Bronker of the Issues of Jurors not appearinge throughout England.

4. Concernynge my Lord Admyralle his Lycence to sell wynes by Retaile at a greater price then the Lawes nowe in force allowe.

5. Concernynge a pattent w[ch] permitteth the vse of a stuffe for dyinge, made of a mixture of Lockwood or Blockwood with other things, which, in that manner vsed, is alleaged to be good and proffitable for dying.

6. Concernynge the Raysing of his Ma[tie's] Customes.

7. Touchinge the Imposycion vpon Currantes.

8. Concernynge the Imposycion vpon Tobaccho.

9. Touchinge a pattent graunted to the Duke of Lynoxe for the searchinge and sealinge of dyverse stuffes by the name of the Newe Draperies.

10. The great Chardges that Shereffes of Counties are putt to by the Clarkes and offycers in the Escheaquer vpon their accountes w[ch] are made meerlie for the kynge's service.

11. Concernynge Muster Masters.

12. Concernynge pre-empcion of Tynne.

13. Concernynge the pattent of Makinge of Smalte or blue starche.

14. Concernynge purveyances.

15. Concernynge lycencynge of transportacion of Iron Ordynance and Bulletts.

16. Concernynge the abuses Committed by the Salt Petermen.

*S.P. Dom., James I, xxiii, no. 66.

VII. THE BOOK OF BOUNTY OF JAMES I

By the King

A DECLARATION OF HIS MAIESTIES ROYALL PLEASURE, in what sort he thinketh fit to enlarge, or reserue himselfe in matter of Bountie.

Hauing so particularly descended into the consideration of our Estate, (respecting Treasure, and Reuenue,) as we finde it full of difficulty to reduce the same, to the termes that are to be wished, by any such sudden or certaine meanes, as will not require some length of Time, and change of former Customes, both in the maner of our Expence, and of our Bountie; Wee haue thought it one of the best parts of the Care, not onely to resolue with our selues, to decline from all maner of Expence that shall not bee necessary for the safetie of Our Crowne, and honour of that Estate and dignitie (which no King can suffer to fall, but hee must run into contempt both abroad and at home) but also to take such further course as may make knowen to Our Seruants and Subiects; that although it is farre from Our intention to stop all liberalitie from Our well deseruing Seruants. Yet Wee meane not in respect of the vaine or vnnecessary Expence, of any priuate man (or upon false suggestion of former seruices) to be drawen either by the mediation of friends, or by the importunitie of any partie innecessitie, so farre to respect or commiserate others, as to cast Our Selues and our Posteritie into those wants or streights, which may driue Vs to lay burdens on Our People, to whom Wee desire to endeere Our Selues by all the Princely offices of Fauour and Protection which any earthly King can affoord vnto his Subiects. And therefore as We doe on the one part expressely forbid all Our Seruants and Subiects (of what condition soeuer they be) to propound or offer any Suites to Us, by which Our People in generall may be impouerished or oppressed: So on the other part We doe likewise expressely forbid.all persons whatfoeuer, to presume to presse Us, for any thing that may either turne to the diminution of Our Reuenew and setled Receipts, or lay more charge vpon Our Ordinarie, vpon paine to be helde and reputed in either of those two kindes, as persons vnworthy to enjoy Our Fauour or Presence for euer. In which consideration, because Wee know not whether We may vnawares, or vpon multiplicitie of businesse, chance to passe any Graunt or Warrant, contrary to the Order set downe herein:

> Wee doe not onely forbid all persons whatsoeuer, (either Officer or others) to receiue any such Petitions, or Warrants, as shalbe of those natures that are forbidden in the schedule hereunto annexed (vpon that perill which is due to such presumption) but We doe forbid our Secretarie of Estate, the keeper of Our priuie Seale, and Our Chancellour of England, to seale any such Graunt or Warrant, before they

haue enformed Us particulerly, and receiued a new signification of Our Pleasure by a new Warrant vnder Our hand. And because We have obserued also, that the swiftnesse in preparing Warrants before the Suites be mooued, (a course contrary to all good order,) is oftentimes a meane to hinder the examining and distinction of mens Suits: We doe likewise command Our principall Secretarie, Our Masters of Requests, and all other Ministers imployed vnder Our Secretarie in that seruice, not to suffer any Warrants to be made for any Suite, before the matter haue bene mooued vnto Us by petition, and Our pleasure signified for that

EXCEPTION

Warrant which is to passe Our hand: Except it be for any such Warrants or priuie Seales, as serue to direct or appoint any summes of money to bee issued for paiments, that concerne any present feruice for Our selues, or Our Estate, which are things of other nature, and of greater expedition then matters of Reward.

TO PREUENT CHARGE OF SUITORS

And in asmuch as We are desirous to prevent the needlesse attendance of suiters, to their charge and disappointment, (which is little better, if not more preiudiciall, then a meere deniall,) or to leaue men incertaine, within what natures of Suites, they may containe their hopes, and when and where, they may resort for answere or dispatch: Wee have thought good, to conceiue and declare in another Schedule, (hereunto annexed) the natures of such Suits wherein We are pleased to be moued. And for the maner of propounding or mouing them, We doe further declare, that either Our Principall Secretarie for the time being, or some by Our appointment for him, and the Master of Requests then attending, shall haue audience of Us for all Suits that doe concerne Our Bounty once in euery weeke at least: At which time if the same shall appeare, to be

LIMITATION

within the natures aboue limited for Reward, Our Pleasure shall be so declared to those that doe prevent them, as the Suitors shall know what they may looke for, and where they shall be dispatched, according to the nature of the

EXAMINATION

Suite that is moued: But if any of those Suites shall require further examination or information from any of Our Officers or Commifsioners, whose knowledge therein may be necessary, for giuing Us further light of the Value and Nature thereof, they shall then be referred to those whome it concerneth, vpon whose Answeres and Certificates Wee will signifie Our further Pleasure, as cause shall require.

MIXED SUITES

And because there may be Suits, which doe not fall within the knowledge or distinction of proper Officers and Offices (in which cases it may be convenient to referre the Examination of them to some such persons as may conferre with the parties, that doe present the said Suits, or those that may haue some particuler interest in the same, either in respect of trade or otherwise.) Wee haue thought meet (in that respect) to appoint a certaine number of Commissioners, to examine and consider of all such particulers, as shall be referred vnto them by Vs or Our Counsell. And to preuent the passing or graunting of any thing which should be contrary to our Lawes, We haue made Our choice of persons seuerally qualified, both in the vnderstanding of our Lawes, and other knowledges, that they may be so much the better enabled, to report the quality of such Suits, to Our Priuy Councel after conference with the Suitors, and Examination of their seuerall natures, and the Circumstances depending thereupon, which would take too much time, from Our sayd Priuy Councell, if they should not be first prepared and digested by that course which is herein expressed.

COMMISSIONERS

RESERUATION FOR ABSENT MEN

Lastly, because We would be loth that those that haue not dayly accesse vnto Us, should thinke themselues in danger still to be preuented by others, who haue more meanes to mooue Suites for themselues then they haue; We doe declare hereby, that (except it be in Cases wherein some speciall industry of discouery may mooue Us more properly to respect the first Suitor then any other) Wee will not suffer any such aduantage to be taken by one mans neerenesse more then another, as not to make it one of Our owne Cares (whosoeuer be the Moouer) to stay either the whole, or part for others, that deserue well, though they bee absent, according as Wee shall obserue, that Wee haue beene good vnto such a Suitor before, in some things else, or shall finde the Suites themselues to be of such Value, as may content more then one.

A MEMORIAL OF THOSE SPECIALL THINGS for which Wee expresly command that no Suitor presume to moue Us, being matters either contrary to Our lawes, or such principall Profits of Our Crowne, and setled Reuenue, as are fit to be wholly reserued to Our owne vse, vntill Our Estate be repaired.

¶ THINGS CONTRARY TO OUR LAWES

1. Monopolies.
2. Graunts of the benefite of any Penal Lawes, or of power to dispence with the Lawe, or compound for the forfeiture.

¶ RESERUED TO OUR OWNE VSE

3. Rents, Lands, and Leases, in possession or Reuersion, not barring the Tenants in possession, to renew their Estates, for xxj.yeeres, or three liues, as hath bene vsed heretofore.
4. Al lands entailed vpon the Crowne.
5. Customes, Impositions, and Seisures for the same.
6. Licences to Import, or Export commodities prohibited by the Law, or any lawfull Commodities, without paying the due Custome.
7. Profits rising out of Our Tenures, Alienations, and Fines Leuied, or Recoueries, either Common Recoueries, or other.
8. Profits answered vnto Vs, from any of Our Seales.
9. Assarts, and Defectiue Titles, as things onely fit to be measured by the rules of Our owne conscience.
10. Debts and Accompts wherupon there is any Seisure or Stallement, and all other Debts and Accompts accrued since the xxx.yeere of Q. Elizabeth.
11. The Fines of the Starre Chamber.
12. No newe Pensions to bee granted.

Neuerthelesse, out of the Generalitie of the Natures abouesaide, We intend to be excepted the Particulars expressed in the Schedule next ensuing, in which We haue conteined all the Natures, that Wee meane to haue reserued for our Bountie.

A MEMORIAL OF THOSE SVITS wherein We are contented to bee moued by Our Seruants and Subiects, and to reward them according to the particular merit of the Suitor.

---

1. Gifts of Offices in Our Gift, to meet and worthy persons.
2. Keeping of Parkes and Walkes in Chases and Forrests, and keeping of Castles, Forts or Houses.
3. Forfeitures of Landes and Goods that shal grow hereafter by Murthers or other Felonies, wherin Neuerthelesse Wee doe straightly forbid all persons whatsoeuer they be, that shalbe Suitors to Vs for any such Forfeitures, if there shalbe any motion made before the Offendours bee duly conuicted, that they do not in any sort resort to any of Our Iudges, Iustices, learned Councell, or other ministers of Iustice, nor intermeddle directly or indirectly in the prosecution of the Cause, before the Offendors be duely conuicted, vpon paine both to bee disabled to obtaine their Suite or any part thereof, or otherwise to incurre Our displeasure for their contempt in that behalfe.
4. Pardons in Cases appearing vnto Vs by due Certificate and Commendation, to be fit to receiue Our Mercy.
5. Escheats that shall growe due for want of Heire by Bastardie or otherwise.
6. Lands that shalbe hereafter purchased by Aliens.
7. Denization of such persons as shall be thought fit.

8. Forfeitures of Outlawries of such as shall bee hereafter Outlawed after Judgement, and stand so outlawed by the space of sixe moneths, after the Outlawrie returned, and likewise of such as are already outlawed after Iudgement, and shall not discharge such outlawrie within sixe moneths next after the date hereof: with Cautions and Prouision that the true Creditors shall bee first payd their debts, and that none of Our Subiects shalbe sued by force of such Graunt, for any debt or other cause in Our Name, but onely in the name of the Grauntee, and with a Clause to be conteined in such our Grants, for submitting the fame to Our Court of Exchequer, for the mitigation of the extremitie of the forfeiture, a tenth part of the benefite of such outlawrie so mitigated to be reserued to Our owne Vse.
9. Proiects of new inuention, so they be not contrary to the Law, nor mischieuous to the State, by raising prices of commodities at home, or hurt of trade, or otherwise inconuenient.
10. Debts due before the xxx.yeere of Q. Elizabeth, whereupon there is no seisure or Installement.
11. Also, whereas in the Schedule of things reserued from Suit, We haue made mention of Assarts and Defectiue Titles, as cases fit onely to be measured by Our owne conscience; Yet We do hereby declare, that We do not vnderstand (as comprehended in that Our reseruation) such intrusions as haue bene made vpon Our possessions by colour of any Intaile, where the Intaile is spent, or by colour of any terme, where the terme is expired, being matter of plaine disinherison vnto Vs, and that which no Subiect in his owne interest would indure: And therefore We are well pleased, That Our Seruants and Subiests do moue Vs in cases of those two natures. Prouided alwaies, that they do not fal vpon any those particular Titles which are already made knowen vnto Vs, and Registred into a Booke, sined by the hand of the Chancellour of Our Exchequer, to the view whereof, as occasion shall serue, the suiter may be admitted, to the intent he may thereby see, there is no cause to reward him for discouery of that, which is already knowen; neither also that they meddle with any more ancient Intrusions, but onely such, where the Intrusions haue bene made, since the first yeere of K.H 8. And that the Suitors submit themselues to such composition, as shalbe made by our Commissioners, And a tenth part of the benefit of such Composition as shall accrue to bee reserued to Our selues, and Our successours, and the parties in possession, to take a new Patent, with the former Tenure reserued.

And because We are willing that those moneys which doe arise by the faults of offendours, may sometimes serue for matter of Bountie, (to a well deseruing seruant) after they are leuied in a course of Iustice, and moderated by those rules of equitie and discretion, with which the publique ministers doe temper the seueritie and rigour of the Lawes, and not pursued or prosecuted by priuate men, who for the most part care not how they molest, or straine the Subiect in such cases: Wee doe first declare, that Wee are pleased, That all such moneys as shall here after come into Our Exchequer, growing either vpon forfeitures, or vpon Fines inflicted by any of Our Courts of Iustice for notorious crimes, and misdemenours (Our Court of Star-chamber onely excepted) shall be so distinguished and seuered in the Receipt (without being mingled with any other Treasure, nor issued for any Our owne occasions) as Wee may distribute such portion thereof, as shall seeme good vnto Us, vpon any man that meriteth Reward. Wherein, although Wee know Wee shall depart with many branches of those Receipts, which haue come vnder the Title of ordinary casuall Reuenue of the Kings of England; Yet Wee haue thought it more agreeable to Honour and Iustice, and to the presidents of the greatest and wisest Princes, (aswell Our neighbours, as Our Predecessours) when Wee are disposed to Reward any man out of such casualties, to vse Our owne Iudgement for the quantitie, and not to leaue the prosecution in such cases to priuate men, lest when they know the particular nature of that offence from which their benefit should be diriued, they may take some such indirect and violent courses, (in respect of their owne gaine) as is farre contrary to that Clemencie, which Wee haue euer vsed, and intend to doe to all Our louing Subiects; hauing euer thought it as proper for Us, (respecting Our Kingly Office) to be the moderatour of the rigour of Our Lawes, as to preserue them from neglect, the one leading to oppression of many, and the other to the ouerthrow and dissolution of the whole.

In which consideration also, whereas Wee haue beene contented heretofore (and so are still determined) to bestow vpon diuers persons according to their merit some portion of that Benefit which the Lawes haue giuen Us, vpon the conuiction of Recusants. Wee doe first expressly signifie Our great dislike of such as out of desire of their owne priuate profit, haue taken, or shall take vndue and extreme courses against any of Our Subiects, aswell by inditing them in places where they haue no residence, as otherwise; And next, because Wee haue bene also informed, That some others, to whome Weee haue passed such Graunts, haue somuch abused Our fauours, as to presume to compound with diuers ill affected, for light summes, before any Conuiction, (whereby the offendours in that kinde haue beene the more backeward to conforme themselues: which is contrary to the godly ende and purpose of Our Lawes, that aymed not at their punishment, but at their reformation: Wee doe hereby command, that in all Graunts of like nature hereafter, a speciall Clause be inserted, that no such Graunts doe in any wise proceed to Composition with any Recusant before a lawfull Conuiction. And further, that sufficient Caution and Securitie be giuen, that We be duely answered of a third of those Forfeitures or Compositions, for the better vpholding and continuing of that proportion of Reuenue which We haue heretofore receiued.

IMPRINTED AT LONDON
by Robert Barker, Printer
to the Kings most Excel-
lent Maiestie.
Anno Dom. 1610.

VIII. PROCLAMATION OF JAMES I, JULY 10, 1621, REVOKING CERTAIN MONOPOLIES*

A Proclamation declaring His Maiesties grace to his
Subiects, touching matters complained of, as publique greeuances.
Whitehall: 10 July (1621)

Parliament not being able in the time of sitting to settle grievances, the King will redress some of the most urgent. Directions have been given as to the proper use of Informers and of Writs of Certiorari and Supersedeas, and the abatement of fees. The Privy Seal to the Masters in Chancery (fees) has been revoked. The Patents for 'gold and silver foliat, the licensing of pedlers and pettie chapmen, the sole dressing of common armes, the exportation of lists, shreds, and other like things, the sole making of tobacco pipes, the hotte presse, the manufacture of playing cardes and brogging of wooll' have been surrendered. Warrant granted under Great Seal for dispensing tradesmen from serving apprentice, converting arable into pasture, licensing wine caske, making denizens, granting leets, passing parks and free-warrens, granting fairs or markets, tolls, stallages, and other like duties, leasing tithes, passing concealments, intrusions, encroachments, lands out of charge, &c., have been revoked. Privileges for 'gilding and printing of leather, printing vpon cloth, the making of pauing tyles, dishes, pots, garden poasts, and vessels of earth; the making of stone pots, stone jugs, and the like; the importing of pikes, carpes, eeles, and scallops; the making of racket hoopes, rackets, and cloth balles; the making and selling of oyle, inuented for keeping armour, the importation of sturgeon, the making of garments of beauer, the making of hard waxe, the making of chamlets, the making of backe screenes, the making of fortage and lineage of paper, the measuring of corne, coale, and salt, the printing of briefs, and many other things vpon one side of paper, the weighing of hay and straw, the discouerie of annoyances in the Thames, and ballasting ships' cannot be pleaded against any injury to the Subjects. With the consent of the Merchant Aventurers the outports may share in the trade of new draperies, and in all commodities which they traded in temp. Elizabeth, not paying the threepence on each Perpetuana.

The Proclamation 26 September 12 Jac. I[1] is quickened and affirmed, prohibiting the exportation of wool and fuller's earth. The order obtained by the Drapers of Shrewsbury limiting the trade in Welsh clothes, cottons, freeses, lynings, and plaines is withdrawn. Butter may be brought out of Wales when the price does not exceed threepence per pound from April 30th to November 1st, and fourpence from October 31st to April 1st. The export of iron ordnance is prohibited.

*Steele Proc. no. 1314; Rot. Pat. p. 13. m. 17.d.

[1]Proclamation of James I, September 26, 1614 prohibiting the Exportation of Sheepe, Woolls, Wool-fells, and Fuller's Earth. Rot. Pat. p. 5. m. 1. d. See Steele Proc. no. 1150.

IX. PROCLAMATION OF JAMES I, FEBRUARY 14, 1622-23*

A Proclamation declaring His Maiesties grace to His Subiectes for their reliefe against publique Grieuances.

In face of the complaints against monopolies, excessive fees, and other matters, and the Proclamation 10 July 19 Jac. I, the King sees fit to give his subjects an easy way of bringing their complaints before him. George Marquess of Buckingham Lord High Admiral, Thomas Earl of Arundel and Surrey Earl Marshal, William Earl of Pembroke Lord Chamberlain, Lancelot Bishop of Winchester, and William Bishop of St. David are to sit once a week, or two or more of them, to receive petitions of those aggrieved. No cases having legal remedies and no causeless clamours will be heard.

*Rot. Pat. p. 16. n. 14.d.; Steele Proc. no. 1350.

X. THE STATUTE OF MONOPOLIES*

An Act concerning Monopolies and Dispensations with penall Lawes and the Forfeyture thereof.

Forasmuch as your most excellent Majestie in your royall judgment and of your blessed disposicion to the weale and quiet of your subjects, did, in the yeare of our Lord God one thousand six hundred and ten, publish in print to the whole Realme and to all posteritie, that all graunts of monapolyes and of the benefitt of any penall lawes, or of power to dispence with the lawe, or to compound for the forfeiture, are contrary to your Majesties lawes, which your Majesties declaracion is truly consonant and agreeable to the auncient and fundamentall lawes of this your Realme: And whereas your Majestie was further graciously pleased expressely to commaund that noe suter should presume to move your Majestie for matters of that nature; yet nevertheles uppon misinformacions and untrue pretences of publique good, many such graunts have bene undulie obteyned and unlawfullie putt in execucion, to the greate greevance and inconvenience of your Majesties subjects, contrary to the lawes of this your Realme, and contrary to your Majesties royall and blessed intencion soe published as aforesaid: For avoyding whereof and preventinge of the like in tyme to come, may it please your most excellent Majestie at the humble suite of the lords spirituall and temporall and the commons in this present Parliament assembled, that it may be declared and enacted, and be it declared and enacted by the authoritie of this present Parliament, that all monapolyes and all commissions graunts licences charters and letters patents heretofore made or graunted, or hereafter to be made or graunted to any person or persons bodies politique or corporate whatsoever of or for the sole buyinge sellinge makings workinge or usinge of any thinge within this Realme or the dominion of Wales, or of any other monopolies, or of power libertie or facultie to dispence with any others, or to give licence or toleracion to doe use or exercise any thinge against the tenor or purport of any lawe or statute, or to give or make any warrant for any such dispensacion licence or toleracion to be had or made, or to agree or compound with any others for any penaltie or forfeitures lymitted by any statute, or of any graunt or promise of the benefitt profitt or commoditie of any forfeiture penaltie or somme of money that is or shalbe due by any statute before judgment thereuppon had, and all proclamacions inhibicions restraints warrants of assistance and all other matters and things whatsoever anyway tendinge to the institutinge erecting strengtheninge furtheringe or countenancinge of the same or any of them, are altogether contrary to the lawes of this Realme, and so are and shalbe utterlie void and of none effecte, and in noe wise to be putt in ure or execucion.

*21 Jac. I, c. 3.

II. And be it further declared and enacted by the authoritie aforesaid that all monopolies and all such commissions graunts licences charters letters patents proclamacions inhibicions restraints warrants of assistance and all other matters and things tendinge as aforesaid, and the force and validitie of them and every of them ought to be, and shalbe for ever hereafter examyned heard tryed and determined by and accordinge to the common lawes of this Realme & not otherwise.

III. And be it further enacted by the authoritie aforesaid that all person and persons bodies politique and corporate whatsoever, which now are or hereafter shalbe, shall stand and be disabled and uncapable to have use exercise or putt in ure any monopolie of any such commission graunt licence charters letters patents proclamacion inhibicion restraint warrant of assistance or other matter or thinge tendinge as aforesaid or any libertie power or facultie grounded or pretended to be grounded upon them or any of them.

IV. And be it further enacted by the authoritie aforesaid that if any person or persons at any tyme after the end of fortie dayes next after the end of this present session of Parliament shalbe hindred greeved disturbed or disquieted, or his or their goods or chattells any way seised attached distreyned taken carryed away or deteyned by occasion or pretext of any monopolie, or of any such commission graunt licence power libertie facultie letters patents proclamacion inhibicion restraint warrant of assistance or other matter or thinge tendinge as aforesaid, and will sue to be releeved in or for any of the premisses, that then and in every such case the same person and persons shall and may have his and their remedie for the same at the common lawe, by any accion or accions to be grounded uppon this statute, the same accion and accions to be heard and determyned in the Courts of Kings Bench Common Pleas and Exchequer, or in any of them, against him or them by whome he or they shalbe so hindred greeved disturbed or disquieted or against him or them by whome his or their goods or chattells shalbe soe seized attached distrayned taken carried away or deteyned, wherein all and every such person and persons which shalbe soe hindred greeved disturbed or disquieted, or whose goods or chattells shalbe soe seised attached distrayned taken or carryed away or detayned, shall recover three tymes soe much as the damages which he or they susteyned by means or occasion of beinge soe hindred greeved disturbed or disquieted, or by meanes of havinge his or their goodes or chattells seised attached distrayned taken carryed away or deteyned, in double costs; and in such suits, or for the staying or delaying thereof, noe essoine proteccion wager of lawe aydeprayer priviledge injunccion or order of restraint shalbe in any wise prayed graunted admitted or allowed, nor any more than one imperlance; and if any person or persons shall, after notice given that the accion dependinge is grounded uppon this statute, cause or procure any accion at the common lawe grounded uppon this statute to be stayed or delayed before judgement, by coulor or meanes of any order warrant power or authoritie, save onely of the Court wherein such accion as aforesaid shalbe brought and dependinge, or after judgement had uppon such accion shall cause or procure the execution of or uppon any such judgement to be stayed or delayed by coulor or meanes of any order warrant power or authoritie, save onelie by wirtt of error or attaint, that then the said person and persons soe offendinge shall incurre and sustaine the paines penalties and forfeitures ordeyned and provided by the Statute of provision and premunire made in the sixteenth yeare of the raigne of King Richarde the Second.

V. Provided neverthelesse and be it declared and enacted, that any declaracion before mentioned shall not extend to any letters patents, and graunts of priviledge for the tearme of one-and-twentie yeares or under, heretofore made of the sole workinge or makinge of any manner of newe manufacture within this Realme, to the first and true inventor or inventors of such manufactures which others att the tyme of makinge of such letters patents and graunts did not use soe they be not contrary to the lawe nor mischievous to the State by raisinge of the prices of commodities at home, or hurt of trade, or generallie inconvenient, but that the same shalbe of such force as they were or should be if this Act had not bene made and of none other; and if the same were made for more than one and twentie yeares, that then the same for the tearme of one and twentie years onely, to be accompted from the date of the first letters patents and graunts thereof made, shalbe of such force as they were or should have byn yf the same had bene been made but for tearme of one-and-twentie yeares onely, and as if this act had never bene had or made, and of none other.

VI. Provided alsoe and be it declared and enacted, that any declaracion before mencioned shall not extend to any letters patents and graunts of privilege for the tearme of fowerteen yeares or under, hereafter to be made of the sole working or makinge of any manner of new manufactures within this Realme, to the true and first inventor and inventors of such manufactures, which others at the tyme of makinge such letters patents and graunts shall not use, soe as alsoe they be not contrary to the lawe nor mischievous to the State, by raisinge prices of commodities at home, or hurt of trade, or generallie inconvenient; the said fourteene yeares to be accomplished from the date of the first letters patents or grant of such priviledge hereafter to be made, but that the same shall be of such force as they should be if this Act had never byn made, and of none other.

VII. Provided alsoe, and it is hereby further intended declared and enacted by the authoritie aforesaid that this Act or anything therein conteyned shall not in anywise extend or be prejudiciall to any graunt or priviledge power or authoritie whatsoever heretofore made graunted allowed or confirmed by any Act of Parliament now in force, so long as the same shall so continue in force.

VIII. Provided alsoe, that this Act shall not extend to any warraunt or privie seale made or directed, or to be made or directed by his Majestie his heirs or successors, to the Justices of the Courts of the King's Bench or Common Pleas, and Barons of the Exchequer, Justices of assize, Justices of oyer and terminer, and goale deliverie Justices of the peace, and other justices for the tyme being, having power to hear and determyne offences done against any penall statute, to compound for the forfeitures of any penall statute depending in suite and question before them or any of them respectively, after plea pleaded by the partie defendant.

IX. Provided alsoe, and it is hereby further intended declared and enacted, that this Act or any thing therein contayned shall not in any wise extend or be prejudiciall unto the city of London, or to any cittie borough or towne corporate within this Realme, for or concerning any graunts charters or letterspatents to them or any of them made or granted, or for or concerning any custome or customes used by or within them or any of them, or unto any corporacions companies or fellowshipps of any art trade occupacion or mistery, or to any companies or societies of merchants within this Realme, erected for the mayntenance enlargement or ordering of any trade of merchandize, but that the same charters customes corporacions companies fellowshipps and societies, and their liberties, privileges power and immunities, shalbe and continue of such force and effect as they were before the making of this Act, and of none other; Any thing before in this Act contayned to the contrary in any wise notwithstanding.

X. Provided also and be it enacted, that this Act or any declaracion provision disablement penaltie forfeiture or other thing before mencioned, shall not extend to any letters patents or grants of priviledge heretofore made or hereafter to be made of for or concerning printing; nor to any commission graunt or letters patents heretofore made or hereafter to be made of for or concerning the digging making or compounding of saltpeter or gunpowder; or the casting or making of ordinance or shot for ordinance; nor to any graunt or letters patents heretofore made or hereafter to be made of any office or offices heretofore erected made or ordayned, and now in being and put in execucion, other then such offices as have been decryed by any his Majesties proclamacion or proclamacions; but that all and every the same graunts commissions and letters patents, and all other matters and things tending to the maynteyning strengthening or furtherance of the same or any of them, shalbe and remayne of the like force and effect, and no other, and as free from the declaracions provisions penalties and forfeitures contayned in this Act, as if this Act had never ben had nor made, and not otherwise.

XI. Provided also and be it enacted, that this Act or any declaracion provision disablement penaltie forfeiture or other thing before mencioned, shall not extend to any commission graunt letters patents or privilege heretofore made or hereafter to be made of for or concerning the digging compounding or making of allome or allome mynes, but that all and every the same commissions graunts letters patents and privileges shalbe and remayne of the like force and effect, and no other, and as free from the declaracions provisions penalties and forfeitures conteyned in this Acte, as if this Act had never byn had nor made, and not otherwise.

XII. Provided also and be it enacted, that this Act or any declaracion provision penaltie forfeiture or other thing before mencioned, shall not extend or be prejudicall to any use custome prescripcion franchise freedome jurisdiccion immunitie libertie or priviledge heretofore claymed used or enjoyed by the governors and stewards and brethren of the fellowshippe of the hoastmen of the town of Newcastle uppon Tyne, or by the auncient fellowshipp guild or fraternitie commonlie called hoastmen; for or concerning the selling carrying lading disposing shipping venting or trading of or for any seacoales stonecoales or pitcoales forth or out of the haven and ryver of Tyne; or to a graunt made by the said governor and stewards and brethren of the fellowshipp of the said hoastmen to the late Queene Elizabeth, of any dutie or somme of mony to be paid for or in respect of any such coales as aforesaid; nor to any graunts letters patents or commission heretofore graunted or hereafter to be graunted of for or concerning the licensing of the keepinge of any taverne or tavernes or selling uttering or retayling of wines to be drunke or spent in the mansion house or houses, or other place, in the tenure or occupacion of the partie or parties so selling or uttering the same; or for or concerning the making of any composicions for such licenses, so the benefitt of such composicions be reserved and applyed to and for the use of his Majestie, his heirs or successors, and not to the private use of any other person or persons.

XIII. Provided alsoe and be it enacted, that this Acte or any declaracion provision penaltie forfeiture or other thing before mentioned shall not extend or be prejudiciall to a graunt or priviledge for or concerning the making of glasse by his Majesties letters patents under the Greate Seale of England bearing date the two and twentith day of May in the one and twentith yeare of his Majesties raigne of England made and graunted to Sir Robert Maunsell Knight, Vice Admirall of England; nor to a graunt or letters patents bearing date the twelveth day of June in the thirteenth yeare of his Majesties raigne of England, made to James Maxwell Esquire, concerning the transportacion of Calves Skinnes but that the said severall letters patents last mencioned shalbe and remaine of the like force and effect, and as free from the declaracions provisions penalties and forfeitures before mencioned as if this Acte had never byn had nor made and not otherwise.

XIV. Provided also and be it declared and enacted that this Act or any declaracion provision penaltie forfeiture or other thing before mencioned shall not extend or be prejudiciall to a graunt or priviledge for or concerning the making of Smalt by His Majesties letters patents under the greate Seale of England bearing date the sixteenth day of February in the sixteenth yeare of his Majesties raigne of England made or graunted to Abraham Baker; nor to a graunt of priviledge for or concerning the melting of Iron Ewer and of making the same into castworkes or barres with seacoales or pitcoales by his Majesties letters patents under the great seale of England bearing date the twentith day of Februarie in the nyneteenth yeare of his Majesties raigne of England, made or graunted to Edward Lord Dudley, but that the same severall letters patents and graunts shalbe and remayne of the like force and effect and as free from the declaracions provisions penalties and forfeitures before mencioned as if this Act had never byn had nor made, and not otherwise.

XI. PROCLAMATION OF CHARLES I, APRIL 9, 1639*

A Proclamation, declaring his Majesty's Gracious Pleasure, touching sundry Grants, Licences, and Commissions, obtained upon untrue Surmises.

Whereas divers Grants, Licences, Privileges, and Missions, have been procured from his Majesty, some under his Great Seal of England, and some others under his Privy-Seal, Signet, or Sign Manual, upon Pretences that the same would tend to the common Good and Profit of his Subjects: which since upon experience have been found prejudicial, and inconvenient to his People, contrary to his Majesty's Gracious Intention in granting the same. And whereas also upon like Suggestions, there have been obtained from his Majesty, and the Lords, and others of his Privy Council, divers Warrants, and Letters of Assistance for the execution of those Grants, Licences, Privileges, and Commissions, according to his Majesty's good Intention and Meaning therein. Forasmuch as his most excellent Majesty (whose Royal Care and Providence is ever intentive on the publick Good of his People) doth now discern that the particular Grants, Licences, and Commissions hereafter expressed, have been found in consequence far from these Grounds and Reasons whereupon they were founded, and in their execution have been notoriously abused, he is now pleased of his meer Grace and Favour to all his Loving Subjects (with the Advice of his Privy Council) by his Regal Power to publish and declare the several Commissions and Licences hereafter following, whether the same have passed his Great Seal, Privy-Seal, Signet, and Sign Manual, or any of them, to be from hence utterly void, revoked, and hereby determined; that is to say,

A Commission touching Cottages and Inmates.

A Commission touching Scriveners and Brokers.

A Commission for compounding with Offenders touching Tobacco.

A Commission for compounding with Offenders for transporting of Butter.

A Commission for compounding with Offenders in the importing or using of Logwood.

A Commission to compound with Sheriffs, and such as have been Sheriffs, for selling their Under-Sheriffs Places.

A Commission for compounding for Destruction of Woods in Iron-Works.

A Commission for Concealments and Incroachments within twenty Miles of London.

A Licence to transport Sheep-Skins and Lamb-Skins.

A Commission to take Men bound to dress no Venison, Pheasants, or Partridges in Inns, Alehouses, Ordinaries, and Taverns.

A Commission touching the licensing of the use of Wine-Cask.

*Rot. Pat. p. 23. n. 9. d.; Rush. II 915; Steele Proc. no. 1800.

A Commission for licensing of Brewers.

A License for the sole transporting of Lamperns.

And that all Proclamations, Warrants, or Letters of Assistance for putting in execution any of the said Commissions or Licenses, be from henceforth declared to be void, determined, and hereby revoked to all Intents and Purposes.

And his Majesty in like favour and ease of his Subjects, is farther pleased to declare his Royal Will and Pleasure to be, that the particular Grants hereafter mentioned (upon feigned suggestions obtained from him to publick damages) whether the same have passed his Majesty's Great Seal, Privy-Seal, Signet or Sign-Manual, or any of them, shall not hereafter be put in execution, viz.

A Grant for weighing Hay and Straw in London and Westminster, and three Miles compass.

An Office of Register to the Commission for Bankrupts in divers Counties of the Realm.

An Office or Grant for gauging of Red-Herrings.

An Office or Grant for the marking of Iron made within the Realm.

An Office or Grant for sealing of Bone-Lace.

A Grant for marking and gauging of Butter Casks.

A Grant of Priviledge touching Kelp and Sea-Weed.

A Grant for sealing of Linnen-Cloth.

A Grant for the gathering of Rags.

An Office or Grant of Factory for Scotish Merchants.

An Office or Grant for Searching and Sealing of Foreign Hops.

An Office and Grant for the Sealing of Buttons.

All Grants of Fines, Penalties, and Forfeitures before Judgment, granted or mentioned to be granted, by Letters Patents, Privy-Seals, Signet, Sign Manual, or otherwise.

All Patents for new Inventions, not put in Practise within three years next after the date of the said Grants.

And the several Grants of Incorporation made unto Hatband makers, Gutstring-makers, Spectacle-makers, Comb-makers, Tobacco-Pipe-Makers, Butchers and Horners.

And his Majesty doth further require and command, that there shall be a Proceeding against the said Patentees by quo warranto, or Scire facias, to recall the said Grants and Patents, unless they will voluntarily surrender and yeild up the same.

And also all Proclamations, Warrants, or Letters of Assistance obtained from his Majesty, or the Lords and others of his Privy-Council for execution thereof, from henceforth utterly to cease and be determined, and are hereby absolutely revoked and recalled.

And his Majesty doth further expresly charge and command all and singular the Patentees, Grantees, or others any ways interested, or claiming under the aforenamed Grants, Licenses, or Commissions, or any of them, and their Deputies, that they or any of them do not at any time hereafter presume to put in ure or execution any of the said Grants, Commissions, or

Licenses, or any thing therein contained, or any Proclamations, Warrants, or Letters of Assistance obtained in that behalf, upon pain of his Majesty's Indignation, and to be proceeded against as Contemners of his Majesty's Royal Commands, whereof he will require a strict account.

Given at our Manour at York, the 9th Day of April, in the 15th Year of our Reign, 1639.

XII. LIST OF PATENTS ORDERED TO BE BROUGHT IN TO THE PRIVY COUNCIL BY ORDER DATED APRIL 10, 1640*

The Commission for Brewing and Malting.

A Patent of Register to the Commission for Bankrupts in divers Counties.

The Patent for marking and Gaging of Butter Cask.

The Hatband-makers Grant.

The Patent for making Brick.

The Patent for Kelp and Sea-weed.

The Patent for Sealing of Linen-Cloth.

The Privy-Seal for Buttons.

The Patent for Gutstring-making.

The Horners Patent.

The Patent for Lampreys.

The Patent for Transportation of Butter.

The Patent for Gathering of Rags.

The Patent for Hay and Straw.

*Rush. III 1103.

XIII. ARTICLES OF IMPEACHMENT AGAINST STRAFFORD

Articles of the Commons Assembled in Parliament against Thomas, Earl of Strafford, in Maintenance of their Accusation, whereby he stands charged with High Treason.

XI.

That the said Earl, in the Ninth Year of His Majesties Reign, did by his own Will and Pleasure, and for his own Lucre, restrain the exportation of the Commodities of that Kingdom without his License, as namely, Pipe-staves, and other Commodities, and then raised great Sums of Money for Licenses of Exportation of those Commodities, and dispensation of the said Restraints imposed on them, by which means the Pipe staves were raised from four pound ten shillings, or Five pound per thousand, to ten pounds, and sometimes Eleven pound per thousand; and other Commodities were enhanced in the like proportion, and by the same means, by him the said Earl.

XII.

That the said Earl, being Lord Deputy of Ireland, on the Ninth day of January, in the Thirteenth Year of His now Majesties Reign, did then under colour to regulate the Importation of Tobacco into the said Realm of Ireland, issue a Proclamation in His Majesties Name, prohibiting the Importation of Tobacco, without License of Him and the Council there, from and after the First day of May, Anno Dom. 1638. after which Restraint, the said Earl, notwithstanding the said Restraint, caused divers great quantities of Tobacco to be Imported to his own use, and fraughted divers Ships with Tobacco, which he Imported to his own use: and that if any Ship brought Tobacco into any Port there, the said Earl, and his Agents, used to buy the same to his own use, at their own price; and if that the Owners refused to let him have the same at under values, then they were not permitted to vent the same there; by which undue means, the said Earl having gotten the whole Trade of Tobacco into his own hands, he sold it at great and excessive prizes, such as he list to Impose for his own profit.

And the more to assure the said Monopoly of Tobacco, he the said Earl on the Three and twentieth day of February, in the Thirteenth Year aforesaid, did issue another Proclamation, commanding that none should put to sale any Tobacco by Whole-Sale, from and after the last day of May, then next following, but what should be made up into Rolls, and the same sealed with two Seals by himself appointed, one at each end of the Roll. And such as was not sealed, to be seized, appointing six pence the pound for a Reward to such persons as should seize the same: and the persons in whose custody the unsealed Tobacco should be found, to be committed to Gaol; which last Proclamation was coloured by a pretence for the restraining of the sale of unwholesome Tobacco, but it was truly to advance the said Monopoly.

Which Proclamation the said Earl did rigorously put in execution, by seizing the Goods, fining, Imprisoning, Whipping, and putting the Offenders against the same Proclamation on the Pillory; as namely, Barnaby Hubbard, Edward Cavena, John Tumer, and divers others; and made the Officers of State, and Justices of Peace, and other Officers to serve him in the compassing and executing these unjust and undue Courses, by which Cruelties, and unjust Monopolies, the said Earl raised 100000 *l*. per annum gain to himself. And yet the said Earl though he enhanced the Customs, where it concerned the Merchants in general, yet drew down the Impost, formerly taken on Tobacco, from Six pence the pound to Three pence the pound, it being for his own profit so to do.

And the said Earl, by the same, and other rigorous and undue means, raised several other Monopolies and unlawful Exactions for his own gain, viz. on Starch, Iron-pots, Glasses, Tobacco-pipes, and several other Commodities.

XIII.

That flax being one of the principal and Native Commodities of that Kingdom of Ireland, the said Earl having gotten great quantities thereof into his hands, and growing on his own Lands, did issue out several Proclamations, viz. the one dated the One and thirtieth day of May, and the Twelfth of His Majesties Reign; and the other dated the One and thirtieth day of January in the same Year, thereby prescribing and enjoyning the working of flax into Yarn and Thread, and the Ordering of the same in such ways wherein the Natives of that Kingdom were unpracticed and unskilful: which Proclamations so issued, were by his Commands and Warrants to His Majesties Justices of Peace, and other Officers, and by other rigorous means put in Execution, and the Flax wrought or ordered in other manner than as the said Proclamation prescribed, was seized and employed to the use of him and his Agents, and thereby the said Earl endeavoured to gain, and did gain in effect the sole Sale of that Native Commodity.

XIV. ORAL DEFENCE OF EARL OF STRAFFORD TO ACCUSATIONS RELATING TO ABUSE OF MONOPOLIES*

The next is the 11th Article, concerning Pipe-Staves, and that is by them waved: and well they may; for the plain truth is, if it had been proceeded in, it would have appeared, that there is come Fifteen hundred Pounds Gain to the King, and Four hundred Pounds Loss to myself, and preserving of Woods, and that is all that would be made from that Article.

The next is, the business of the Tobacco, which is not appliable to Treason in any kind: But because I would be Clear in every Man's Judgment that hears me, I beseech your Lordships to call to mind, it was the Petition of the Commons House of Ireland, That the Grant of Impost on the Tobacco should be taken in and converted to the King's Use; so that whatsoever was done, was pursuing their Intention and Desire.

That there was no way but this, to make Benefit and Profit of it, is most manifestly shewn, that there was a Proclamation in England of the like nature, and a Command of the King to proceed in it accordingly; and an Act of Parliament transmitted here, for Passing it to the Crown, according to the Intention of the Commons House; and, for the greatness of the Bargain, no Proof hath been offered to your Lordships, but only the Estimate of a Merchant; and, how far your Lordships will be guided by the Estimate of a Merchant, I know not; but, I have had trial of some of them, and their Estimates never hold; for, they have always told me, I shall gain much, and when I came to the point, I gained nothing: and if Sir George Ratcliffe should be sworn to the Point, he should say confidently, that we are Fourscore and six thousand out of Purse, and when he came out of Ireland, but Fourscore thousand Pounds received; and this is the Profit estimated by the great Merchants, at a Hundred and forty thousand Pounds a Year: But, at the worst, it is but a Monopoly, and a Monopoly of the best condition, because it was begun by a Parliament. I have seen many Minopolies question'd in Parliament, and many overthrown in Parliament, but, I never heard a Monopoly charged for a Treason.

My Lords, The next is the 13th Article, and that is concerning the Flax business; For that, my Lords, if I had thought it any way concerning me, I could have cleared it in a very great measure; But I had no private Interest in the business, much less of private Profit; but only an endeavour and desire to bring in the Trade of Linnen-Cloth to that Kingdom, which would be much Advantage to both Kingdoms, and no Prejudice to this Kingdom, which a Woollen Trade would have been, if set up there.

And, the Proclamation, when it was found not so well-liking to the People, was called in of our own accord, before it was question'd, and so laid aside, and given over.

*Rush. VIII, 652.

For any matter of private Benefit, you have no Witness but Crokay, a Fellow brought out of Prison; Here is but a single Witness, and a sorry one; a Fellow, who, by misbehaving and misusing the Trust committed to him, was turned out; and, upon the turning of him out, the Proclamation was absolutely called in; and, now he comes to be a Witness, being himself the only offended in the Cause.

But, I beseech your Lordships to think, I have not lived with so mean a heart in the World, that I should look to gain Four Nobles, more or less upon a Cart Load of Flax; It is very well known my thoughts have carried me free enough from gaining so poor and petty a matter, as that is. I know nothing in the World of it, no more than the Man in the Moon; but, when it comes to be heard, your Lordships will find me extreme pure in that; for I thank God I have clear hands, I assure you.

XV. REPLY FOR THE PROSECUTION BY JOHN GLYN, RECORDER OF LONDON*

The next Article in number was the Eleventh, and I wou'd be glad my Lord had not mention'd it; it concerns the Pipe-Staves, wherein he pretends he did the King great service, and that (he says) was the reason of our passing over it: But that was not the reason; it had been a foul business, if we had opened it; but having enough besides, we made not use of it: for the substance of the Proofs, by multiplicity of Witnesses, had been, that the parties themselves who bought the Pipe-staves for four Pound odd Money, were fain to sell them to his Instruments for six Pounds, and after to buy them again for ten Pounds, else there must be no License to export them: but that I would not have mention'd, if he had let it slip over.

I come to the Twelfth Article, and that is concerning the Tobacco, wherein he pretends the King's service, and, if my memory fail me not, the desire of the Parliament, that he should take this into his hands for the King.

My Lords, Therein, under his favour, he hath misrecited the Evidence, and spoken what he cannot justifie; for he can shew no such desire of the Parliament. It is true, there was a desire of the Parliament, that the King would be pleased to take his Customs into his hands, for the advancement of his Revenue, that it might go to maintain himself, and he might not be abused, and others live by it; but to take the Tobacco into his hands, he never did, nor can produce a Witness to prove such their desire: and therefore, under favour, he fixes a Wrong upon the Parliament, and injures your Lordships, by his reciting what he neither did nor can make good; for there was no such thing.

But if you observe the course he takes, he makes Proclamation to hinder the Importing of Tobacco into Ireland; that if it be Imported, it must be sold to him at his own rate; and by this means he first hinders the liberty of the Subject from doing what the Law allows him, and so takes on him an Arbitrary Power; And, secondly, he ingrosses this Commodity to himself, deceiving his Majesty, to whom he professeth so much Fidelity; for whereas there is 5000 *l.* Rent to the King, he, by the computation of Merchants, receives near 14000 *l.* a Year: And because their computations are not always true, I do not care if I allow him 4000 *l.* mistaken, and then he will gain near 10000 *l.* So that if he intends the King's Benefit, it is wonder he told not His Majesty of the great Profit that might thereby have arisen, and let him partake of it, as in Justice he should have done, according to the Trust reposed in him: but you have heard of no such matter. And surely my Lord of Strafford would not have omitted it, if it had been for his advantage, especially in this Presence, where he omits nothing to clear himself, or to insinuate with His Majesty.

*Rush. VIII, 719.

Now I come to the Thirteenth Article, the Article concerning Flax, which I know is fresh in your Lordships memories, and I believe will be so in the memories of the Subjects of Ireland for many Years, how he ingrossed it into his hands, and interrupted the Trade of the poor People, whereby such Miseries and Calamities befel many of that Nation, that, as you have heard it proved, thousands die in ditches, for want of bread to put in their mouths. And whereas he pretends that this was proved but by one witness, and that man to be imprisoned, and of no credit, tho' he was his own instrument; your Lordships remember Sir John Clotworthy his testimony, and another's, and his own Warrant produced, and acknowledged here to justifie the execution of it; and such a thing was thereby taken into his own hands, that I profess I never heard the like, that the poor People should be constrained to use their own as he pleased; and that pleasing of himself, laid an impossibility on the People to execute his pleasure; which was a bondage exceeding that of the Israelites under the Egyptians, for there was not laid so much upon the Children of Israel, but there was a possibility to perform; they might, with much labour, perchance get Stubble to burn their Brick, but the Natives here must have a charge laid upon them, without possibility to perform, and the disobedience must cost them no less than the loss of their Goods, which drew with it ev'n the loss of their Lives for want of Bread. This was not proved by only one Witness, but by many. And your Lordships remember the Remonstrance of that Parliament of Ireland, which declares it to a greater height than I have open'd it.

XVI. THE GREAT CASE OF MONOPOLIES: *THE EAST INDIA CO.* v. *SANDYS**

This was a special action on the case which declared that the King by letters patent had confirmed the earlier charter of the East India Company and had constituted the members thereof a corporation perpetual, granting to them, their sons, apprentices, factors, and servants, the whole, entire, and only right to trade into and from the East Indies, and into and from the islands, havens, cities, creeks, towns, and places of Asia, Africa, or America, or any of them, beyond the Cape of Bona Esperanza, to the Straits of Magellan, as by the court of the Company should from time to time be limited and agreed; and with a prohibition against others from trading in the said territories on pain that any who did trade to any part within the patent, should forfeit his goods and ship, one moiety to the King, and the other moiety to the company, and further be imprisoned at the King's will, and to give security that for the future he would not trade.

Notes of the judgments of Walcot, Holloway, and Withins, JJ., will be found in Skinner's Reports at 223, as well as at 10 State Trials, 516. The judgment of Jefferies, L.C.J., is not, however, given by Skinner but will be found in full at 10 State Trials commencing at page 519.

The relevant parts of the judgments may be extracted as follows.

Holloway, J., 10 State Trials, 517 observed:

No parliament ever looked on this as a monopoly, nay, so far from it, as in the 14 Car. 2, Cap. 24, this Company, &c. are said to be an advantage to the public; and that act was made, that the persons of this Company, &c. should not be discouraged in those honourable endeavours, for promoting public undertakings; then how can this be a monopoly?

It never hath been questioned as such by parliament, though they have looked narrowly into the king's prerogative, even to the questioning some things that were his undoubted rights; and concludes *pro Quer.*

The report of the judgment of Withins, J., 10 State Trials, 518 is in the following terms:

As to the second, whether a monopoly: he says, a monopoly is no immoral act, but only against the politic part of our law; which if it happened to be of advantage to the public, as this trade is; then it ceases also to be against the prohibiting part of the law, and so not within the law of Monopolies.

The company hath been in possession of this trade near one hundred years, and that possession will in time give a right: and cited 'Grotius de Jure Pacis', &c. and concludes *pro Quer.*

*(1648) 10 St. Tr. 371; Skinner, 132, 165, 197, 223.

The main points in the case are stated in the judgment of Withins, J., as being:

(1) whether Letters Patent giving a sole trade to a company exclusive to others be good,

(2) whether in case if they be good, an action lies.

In giving judgment upholding the validity of the charter and the right of the Company to maintain the action, Jefferies, L.C.J., discussed a number of points which are not of importance in a discussion of monopolies. Those parts of his judgment which relate to the subject are here extracted and occupy the remainder of this appendix. 10 State Trials, 522, 523, 538, ff., 552, 553:

The first and great point in this cause, is, whether this grant of the sole trade to the Indies, to the East India Co., exclusive of all others, be a good grant in law or not, and I am of opinion it is.

And for the better communicating my thoughts upon this subject, I will proceed by these steps:

1. I will very briefly consider of the inland trade within this kingdom, and the foreign trade with other nations; and therein observe, that the king's prerogative is concerned in both, and that there is a great difference between both, allowed by the municipal laws of this Kingdom.

2. I shall show that the liberty of foreign trade may be restrained.

3. That foreign trade and commerce being introduced by the law of nations, ought to be governed and judged according to those laws.

4. That by the laws of nations, the regulation and restraint of trade and commerce is reckoned inter Juris Regalia; i.e., the prerogative of the supreme magistrate.

5. That though by the laws of this land, and by the laws of all other nations, monopolies are prohibited, yet societies to trade, such as the plaintiffs, to certain places exclusive of others, are no monopolies by the laws of this land, but are allowed to be erected both here, and in other countries, and are strengthened by the usage and practice of both in all times.

The true question is, Whether this be a good grant to the plaintiffs, of a sole trade to the Indies, were the inhabitants thereof Christians or infidels, exclusive of others?

And therefore I proceed to the next step, that though unlawful engrossing, and monopolies, are prohibited by the laws of this, and all other nations; yet I do conceive, that the charter now in question, of a sole trade exclusive of others, is no such unlawful engrossing, or monopoly, but is supported and encouraged, as conducing to public benefit by the law, practice, and usage of this and other countries, And herein, by the way, though the word Monopoly, or Engrossing, generally spoken of is odious in the eye of our law, yet some engrossings, and so some monopolies, are allowed of in our books; and so I desire to be understood, when I say a lawful or unlawful monopoly or a lawful or unlawful engrossing. And in as much as this is the great, and as I think, the only objection that either hath, or can be made against the present charter, I shall be the more particular in giving my opinion therein, with the reasons and authorities that have induced me thereunto.

I premise only this, that in all those countries, where societies of trade are erected by the supreme power, exclusive of all others, as the case at the bar, monopolies are forbidden; and are as severely punished by their laws, as they can be by the common and statute laws of England, (viz.) in Holland, Germany, France and Spain, etc.

And so wherever the civil law prevails, monopolies are punished with confiscation of goods, and banishment. C. de Monopoliis et Cens. forens, part 1, fol. 497.

Now though monopolies are forbidden, yet that cannot be understood to be so universally true, (as no general law can ever be) that it should in no respect, and upon no occasion or emergency whatsoever, admit of any exception or limitation.

The exceptions thereof may be such as these:

1. Though no private persons can have the sole trade to themselves, by their own private authority, yet this may be granted to a public society, by the prerogative of the prince; if,

2. It be upon good cause, and for the public advantage of the kingdom.

3. From the necessity of beginning and carrying on such trades and foreign commerce, which can be only done by companies and societies.

4. Such companies and societies ought to be continued and supported upon the natural equity and justice, that no other persons should be permitted either to reap the profit, or to endanger the loss of what hath been begun, and been carried on by them, with great hazard and expence.

Now in as much as foreign trade can never be of advantage to this kingdom, except the balance be kept equal between this and other countries; which can never be done, but by keeping up to proportionable rules for the regulation thereof with the other countries: and because, as I said before, the municipal laws of this realm seem too scanty for that purpose, I will therefore first consider how this question stands, as to the law of nations; and then how it is considered by our law, producing authorities in both to make good my assertion. And because I thought the former more natural and effectual for the decision of this question, made me more inquisitive than otherwise I should have been. Cujacius, lib. 16, Obser. 23, distinguishes inter 'Monopolia licita et illicita.'

'Licitum Monopolium,' says he, 'est, si certis personis vel quod potius est certo Collegio concesserit Princeps ut ei soli jus sit vendendae certae mercis'; and therefore recites a law of the emperors Theodosius and Valentinian, by which certain governors of commerce were appointed; 'Edictali Lege sancita, ut nulli Mercatori nisi ad designata loca temporibus praestitutis ad negotiationis suae species distrahendas passim liceret accedere.'

Carpzovius, in his Decisions before-mentioned, lib. 2, Decis. 105, N. 13 and 14, makes this no new case; 'Et certe (non est novum) modum commerciis (quae tamen liberrima esse debent) poni ex causa nimirum publicae utilitatis vel necessitatis, ex quo Monopolia alias prohibita jure subsistunt.'

And again, 'Exempla haud rara sunt ubi necessitate et Edicto principis Monopolia quandoque probari: Commercia ad certas personas et loca restringi videmus.'

Idem, Decis. 4 N. 10. et N. 13. 'Nimirum Exercitium ac permissio Monopoliorum à Principis arbitrio dependet,' etc. Scacca de Commerciis, Q. 7, fol. 301, N. 15. 'Hoc non procedit in Monopolio, autoritate Principis sive Reipub. contracto, quia sicut monopolia, privatâ autoritate contracta Reipub. sunt perniciosa: Ita haec quae Legis Autoritate, ex justa contrahuntur, Causa Reipub. valde utilia sunt.'

Grotius de J.B. et P. lib. 2, cap. 12, sect. 16. 'Monopolia non omnia cum Jure naturae pugnant: nam possunt interdum à summa potestate permitti, justa de causa et pretio.'

He gives amongst others these two examples:

1. From the history of Joseph, when he was vice-roy in Egypt; which is, says he, an illustrious instance of this matter.

2. That under the Romans, the Alexandrians had the sole trade of all Indian and Ethiopic commodities.

So Thuanus, lib. 32, gives an instance of a grant from the French king, Ann. 1604, for the sole trade into Canada, or New France; for which he gives this reason, 'Ne gravis esset aerario ad sublevandos navigationis illine institutae sumptus.'

Which I conceive will go a great way in supporting all such trading companies as cannot be begun but by a public expence.

C. de Monopoliis, the prohibition is expressly limited, 'Nisi Privilegium vel alia consuetudo in utilitatem publicam vergens resistat.'

'Mercatura est res indifferens, in qua Magistratus, vel in vetando vel permittendo suam pro Commodo Reipub. potest interponere autoritatem.' Salmas. de Foen. Trapezit. fol. 236. 'Hoc solum permissum est Regi ut possit prohibere, ne aliis vendat salem.' Alciat. in Q. inter publica 17, in Fin. F. de Verb. Sign. as it is at this day practised in France, Thuan. lib. 5.

'Sic in Sale Vendensi, Monopelia etiam hodie in Italia licite exerceri è Superiorum permissione.' Scacca de Mercat. part 4, N. 30.

'Sic in Repub. Lubecensi, certis quibusdam Mercatoribus ob praedictas rationes jus coquendi sacchari, et salis speciali Privilegio concessum est.' Marguard. lib. 4, c. 7, N. 29.

And then as to the usage:

'Haec est communissima omnium, nullo prorsus reluctante Doctorum sententia, quod jura hujusmodi Emporalia et Regalia possunt acquiri non modo per Concessionem summi Principis, sed etiam Consuetudine et Praescriptione.' Lessius de Justitia, lib. 2, c. 22, Dub. 21.

By the imperial laws commerce and traffic have received several other limitations; sometimes the subjects of the Empire have been forbidden to trade to certain places, particularly named; and in general by other constitutions, forbidden to export coin, gold, or arms, to any of the barbarous nations.

And that the law or customs of nations is so, the practice does evince.

And first in Germany, where the law prohibiteth all monopolies; yet see how the law there stands in respect of our case.

'Circa Monopolia autem, quae exercentur adversus Cives, observandum, non esse illicitum, si non cuivus quodvis negotiationis genus exercere conceditur, sed illis duntaxat qui ad idem exercendum juxta instituta Civitatis sibi jus quaeriverunt, quemadmodum in rebus pub. Europaeis tecta quaedam praestitisse oportet eum, qui mercatorium aut opificium aliquod tollere vult.'

This as to Corporations.

As to trading Societies thus:

'Sed et fieri potest ut a summa potestate Societati mercatorum indulgeatur certum genus Mercium & certis locis advehere, exclusis reliquis cujus privilegii concedendi variae possunt esse causae.

'1. Nam Commercia quae ad loca remotissima instituerentur, priusquam rite stabiliantur magnos requirunt sumptus, & ancipiti eventui initio sunt obnoxia; ergo authoribus talium commerciorum cavendum est, ne quod ab ipsis constitutum magno cum periculo, & sumptu sunt, alii gratis intercipiant.

'2. Ac praeterea ejusmodi Societates privilegiatae opibus suis Reipub. exigente necessitate, felicius possunt quam singulà succurrere.

'3. Videntur etiam meliori fide commercia tractari, ac majorem copiam mercium hoc modo posse advehi, neque de tot fraudibus et compendiis cogitare necessum habent quorum lucrum in commune velut aerarium redactum aequalibus portionibus distribuitur. Puffendorff de Jure Naturae & Gentium. lib. 5. fol. 655.'

A learned author does more at large describe it.

It has been a question sometimes debated, whether the society entered into by the Hans Towns were not against law? 'Quippe quod speciem Monopoli prae se ferre videtur, ut certis locis merces emant confaederati quae rursus pretio eo, quo volunt, vendant.'

This is the same objection now made against the charter at the bar.

But the answer given was twofold, and will come home to this case.

1. That the emperior Charles 4. has given his approbation, and made it lawful by his authority.

2. That they had continued in possession of this society so long, that now the length of time (together with the prince's consent) removed all doubt whatsoever: Carpzovius de lege Regia Germanorum, cap. 6. sect. 10. And the charter now in question, and other charters of like nature granted by the kings of England, which I shall have occasion to remember by-and-bye, remain undisturbed without the least interruption, as long as this society did before this question was stated.

And though, according to the rules of our laws, such a length of time does not obtain the credit of a prescription; yet by the law of nations, and the practices of all other countries which are only adapted for this purpose, it is otherwise. 'Praescriptio enim tam longi temporis vim legis obtinet, imo tollit omne vitium.'

'Praescriptio temporis immemorialis, quae privilegiata est et ex vitioso etiam titulo dominium et jus tribuit, omnesque solemnitates, etiam extrinsecus, negotio accessisse, praesumit tanti temporis antiquitas, num. 10. n. Atque omnem Monopolii respectum consuetudo immemorialis vel Caesarum approbatio excludit, n. 10. 26.

'Quia consuetudo immemorialis Caesarum scitu et concessu haec antiqua societas fulcitur, omnis Monopolii respectus etiam minimus laeserat.' Marg. lib. 4. c. 7, n. 50.

And as these Hans Towns were one of the first corporations of trade I have read of, so was it thought the interest of England to support and encourage them. I find above sixty (some say eighty) towns and cities united their stocks, making Lubeck, Brunswick, Dantzic, and Cullen, the chief places of their residence; and so great was their trade and credit under that constitution, that many princes granted them large privileges, and they kept courts by their deputies and councils at Bergen.

By the laws of Spain, all monopolies are forbidden and under the same penalties appointed by the civil law: yet there also a right may be acquired to a sole trade, by licence obtained from the king, or by prescription.

Quinta partida Tit. 7. leg. 2. membris hoc Commercium Maritimum exclusis caeteris ad 20. annos concederetur. 'Neque ulla re se magis prodidit Imperii odium Batavicae nostris diebus, (Deo ita volente) constituti magnitudo et felicitas, quam Navigationum in Indias Orientales susciptarum constantia et successus, ad quas ut aerario parceretur, societates institute, cautumque tandem, ut sub unam societatem omnes coirent, quod alioque experimento constitisset, Aromatum pretia ab insularis ob emptorum frequentiam augeri, et cum alii aliis praevertere, et lucrum ad se aliorum damno derivare satagerent, ubi concordia maxima est opus, aemulationum et dissidii semina spargi.'

I come in the next place to make it appear, that as the law of nations, and the practice of all other countries, warrants the like grants and restrictions with the case at the bar; so I conceive this charter of sole trade to the Indies, excluding others, is neither opposed by the common law, or prohibited by any act of parliament; but is supported by both, as will more evidently appear by the practice and constant usage in all times.

Therefore, though ingrossing be a crime, odious in the law, and punishable, yet all manner of ingrossing is not.

Therefore in the case of foreign trade, which is only applicable to the case at the bar; it was resolved by all the judges of England, 3 Instit. 196. That merchants may buy beyond sea in gross, and sell here again in gross also. I say, that all monopolies are not unlawful. Generally speaking they are, and therefore, I will admit the description of an unlawful monopoly made by my lord Coke, 3 Instit. 181.

A monopoly is an institution or allowance by the king, by his grant, commission, or otherwise, to any person or persons, bodies politic, or corporate, of, or for the sole buying, selling, making, or using any thing; whereby any person or persons, body politic or corporate, are sought to be restrained of any freedom or liberty they had before, or hindered in their lawful trade.

Now if the subjects of England had not, before this grant, a freedom and liberty to trade to the Indies, against the king's royal pleasure, the charter at the bar will be no monopoly within that rule.

Now that they had no such liberty, hath been sufficiently proved by the several prohibitions mentioned before; and the many more instances thereof cited by Mr. Attorney and Mr. Solicitor; and it would be very strange that the king might prohibit foreigners from coming here into England, and not prohibit his own subjects from going into foreign countries.

And it is not denied, but if the king should proclaim a war with the Indians, that then it would be a prohibition to all his subjects to have any commerce with them; nay, and he might continue that war as long as he pleases; and by that means all his subjects would be as well prevented of any of the commodities of that country; and also of exporting any of our commodities thither. So that surely this charter, with these restrictions, is much better than a total exclusion; and therefore foreign trade is not like our home trade, to which the word monopolies is properly applicable; for that cannot be totally excluded for any time, though never so small, by any act of prerogative.

Object. Ay, but, say the defendant's counsel, though the King can by his prerogative prohibit all trade to any country, upon such great emergencies as war and plague, etc. yet to grant liberty to some, and exclude others, that makes the grant at the bar be thought a monopoly. Which is still begging the question, for if the king, by his prerogative, have the power of restraining and disposing foreign trade, where acts of parliament have not interposed; as by the precedents already cited I conceive clearly he has, as inherent to his crown; therefore, as he may restrain all, so he may restrain any part by the same parity of reason.

If the king proclaims a war with any country, which is a general prohibition of trade, and should order that John a Style, or a dozen, or any greater number of his subjects, etc. and give them instructions to treat for a peace, and the persons so appointed should carry on a trade, would not Mr. Sandys, do you think, have as much reason to murmur that he was none of those ambassadors, as he has now by being not comprized within the charter? And would it not be thought an arrogancy and sauciness in him, to demand an account of the instruction given by the king to such ambassadors? Or durst he trade there till a peace were proclaimed with that country?

And the gloss of that law says, 'Mercatores non faciant inter Monopolium de re non vendenda nisi pro certo pretio, vel de non excercendo officium nisi per eos recicpiatur officiales et socios: Possunt tamen haec facere cum concensu et scientia Regis et contra facientes perpetuo exulabunt, et eorum bona Regi applicantur. Ex privilegio ergo Regis possunt similiter et consuetudine vel prescriptione, quia quod privilegio acquiritur, etiam praescriptione acquiri potest.'

And there quotes 'ubi dicitur, quod potest concedi privilegium; quod quis solus piscetur in certa parte Maris, et aliis potest prohiberi.'

In France Monopolies are prohibited also, 'Sub poena Confiscationis corporis et bonorum indict' Const. Fr. 1, Art. 191.

Notwithstanding which, there are established several corporations for trade; I will name but two. Anno. 1657, the French king makes a grant of the sole fishery in his dominions to a society, excluding others upon pain that interlopers shall incur the penalty, 'de Confiscation des Vaisseaux et Merchandizes et de dix mille Livres d'Amende'. Aytz. vol. 4. pag. 207. And in the year 1664, the East-India Company, by his declaration, with an exclusion to all others, like our East-India Company, page 74, 75.

In the United Provinces, the laws against monopolies are the same, yet there always were several trading corporations exclusive of all others. 3 June 1621, in the charter of the Dutch West-India Company it is granted thus: 'and in case any one shall go to, or negotiate in any of the aforesaid places granted to this Company, and without consent of the said Company, it shall be upon pain and forfeiture of such ship and goods, as shall be found to trade in those coasts and places, which being presently and on all sides, on the behalf of the said Company, set upon, taken and forfeited, shall be and remain to the use of the said Company', Aytz. vol. 1. p. 62. sect. 1.

And in case such ships or goods be sold, or fly into lands or havens, the riggers and part owners thereof shall and may be distrained to the value of the said ship and goods.

That the aforesaid Company shall within the said limits make governors, officers of war and justice; and for the other necessary services for the preservation of the places, and maintaining of good order, policy and justice, and the advancement of their trade, shall appoint, dispose and displace, and substitute others in their places, as they shall find their affairs do require.

All ships coming to any place where the Company have their garrison and government shall not transport thence any men, goods, or money, without leave and consent of the council, upon the pain and forfeiture of six months wages, etc.

In the grant to the Dutch India Company 20 Mar. 1602, that no body of what quality or condition soever, shall for the space of twenty-one years pass Eastwards of the Cape of Good Hope, upon forfeiture of ships and goods, Aytz. 1 vol. fol. 157.

That the said Company may appoint governors and officers of war and justice, and for other necessary services, for the preservation of their places and maintenance of good order, policy and justice.

The said officers to take the oath of supremacy to the states general; and of fidelity, as to what concerns trade and traffic, to the Company.

And afterwards. the 9th of Sept. 1606, a Placart was published, that nobody, directly or indirectly, shall pass or trade beyond the Cape of Good Hope, upon pain of death, and forfeiture of their ships or goods, which shall be found to have done or to do so. And though they should absent themselves out of the United Provinces, yet the sentence shall go on, and be decreed and executed, with the present confiscation and selling of their goods, actions, and credits.

Idem, page 158. And surely the Dutch have been always by us esteemed as our greatest and most dangerous rivals in trade.

And as for the reason and necessity of establishing this way of trading by companies, see the judgment of Thuanus, lib. Hist. 124 and 130, where making mention of the East-Indies, he saith thus: 'Diversis itineribus hujus Regionis Incolarumque Ingeniis cognitis tanta frequentiâ à privatis haec ipsa Navigatio et Commercium exercitum fuit, ut alter alterum fere ivisset perditum. Ad obviandum itaque huic malo visum fuit, An. 1602. quibusdam hujus Navigationis mercatoribus, praepotentum ordinum consensu certum constituere corpus, cujus tantummodo, etc.'

The Indians being infidels are by law esteemed common enemies; and the opinion of my lord Coke in Michelborne's case, I think, therefore, to be law, notwithstanding the objections that have been made against it, which none of our books warrant; now the king by his charter makes the plaintiffs as it were his ambassadors to concert a peace, and Mr. Sandys murmurs because he is not one of them.

The king may grant a fair or market to every subject he has; but because he grants that privilege to some of his subjects, have the rest any just ground of complaint? because the king may pardon every offender, but will not pardon any highwayman now in Newgate, must those gaol-birds, therefore, think themselves injured in their liberty and property? because the king granted to his town of Hull, that no other ships should be there freighted for foreign parts, till the ships of that town were first freighted; as he did, Rot. Claus. 41 E. 3, memb. 25. did London, Dover, or any other town of trade complain? Would any of these gentlemen that contend for this liberty of trade, adventure with their fortunes to Algiers, and when they are seized upon by the Algerines, tell them we are Englishmen, and have by the common law of England, and many statutes of our kingdom, which support the liberty of the subject, a freedom to trade wherever we please? Or would not they rather say, we have a pass from the king of England, and rely upon that, which presumes treaties, leagues, and truces between princes; and in case that will not prevail, the king will see them righted? And in the charter that is now before us, there is a particular restriction and limitation of trade to any prince in amity with our king. Now as the constant usage and practice of other countries warrants such societies as these, so does ours too: For, as I said, the Hans towns were some of the first corporations of trade that we read of in history; so was it thought the interest of England to support and encourage them.

King H. 3, gave them great privileges, and the Still-yards for their residence, which they enjoyed near 300 years, managing their trade by an alderman and counsel called The Guild of the Hans, ingrossing the trade of England for grain, cables, masts, pitch, tar, etc. and under that colour the Jacobsons at this day claim several privileges.

It is observed by many historians, that the most flourishing trades have been begun by united stocks and policies.

In this kingdom a patent was first obtained for the erecting the staple, from E. 3, before any act of parliament intermeddled in that trade, and proceeded under several regulations till the time of queen Elizabeth. In the book I cited before, Malyn's Lex Mercatoria, fol. 150. says, This company of merchants are above 400 years standing, as that book reckons from 1248, when the said merchants obtained privileges of John duke of Brabant, and were called the brotherhood of St. Thomas Becket of Canterbury; which were confirmed by king E. 3, H. 4, H. 5, H. 6, E. 4, R. 3, H. 7, who gave them the name of Merchant-Adventurers; and after him confirmed by H. 8, E. 6, Q.M., Q. Eliz. and king James, not without many enemies and opposers;

especially, says that book, of late taxing them to be monopolies, and unprofitable to the commonwealth, being that all our cloths are not dressed and dyed in England; yet it still prevailed, as being thought for the public good.

And it is observable, that queen Elizabeth did not only confirm what was done by her predecessors, but augmented and grettly enlarged the privileges of this ancient company; and confirmed the charter of the Muscovy company, granted by Philip and Mary; and set up several other companies, as that of Exeter, mentioned at the bar; the East-India company, and the Levant and the Eastland company. And although that ancient and beneficial company of staplers was often opposed by particular persons, and complained of as a monopoly intrenching upon the liberty of the subect, in several parliaments, in the time of H. 4, H. 7, E. 6, and queen Mary: yet all parties being heard, these complaints were fully answered, and the Company's privileges ratified and enlarged.

Again, in queen Elizabeth's time, the clothiers having prevailed against the company, the clothing countries were almost quickly ruined, and reduced to that extremity, that in 29 Eliz. the lords of the council sent for the members of that Company, desiring them to reassume their privileges, and chearfully to proceed in their society; with assurance of all countenance and assistance from the government. And in the reign of king James, after several interlopers had endeavoured to destroy the Company, the king published his proclamation to restore the Company to its ancient privileges.

So did king Charles 1, 7th Dec. 1634, reciting, 'Whereas we have taken into our princely consideration the manifold benefits that redound to this kingdom; and finding how much order and government will conduce to the encrease and advancement of the same, we have thought fit, with the advice of our privy-council', etc. There he gives an establishment to the Company, and prohibits any to intrude upon their privileges, upon pain of such punishmentss at the Star-chamber shall inflict.

Since this, it may be worth consideration, whether the breaking of this Company, has not occasioned the great decay of our trade in wool: it being agreeable to reason, that as no law can be effectual without courts of justice to put them in execution; nor a straggling army subsist without discipline: so a straggling trade managed by particular persons, whilst every one strives to advance his own private interest, will ruin the trade in general, especially such a hazardous trade as this to the East-Indies which already hath been so chargeable, and can only be prevented by the conduct and government of a public society: and surely to look after and settle these matters, properly belongs to the care and prudence of our governors.

Now I shall observe, how the practice has been both in queen Elizabeth's time, and ever since, and that although many charters like ours at the bar have been granted; and none ever demanded by a judgement in Westminster-hall, or so much as objected against, save only that of the Canary patent, till this cause at the bar; and though several attempts have been made both in parliament, and in the courts at Westminster-hall, against monopolies; yet this charter and others of the like nature, were never looked upon under that character. For instance,

1. A charter was granted 2 Eliz. to the merchants of Exeter for the sole trade to France, excluding all other merchants of Exeter not of that company, continued undisturbed, and prevailed against a great opposition that was made against it in parliament. King Edward 6, and king Philip and Mary, having granted a charter like ours to the Russia company, which continued in peace till the eighth of queen Elizabeth; when the parliament taking notice of that patent, thought fit to confirm it with all the commendations imaginable; and was so far from thinking it a monopoly, that it says, the commonwealth before that time had received great advantages by it; and grants, and inflicts greater and other penalties than were or could be inflicted by the letters patent: and it is observable, that there were some interlopers upon that trade in those days, and had been liable to the forfeitures inflicted by those letters patent, and were therefore forced to apply themselves to that parliament, and did obtain a special proviso to excuse those forfeitures, which, had not that act of parliament been made, they had been liable to; which I take to be an authority full, as to the case at the bar.

Queen Elizabeth, during her reign, granted several charters of the like nature, which passed the perusal of her attorney and solicitor, learned men in our profession. In the beginning of her reign my lord chief-baron Weston was solicitor, sir Gilbert Gerrard attorney-general, and passed those patents both to the Russia and Exeter companies: 23 Eliz. my lord chief-justice Popham was attorney, and the lord-chancellor Egerton solicitor, in whose time some few such charters were also granted like to this at the bar. And then my lord Coke was attorney-general, and my lord chief-baron Fleming solicitor-general, who approved thereof; and it is observable, that in the 43 and 44 of the queen, the parliament took notice of many patents of monopolies, as it appears by the book cited at the bar; Townsend's Collections, 244 and 245. The parliament seemed to be as high as ever they were in any age before, and particularly were incensed by those patents. A list of all were brought in by Mr. Secretary Cecil, that were thought grievous or prejudicial to the commonwealth; and though there were a catalogue of forty or fifty, amongst whom that of Darcy is one, yet the parliament, nor none other, complained of any charter granted to corporations, but they continued undisturbed. And by the way it is not amiss to observe, that Darcy's patent was not immediately damned in parliament, but referred to take its fate in Westminster-hall; the great reason that guided that judgment was, the restraint that was put upon the home trade; and so it appears in More's Report, 672. And thus stood these charters; the China charter, the Turkey company, the Barbary company, the Guinea company, all charters of sole trade, excluding others, remained in trade during all queen Elizabeth's time.

But in the third year of king James was the first act made for opening a general trade to Spain, Portugal, and France, to all the king's subjects; which could not be done in Westminster-hall, as appears by the preamble to that act; nor does that act call those charters monopolies, or open a free trade to any other parts of the world, but leaves all charters of foreign trade, save to Spain, Portugal and France, to remain as they did before. And in the 4th of Jac. cap. 9, there is notice taken particularly of the charter granted to the Exeter merchants of the sole trade to France; and because it was thought to be damned by the general words of that statute E. 3, yet it is there enacted and declared, that the said statute of patents, neither did nor should dissolve, annihilate or impeach the said charter, or the said company in any of their privileges, liberties or immunities, granted unto them by the said charter, any thing contained in that general act to the contrary notwithstanding; and from this act of parliament I observe two things:

I. That the parliament thought that the charter to Exeter for sole trade to France, exclusive of others, was for the public benefit and weal of that city.

II. That the letters patent were good in law, and did not want the assistance of an act of parliament to support them; for that act does not confirm those letters patent, but provides only, that the statute 3 Jac. should not by general words be thought to impeach or destroy them. Now had the parliament thought the charter void or infirm, they might have confirmed or strengthened it, as the Russia patent was; but they concluded, that had it not been for the statute of Tertio, the charter was good to all intents and purposes: and this I take to be full authority in the case at the bar. But to proceed, the Greenland patent for sole fishing, exclusive of others, granted by queen Elizabeth, is held good, Rolls, Part 5, fol. 3. Taylors of Ipswich's case, and the case of the abbot of Westminster, is agreed to be law; in Darcy's case, More, 673, by Mr. Justice Dodderidge: and by the way he gives good advice to all persons that dispute the king's prerogative; and for the friendship I bear to Mr. Sandys, and others that are now in court, and I think need the advice, I shall read the very words of the book: he that hews above his hands, chips will fall into his eyes; 'Et qui Majestatem scrutatur principis, opprimetur splendore ejus.'

In king James's time, many grants, like ours were made, but particularly in 7 Jac. the patent granted to the East-India Company by queen Elizabeth, was, by the advice of her council, as well as by my lord Hobart, then attorney-general, and sir Francis Bacon, solicitor-general, confirmed and allowed with the same clauses as the charter at the bar; and so remained undisturbed and uninterrupted all king James's reign, and was not thought to be any whit touched or aimed at by the proviso in the statute, 43 Eliz. cap. 1, sect. 9, that act only pointing at the monopoly patents complained of in that parliament of 43 of the queen, which I mentioned before. Then comes the statute so much insisted on by the defendant's counsel, commonly called the statute of monopolies, Stat. 21 Jac. cap. 3, which certainly doth not at all effect the case at the bar. For first, this charter is not a general grant for the sole buying, selling, making, using of any thing within this realm, which are the very words of the acts: nor does this charter give the East-India Company licence or toleration to do, use, or exercise any thing against the tenor or purport of any law or statute, which are the only things provided against by that act. But the parliament then seemed to take the same general care of all such charters as this at the bar, as the parliament did in 3 Jac. of that particular charter of Exeter; and therefore, to the end that those words in the beginning of this act of monopolies might not be thought to extend to charters, to corporations for trade, there is a proviso, sect. 9, that that act should not extend to any corporations, companies, or fellowships, etc. erected for the maintainance, enlargement, or ordering any trade or merchandize, but leaves the same as they were before that act, without any immutation: and it is observable, that the parliament then thought a general saving sufficient to support those charters that were then in being, to corporations for trade and merchandize; but made particular provisos for the saving of patents for inland commodities, viz. such as salt, gunpowder, ordnance, shot, and the like.

So that this company was in full possession of their privilege of sole trade, exclusive of others, all king James's and king Charles 1st's time, till all the prerogatives of the crown were invaded, and the crowned head too was taken off by traitors and rebels. But the providence of God having restored us our king, and re-invested him with all his undoubted prerogatives as well as restored us to our ancient rights and privileges, and scarce, as I may say, warm in his throne, but amongst the other considerations that he had for the public weal of his subjects, he considers the public advantage of this kingdom arising by trade, and amongst them, one of his first thoughts are fixed upon this Company. For 3d of April, 1661, he by his letters patent taking notice of the charters of queen Elizabeth, and king James, granted to the East-India Company, and of the injuries that were done to them by the late troubles; with the advice of his council, and approbation of Mr. Attorney Palmer, and my lord-chancellor Finch, he granted and confirmed to them all their privileges. The 27th of May, in the 20th of his reign, lord-chancellor Finch being attorney, and my lord-keeper, that now is, solicitor, he confirms this charter; and grants to the East-India Company other privileges by another charter in the 28th year of his reign; at which time the Lord-Keeper was attorney, and sir William Jones, solicitor; he confirms the former, and grants more privileges: and in the 25th year of his reign, by the charter now in question, passed with the approbation of the present attorney and solicitor, men of great ability in their professions, and of whom, were they not present, I should say much more; the charter to this company was confirmed with additional privileges.

Nor has this charter passed only the approbation of his majesty and council, since his happy restoration, but the parliament has likewise taken notice of it; the statute 14 Car. 2, cap. 14, takes notice of it to be of great advantage to the public. The stat. of the 29th of this king for poll-money, taxes them with twenty shillings for every hundred pound in stock. In the great case between Skinner and the East-India Company, the House of Commons defended them, even to an eruption between the two houses.

Mr. Jenks and some other linnen-drapers and tradesmen of London, taking the advantage of the heats that too frequently possessed the House of Commons of late years, especially against the point of prerogative, did furiously attack the East-India Company, but without any success, and this company was never assaulted in Westminster-Hall till this cause at the bar. I cannot help therefore this observation, that as the king by his charter 1667, takes notice, that the charters granted by queen Elizabeth and king James remained uninterrupted till the late rebellion; so the interlopers against the king's prerogative in this particular, and the horrid conspirators against the king's life in this last hellish conspiracy, first appeared in Westminster-Hall about the same time.

* * *

From what has been said, I hope it doth plainly appear that since the law of this land, and the law of nature and nations, allow the power of making companies to manage traffic, exclusive to all others to be in the prince, that this is reckoned to be 'inter Jura Regalia'; that no act of parliament does restrain this prerogative; that the practice of all Europe has been accordingly; that particularly such companies have been erected in England, and those companies have been in quiet possession of their privileges for such a number of years; that they have passed the approbation of many learned men; that they have been thought for the public advantage of the nation, by so many kings and princes, with the advice of their council, both in and out of parliament; that all statutes and authorities of law that we can meet with in our books affirm it, and none that I can meet with oppose it.

* * *

So that I conclude the first, and, as I conceive the only point in this case that letters patent which gave licence and liberty to the plaintiffs to exercise their sole trade to the Indies, within the limits of their grant, exclusive of all others, is a good grant in law.

2. I do conceive, that the defendant trading to the Indies, contrary to this charter, may be punished by information at the suit of the king; and that this action by the plaintiffs is also well brought; but in as much as I have detained you so long upon the first point, I shall trespass upon your patience but a few words to this.

1. Therefore I conceive, the plaintiff need not alledge any special damage, no more than the grantee of a fair, market, or any other franchise.

2. The action is brought, and grounded upon the grant of the sole and entire trade; which, as I conceive is a franchise the king may grant, and is like the case of new inventions; upon which letters patent actions are brought by every day's experience; and the prohibiting clause is added, only to make the thing more notorious: and that interlopers, in case they should be prosecuted at the king's suit, should be more inexcusable. And until you can imagine there be as many East-India Companies as there are commoners and school-masters in England, Mary's case, Coke 9. can never be thought an objection. As to the objection in the 11 Rep. 88, Rolls Abridg. part 1. p. 106. Darcy's case, that admitting the grant or dispensation to Darcy had been good, for the sole importing of foreign cards: yet that being only a dispensation to the stat. of Ed. 4. and did only exclude Darcy from the penalty of that act, he could not maintain the action: but if in case that grant had vested an interest, as our grant at the bar does, he might have brought an action, as my lord Rolls says in the next paragraph, may be collected out of Darcy's case.

The case upon patents of new inventions, are full authorities in the case at the bar: and so is that case of the abbot of Westminster, wherein the grant of the market for thirty days, exclusive of others, is particularly set forth in the action. And the Salisbury man that brought cloth to London, and sold the same contrary to that charter, is prosecuted in an action of trespass upon the case, at the suit of the abbot; and the writ concludes, (supposing the grant good) 'In nostri contemptum et praedicti Abbatis grave damnum ca Fr. et libertatum suarum praedictarum laesionem manifestam'; which is an authority full as to this point.

Upon the whole matter, I am of the same opinion with my brothers; and do conceive, that that grant to the plaintiffs of the sole trade to the Indies, exclusive of others, is a good grant, and that the action is well brought:

And therefore let the Plaintiff take his Judgment.

BIBLIOGRAPHY

ABBOTT, B. V. *American and English Patent Cases 1602-1833.* Washington, 1887.

ADAMS, G. B. and STEPHENS, H. M. *Select Documents of English Constitutional History.* New York, 1914.

AKERMAN, C. *L'Obligation d'exploiter et la licence obligatoire en matière de brevets d'invention.* Paris, 1936.

ARBER, EDWARD. *Transcripts of the Registers of the Company of Stationers of London, 1554-1640.* London, 1875-94.

ARISTOTLE. *Oeconomica.* Ed. Edward Walford, London, 1880.

——— *Politics.* Jowett tr. Oxford, 1908.

ASHLEY, W. J. *An Introduction to English Economic History and Theory.* London, 1912.

BACON, FRANCIS. *Works.* Ed. Basil Montagu. London, 1825-43.

BACON, M. *New Abridgement of the Law.* 7th ed. London, 1832.

BAGEHOT, WALTER. *The English Constitution.* London, 1867.

BARNETT, O. R. *Patent Property and the Anti-Monopoly Laws.* Indianapolis, 1943.

BIGGAR, O. M. *Canadian Patent Law and Practice.* Toronto, 1927.

BLACKSTONE, Sir WM. *Commentaries on the Laws of England.* 12th ed. London, 1795, book IV.

BOECKH, AUGUST. *Staatshaushaltung der Athener.* Berlin, 1851.

——— *The Public Economy of Athens.* London, 1828.

BRENTANO, L. *History and Development of Gilds.* London, 1869.

CAMPBELL, Lord JOHN. *Lives of the Lord Chancellors of England.* 3rd ed. London, 1848.

CAMPBELL, WM. *Materials for the Reign of Henry VII.* London, 1873-7.

CARR, C. T. *Select Charters of the Trading Companies (1530-1707).* Publications of the Selden Society, vol. XXVIII. London, 1913.

CASALONGA, ALAIN. *Traité de la brevetabilité : Le concept de cause et le brevet d'invention.* Paris, 1939.

CHAMBERLIN, EDWARD. *The Theory of Monopolistic Competition.* Harvard, 1938.

CHAPMAN, S. J. *Outlines of Political Economy.* London, 1911.

CHITTY, J. *Law of the Prerogatives of the Crown.* London, 1820.

CHURCH, R. W. *Bacon.* (English Men of Letters series.) London, 1910.

CLARENDON, Earl of. *The History of the Rebellion and Civil Wars in England (1609-1674).* Oxford, 1819.

COKE, Sir EDWARD. *Institutes of the Laws of England.* 18th ed. London, 1797-1823.

COLLIER, JOHN DYER. *Essay on the Law of Patents.* London, 1803.

COMYNS, Sir JOHN. *Digest of the Laws of England.* Dublin, 1785.
CRAIK, G. L. *History of British Commerce.* London, 1844.
CUNNINGHAM, W. *Alien Immigrants to England.* London, 1897.
——— *The Growth of English Industry and Commerce during the Early and Middle Ages.* 5th ed. Cambridge, 1915.
——— *The Growth of English Industry and Commerce in Modern Times.* Cambridge, 1912.
D'EWES, Sir SIMONDS. *Journals of all the Parliaments during the Reign of Queen Elizabeth.* London, 1682.
——— *Journal, from the Beginning of the Long Parliament to the Opening of the Trial of the Earl of Strafford.* Ed. Wallace Notestein. New Haven, Conn., 1923.
——— *Journal, from the First Recess of the Long Parliament to the Withdrawal of King Charles from London.* Ed. W. H. Coates. New Haven, Conn., 1942.
DU CANGE, C. D. *Glossarium Mediae et Infimae Latinitatis.* Niort, 1885.
FAY, C. R. *Great Britain from Adam Smith to the Present Day.* London, 1928.
FOX, HAROLD G. *The Canadian Law and Practice Relating to Letters Patent for Inventions.* Toronto, 1937.
——— *The Canadian Law of Trade Marks and Industrial Designs.* Toronto, 1940.
——— *The Canadian Law of Copyright.* Toronto, 1944.
FRANCOTTE, HENRI. *L'Industrie dans la Grèce Ancienne.* Brussels, 1901.
FRANK, JEROME. *Law and the Modern Mind.* New York, 1936.
GARDINER, S. R. *Constitutional Documents of the Puritan Revolution, 1625-1660.* 3rd ed. Oxford, 1906.
——— *History of England from 1603-1642.* London, 1893.
GIBBINS, H. de B. *Industry in England.* 8th ed. London, 1913.
GNEIST, R. von. *History of the English Constitution.* London, 1886.
GOODEVE, T. M. *Cases Relating to Letters Patent for Invention.* London, 1884.
GORDON, J. W. *Monopolies by Patents.* London, 1897.
GREAT BRITAIN, HISTORICAL MANUSCRIPTS COMMISSION. *Report on the Cholmondeley Papers.* Appendix, 5th report. London, 1876.
——— *Report on the Manuscripts of the Duke of Buccleuch and Queensberry.* London, 1899-1926.
——— *Papers of the Earl of Lonsdale.* 13th report. London, 1893.
GREAT BRITAIN, HOUSE OF COMMONS. *Journals.* Vol. I, 1547-1628. Vol. II, 1640-2. London, 1803.
GREAT BRITAIN, HOUSE OF LORDS. *Journals.* Vol. III, 1620-8. London, 1629.
GREEN, JOHN R. *History of the English People.* London, 1874.
GRENFELL, B. P. (ed.). *The Revenue Laws of Ptolemy Philadelphus.* Oxford, 1896.
GRIFFIN, R. *Cases Relating to Letters Patent for Inventions.* London, 1887.

GROSS, C. *The Gild Merchant.* Oxford, 1890.

HALLAM, HENRY *Constitutional History of England.* Everyman edition. London, 1827.

——— *View of the State of Europe during the Middle Ages.* London, 1818.

HAWARDE, JOHN. *Les Reportes del Cases in Camera Stellata, 1593 to 1609.* Ed. W. P. Baildon. London, 1894.

HAWKINS, W. *Pleas of the Crown.* 8th ed. London, 1824.

HERBERT, WILLIAM. *History of the Twelve Great Livery Companies of London.* London, 1836-7.

HOLDSWORTH, W. S. *History of English Law.* London, 1922-6.

HOLMES, Mr. Justice O. W. *Collected Legal Papers.* New York, 1920.

HOUSE OF LORDS. *Calendars of House of Lords Manuscripts down to 1693.* London, 1887-94. See Appendix to Report I of the Historical Manuscripts Commission, 1-4.

HOWELL, J. (ed.). *Cottoni Posthuma: Divers Choice Pieces of that Renowned Antiquary, Sir Robert Cotton.* London, 1651.

HUME, DAVID. *History of England.* Dublin, 1772; London, 1803.

ILLINGWORTH, WILLIAM. *Inquiry into the Laws Respecting Forestalling, Regrating and Ingrossing.* London, 1800.

JAMES I, King of England. *Declaration Concerning Matter of Bounty.* London, 1610.

KAEMPFFERT, W. B. *Invention and Society.* Chicago, 1930.

KLOSTERMANN, ERICH. *Das Patentgesetz für das deutsche Reich.* 1877.

KOHLER, JOSEF. *Handbuch des deutschen Patentrechts.* Mannheim, 1900.

LE ROSSIGNOL, J. E. *Monopolies Past and Present.* New York, 1901.

LEVY, HERMANN. *Monopoly and Competition.* London, 1911.

LIPSON, E. *The Economic History of England.* London, 1929.

LODGE, EDMUND. *Illustrations of British History.* 2nd ed. London, 1839.

LONGMAN, WILLIAM. *The History of the Life and Times of Edward the Third.* London, 1869.

MACAULAY, T. R. *History of England.* London, 1849-61.

MACRORY, E. *Cases Relating to Letters Patent for Inventions.* London, 1859.

MADOX, THOMAS. *Firma Burgi: Or an Historical Essay Concerning the Cities, Towns and Boroughs of England.* London, 1726.

MAITLAND, F. W. *Domesday Book and Beyond.* Cambridge, 1897.

——— *Constitutional History of England.* Cambridge, 1913.

MALAPERT and FORNI. *Nouveau Commentaire des lois sur les brevets d'invention.* Paris, 1879.

MARSHALL, ALFRED. *Economics of Industry.* London, 1913.

MARTIN, W. *The English Patent System.* London, 1905.

MILL, JOHN STUART. *Principles of Political Economy.* London, 1848.

MORE, Sir THOMAS. *The Utopia* (1518). Tr. Ralph Robynson, 1551. Ed. J. H. Lupton. Oxford, 1895.

MOULTON, H. FLETCHER. *Law Relating to Letters Patent for Inventions.* London, 1913.

MUND, V. A. *Monopoly: A History and Theory.* Princeton, 1933.

MUNRO, W. H. *The Seigneurs of Old Canada.* Toronto, 1920.

MURDIN, WILLIAM. *Burghley's State Papers.* London, 1759.

NICHOLAS, EDWARD. *Proceedings and Debates of the House of Commons in 1620 and 1621, Collected by a Member of That House.* Ed. T. Tyrwhitt. Oxford, 1766. (Nicholas's notes of the parliamentary proceedings of March 14 to 16, and Nov. 20 to Dec. 19, 1621 are S.P. Dom. Jac. I, cxxv. Notes by Nicholas for the session of 1624 are S.P.Dom. Jac. I, clxvi; of 1628 and 1629 are S.P.Dom. Car. I, xcvii and cxxxiv.)

NESBITT, ALEXANDER. *Glass.* London, 1878.

Parliamentary History of England. Vol. I, 1066-1625. Vol. II, 1625-1642. Vol. III, 1642-1660. London, 1806-8.

PERSSON, A. W. *Staat und Manufactur im römischen Reiche.* Lund, 1923.

POOLEY, Sir ERNEST. *Guilds of the City of London.* London, 1945.

PRICE, W. H. *The English Patents of Monopoly.* Harvard, 1913.

PROTHERO, G. W. *Statutes and Constitutional Documents of the Reigns of Elizabeth and James I, 1558-1625.* 3rd ed. Oxford, 1906.

RAUMER, F. L. G. von. *Geschichte der Hohenstaufen und Ihrer Zeit.* Leipzig, 1844.

RENOUARD, A. A. *Traité des brevets d'invention,* (1844). 3rd ed. Paris, 1865.

RIEZLER, KURT. *Finanzen und Monopole im alten Griechenland.* Berlin, 1907.

RILEY, HENRY THOMAS. *Munimenta Gildhallae Londoniensis; Liber Albus, Liber Custumarum, et Liber Horn.* London, 1859-62.

ROBINSON, W. C. *The Law of Patents and Useful Inventions.* Boston, 1890.

ROGERS, JAMES E. T. *Six Centuries of Work and Wages.* London, 1884.

ROLLE, Sir H. *Abridgement des plusieurs cases et resolutions del common ley.* London, 1668.

ROSTOVTZEFF, M. *The Social and Economic History of the Roman Empire.* Oxford, 1926.

RUSHWORTH, JOHN. *Historical Collections 1640-44.* London, 1721.

RUSSELL, Earl. *English Government and Constitution.* London, 1821.

RYMER, THOMAS. *Foedera, conventiones, literae et cujuscunque generis Acta Publica, inter Reges Angliae et alios quosvis Imperatores, Reges, Pontifices, Principes, vel Communitates, ab ingressu Gulielmi I in Angliam, A.D. 1066, ad nostra usque tempora.* London, 1727.

SCHECHTER, F. I. *Historical Foundations of Trade-Mark Law.* Columbia, 1925.

SCOBELL, HENRY. *Memorials of the Method and Manner of Proceedings in Parliament.* London, 1670, 1689.

SCRUTTON, Sir T. E. *The Elements of the Law Merchant.* London, 1891.

SHEPPARD, WM. *Abridgement of the Common and Statute Law of England.* London, 1675.

SMITH, J. W. *Compendium of Mercantile Law.* London, 1834-1931.

STEEHOLM, C. and H. *James I of England.* New York, 1938.

STEELE, ROBERT. *Tudor and Stuart Proclamations, 1485-1714.* Oxford, 1910.

STRAFFORD, Earl of. *Letters and Despatches.* Ed. Wm. Knowler. London, 1739.

STRYPE, JOHN. *Annals of the Reformation.* Oxford, 1824.

STUBBS, W. *Constitutional History of England.* 5th ed. Oxford, 1903.

STUBBS, W. *Select Charters of English Constitutional History.* 2nd ed. Oxford, 1874.
SUETONIUS. *History of the Twelve Caesars.* Holland ed. London, 1899.
TASWELL-LANGMEAD, T. P. *English Constitutional History.* 7th ed. London, 1911.
TAUSSIG, P. W. *Inventors and Money Makers.* New York, 1915.
TAYLOR, HANNIS. *Origin of the English Constitution.* Boston, 1889.
TERRELL, T. *Law and Practice Relating to Letters Patent for Inventions.* 8th ed. London, 1934.
TREVELYAN, G. M. *English Social History.* London, New York and Toronto, 1942.
UNWIN, GEORGE. *Industrial Organization in the Sixteenth and Seventeenth Centuries.* Oxford, 1904.
——— *The Gilds and Companies of London.* London, 1908.
VANDER HAEGHEN, G. *Le Droit intellectuel.* Brussels, 1936.
VEBLEN, THORSTEIN. *The Theory of Business Enterprise.* New York, 1904.
VINER, C. *General Abridgement of Law and Equity.* Aldershot, 1741-53.
VOJÁCĚK, J. *A Survey of the Principal National Patent Systems.* New York, 1936.
WALKER, A. *Patents.* Deller's ed. New York, 1937.
WEBSTER, THOMAS. *Reports of Patent Cases.* London, 1844.
——— *Law and Practice of Letters Patent for Inventions.* London, 1841.
——— *On the Subject-Matter of Letters Patent for Inventions.* London, 1851.
WHEELER, JOHN. *A Treatise of Commerce.* London, 1601; reprinted New York, 1931.
WILCKEN, ULRICH. *Griechische Ostraka aus Ägypten und Nubien.* Leipzig and Berlin, 1899.
——— *Grundzüge .. und Chrestomathie der Papyruskunde Gewerbes im hellenistischen Ägypten.* 1913.
WRONG, G. M. *The Canadian Manor and its Seigneurs.* Toronto, 1908.
ZOUCH, R. *Jurisdiction of the Admiralty of England.* London, 1663, 1685.

ARTICLES IN PERIODICALS

Anon. "Comments on 'Standard of Invention' " (1944) 26 *Journal of the Patent Office Society,* 619.
ARNOLD, T. W. "The Abuse of Patents" (1942) 170 *Atlantic Monthly,* 14.
BRODHURST, B. E. S. "The Merchants of the Staple" (1901) 17 *Law Quarterly Review,* 56; (1909) 3 *Select Essays in Anglo-American Legal History,* 16.
BROWN, W. J. "Law and Evolution" (1920) 29 *Yale Law Journal,* 400.
CASTELLAN, C. A. "The Shifting Sands of Skill and Ingenuity" (1946) 28 *Journal of the Patent Office Society,* 416 at 419.
DAVIES, D. S. "Further Light on the Case of Monopolies" (1932) 96 *Law Quarterly Review,* 397.

DAWSON, C. W. "Some Notes on the Doctrine of Aggregation" (1944) 26 *Journal of the Patent Office Society*, 838.

DUFT, H. C. "Supreme Court Announces Rule for Measuring Invention and then Fails to Apply It" (1945) 27 *Journal of the Patent Office Society*, 779.

ENCYCLOPÆDIA BRITANNICA. 14th ed. Articles on "Guilds" and "Hanseatic League."

EVANS, E. A. "Disposition of Patent Cases by the Courts" (1942) 24 *Journal of the Patent Office Society*, 19.

FAIRMAN, T. O. "Early English Inventions" (1885) 12 *The Antiquary*, 1.

FENNING, K. "The Origin of the Patent and Copyright Clause of the Constitution" (1929) 17 *Georgetown Law Journal*, 109.

FOX, H. G. "Abuse of Monopoly" (1945) 23 *Canadian Bar Review*, 353.

GARDINER, S. R. "On Four Letters from Lord Bacon to Christian IV, King of Denmark, Together with Observations on the Part Taken by Him in the Grants of Monopolies Made by James I" (1867) 41 *Archaeologia*, 219.

H., M. J. "Standard of Invention" (1944) 26 *Journal of the Patent Office Society*, 439.

HEARD, N. "Uniform Standard of Invention" (1943) 25 *Journal of the Patent Office Society*, 676.

HULME, E. W. "The Early History of the English Patent System" (1896, 1900) 12, 16 *Law Quarterly Review*, 141, 44; (1909) 3 *Select Essays in Anglo-American Legal History*, 117.

JENKS, EDWARD. "The Early History of Negotiable Instruments" (1893) 9 *Law Quarterly Review*, 70; (1909) 3 *Select Essays in Anglo-American Legal History*, 51.

JEWETT, F. B. "The Relation of Research and Invention to Economic Conditions" (1939) 21 *Journal of the Patent Office Society*, 195.

MACAULAY, T. B. "Lord Bacon" (1837) July *Edinburgh Review*.

——————— "Burleigh and His Times" (1832) Apr. *Edinburgh Review*.

MULLER, C. B. " 'Invention' Crux" (1942) 24 *Journal of the Patent Office Society*, 795.

POSTAN, M. "The Fifteenth Century" (1939) 9 *Economic History Review*, 165.

POTTS, H. E. "The Definition of Invention in Patent Law" (1944) 7 *Modern Law Review*, 113.

PRAGER, F. D. "A History of Intellectual Property from 1545 to 1787" (1944) 26 *Journal of the Patent Office Society*, 711.

RICE, W. B. "A Constructive Patent Law" (1939) 16 *New York University Law Quarterly Review*, 179.

SCHRAMM, F. B. "Patent Laws and the Chemist" (1945) Mar. *Chemical and Engineering News*, 537.

SHELLEY, K. E. "Patent Injustice" (1942-3) 61 *Transactions of the Chartered Institute of Patent Agents*, 17.

WIGMORE, J. H. "The Public Interest in a Sound Patent System" (1943) 195 *Journal of Commerce* (no. 15082), 24.

WOODLING, G. V. "What's a Good Yardstick for Patentability" (1944) 29 *Journal of the Patent Office Society*, 320.

WOODWARD, W. R. "A Reconstruction of the Patent System as a Problem of Administrative Law" (1942) 55 *Harvard Law Review*, 950.

YNTEMA, H. E. "The Hornbook Method and the Conflict of Laws" (1928) 37 *Yale Law Journal*, 468.

ZITVER, L. "Judicial Review of 'Invention' and a Proposed Alternative" (1943) 25 *Journal of the Patent Office Society*, 318.

INDEX

Cases are not indexed in the following pages. All cases may be referred to at the beginning of the volume in the Table of Cases.

www.ingramcontent.com/pod-product-compliance
Lightning Source LLC
LaVergne TN
LVHW090800070826
844660LV00022B/1043

* 9 7 8 1 4 8 7 5 9 8 7 4 7 *